THE ETHICS OF DEATH

D1319887

THE ETHICS OF DEATH

LLOYD STEFFEN AND DENNIS R. COOLEY

Fortress Press
Minneapolis

THE ETHICS OF DEATH

Religious and Philosophical Perspectives in Dialogue

Cover image: Aerial photograph of headstone and shadows/Cameron Davidson/Corbis

Cover design: Laurie Ingram

Library of Congress Cataloging-in-Publication Data

Print ISBN: 978-0-8006-9919-2

eBook ISBN: 978-1-4514-8757-2

The paper used in this publication meets the minimum requirements of American National Standard for Information Sciences — Permanence of Paper for Printed Library Materials, ANSI Z329.48-1984.

Manufactured in the U.S.A.

This book was produced using PressBooks.com, and PDF rendering was done by PrinceXML.

Dennis Cooley:
To my sisters—Lori, Faith, and Ami

Lloyd Steffen:
To Samuel Atticus, Hannah, Paul
and in memory of William "Bill" Ballou Cranshaw (1988–2011)
ex morte amici magnus dolor nascitur

CONTENTS

Introduction

The title of this book is odd. Although ethical issues often take center stage in discussions of dying, particularly around actions to hasten, inflict, or prevent death, the idea of an "ethics of death" is peculiar. Ethics is to a large extent concerned with action, and death is not an action. It is more like a state, but to call it a state implies a state of being—namely, the state of being dead—and that is not quite right either.[1] Ethics is concerned with decision making, and while we can make decisions about what to do with someone who has died, treating the dead as an object of our deliberation, ethics is meant to help living human subjects decide what to do, who to be, and how to act: what can ethics possibly means to a human subject who has died and is thus incapable of decision making? How can there be an ethics of death when death seems to cancel the possibility of all the things we associate with ethics: being an agent, a person who reasons, acts, exercises volition, experiences the world, and engages others through various forms of relationship. Even the idea of "being dead" seems odd. We can acknowledge "being toward death" with death a future prospect, but once death comes, the "being toward" appears to be canceled. Death obliterates the "being"—how can we have an ethics without being? [2]

We—the two authors of this book—have an answer to these questions, although it is tentative and may not satisfy all readers. Here goes: in focusing our attention on what we call the ethics of death, we are claiming that *death is an experience for the living*.

No doubt people go through the experience of dying, but whether those who die actually experience their own deaths is at least an unknown.[3] What we do know is that the living experience death, but always the *deaths of others*. *Others* is a term important in ethics. The moral point of view would insist that

1. Death is considered by some philosophers as a process rather than an event.

2. The first-person past-tense linguistic utterance "to die" is odd as well. "I died" is grammatically correct but philosophically contradictory. No one can coherently utter the words "I died" or "I have died" meaningfully in a literal way, although we use such expressions as "I was so embarrassed that I just died" or "That joke just killed me" as linguistic intensifiers.

3. The claim that people who have near-death experiences actually die overlooks that the individuals who have these experiences are *near death*. Near-death experiences, whatever they are empirically—and there is no reason to doubt them as experiences people have—are well termed as "near death" and are best associated with peculiarities in the dying process rather than with "death" or "being dead."

our decision making take into account others, and even principles in ethics like universalizability—that what is good for me to do is good for anyone to do—or utilitarian calculation—acting to achieve the greatest good for the greatest number—clearly center deliberation on our relationships to others. If there is, as Kierkegaard offered, a moral "sphere" or stage of life, it is a sphere that is concerned specifically with self-other relations. The relationship of the self to others is what defines the very context for moral thinking and ethical reflection.

So, in human experience, human beings we know—some we love—die. These "others" who are not me go through a dying process of various durations under various circumstances. When that dying process comes to an end—which it does—we, who have not gone through that process, speak about the death of others and what that death means and how it affects what we do, who we are, and how we act. In this sense, death is an experience for the living.

This book is written to think about how we, the living, experience death as we encounter it through our involvements and reflections with those others with whom we are in relationship, which is to say the whole moral community broadly speaking. Our effort in these pages is to deliberate on the moral meaning of death for the living. For we, the living, confront death in our own lives and in the lives of others, and we ask questions about what is good, right, and fitting as persons—even we ourselves—face death. When others die, the living are left with moral questions that reflect back on the movement toward death, which comes to have standing as a moral project in people's lives whether we recognize it as such or not; we, the living, will even judge whether a particular death was a "good death," or whether it was a tragic death, a justified death, a wrongful death, a terrifying death, or a peaceful death. Death looms before all and presents us with the prospect of losing what is most important—our own life and the lives of others, many of whom we love. Although death will one day include each of us, the experience of anyone's actual death, even our own, will be someone else's. Another way to put this is that my death—your death—will be experienced by someone other than me—or you.

Having opened the idea of an ethics of death to reflection on the deaths of others as experienced by the living, we have undertaken to examine the deaths that all of us witness and involve ourselves in as members of the moral community. Death takes many forms. It comes to us through natural processes, such as disease, and through human action, such as killing. But in the processes whereby human beings come to death, decision making and questions of moral meaning are constantly present. Heart disease and cancer, for instance, are natural occurrences that can lead to death, but people make all kinds of decisions about what to do once they are handed a diagnosis: whether or not to treat, how aggressively to treat, and so on.[4] These may look like purely scientific questions, but medical science is actually providing information for deliberation and interpretation as well as treatment options: what is to be done with that information is a moral question. The physician who says to a patient, "This is what we should do," is acting as a member of the moral community hoping to persuade another person with whom the physician is in relationship to act in such a way that the good of life might be preserved. The physician wants to see the patient flourish, which is to say that by taking one course of action over another the physician believes that the patient might continue to enjoy life and the many goods of life—friendship, aesthetic experience, bodily and psychological integrity, and so on. Ordinarily, reasonable persons want to avoid death—not only their own but the death of others—for as long as possible, since life is good in and of itself. There are many intrinsically good things in life, and death puts an end to those and grieves us with the pain of loss, which can be devastating and even at times unendurable. The pain of loss, which is part of the experience of death for the living, leads often to the conclusion that death is itself a great evil, but death can be thought of more neutrally, say, as a terminus in the life process, and it is known throughout nature among all life forms. Human beings can do things that bring about death in ways that challenge moral sensibilities and upset the possibility of human flourishing. This book investigates an ethics of death by examining those challenges.

In the pages ahead we examine such issues as suicide, physician-assisted suicide, euthanasia, capital punishment, abortion, and war—all areas of life where death poses moral challenge. Each author comes at the issue of deciphering moral meaning in a different way. Dennis Cooley, a professor of philosophy and ethics at North Dakota State University (NDSU) and associate director of the Northern Plains Ethics Institute, has written on ethical issues at the end of life from the perspective of a philosopher. Lloyd Steffen, a professor of religion studies at Lehigh University, has also written on end-of-life issues, and he does so as an ethicist concerned about philosophical issues but also as a religion scholar who refers ethical issues to religious values and frameworks. We actually met in Salzburg, Austria, in 2008 at the sixth global Making Sense of Dying and Death conference, agreed to coedit the proceedings of that conference, which was published as *Re-Imaging Death and Dying: Global Interdisciplinary Perspectives*, and then decided to pursue a new

---

4. Although the idea of such diseases as "natural" is made more complicated when they are caused by human action such as smoking or eating imprudently.

project—an interdisciplinary and dialogical inquiry into the ethics of death.[5] This book is the product of a two-year dialogue between a philosopher whose discipline is well defined and a religion scholar who works in a "field" rather than a discipline and who brings the perspectives of a philosopher of religion and ethicist to bear on a topic of importance in the study of religion: death.

From the beginning, dialogic engagement motivated this project. Both of us were committed to the idea that the book would be an exchange, a give-and-take, around ethical ideas involving the meaning of death for the living. Each author would provide background by laying out the ethical perspective to which he was committed, then address in an essay each of the topics taken up in individual chapters in the volume. At the close of the essays, each author would ask of the other person questions provoked by the essay, then each would respond and offer questions back. Much of what is found in this volume is a dialogue in which two scholars interrogate one another on topics of common interest but through different perspectives. The questions we ask of each other reflect differences in training and methodological commitment.

We undertook this project believing that scholars and students as well as more general readers would find this a valuable contribution to a cross-disciplinary discussion of issues related to the ethics of death. In the pages ahead, readers will encounter authors who are concerned to lay out how they go about analyzing ethical problems in light of theoretical commitments, and readers will discover quickly that different approaches are used in the examination of the moral questions at issue. The authors at times disagree with one another, sometimes over questions of analysis, sometimes in ethical outcomes. We ourselves found challenge in the other's perspectives, essays, questions, and remarks. Readers may be interested to see what a philosopher wanted to know about religious attitudes and what sustains those attitudes in questions of life and death (and afterlife), as well as how a religion scholar presents a diversity of views from different religious traditions that may or may not provide clarity on particular philosophical questions. As we exchanged files via e-mail (and tried not to mix up or lose the latest version of a chapter), we found the ongoing conversation engaging, even fun at times, and both of us hope that in these pages readers will find a model for how to engage and inquire, push and disagree with civility and good will. There is no rancor in these pages, and neither of us engaged in critical inquiry of the other's

5. Here is the full publication information for the conference proceedings: Dennis R. Cooley and Lloyd Steffen, eds., *Re-Imaging Death and Dying: Global Interdisciplinary Perspectives* (Oxford, UK: Inter-Disciplinary, 2009). This e-book may be found at http://www.inter-disciplinary.net/publishing/id-press/ebooks/re-imaging-death-and-dying.

perspective with an eye toward criticizing for the sake of criticizing, as if that were the hallmark of "critical thinking." Some ideas put forward in the pages ahead may surprise readers, but even controversial ideas are given a fair hearing and not rejected out of hand—we have tried to clarify issues and perspectives through the process of analysis and back-and-forth deliberation.

As a word of thanks, we want to express our gratitude for the global dying and death conference mentioned above that turns out to have been the true origin of this volume. This conference still meets yearly and is sponsored by Inter-Disciplinary.Net, with Dr. Rob Fisher and Dr. Nate Hinerman the primary organizers. We are also grateful for the support of Fortress Press throughout this project and to readers who offered helpful comments and suggestions that have improved what is offered in these pages.

Dennis Cooley would like to thank his department colleagues in the philosophy-humanities and the religious studies programs at NDSU and Catherine Cater, NDSU professor emeritus, who spent so much time discussing various positions and arguments with him and then kept him from making too many mistakes.

Lloyd Steffen would like to thank friends and scholars at Lehigh University, especially Kenneth Kraft, who provided a helpful assist on ethical issues in Buddhism, Dena Davis, who introduced him to the Jain practice of *sallekhana,* which finds its way into the suicide chapter, and Barbara Pavlock, for her instructive Latin lesson; and members of the ethics committee at St. Luke's University Hospital in Fountain Hill, Pennsylvania and colleagues at various conferences with whom he has discussed dying and death issues. He is, as always, grateful for the support of his spouse, Emmajane Finney, and his sons Nathan, Sam, and Will.

1

Ethical Perspectives

INTRODUCTION

In all moral decision making, there are two necessary components: a value theory and a normative theory. The value theory tells us what things, including objects and properties, such as being pleased or being a living thing, have a worth that should be taken into account in some way when making a decision. Basically, values serve as the data in ethics. Normative theories, on the other hand, say how to use the data. Normative principles classify actions as morally right or wrong, or morally required, forbidden, or permissible. They also classify people, actions, and objects as good or bad. But the principles could not fulfill this function without values. As will be seen in what follows, some ethicists believe that an action is morally right because in performing the action, no moral agent was treated in an inappropriate way. In other words, everyone affected was respected for their intrinsic worth. So here value is found in being a person, and the normative principle states that we have to respect that value in order to do the right thing.

Below, we will develop normative principles we or others find useful in making moral decisions about death. We shall also develop a value theory that allows the normative theories from this chapter to be applied in theoretical and, more importantly, real-world situations.

STEFFEN

The question at the heart of ethics is this: "Why do you do what you do?"

This question may look simple, but consider all the other questions that it opens: What are our motives, our intentions, and our purposes? Why do we act one way rather than another? What goes into making a decision? Do we have to deliberate in a conscious reflective mode when we act or do our actions flow from something more basic and unreflective, as if the way we act is somehow a part of our personality, our habits and character? If what we do—our actions—reveals our character and character is built up over years of experience and interaction with others, what does it mean to say that what we do flows from decisions we make? Do we really deliberate over actions or do we act out of habit, almost out of moral instincts, and are we forced to hunker down and think things through only occasionally, when confronted for the first time with a really serious issue out of the ordinary?

And the questions continue. Can we change character—and why would we want to if we are feeling comfortable with our own sense of identity? Do we really aim at goodness in what we do? What role do emotions play in choosing how to act? What role does reason play in decision making, and what role does it play in decisions that seem to be grounded in emotion? Are reason and emotion really so different if both involve perceptions that entail judgments, evaluations, and interpretations of those things we perceive to be objects of fear, resentment, anger, or love? What authority do we try to serve when we act one way rather than another? Do we always try to choose the good thing to do, the best thing—and what is that, and how can we possibly know? Is the good action the one that promotes my interest, or is it the one that promotes the interests of my community, or of everyone taken altogether? Can we deceive ourselves about what is good so that sometimes we do something wrong, hurtful, or injurious to others or even ourselves while thinking that action is a good thing? Is being selfish or self-interested a good reason to act one way rather than another? Can I calculate goodness and make a decision by running the numbers? If I want no one else to enjoy the benefits I receive from some action, can the action be said to be good? Why do bad things happen to good people and why do good people sometimes do bad things? We can stop now with the questions. We have just started, but the questions go on and on.

The variety and breadth of the questions that arise in thinking about how we are to live well are what make ethics an intellectually demanding and even exciting arena of inquiry. It is worth noting at the outset, however, that ethics does not claim to be doing new things. New problems demanding ethical attention arise all the time, many of them created by technology or new political, social, or scientific advances. Kant never had to deal with a heart-lung machine and wonder when it might be justifiably turned off. Aristotle never had to contemplate a justification for a public policy on carbon emissions aimed at reversing global warming. These are our problems, not those of Kant or Aristotle, yet both Kant and Aristotle contemplated the meaning of ethical living and made contributions to moral philosophy that are still being used—and appreciated—today. Ethics adapts to address new issues and problems, but it is concerned with timeless issues that have preoccupied thoughtful people over the ages and probably before we even began thinking about ages and time, old issues such as the meaning of the good life and what is required to live life well.

Those old questions at the heart of moral inquiry may make the field of ethics look like it avoids innovation, which it does to a considerable extent, and they may lead the newcomer to the field to suspect that this is a subject area dominated by a lot of old fuddy-duddy philosophical types—probably male and privileged in one way or another—and from there it is an easy inference to the suspicion that ethics is boring. How could it not be if it is relying on the insights of thinkers who lived twenty-five-hundred years ago in the case of Aristotle or over two hundred years ago in the case of Kant? In a world where we expect change as rapidly as we expect to see a new advertisement proclaiming this year's pair of jeans to be vastly superior to last year's, the idea that we could benefit from philosophical thought about living well formulated in a faraway land two millennia ago seems itself far-fetched. But before stopping there, note that in this field, unlike many others, there are some actual proposals on the table for considering questions that, truth be told, really are of interest to just about everyone. In ethics, the question, "What is it that makes life worth living?" is a question worthy of consideration, and ethicists actually do answer it. When, at the end of this section, I share one of the most common answers ethicists offer, I hope that the reader who responds by saying "That's it?" will also go on to say, "Well, of course, but that just opens up a lot of questions."

What makes ethics interesting is not the answers but the questions—and the questions can be challenging. We cannot think about the topics that are the subject of this book—dying and death—and not realize that these topics raise hard questions. Dying and death are realities and prospects in life that have or will involve us all, and ethics reminds us that at the heart of these topics are real people in difficult, sometimes tragic situations. They often do not know what to do or what they should do, but decision making is inescapable. So ethics is going to prompt a series of questions: Why will people facing dying and death do what they do? How will they justify their actions? How will they present their positions so that we will agree with them and support them, or perhaps criticize them and even want to prevent them from enacting their decisions?

Before we enter into discussions and debate over the particular issues that will be addressed in this book—all those big and messy issues: abortion, capital punishment, physician-assisted suicide, just to mention a few—we should pause to inquire about ethics and its resources.

ETHICS AND MORALS

Ethics is a field of philosophy that inquires into the meaning of action and all that bears on reasons for action. Ethics has been described as the philosophical study of morality, with morality in this formulation pointing to behaviors—those things human beings actually do. In *descriptive ethics*, we take the pulse of the world and note how the world is filled with different kinds of behaviors, justifications, and systems of justification for those behaviors. In *metaethics,* philosophers analyze the nature of moral judgments and consider the adequacy of theoretical systems. And *normative ethics*, which will be the focus of this book, tries to establish which moral views are justifiable so that we can prescribe the good, right, and fitting thing to do, which one hopes will be a good action but which may sometimes be the least bad action.

In ethics we use prescriptive language, the kind of language physicians use when they direct a patient to take a medication three times a day: here is a prescribed action and this is what you ought to do. By saying that ethics uses prescriptive language—a language of *shoulds* and *oughts*—we are also saying that our aim is to arrive at a position where we can recommend some action to others as the best thing to do, just as the physician will say, "Take one pill three times a day—do not skip a day or take three pills at a time."

To begin an ethics book by talking about prescriptive language may seem odd and out of step, especially when the view is widespread that ethics is really about opinions and the need to respect the diversity of opinion. We are rightly suspicious of a judgmentalism that can reveal ethnocentrism or, worse, cultural imperialism. We have learned the importance of toleration, respect for diversity, and the value of being nonjudgmental toward other viewpoints, all good things we could actually show to be good ethically speaking. Ethics, however, is filled with *oughts* and *shoulds* that commend certain kinds of actions and attitudes, such things as these: we ought not to tell lies, we should be kind to others and respect other persons, we ought to be tolerant of a position we disagree with but recognize as reasonable, and we ought not be judgmental in this situation for the reason that the facts are not all clear or known. Although normative ethics involves more than compiling a list of shoulds and oughts, it is still inescapable that analyzing situations and problems to establish what one should do is very much its aim. Moral inquiry pushes us to discern, establish, and then commend to others why we ought to do this rather than that. We are looking for reasons, the best reasons—which means the most justifiable reasons—for our actions, and what we determine to be the best, most fitting, and right thing to do is what we *should* do and others *ought* to do as well. It's only logical.

Normative applied ethics seeks to resolve particular moral issues, and this book is about particular moral issues related to very specific topics familiar to everyone—abortion, suicide, euthanasia, war. What should one recommend in thinking about physician-assisted suicide or abortion or war? Are such activities allowable, not allowable, sometimes allowable? How do we know? How do we determine when such an activity is justified and, if so, under what circumstances? When we ask what is right and what is wrong, we are applying *normative ethics* to particular issues, and that is our purpose in the pages to follow. Readers may disagree with us, but when they do so, their disagreements should be based on an analysis of the strengths and weaknesses of the positions being offered. Disagreements should be welcomed if one encounters better arguments or questions that either were not raised or still are not satisfactorily answered. The work of applied normative ethics requires engagement with problems and with people who are confronting problems. Those who would study ethics and engage the problems that people face need to bring to their work of critical analysis clarity, constant questioning, and the envisioning of possible answers or imaginative solutions.

ETHICS EDUCATION

We learn to be moral persons by all that intersects with us in our relations with others. We are schooled in what constitutes acceptable and unacceptable behaviors. We learn to be moral persons from our parents and families, our friends, our schools and religious institutions, groups we join, the books we read, and the people who become friends, critics, or even enemies. We are educated into the moral life and then come into the study of ethics already formed as moral persons. The task of ethics is not to provide the moral education we associate with behavioral training, but ethics education is itself a good thing in the moral sense of "good." For ethics education requires that we engage practical reason to consider action and justifications, values and behaviors, and engage processes whereby people create moral meaning. This book is an ethics education project, and as such it is meant to benefit those who will make use of it, for it is designed to contribute to the efforts each of us makes to live well in relation to both ourselves and others. The authors of this book both believe that ethics is important to the life projects every one of us undertakes. This book, then, as an exercise in ethics education, is a contribution to thinking about the good life (and perhaps, given our subject matter, a "good death").

Ethics education—education into ethical thinking and reflection—is itself an activity that can be subjected to ethical critique. Ethics education is what allows us to construct an argument against the position of the reader who, in reflecting on the claim made just a short time ago that ethics might be boring, concluded that the study of ethics must therefore be a waste of time. A response to that position would point out that ethics education contributes to life projects aimed at living fulfilled and meaningful lives, and engaging with the meaning of one's own life is the central task we face as moral persons. Individuals suffering from psychological distresses that prevent them from finding pleasure and enjoying life—Freud called such states "anhedonia"—might of course find such a task boring, but we might be concerned about such persons, make judgments about their condition, and wish to help them reinvigorate their existential passion for living. Our life projects are not boring, and boring is not bad in any case: persons who have faced an adrenaline rush caused by the possibility of mayhem or a threat to their lives could probably speak eloquently to the issue. Let us dwell there no further and turn instead to ethics education as it contributes to life projects aimed at life lived well and meaningfully.

We derive several benefits from ethics education, the first of which is that we increase our sensitivity to the needs and desires of others. That increase in sensitivity, which also represents increasing self-awareness, is made possible by learning to identify the various kinds of ethical issues that arise in the context of our relationships with self and others. Ethics education helps people learn about and identify a wide variety of such issues, and then provides some of the tools for analyzing those issues and considering responses. Involving oneself in an ethics case study, for instance, results in finding out about moral complexity and the many options for action people face when confronting problems and dilemmas. As life itself is complex, so too is the moral life. Deliberating on options for action increases our own awareness of the problems both we and others will face. Becoming sensitized to complexity may help us identify moral issues however they arise—in our personal life, in work or professional life, even in our downtime as we grapple with moral issues at the heart of the literature we read, the films we watch, and the video games we play. Moral complexity is central to any form of entertainment we judge to be challenging and ennobling, and grappling with that complexity contributes to our desire to live well.

Another benefit of ethics education is learning about ethical theories and systems of analysis. All ethical theories have strengths and weaknesses. Learning to use these theories and apply them to real-life issues makes them resources for ethical living. Ethical theories provide action guides that affect decision making.

They articulate principles that people actually use to justify acting one way rather than another. I shall discuss ethical theories shortly.

Ethics education benefits us by helping us analyze the moral meaning of everyday activities. The more educated we are in ethics, the more able we are to apply theory to practice and refer actions to theory. As we apply the best in these theories to our everyday lives, we grow more confident of our moral reasoning abilities and powers. Ethics education seeks to nurture the processes of reasoning that lead us to accept ethical principles and then apply those principles to real-life situations and problems.

Finally, we must note that the study of ethics—this process of ethics education, of which this book is a part—may not lead us to consensus with others about what to do on so thorny a problem as, say, abortion. Yet the increase in ethical awareness may alter ethical behavior. This cannot always be assured, but ethics often presents situations other people confront even though they are not part of our personal experience. By making us think about the principles or action guides relevant to a particular situation, we may be shaped in new ways in our own thinking about how we would or should act. Ethics education is, after all, education. As such, the acquisition of ethical knowledge and understanding may enlarge our sense of empathy for those facing complex situations. That increase in empathy contributes to the possibility that what we learn will affect not only our understanding but our decision making and our behavior. Learning changes people. Going from not knowing to knowing, and from not understanding to now understanding, alters outlook, framework, and awareness. The reader should expect to be changed by studying ethics, even if he or she already knows that it is good to be kind to people and wrong to lie. Ethics education does not so much change basic moral commitments and orientation as it does increase understanding, deepen awareness, and expand empathy toward others. By sensitizing us to moral dynamics and ethical nuance, such education affects how we think, and it may very well affect how we live.

ETHICAL THEORIES

Ethics education presents various ethical theories for our consideration. These theories create a structure within which we can analyze moral issues and problems, and they provide working tools in the form of action guides or principles that we can apply to behavioral dilemmas. Ethical theories make it possible to sort out what is at issue when moral questions and perplexities arise. They help us propose options for action so that we might do what is good, right, and fitting. Theories, in other words, can help us determine the reasons to do one thing rather than another when faced with a choice. Ethical theories help determine why people do what they do, and they also provide the assessment tools to determine if those decisions, either proposed or already accomplished, are, or were, the best thing to do.

We shall examine four ethical theories that are worthy of attention because they are commonly discussed and studied by those who work in ethics. More importantly, however, these theories provide the ethics handles that people actually use in their everyday lives. The theories claim reason as their foundational authority. Deontological ethics, utilitarian ethics, virtue ethics (axiological ethics), and natural law ethics all claim to be reasonable and reason-based ethical structures. This distinguishes them from religiously based ethics, which, however reasonable they may be, do not look primarily to reason but to transcendent revelation and divine command as their source of authority.

DEONTOLOGICAL ETHICS OR KANTIANISM

Deontological ethics is associated with the ethical writings of Immanuel Kant (1724-1804), the eighteenth-century Prussian philosopher who formulated two versions of what he called "the Categorical Imperative." Kant's ethics proposes a formal prescription for discerning what is and what is not the good, fitting, and right thing to do, and he put it this way:

- Act on that maxim through which you can at the same time will that it should become a universal law.
- Act in such a way that you always treat humanity, whether in your own person or in the person of any other, never simply as a means, but always at the same time as an end.[1]

These two principles are the core of Kant's deontological or duty-based ethic. The ethic articulates two principles that establish the formal reasons for making decisions and then acting one way rather than another. The first principle is often called the *universalizability principle*, the second the *respect for persons principle*.

When contemplating an action under the universalizability principle, the Kantian constructs a maxim, or rule, and applies it universally. That means that if the rule is good for me to do, as in "Cheating is a morally good action because it contributes to many good results not only for myself but for others," it is good

---

1. Immanuel Kant, *Groundwork of the Metaphysics of Morals*, trans. H. J. Paton (New York: Harper and Row, 1964), 88, 96.

for everyone else to do. My thinking might go like this: if I cheat I will improve my grade and help myself get into medical school; and if I get into medical school and become a doctor, many good things will accrue to me and those I will help as a doctor. The benefits look to be incalculable. Therefore cheating is a good thing, a morally good action as our maxim or rule states.

The principle of universalizability operates by taking the rule one has devised and making it universally applicable, like a "law of nature" as Kant put it. Perhaps Kant had in mind gravity, which is a constant, so when we talk about the law of gravity, we do not say it applies to left-handed people one way and to blue-eyed people another, but to everyone everywhere in a similar way. The rule about cheating, which is akin now to the law of gravity in that it applies to everyone, specifies a morally good action *if* it is good for everyone. If, however, it is not good for you to do it, or for everyone to do, then it is not something that I should do. In fact, if I apply the rule and find out that it will not apply universally, I must conclude that it is not good for anyone to do. That is how we identify under the rule of universalizability an immoral or wrongful act. What is immoral is whatever fails to pass the universalizability test. So if I am going to justify cheating, I can only do so by acknowledging the goodness of cheating for everyone, thereby authorizing everyone who is similarly situated to cheat.

But this will not work. The people who contemplate cheating do so because they want to increase their advantage over others, but the universalizability principle exposes a contradiction. On the one hand, I want to cheat to gain advantage for myself over others. On the other hand, if I universalize a rule that endorses cheating so that everyone is entitled to cheat, I am allowing others to seek their advantage by cheating me, and that makes no sense. A person who decided to cheat, therefore could not reasonably want someone else to cheat, for by allowing someone else to cheat the original advantage to be gained over others by means of cheating is lost.

The universalizability principle insists that this is how ethical determinations must be made. In the case of cheating, I have to admit that I do not want others to do what I want to do because cheating only "works" if other people are honest and do not cheat. In the logic of cheating, one gains the advantage only if others refuse to cheat. When we analyze cheating, the point of the behavior is to gain over others an unfair advantage, but reasonable people would not want others to take advantage of them in this way. If people do not want to be taken advantage of by others, then, on Kant's viewpoint, neither should they act in a way that allows them to receive an unfair advantage. This analysis shows that cheating fails the test of universalizability, and that is why cheating, for Kant, is wrong.

On the principle of universalizability, one ought not to cheat. And on the second "respect for persons" principle, one ought not cheat because by doing so one is treating all those who do not cheat disrespectfully. They are actually harmed by the cheater because they are being put in a position of inequality and disadvantage—the playing field is not level, the deck is stacked and the cards are marked. When this happens, the noncheater is actually harmed by the cheater who treats others unjustly by taking unfair advantage of them. To cheat is to treat others as a means to an end. The cheater seeks to promote his or her own benefit and create through the act of cheating a situation in which all who do not cheat are disadvantaged. Cheaters act as if the rules that establish a level playing field do not apply to them, and they act as if they were superior to others. Who would willingly agree to have his or her own dignity assaulted as the victim of such an injustice? When someone cheats, those who do not cheat are being treated disrespectfully.

UTILITARIANISM/CONSEQUENTIALISM

In Kant's ethic, no attention is paid to the consequences of an action. Attention is paid to intentions—the good will. The focus of the ethic is on motives and intentions because they are under rational control, and reason tells us that we can never truly foresee the consequences of our actions. One wants to do what reason bids, to do one's duty and obey the moral law as formulated in the Categorical Imperative. Another reason-based Enlightenment ethic, utilitarianism, does pay attention to consequences and bases determinations of what is and what is not moral solely on the "greatest good for the greatest number" of people. Utilitarianism, associated with Jeremy Bentham and John Stuart Mill, proposes that what is moral—what is good, right, and fitting to do—is what reason is able to establish as the best possible anticipated or foreseen consequences of an action for the greatest number of people. That is the sole determinant of moral meaning. The content of the principle of utility ("usefulness") may be defined as happiness or pleasure, or even in Christian "situation ethics" as the act that shows itself to be the most loving, but moral meaning is always the result of assessing consequences. Although utilitarian consequentialism does not pay attention to intentions or principles of human dignity, it does understand human beings, because they possess the rational capacity, to have standards of happiness above those of other animals—better a dissatisfied human being than a satisfied pig, John Stuart Mill famously said, but the ethic determines moral meaning by rational calculation. If a utilitarian were to consider intentions, as in saying that physicians should intend to show kindness as they approach patient care, the showing of kindness would not be intrinsically valuable but would be justified as the best way to maximize the good of physician care.

Both Kantianism and utilitarianism are Enlightenment-era ethics grounded in reason, but they are not thereby compatible with one another. They engage reason in service to two quite divergent purposes. Both seek to provide a means for understanding good action and provide the tools for realizing what is good and morally appropriate, but they have no truck with one another. If one is a consequentialist, one is by necessity not a deontologist. Many students of ethics decide between these options, choosing which side of this ethical divide they will commit to, so we have deontologists—Kantians—on one side, utilitarian consequentialists on the other. They often arrive at the same conclusions about what to do in a particular situation. That student cheating on a test to get into medical school does not fare well on the utilitarian ethic any more than on the deontological side, since a consequentialist would question how much good comes from allowing a student to enter the medical profession when he or she is not in command of the body of knowledge required in physician training. Consider all the harm such an individual could do to patients and to the profession, and we can ask, "Would I, or any reasonable person, want to have as a physician someone who cheated to get through medical school?"

The consequentialist considers the greatest good for the greatest number—all those prospective patients who might one day have a doctor who cheated his or her way into the profession and who, if found out, would bring disgrace to the profession. The individual who cuts corners in study may be revealing a propensity to harm future patients by similar acts of dishonesty. A utilitarian, then, would on consequentialist grounds object to the cheating as well, though for different reasons than the Kantian. Consequentialism must not be thought of as a form of ethical egoism where moral meaning is determined by placing inordinate weight on the consequences for oneself. On the contrary, in the weighing of consequences, one's personal interests are no weightier than anyone else's, and what one might personally prefer for an outcome might be thwarted by a rational consideration of consequences generating the greatest good for the greatest number, which might be quite contrary to one's own preferences. The utility of allowing a cheater to cheat for some supposed good end would in all likelihood not withstand scrutiny, and utilitarianism would adjudge the act of cheating as disallowable and, yes, immoral.

But utilitarianism does not, in a formal way, say that there is any act that is intrinsically wrong, and an act utilitarian, that is, one who calculates the foreseen consequences of a particular action, might determine on consequentialist grounds that an otherwise immoral action is justified in a certain situation—lying to save a life, say, or intentionally killing one person to save five others. A Kantian could not easily make that move, for a wrong act, one that disrespects persons or fails the universalizability test, is an act that ought not be performed. Both theories have advantages, but both have problems as well. Utilitarianism will not provide us with any notion of human rights, which Kantianism does, but Kantianism also has a tendency to move toward ethical absolutes—as if there were never an occasion or situation so morally challenging that a lie could not be told or cheating could not be justified. Logically, the Kantian could conceivably accede to even an immoral action as long as it were universally adopted (such as stealing as long as it is not detected)—a criticism John Stuart Mill made of Kant. Kant does not deal with the problem that universalized rules or maxims might actually come into conflict with one another, so when confronted with, say, hiding a Jew from a pursuing Nazi, how does the Kantian reconcile the maxim not to lie with the maxim to save a life? The Kantian cannot appeal to consequences.

The obvious problems with these theories include the inevitable failure of the utilitarian to foresee all the consequences of any action while refusing to acknowledge any act as intrinsically wrong, instead viewing such an act as only consequentially bad. Kantians, on the other hand, can become so strict in regard to principles that they refuse to make exceptions to rules, so that lying, when it might be necessary to save a person's life, is impermissible; and the idea that there are foreseen evil consequences is sloughed off as something that the person with good intentions is simply not responsible for—because one can never tell all that might happen and responsibility extends only as far as preserving a good will in one's own decision making. The problem is that sometimes we can foresee evil consequences. We can see that what is going to happen is harmful or destructive. We are so situated that not to act is to act, and the refusal to act on grounds of moral purity contributes to the wrongdoing despite our protests to the contrary. In sum, the two theories have internal problems, and each is lacking something for which the other provides some kind of compensation with respect to moral meaning. Beyond that, they are antagonistic toward one another, and each excludes the other.

VIRTUE ETHICS

Frustration with the problems created by these ethical theories led to a revitalizing of Greek virtue ethics several decades ago. If Enlightenment ethical theories focus on action and direct attention to the central ethics question—"Why do we do what we do?"—virtue ethics offers a corrective. This ethical theory considers being rather than action as the central category. The question in virtue or axiological ethics is not "What should I do?" but "Who should I be?" Ethics now directly focuses on issues of personal character; it seeks to develop habits conformed to behavioral ideals. Virtues are themselves excellences of character. In Aristotle's formulation, ethics seeks to develop virtues that are means between extremes of excess and deficiency, and the moral life is a process of engagement whereby one works to become a person of virtue. Aristotle believed that cultivating virtue is the only way to happiness, and happiness is the end toward which reason and human striving are directed. Since I earlier promised to provide an answer to the question about the meaning of life, this is the ethicist's answer, Aristotle's answer—happiness. It may not be the only answer, but it is a good answer, perhaps the best answer. What people want out of life is happiness, and the ethic Aristotle and other virtue ethicists propose seeks to attain that end. To acquire happiness, one must develop and cultivate the virtues. We become ethical persons to the extent we work to become wise, courageous, temperate, generous, honest, and just in dealings with others. Conversely, the achievement of happiness will come about to the extent that we also work to avoid those things that represent either excesses or deficiencies of these virtues, as cowardice is a deficiency of the virtue of courage and rashness is its excess.

Virtue ethics points to the inward development of persons in moral community, and it too has problems. It downplays external action by focusing on internal development, though, truth be told, the test of internal virtue "cultivation" must always be publicly observable behavior. A person cannot cultivate honesty inwardly and be dishonest in his or her actual dealings with other people. Virtue ethics focuses on internal virtue development, but the presence of virtue can only be established by outward behavior. There are more serious problems, however, one of which is that communities formulate through societal commitments and organization various ideas of what constitutes virtuous behavior. The problem then is that the prejudices and pathologies of communities may determine what we mean by a virtue at this time or in that place. One can imagine a society that rewards those who report to political authorities persons who hold dissenting political ideas; such a society would then cultivate in children the "virtue" of betraying the trust of "dissident" friends. Racist and sexist attitudes have certainly been deemed virtuous at different times and in various places. Virtues, we would think, need to conform to goodness to be virtues, but that need not always be the case. We can even imagine, as was done in the film *The Firm* (1987), a community that transforms a classic vice into a virtue: "Greed is good."[2] Greed cannot be universalized; it does not show respect for persons, and it leads to great harm with respect to the "greater good." We can understand why ethical theory would seek development beyond consideration of virtues, and Kantianism and utilitarianism both offer correctives to these problems we find in virtue ethics.

NATURAL LAW

Another proposal for ethics, one that I subscribe to, derives from the ancient tradition of what is called *natural law*. Natural law asserts the primacy of reason as the foundation for ethical insight, the claim being that human beings are so constituted as reasonable beings that they have a natural capacity to discern goodness and direct themselves toward action we would describe as good, right, and fitting. William Blackstone, the famous English legal scholar of the eighteenth century and author of the influential *Commentaries on the Laws of England*, acknowledged a law of nature that held "that we should live on, should hurt nobody, and should render unto everyone his due," insisting then that "no human laws are of any validity if contrary to this."[3] Natural law makes a serious claim on the idea that ethics should reflect the way the moral life is actually lived. This may seem obvious, but although ethical theories can present action guides that appear very clean and precise, the moral life as it is actually lived is very messy indeed. We are often perplexed about what to do, and our theories seem unhelpfully abstract when we face troubling circumstances. Natural law approaches ethics from the view that reason is by natural endowment capable of discerning various goods of life, including not only the good of life itself but several other goods universally recognized as good and without which human life would be impoverished. Such goods include friendship, bodily and psychological integrity, aesthetic experience, practical reasonableness, and speculative reason—the list could go on. Using those goods as its foundation, natural law supports actions and attitudes that

---

2. This statement by the character Gordon Gekko, played by Michael Douglas, in Oliver Stone's *The Firm* actually echoes the Berkeley Commencement Address of the previous year, when Ivan Boesky said, "Greed is all right, by the way. I want you to know that. I think greed is healthy. You can be greedy and still feel good about yourself." Boesky was later arrested and sent to prison for insider trading. See Lynn Stuart Parramore, "'Greed Is Good': Top 7 Most Piggish Commencement Speeches," Alternet.org, May 23, 2013, http://www.alternet.org/education/greed-good-top-7-most-piggish-commencement-speeches.

3. Quoted in Robert D. Richardson, *Emerson: The Mind on Fire* (Berkeley: University of Califonia Press, 1995), 497.

conform to and promote the various goods of life. These goods are recognized as good through the exercise of reason's natural capacity. And in the exercise of the good of practical reason, natural law ethicists can formulate basic moral agreements about prospective actions that should cut across cultural divides and express universal moral aspirations.

So a natural law ethic can provide us with some basic moral agreements, and it is reason's chore to articulate them. But this approach to ethics also recognizes that, as I said, life is messy. Our affirmations of universal moral insights may require some further consideration as a result of situation and circumstance, which is to say that this way of approaching ethics will allow us to consider making exceptions to those basic common agreements. We can see this most dramatically in what is called just war theory.

Just war theory is often employed to provide justification for the use of military force and thereby justify war. But as an expression of natural law ethics, just war, were it to be considered a true ethic and not a handmaiden of policy makers seeking to justify force for nationalist or aggressive purposes, has a common agreement supporting it. As an ethic, just war is founded on a common agreement that could easily support practical pacifism: force ought not be ordinarily used to settle conflicts. Natural reason can avow this agreement, and no reasonable person of good will would object to it, whatever the contingency of cultural difference. The problem is that sometimes situations arise where an exception needs to be considered. What happens when the party with whom one is in conflict is unreasonable, acts aggressively, and perhaps poses enormous threats to the safety of innocent persons? In such circumstances one has grounds for considering a use of force.

Just war says that the use of force contemplated must be restrained and rule governed so as to minimize harm, resolve the conflict, and restore the conditions where conflicts can be settled by means other than force, such as mediation and compromise. What this means about just war as a natural law ethic is that reason can determine a common agreement that force is not a preferable way to settle conflicts but that force is sometimes necessary to prevent injustices. The ethic is not absolutist but is open to making exceptions; and the common agreement moral platform immunizes the ethic from ethical relativism. The ethic therefore establishes criteria, which are formal justice-related notions, also avowed by practical reason, that must be argued about and those contemplating force must resolve to satisfy. This approach to ethics asserts the idea that there is a common moral agreement that can be overruled in certain circumstances for reasons of just cause and other justice concerns, which can be articulated as criteria. If this is indeed an approach to ethics, we should be able not only to use it but also to find it being used in all kinds of different situations. So the Oregon Death with Dignity Act, as one example, supports the moral idea that physicians ought not ordinarily help patients commit suicide. Who would disagree with that? Even Jack Kevorkian would not disagree. But that law then imposed over seventy conditions to govern the process of making an exception to this moral agreement. All of the restraining criteria or conditions of justice have to be satisfied before a physician can write a lethal prescription.

In the pages ahead, I will make use of this approach to ethics because I believe it deals with the messiness of life and allows us the ability to use practical reason to figure out what is best to do when confronted with morally difficult problems. Issues involved with death and dying present such problems, and this ethic allows us to affirm aspects of the three other ethical perspectives we have just examined. It allows us to assert and follow a universal, principled common agreement rule, which a Kantian would require. It allows us to consider the possibility of an exception in certain circumstances due to practical justice considerations (criteria) so that consequences play a role—this would involve considerations relevant to utilitarian consequentialists. And this ethic requires that people of good will come together to discuss problems, share information relevant to a conflict or problem honestly and courageously, and reflect on issues wisely, all of which points to virtue. The natural law ethic is a *hybrid ethic* that allows the other ethical theories a part but says none has the final say. On the level of theory this may look to be contradictory, but as an ethic that is taking seriously the problems we confront in the messiness of the moral life, it is actually a guide for proceeding through moral analysis in ways that reflect our actual experience.

A natural law hybrid ethic, because it is open to exceptions, is by definition not an absolutist ethic. Neither is it a situation ethic because it is grounded in principles that are universal and recognizable to reason as such. It conforms to the requirements of an ethic: it respects the principle of universalizability; it is concerned for others (other-regarding) and their well-being (beneficence); it is guided by concerns for justice, which appear in the development of criteria to guide exception making; and it will support a set of normative principles housed in our common agreements, such as "don't settle conflicts by force" or "doctors should not directly kill patients who want to die."[4] This ethic takes advantage of the strength of our other ethical theories—deontological Kantianism, utilitarian consequentialism, and virtue ethics—while avoiding their weaknesses. This

---

4. See the requirements for an ethic, Joseph Runzo, "Religion and Ethics in the Global World," in *Ethics in the World Religions*, ed. Joseph Runzo and Mary M. Martin (Oxford: One World, 2001), 23.

ethic allows us to talk about human rights and intrinsically wrong acts while taking account of consequences and the need for virtuous people to engage in respectful conversation and disagreement.

RELIGIOUS ETHICS

One other moral theory—divine command theory—also merits attention. Divine command theory says that reasons for action should reside in transcendent sources. In other words, I do what I do because God or some other version of ultimate reality has revealed the divine will, and because the will is good and pure and envisioned as incapable of error, one should abide by it and do what it reveals should be done. People all around the world subscribe to such an ethic. And it is a very powerful place to stand, ethically speaking. If one is able to argue that the reason one is holding to an ethical position is because it is commanded by transcendent sources as the good and right thing to do, ethical conflicts disappear, and one can advocate for a course of action that rests in the certainty of divine knowledge and authority. It is hard to argue with God. On the other hand, ethical injunctions derived from divine sources usually come to us through texts that are interpretations of what is perceived to be the revealed will of God—no good theist ever wants to say that human beings have access to God's mind or will the way God does, so God communicates through revelation, and revelations are interpretable. Moses came down from the mountain with God's commands written in God's own hand, but he destroyed those tablets; when he went up again, he took dictation and the commandments that came down the second time were in his hand, not the writing of the divine finger. So the law that came down from Sinai is Moses' interpretation of what God said, and interpretations are disputable. Divine command, as powerful as it is as a place to stand, does not eliminate the problem of conflicting interpretations as to what is right and wrong.

When we approach issues of death and dying and examine how religion might play a role in sorting out ethical issues, we must keep in mind that appeal to divine direction on a particular issue is always going to be an appeal to an interpretation of a divine will that is revealed (and thus somewhat concealed). Thus, any claim that one can speak with absolute certainty about what God as the ultimate arbiter of good and evil, right and wrong wants human persons to do in a particular situation is an interpretation. If we knew for certain God's will on any particular moral conflict, we would be possessed of moral certainty, for God, as we define God, would not be capable of making a mistake and would have no reason to mislead us. So we would have certainty about what to do.

That the divine will is clear, that it has been communicated clearly, and that the ability of human persons to receive without interference from ego or self-interest the divine will as God intended are bold assumptions; religious ethics usually begins with some kind of theological anthropology that insists on human limitation and finitude, especially in the face of the divine. On the issues we shall examine in the pages ahead, we will mention appeals to religious authority and religious grounds for decision making, but we should be clear. Divine command as an ethic is still an ethic, and people have to make decisions to use it and interpret it. In fact, religion itself will insist on a view of human persons as fallible and capable of error and misinterpretation. Even those who claim that they are following a "literal interpretation" of their religion's sacred teachings are identifying by that statement that they are following a particular interpretation, but who says a literal interpretation is the correct one? We may define God as the ultimate arbiter of ethical truth, but it is hard to define human beings as capable of receiving or understanding that truth without error or without using reason to discern or even construct truth.

Religious ethics may very well lead to the same conclusions one finds in secular or nonreligious ethics, but not always. Sometimes a religious ethic may push for action guides ordinary practical reason would not see as a moral requirement. For example, the Christian injunction to "love one's enemy" is central to the religious ethic of Jesus and thus important to Christians. Of course, not all Christians acknowledge it as a live option in their lives because it seems too extreme, as if it is asking too much of mere mortals. Such an ethical requirement appears to be supererogatory—good to do and perhaps even wonderful to do, but a command above and beyond the requirements of reason, not a duty and not really expected. Sometimes religious ethics seem to present what appear to be supererogatory demands.

In addition, religious ethics can come to us in texts and sacred stories, not as principles but as illustrations, parables, or examples. Religious ethics may present narratives that embody ethical ideas of behavior. While it is possible to have clear injunctions or imperatives about what is expected religiously from behavior, as in "Thou shalt not kill," there are also stories that express moral requirements. In Christianity, Jesus tells stories and parables that contain an ideal of behavior and sometimes pose a question that listeners are asked to attend to and reflect on. Religious ethics can often use narrative forms to convey ethical ideals.

In general, religious ethics are important in discussions of ethical issues because religion is one of the most important cultural transmitters of meaning, value, and ethical ideals. Religion addresses expectations for behavior in codes and stories, by means of sacred texts and commentaries, through preaching and the learning of tradition. Beyond the specific appeal religious people may make to an ethic of divine command to justify their decisions about what to do and how to act, religion also conveys ethical norms and expectations to individuals and communities in ways that should not be underestimated.

In the pages ahead we shall see the role that religion can play in shaping ethical responses related to death and dying. What is conveyed should be subject to reasoned analysis. Religion deals with ultimate realities and ultimate power—the power of the divine will that typically is thought incapable of making errors with regard to how to act. The problem that confronts religious ethics is that even if one grants for the sake of argument that God possesses perfect moral knowledge, that knowledge has to be revealed, for no one claims to know the mind of God as God knows God's own mind. And where there is revelation, there is interpretation; and where there is interpretation, there is disagreement and confusion and sometimes even chaos. Things are thus not always clear even when people claim they understand the divine will and its specific instructions.

The fact that an ethical perspective is grounded in religion does not relieve people of the responsibility to analyze that perspective to see whether what is being asked of them is coherent as an ethical perspective and whether the normative ideas for behavior being put forward conform to reasonable ideas about what is good, right, and fitting. What I mean by this is that religious ethics can sometimes advance ideas for action that are contrary to our common and more reasonable ideas of what is good. Religious people can claim that what they are doing is grounded in the divine will and then assert that what they are doing must be good because God is good; finite human beings in their limitations simply lack insight into the good God does through acts that may seem wrong, destructive, or evil. The 9/11 hijackers apparently believed they were doing God's will and what they were doing was good and right and in conformity with God's goodness.[5] While we may want to talk about the compassion ethic of Buddhism or the love ethic of Jesus, we also need to keep in mind that the power of religion is not only great but potentially dangerous, and that people can use religion to construct justifications for actions that reason and an ethics based on reason simply cannot support and justify. So religious ethics are important and perhaps the way most people in the world actually learn an

5. See "Final Instructions to the Hijackers of September 11, Found in the Luggage of Mohamed Atta and Two Other Copies," in Bruce Lincoln, *Holy Terrors: Thinking about Religion after September 11* (Chicago: University of Chicago Press, 2003), 93–98.

ethical worldview, but we must invoke religious ethics with caution and be willing, as ethicists, to subject even a religious ethic to critical analysis.

It is perhaps worth noting that *natural law ethics*, which has a long tradition going back to the Greeks and Romans, Cicero especially, was preserved and developed in the Roman Catholic moral tradition. Rather than appealing to some source of authority that makes clear the divine will on any imaginable moral issue, the natural law tradition would say that reason must be engaged to figure out the moral meaning of any decision and action. Natural law ethics, which is related both to secular and religious ethics, holds that human beings possess a natural endowment—reason—that enables them to discern goods of life and to formulate common moral agreements through the use of reason—that is the divine gift to humanity and the contribution of "ultimate reality" to the work of ethics. We shall make use of the concerns and values of religious ethics in the pages ahead, but it is part of religious ethics to see reason itself as a reflection of that which is the divine within us—the *imago Dei* for many Christian and Jews—and such a view is not alien to religious traditions the world over.

COOLEY

Before spending much or any time figuring out which actions are morally right or wrong or what is morally good or bad, we should first answer the question, what is the purpose of morality? Without that knowledge as a benchmark, we could wander in the wilderness trying to discover what we should do and be, and why we should do it and be it. The vagabond life might have some appeal to us, but without a measure for telling what counts and what does not count, we have as much chance of succeeding in being good and doing right as someone trying to assemble an elephant who has only heard vague rumors as to what such a creature looks like.

Not to waste too much time, I will stipulate that morality, much like etiquette, exists to help people and society to function better. In a very densely populated area, etiquette allows people who do not know each other to interact more efficiently so they can lead better lives and the society can improve. For example, if we did not have rules about holding doors open for others, there would be a lot more hurt feeling and noses than would exist with the social rule to hold the door open if there is someone in sufficient proximity at the moment you enter the doorway. So, etiquette makes our lives better.[6]

Morality is based on the same idea but it has a much more important mission. By being ethical, we make our lives better in much more significant ways. First, by doing the right thing, we do not bear the burden of wrongdoing and the residual debts owed because something impermissible was performed by us. More importantly, by doing what is right we develop the dispositions or habits of virtue. These, such as compassion, wisdom, and sympathy, are part of our character, which improves our value as individual persons. When Aristotle characterized virtues as excellences, he was saying that a person who has a virtue is more valuable than a person who does not. And we can see this in our everyday moral thinking. A person who is selfish is considered to be a lesser person than someone who is generous, for example.

Most importantly, as we improve ourselves morally, we simultaneously advance the communities and societies in which we live, although we might not intend our actions to have this effect. But the improvement must occur if we do the right thing or are the right kind of person. Societies and communities are merely collections of people sharing sufficient common ideas that bind them together for a general purpose. If one person improves herself, then the society's value must also increase because it has a more valuable member than it did before that enhancement.

In addition, greater value can accrue based on the impact that one person's action has on the rest of the community. Think of it as throwing a stone into the middle of a calm pond. There is a big splash next to where the stone went in and ripples going out from the origin point in smaller and smaller waves as they spread out. If that one person can help others improve by being a role model, teaching others to do the right thing at the right time for the right reasons, and just doing the ethical thing in her social interactions, then the society as a whole continues to become better.

Finally, it is important to point out the integrated nature of people within a society or community and how that does and should impact our thinking about morality. We don't want to believe that people are merely autonomous islands without relationships to others within their various communities because that is not how people truly are. In order for a person to do the right thing or become a better person, part of that action or improvement has to be focused on the community and societies in which she lives. That is, we cannot be totally self-oriented to improving ourselves because each of us exists in a web of interrelated, complex relationships that are part of who we are. So when we act, we must realize that we are part of a greater whole that will be affected by our actions. Since we are not merely a distinct and complete individual without connections to others, we must, in order to be good persons and act

---

6. Of course, etiquette can crush improvement by thoughtlessly maintaining the status quo. It is here that morality and etiquette part ways.

ethically, consider the greater whole of which we are an integral component. The fact that being part of a community automatically makes us think about others in the community makes it easier to fulfill this role. Just as we think of our family members when we are making major decisions in our lives—because we know that our actions will affect them and we care about how the actions affect them—we should think of other community members and what will happen to them when we act. We do not care for them in the way that we do our family—those familial relationships have stronger emotional ties—but in the way we do for others with whom we share common cause and sense of community. This is what makes us part of the community in the first place. We care as community members about what happens to those in our community because we identify with them through the common cause. That empathy helps drive our consideration for what should happen to them and therefore is part of our ethical thinking in general. Part of each community's common cause is morality.

Regardless of who one is, in general, there are two distinct ways of thinking about ethics and morality that are used by all moral agents or persons. The first is consequentialism, which is the theory that considers only the consequences of actions and our other activities in determining the morality of what we have done. Generally, the idea here is that we should maximize those consequences that are intrinsically good while minimizing those consequences that are intrinsically bad. An intrinsic good is something that is good in and of itself, for its own sake, or as an end in itself. Basically, something is intrinsically good just because it is good without having to resort to saying that it is good for something else. Caring for others who deserve such care is just good in and of itself; therefore, just care is an intrinsic good. Money, on the other hand, is an extrinsic good because it is a good way to get things we want, such as food, cars, and houses. To have something intrinsically good is to have something that is excellent, all things considered. Possession of it improves our moral worth as persons and makes the world a better place.

The idea of consequentialist moral thinking is to maximize intrinsic good over intrinsic evil. In other words, it is a cost-benefit analysis used by businesses and each one of us every day of our lives. We are constantly choosing what we should be and what we should do based on what seems the best thing for us to do at that time and in those circumstances—although we might not consciously be saying that to ourselves. Why should you do one thing over another? If you said that you should do so because one action is better than the other, then you just used a consequentialist principle.

If how our brains function is any indication, we are geared toward being consequentialists in certain circumstances. Consider the following. Trolley problems were created in the 1960s by Philippa Foote but developed in much more detail by Judith Jarvis Thomson.[7] The first one we shall consider involves you as the conductor of a trolley. On the track ahead of you are five small children who have wandered away from their daycare center. If you do not turn the trolley onto another track, then you will hit the five children, likely killing all of them. The good news is that you can turn the trolley onto a branching track, which will keep the five from being hit. The bad news is that on that track is a sixth child from the daycare center who will be seriously harmed through your action. So, what do you do?

Most people choose to turn the trolley onto the track with the one child. Their reasoning is based on the fact that, when one is forced into making a decision with only the two choices, it is right to save five children even though it will sacrifice one child. This is an example of consequentialism at work. Five minus one is a net gain of four children left alive. On the other hand, one minus five is a net loss of four children. Neither one of these outcomes is something anyone would desire—our empathy is always heavily engaged when it comes to endangered children—but most people will take the least tragic or overall bad outcome when they are faced with only evil outcomes.

However, you will notice that I said only that most people will take this option, not that all people will do so. Does this mean that those who would not turn the trolley onto the branching track have somehow made a wrong decision? An unethical decision? Not really; they have focused on other moral values or have made a distinction between acts of omission and acts of commission. An act of omission is one in which a person allows something to happen rather than taking an active part in bringing the action about. In the trolley problem, keeping the trolley on its original course is an act of omission. Acts of commission, on the other hand, require a more active role for the moral agent. He or she has to do something, such as turn the trolley. The moral distinction people often assume exists is between letting something happen and making something happen. The latter seems to give people dirty hands whereas the former keeps them from being responsible. In the former, they have to take an active hand in bringing the action about—which makes them responsible for the action, it seems—and in the latter, they appear to be merely a victim of circumstances.

7. Philippa Foot, "The Problem of Abortion and the Doctrine of the Double Effect," in *Virtues and Vices* (Oxford, UK: Basil Blackwell, 1978). Judith Jarvis Thomson, "The Trolley Problem," *Yale Law Journal* 94 (1985): 1395–1415.

The moral distinction between acts of commission and omission was shown to be false by James Rachels in his famous example of Smith and Jones and their two unfortunate cousins.[8] Smith and Jones each have a young child cousin who inherits a vast estate. If each child dies, then both Smith and Jones would inherit their respective dead cousin's money. Smith creeps into his young cousin's house, up the stairs, and into the bathroom in which his cousin is taking his evening bath. Smith holds his cousin's head underwater until the child drowns. All of us would say both that Smith is responsible for the child's death and that this is a clear act of commission that is a murder.

Now let us take a look at what happens in the case of Jones. Jones acts exactly the same as Smith up to the point in which Jones enters the bathroom, but, in this case, he notices that his young cousin has slipped on a bar of soap, struck his head, and is drowning in the tub. If Jones does nothing, his cousin will die. To save the child, all Jones has to do is raise his cousin's head out of the water, which is a physically easy thing to do for Jones. But Jones does nothing other than watch his cousin drown. Jones, therefore, has committed an act of omission.

In this case, we would say that Jones is as morally responsible for his cousin's death as Smith is for his cousin's death, even though Jones allowed his cousin to die instead of actively killing him. The mere fact that Jones did nothing does not mean that nothing bad happened or that Jones did not act. Jones is responsible for the death of his cousin. By deciding to omit acting, we can be just as responsible for the evil that results—and the good for that matter—as when we perform an act of commission. So there is no safe harbor for us in the alleged distinction between acts of omission and acts of commission when considering the trolley problem above or the variation below. In both cases, we are equally responsible for what happens.

As stated above, some people make their decisions in trolley problems by using moral, nonconsequentialist considerations. These tend to be based on deontological theories of ethics, which we can define here as theories that do not focus solely on the consequences of an action to determine if the action is morally right or wrong. In deontological theories, the consequences can play a major role or no role at all. If consequences are moral factors in whether or not the action is right or wrong, then there have to be other moral considerations as well, such as justice or respect for people or moral rights. For example of a deontological principle with consequentialist elements, a person has to

8. James Rachels, "Active and Passive Euthanasia," *New England Journal of Medicine* 292 (1975): 78–80.

maximize utility, while at the same time making sure that everyone affected by her action is treated as an intrinsically valuable entity should be treated.

Let us take a look at a different trolley problem. We are going to keep the trolley and the five daycare children on the tracks but make a few significant changes. You are no longer the conductor. You are merely standing on a pedestrian bridge overlooking the track. Standing beside you is a very fat man who is leaning precariously over the bridge's guardrail. You see that if the trolley is not stopped, the five children will be struck and killed. You yell down to the conductor, but he is unable to stop the trolley in time. However, all that is needed to help stop the trolley—and therefore save the innocent children—is for a very large object to fall in front of the trolley. The resulting wedged weight, along with the trolley's brakes, will overcome the trolley's momentum in the nick of time. So, do you push the fat man over the edge or not? If he falls in front of the trolley, which will happen if you push him, then his body will act as the needed weight. However, it will kill him.

Generally, the response to this trolley problem is different from that of the first. Most people vote for not pushing the fat man even though it will result in five children being killed. The reason for this change in decision is based on justice or some other value that conflicts with consequentialist thinking. Many state that it is wrong to use the man for the end of saving the children because it is not fair or he does not deserve to be treated in this manner. Others state that by pushing him, we have violated his right to life. Yet others claim that when he is pushed by us, we do not respect his value as a person. Even though we save more lives, the value of one life cannot be compared to the sheer quantity of the other lives. In fact, the reasoning goes, by making it a cost-benefit analysis we degrade the fat man's true value—and maybe even ourselves by allowing ourselves to act in this manner and being people who would sacrifice one person to save five others. The result here shows that people do not always primarily use consequentialist thinking to make their moral decisions, whereas the first trolley problem shows that people do, at least sometimes, primarily use consequentialist thinking to make their moral decisions.

The big question now is what these two trolley problems tell us about how most people view morality. First, and most importantly, I think they show that there are universal ways that people in this country and around the world think about morality. We have a common, universal set of beliefs about value and how morality goes. We think consequentialism works in some cases and deontological theories work in other situations. This reality is very helpful in making decisions that affect wide, diverse swathes of a large society. There will be a common base from which we can discuss the right actions to make ourselves flourish and our society a better place to be. We also have in common universal ideas of virtues and vices. That is, what is a virtue in one place is a virtue in every place, and the same holds true for vices. The difference between groups, communities, and societies is merely which virtues and vices are most important in that society and to whom they apply. But again, the point is that there is common ground for morality that allows us to understand other people's morality and allows them to understand ours—even though neither party might adopt all of the other's views.

Second, even though we might have been neither primarily deontologists for the first trolley problem nor primarily consequentialists for the second, we can still understand why others were. That is, although we would not choose to act in the way that they would, we still can appreciate why they decided that an alternative way of being or acting is morally permissible. More importantly, most of us would not say that making a choice other than ours is evil or wrong for everyone, only that it is inconsistent with our central beliefs about how the world should be. In fact, we recognize that acting in a different way can be as morally permissible as acting in the way we have chosen. This understanding of others' decisions shows that there might be many ethical solutions to a problem rather than merely one. In fact, it is difficult to think of situations in which there is only one right thing to do, unless the circumstances have been described to remove any uncertainty or conflicting values, such as in the case of the institution of slavery always being morally evil. Values not conflicting—or not conflicting in such a way that only one action is right and only one value is good—usually does not happen in real life. Because life and situations in which we decide are always complex, and complexity is generally what causes moral dilemmas in which values and principles conflict, then we should expect that there is not one solution to any particular moral dilemma that prevents all moral residue. For example, in *Sophie's Choice*, Sophie has to decide which of her two children are to live. Selecting either is morally permissible. However, selecting either will also leave Sophie with moral residue caused by not selecting the other, not fulfilling her duties to all of her children, or failing to satisfy all the subjective and objective moral demands placed on her. She will feel guilty even when she does the right thing. We must realize that we might not have chosen the same child as she did, but Sophie did nothing wrong in making her selection. Given the purpose of morality to improve our lives and others' lives in communities, we should respect others' decisions in these complex situations, although we need not agree with them.

The fact that we are deontologists and consequentialists as moral agents thinking about morality should form the basis of any moral code or set of moral principles that tells us what to be and how to act.[9] The main reason I make this claim is based on pragmatism. If people already reason this way and it is not an obviously bad way to think, then it would be easier to design a moral code that incorporates how people are instead of trying to impose a moral code that would work only in an ideal world with ideal people. We, as persons, are not perfect, but we can be good people doing what is right. Therefore, the moral system should be designed for what we are as moral agents rather than for a ideal world that cannot exist.

I propose that the Pragmatic Principle developed here plausibly combines these two seemingly inconsistent foundations into a useful moral principle. Not only will it classify correctly in every situation, it can also be used to create a reasonable argument that all reasonable moral agents can understand and appreciate, although they might use the principle to find a different right action for themselves. In fact, the principle merely points out some of the actions that are permissible for a given situation; it does not give an exhaustive list. There could be equally useful principles that also provide a set of correct answers to any moral situation we encounter, but those will not be discussed here.

The Pragmatic Principle has two necessary criteria. If an action satisfies both, then the action is ethical. The first criterion is what I will call the Quasi-Categorical Imperative (QCI), which is based on Immanuel Kant's work. Kant argues that we must always do our duty each time we act. Doing our duty requires us to act as purely rational persons would act in the same circumstances. Purely rational persons would always treat those entities that have intrinsic value with the respect they deserve because the intrinsic value makes those things worthy of respect. Furthermore, such purely rational persons would value each intrinsically valuable object according to the intrinsic value the object has. For QCI, a person who is much more virtuous than another person has greater intrinsic worth than that other person. Each person has equal intrinsic value as a person, but each can have more or less intrinsic value overall because he or she is an individual person. Our more virtuous person, for example, has value equal to the less virtuous person if we look only at the general intrinsic value of being a person. But if we consider the individual person versus the other individual

---

9. fMRIs have shown that different parts of the brain dominate when a person is thinking primarily as a consequentialist—rational part—and when the person is thinking primarily as a deontologist—emotional part. Joshua D. Greene, R. Brian Sommerville, Leigh E. Nystrom, John M. Darley, and Jonathan D. Cohen, "An fMRI Investigation of Emotional Engagement in Moral Judgment," Science 293 (2001): 2105–8; and Joshua D. Greene, The Secret Joke of Kant's Soul," in Moral Psychology, vol. 3: The Neuroscience of Morality: Emotion, Brain Disorders, and Development, ed. Walter Sinnott-Armstrong, 35–79 (Cambridge, MA: MIT Press, 2008).

person, we can see that the individual who is more virtuous has to be more valuable as a result.

The Quasi-Categorical Imperative, or QCI, is as follows:

> If, in performing an action, the agent does not treat anyone as a mere means, then there is prima facie evidence that the action is morally right.

Treating someone as a mere means is basically understood to entail not treating them with the respect owed to their intrinsic value. But treating others is an internal, not external, thing. That is, morality for Kant is internal—it only involves our mental states. The consequences of our actions, after all, might be altered by unfortunate events over which we have no control, such as a natural disaster or human interference. Since we must be able to control our morality rather than throwing it to the whim of outside forces, then internalizing morality is the only way to go.

Of course, a very large problem is trying to find an adequate definition of what it means to treat people internally as a mere means or to give them the proper respect they deserve as ends in themselves. For the moment, let us practically characterize what this concept means without laying claim to having a definition that can withstand all objections. Basically, we know what it entails because it means the same thing as that exhibited by our desire to be respected in both thought and deed as intrinsically valuable beings. It is how we want to be treated or how we want those for whom we care to be treated in similar situations, whichever is the higher standard of the two. This standard entails that when we act, we must primarily have good intentions, good motives, good mental states, and the feeling of respect for all those affected by the action. Let us briefly examine each of these mental states.

An intention is the purpose or goal of an action. It is what makes that action the particular action that it is. For example, if I intend to say hello to my friend, then my action is to say hello to my friend. If I intend to murder another person, then the intention is what makes the action performed an act of murder. If I kill someone without the intention, then it is a homicide but not a murder. By primarily good intentions, I mean that, taken on the whole, the main goals or purposes of the actions are good overall. We can intend what is evil, but goodness, understood to be increasing our or other's flourishing as good beings, should be our central focus.

Motivations are what cause us to act on our intentions. For example, my saying hello to my friend because I desire her to loan me $10 is a different motivation from saying it because I want to express care for her. The latter is permissible if it is the primary motivation, whereas the former is not if it is primary. Being motivated merely by greed to get something out of my friend does not treat her in the proper way—that is, it does not respect her actual value as a person or as an individual. However, once again, motives can be mixed. As long as the overall whole of motives is good enough in regard to those affected by the action, then this component of treating those people as ends in themselves is satisfied.

The third mental state required to treat people as ends in themselves includes the attitudes we bring to the action. Suppose that we have made a promise to help an elderly neighbor plant her garden, but we really do not want to do it. Our primary intention is to help her, our primary motivation is to keep our word and maintain our honor, but when we assist the neighbor, we are really angry about losing a perfect afternoon to hang out with our friends. This bad attitude or feeling makes the action of helping unethical because we are treating our neighbor as a mere means. We degrade her value by seeing her as a burden rather than as a person deserving the respect any person we have promised to help deserves. This result does not entail that people cannot be a bit put off or have something of a bad attitude to the action. However, the overall feelings must be good, such as being pleased that one is honoring one's word and helping someone who needs help.

Finally, in order for an action to satisfy QCI, we have to have the feeling of respect for those who we foresee will be affected by our actions. This requirement is probably the hardest to identify and then describe, but a comparable instance might cast some light on it. Suppose that you love your parents. Ask yourself how you want your mother and father to be treated by others as your parents go about their daily lives. If they are in a restaurant, do you want the staff to feel respect for them? If they are in line at the bank, do you want the tellers to feel respect for them? That feeling of respect you want strangers to have for your loved ones is the respect that each of us has to have for all the people affected by our actions. It is not a stronger respect based on developed relationships, but rather one that recognizes that each person is a member in the community of personhood.

Morality has an internal element, but we have seen from the trolley problems that it is also external. That is, the consequences of what we do matter as well. That means we must have a consequentialist component for the Pragmatic Principle. If an action is likely to maximize value, according to what at least one reasonable person reasonably believes would maximize utility, then it is a candidate for a morally right action. Let us call this Reasonable

Person Consequentialism, or RPC for short. Put more formally, RPC states the following:

> If a reasonable person in the same circumstances in which the agent finds herself would reasonably believe that the action has at least as much utility as any alternative to the action, then there is prima facie evidence that the action is morally right.

There is a lot to unpack here. First, for the moment, let us put aside what it means to be a reasonable person. Second, what a reasonable person would reasonably believe about utility means that cost-benefit analysis is involved. Recall that consequentialism deals with how the values of each action's consequences are combined in a mathematical formula:

Good – Evil = Overall Value.

That is, each action's value is determined by subtracting the value of all the evil produced by the action from the total value of all the good produced by the action. In order to perform this calculation we would have to know all the consequences that would result from this action and their value.

However, we cannot actually know all the relevant consequences of an action before we do it. Sometimes the situation is so new to us that we do not have enough useful precedence to figure out everything that will happen. Other times, there might be too many consequences for us ever to do the calculations. Even if we do something that we have done in the past, the fact that the world has changed increases the likelihood that the consequences will not exactly match those that occurred in a different situation. With greater changes in the world will come less certainty or lower probability that the consequences will adequately resemble those we have seen for similar actions. Finally, we might not have time to figure out all the real or probable consequences, especially if we are in trolley problem sorts of real-life circumstances. Therefore, to keep consequentialism and make it practical, we are going to focus on what a reasonable person in the same situation would likely think is the best thing we could do. Now we might be that reasonable person, but we might not. Even if we are reasonable people, we might not reasonably believe something about the outcomes. The important consideration to keep in mind is that whatever we actually do in the circumstances has to be something that a reasonable person acting from reasonable beliefs would do.

Reasonable people have general rules they use, which, in many normal circumstances, lead to what is the best outcome. In some circumstances, a reasonable person might reasonably believe that the flourishing of one agent might have to be sacrificed in favor of another's flourishing. This sort of choice happens when only one person can be benefited—for example, when hiring for a job. A reasonable person might reasonably hold that goods could be distributed so that each person affected by the action receives enough to make her life better than it would be in other states of affairs, but none flourishes as much as if she had received all the available goods. The size of the set of rules is limited only by the number of reasonable beliefs about what will reasonably best serve utility. This is why many reasonable people, but not all of them, would turn the trolley so that it hit the one child rather than the five.

One of the dangers of going too far into the consequentialist realm is that people start being treated as numbers rather than as the intrinsically valuable beings that they are. That is why we have the Quasi-Categorical Imperative to retard our progression from correctly including people in our moral decision making to turning them into numbers or objects. From the set of actions created by RPC that would satisfy at least one reasonable person, QCI winnows out options that cannot be morally right and therefore cannot be moral duties. QCI does not allow just anything to be sacrificed on utility's altar. If, in an action's performance, at least one intrinsically valuable entity is treated without the respect it deserves, then it does not matter how well utility is served by the action. The act is wrong. The set of permissible alternatives open to an individual moral agent must contain only those actions that give proper respect to those things deserving it. From that set, whichever actions are likely to maximize utility in the appropriate way are morally right.

Of course, the Pragmatic Principle is merely comprised of two conditions, which taken together are sufficient for morality, although QCI seems a necessary criterion to all adequate moral codes. This limitation entails that there are other principles, theories, and moral codes that could arrive at different results, and do it legitimately. However, our work only needs to show that using the Pragmatic Principle always correctly classifies at least one morally right alternative in each case that can occur or be imagined, which makes the principle a plausible ethical principle to adopt.

Focusing a few moments on what a reasonable person is and how such a creature makes her decisions would help fill out this rather theoretical principle and RPC. A reasonable person has the general flourishing goals that all moral agents have of making the world a better place while at the same time having a good life. In order to make the world a better place, moral agents seek the thriving of the communities, societies, and other complex groups of which the agent is a component. In order to have a good life, moral agents seek the flourishing of the individual as an individual and as a member of the complex groups

To achieve both types of thriving, a reasonable person must have at least eight traits. Since I have stated the ends to be pursued by moral agents, I have to list which characteristics a person must have in order to achieve those goals efficiently. Roughly, the reasonable person is able to do the following:

1. Recognize morality's purpose and what it is all about.
2. Accurately apply her rules of conduct to each situation she encounters.
3. Try to make herself and others better as long as doing so sacrifices nothing of comparable worth.
4. Adopt reasonable goals.
5. Know that reasonable people will have different reasonable views at times and respect those views although she might not agree with them.
6. Strike the proper balance of emotion and reason in decision making.
7. Act with more reluctance to impose risk on others than on herself.
8. Correctly analyze and use the evidence available in the situation.[10]

I have already discussed the first characteristic, but the others could use a bit more development. Let us start with the second trait and then work our way down the list. A reasonable person has rules of conduct that govern her behavior, such as being kind to others and helping the elderly when doing so is appropriate. Part of being reasonable is knowing when such rules should be applied and when they should not, such as not helping an elderly mugger rob a young man, although acting this way is very kind and helpful to the elderly mugger.

The third condition incorporates the goal of flourishing and improving ourselves and the world. This is not a goal that requires the impossible state of perfection. There is a sensible, practical limitation on that idea—the notion of comparable moral worth—which states that each of us should choose actions and other activities that do not make the situation morally worse than it needs to be. Reasonable people realize that there are limitations on what we should do—there are always situations in which a rule might not work. If, for example, you could improve your knowledge of Latin but the effort would cause great

---

10. Dennis R. Cooley, *Technology, Transgenics, and a Practical Moral Code* (Dordrecht, Netherlands: Springer, 2009).

financial hardship to your family, then the improvement to you would be too large a sacrifice of the flourishing of others. It would exceed comparable moral worth. If learning Latin is something that will make the overall situation better than it otherwise would be—knowing Latin makes it easier to learn the Romance languages such as French, Spanish, and Italian, for example—then that improvement could sway the decision in its favor. Comparable moral worth is served when the sacrifice made makes the overall world and person better, but not otherwise.

Adopting reasonable goals makes practical sense. Everyone wants world peace, but having that as a goal is rather silly. Given how the world really is, no one could achieve world peace. This is not to say that peace is not important, but working for something that we can actually bring about is much more productive for ourselves and those around us. Instead of world peace, for example, the person could work so that more people have better lives than they otherwise would. By teaching better farming techniques, tensions caused by a lack of food could be overcome in an area that needs more sustenance.

The fifth characteristic is an important one that has been forgotten far too often in a world in which people think that every moral and political issue has a clear, obvious solution and that those who have the wrong answer are morally defective in an evil way that merits disrespect for them. If we are reasonable people, then we must recognize that we have to live with others. Therefore, it is not a good idea to treat them as demons rather than the people they are. If their ideas are not evil or vicious, then it is no real harm for us to tolerate their ideas even though we might not agree with what they say. In addition, reasonable people know that they are wrong on a lot of issues. This possibility should keep us humble enough to listen to what others say and think. The others might be wrong, but even if we are right, we need constantly to check our conclusions to see if they need to be revised. Even if we should not change our conclusions, then knowing why we are right can enhance our decision-making process for this decision and help us train our minds for better future decisions. Finally, multiple solutions to a problem or issue are morally legitimate at times, as in the case of most presidential or representative elections. The mere fact we like one solution better than another does not mean that someone who disagrees with us is in the wrong—just as we are not in the wrong for disagreeing with that person.

The reasonable person characteristic addressing the need for intellectual and emotional balance might appear at first a bit odd, but there is good reason for it being a necessary feature of each reasonable person. As everyone knows from experience, a person who makes decisions based on purely emotional reactions often makes very bad choices. In every situation, reason has to be used to evaluate evidence, apply principles, and perform all the other requirements of good decision making.

However, we ought not side with the position that pure reason alone should be used to make decisions. Mr. Spock and Data from the *Star Trek* series are interesting science-fiction characters, but we should never forget that they are *fiction*. Real people cannot operate in the same way as those characters. Consider what it really means to make decisions with pure reason alone. That means there are no emotions or desires involved. But how does anyone make a decision if there is no motivation to do so? That is, can we make a decision without caring about choosing? Obviously, if a person does not have the emotions or desires that lead to motivation to choose, then the person cannot choose. Therefore, both reason and emotion are necessary for decision making. To be reasonable persons, we must keep our desires and our reason in the appropriate balance for the particular situation. In many cases, reason will triumph because it is more useful than emotions in finding the right solutions to problems. In other situations, such as doing thoughtful things for our loved ones, emotion is primary. In rare circumstances, they are in perfect balance.

Reasonable people are less likely to impose risk on others than they are on themselves. The basic idea here is respect for people and their autonomy in making life decisions. If each of us wants to do something risky, such as to smoke, then because it is our life, which we control, we are entitled to smoke. However, if we respect people in the way they deserve, we will not expose them to unnecessary risk, such as secondhand smoke, without their consent or for no sufficiently compelling moral reason. Just as we get to decide what happens to us, they have the same right or ability.

Finally, perhaps the most complex characteristic to being a reasonable person is that of using evidence correctly, which requires an ability to evaluate it appropriately. I will merely sketch out what types of evidence a reasonable person will use to make a decision, which will indicate how it is to be used. There are specific types of evidence employed to evaluate situations for what is morally permitted, required, or forbidden. Reasonable people seek out and apply information about the following:

1. The external world society's rules, practices, and customs.
2. Rules and responsibilities associated with specific roles the agent is playing at the time.
3. Claims that others have on the agent and the agent has on others.

4. Maxims growing out of previous judgments that the agent has made, in order to maintain ethical consistency in the person's life and decisions.

5. In situations in which moral values, principles, and other morally relevant factors conflict, what is right on balance.

6. Which consequences are important and the value of those consequences, as well as the value of other relevant things.

7. Which if any mediated consequences count and which do not.[11]

The majority of these evidence types are included as a result of the Pragmatic Principle's two components. Some, such as evidentiary requirements 1 and 3, deal with respecting others. Others, such as 5, 6, and 7, deal with consequentialism. The seventh type of evidence is for situations in which our actions in some way cause other people to act, which then makes the consequences of their actions part of the consequences of our actions—that is, they mediate our actions. For example, if I leave my car running with the windows down while I run into the store for a small purchase and the car is stolen, then the car being stolen is a consequence of my action. The hard part is figuring out if I am morally responsible for what the car thief did. A pure consequentialist would say I am, but a deontologist might reply that the thief had no right to take my car and I had a right to have my car left alone. In other cases, it is clearer that the consequences count, such as when we assign moral responsibility for a bank teller being shot to someone, such as the driver of the getaway car, who willingly helps the actual shooter rob the bank. And in yet other cases, the consequences do not count, as for victims of sexual assaults, who do not bear moral responsibility for their attacker's morally repulsive actions. A reasonable person will make a reasonable decision about which consequences count and which do not.

Each evidential category recognizes the central fact that we are individual people who should seek our own flourishing as individuals in complex groups while at the same time seeking in some way the flourishing of the groups to which we belong.

A benefit of the Pragmatic Principle—based on our definition of it and how it works—is that using it in a reasonable fashion will provide an argument for any decision we make. By weaving the reasonable person features throughout the principle, as well as the basic moral idea on which our universal ethical systems are based, the decisions and why they were made are understandable to any reasonable person. Each reasonable person has the same basic fundamental

---

11. Robert L. Holmes, *Basic Moral Philosophy* (Belmont, CA: Wadsworth, 2006), 215–17.

ideas, so there is a common understanding shared between all reasonable persons. Therefore, using the Pragmatic Principle will lead toward bettering the world through reasonable discourse and understanding of each other. We will know why each of us do what we do and how each of us are what we are in general, as moral agents, and, in particular, as individual persons.

THE VALUE OF DEATH

No one disagrees that death involves harm from loss, but the sticking point arises with regard to what the loss is and who suffers it. Clearly, those who care for a person are most often negatively affected by his or her death, as are others who might feel the injury in different ways, including but not limited to the financial loss of an employer whose employee can no longer work and a society that no longer has a good citizen who helps the society to flourish. But before we can discuss harm from loss, we first must know what is lost.

A THEORY OF VALUE

Although there are many types of value, I will focus on intrinsic value as being most relevant to this discussion.[12] According to William Frankena, a thing is intrinsically valuable if and only if it is good in and of itself, or good because of its own intrinsic properties.[13] A red ball, for example, has the intrinsic property of being red. If it became green, then it would no longer be a red ball; rather, it would have the intrinsic property of being green. Physical features of objects are easy to understand, but what has the intrinsic properties that entail that the thing is good as an end itself?

For the purposes of being inclusive and trying to get as detailed an answer as is practical for our purposes, the theory of value we adopt should be inclusive. If something is reasonably thought to have intrinsic value by a reasonable person, then I will assume that it does until it can be shown not to have such worth. I take this rather liberal stance because I do not want to exclude value that exists. Making a mistake at this basic level leads to severe problems we can avoid by not having to prove beyond a reasonable doubt that something has value. For instance, suppose that we excluded pleasure and pain because

12. Something is extrinsically valuable if it is useful for some ends. Pain, for example, is intrinsically disvaluable because it is bad in and of itself, but it is extrinsically valuable as a means to warn the person experiencing it that something has gone wrong and now needs care to stop the problem causing the pain.

13. William Frankena, *Ethics* (Englewood Cliffs, NJ: Prentice-Hall, 1973), 82.

we cannot show that they are ends in themselves with any certainty that all reasonable people would find compelling—there will always be at least one person who will reject even the most obvious cases of value. If pleasure and pain do have intrinsic value, positive and negative, respectively, then our calculations about what we should do according to reasonable people would be inaccurate, to say the least. As Reasonable Person Consequentialism requires, in order to do what is morally right we must act as a reasonable person in the same situation would reasonably believe would lead to the best outcome. If part of our values were missing, then we would not have sufficient evidence to come to any informed conclusion we could defend. In addition, there is not a consensus as to what, if anything, has intrinsic value; thus, we would have to exclude all possibly intrinsically valuable entities until such time as we could deliver a compelling argument that would eliminate all opposition—which is highly unlikely.

By giving value to entities that might have intrinsic value according to at least one reasonable person with a reasonable belief about the matter, we have the rough material to make ethical decisions that can stand scrutiny. First, although such a decision might in the end turn out to be mistaken, such reasonableness will be recognized by other reasonable people to be reasonable. Hence, they will understand why the decision was made as it was, although they might not agree with the result. Second, we do not make the mistake of ignoring intrinsic value when it exists. One of the most serious moral failings of many people and societies has been to classify people in ways that they should not have been classified, such as those who were enslaved under the false belief that they were not people or the Aristotelian notion that they were people but had a character trait that suited them to slavery. If these individuals had been given the benefit of the doubt, then a lot of horrific evils would never have occurred. Third, even if something is not intrinsically valuable and we reasonably believe that it is, we generally do nothing wrong by believing it is good in and of itself. It might be the case that our utility calculations are off, but they should not be too far in error because they are balanced by those things with actual intrinsic worth. Moreover, by using only those things it is reasonable to suppose have intrinsic value, we cannot have done the wrong thing in our calculations or the actions based on our calculations. We did act reasonably, which must have been the right thing to do even if it proves wrong in an objective mathematical way.

DOES DEATH HARM THE DECEASED?

To put the answer to the above question clearly, the answer is an Epicurean no. Epicurus thought that:

> So death, the most terrifying of ills, is nothing to us, since we exist, death is not with us, but when death comes, then we do not exist. It does not concern either the living or the dead, since for the former it is not, and the latter are no more.[14]

First, death is not a harm for people and organisms because those entities cease to exist the moment that the person or organism dies. Since something cannot be harmed if it does not exist, then there is no way that death can harm these no longer existing entities. That is, in order to be injured as a psychological entity, such as a person, then the being has to be in existence as that psychological entity. Once that entity dies, then it cannot be harmed because it does not exist.

There are those who would argue that there is life after death. Generally, what they mean is that the psychological person continues to exist in some way that allows it to remain that particular psychological person, although it is free from the body and might have enhanced or degraded capabilities or states. It might be in a state in which pain and pleasure no longer matter for the entity, or it may have knowledge it could not have while the psychological person was tied to a body, or it could be in some other enhanced state of being, such as being in the presence of the divine. On the other hand, without the body, the psychological person might not receive as much information as it had when the body was providing stimulation from external world objects through the senses. This might be a bad thing if our information of the outside world comes solely from the senses. Regardless of how a particular view of the afterlife works things out, there is a demand that the predeath and postdeath entities have enough properties in common to be the same entity, just as each of us are the same person now as we were a few minutes ago. That is, identity over time must be preserved in each of these cases.

There is a severe lack of evidence for this empirical claim, however; in fact, belief in the existence of life after death seems based more on faith than evidence. Consider popular culture. There are a number of shows on television that try to show that a building is haunted. Other media venues address the same or other issues of the paranormal or supernatural, such as people having out-of-body experiences. In some situations, people claim to have gone to another place and were greeted by dead people they know. Others claim to be able to

---

14. Epicurus, "Letter to Menoeceus," *Epicurus: The Extant Remains*, trans. In Cyril B. Bailey, 83-93 (Oxford: Clarendon Press, 1926), 85.

have sense experiences of what happened in the room where their body is, at the very same time that they claim that they were not in their bodies. They say that certain external world events occurred during a past time, which is sometimes confirmed by someone who was in the room at that time.

Let us put aside the facts that such experiences are very general and would apply to many situations and that false predictions are ignored by those who want to confirm what the person is saying. In other words, if this is empirical evidence, then it is very unreliable.

The central assumption of out-of-body beliefs, however, is an impossibility. As most of us are aware, those who use out-of-body claims to show an afterlife have to argue contradictorily that the experiencer's brain was not sufficiently functioning to be the cause of sense experience—otherwise we can simply say that their malfunctioning brain deceived them—and that the person was still empirically experiencing the external world. In addition, the person is out of his or her body, yet the experiences the person is having are bodily experiences of sight, sound, and so on. What is puzzling is how these folks are managing to experience any physical event, given that the only way that they could experience such a thing is if their body were working in the proper way to deliver data to their mind or brain, which they already state cannot be the source of these ideas. So we have to accept that the physical world somehow is being experienced by incorporeal people who cannot be in the physical world and cannot receive physical world data from the eyes, ears, nose, and so on.

The same sort of problem applies to ghost and other paranormal beings. The ghosts and other entities are incorporeal, yet they are corporeal enough to be experienced through sense experience or devices, such as electronic meters, that measure physical phenomena. At least this is what those who make money from such "ghost hunting" endeavors want their viewers and advertisers to believe. But we know that such a claim makes as much sense as saying the ground is solid and then trying to prove it is in this state by swimming through it. If these entities are supernatural or paranormal, then the natural or normal cannot capture evidence of them because they are in two different and unconnected realms.

WHAT HARM DOES DEATH DO?

Although death does not harm the person who ceases to exist, except in some of the social person cases, it can cause a great deal of damage to intrinsic value in two ways. Before we consider these losses, it is important to restate that the value loss can only be understood in some given context. For example, the death of a person is a loss of intrinsic value, but in a larger context the loss might serve to increase intrinsic value for that context. I will explain this phenomenon below after dealing with generic and specific harms.

First, in general, the loss of a person as a person is a loss of value in and of itself *because* the person is intrinsically valuable. As was stated above, there are entities that are intrinsically valuable because they instantiate a property that makes them have such worth. If that property is lost without the entity taking on another characteristic that gives them intrinsic value, then there must be overall loss in value of more complex wholes containing the remains of that entity that was once good in and of itself. This loss is what we can feel when we hear of the death of a person we do not know. We have no relationship with such a person or memories or other mental states about the individual person lost, but we have empathy with all of those entities that have intrinsic value. We recognize that when they cease to exist as a generic person something bad has happened to the society or world as a whole.

However, we can never forget what the context is when discussing a death. For example, suppose there is food available to keep only four members of an Antarctic expedition alive until they can receive outside supplies, but there are five members of the team. If all five remain alive until the supplies fail, then all five will die from starvation. If one of the members dies now, then the remaining four can survive. Suppose that one of them decides to make a heroic sacrifice by taking his own life, which he does by leaving the tent for a walk from which he does not return. If we consider his death in and of itself, then there is the loss of intrinsic value from his personhood when the death happens. The remains of the person no longer have the same properties that made it good in and of itself when the properties were instantiated. However, when examining the overall intrinsic value of the team over time—that is, moving to a much wider scope of context—then the overall intrinsic value in which the suicide happens is greater than the situation in which all five died of starvation.

The same sort of idea can be seen, according to Malthusians,[15] when we consider cases in which people die from famine, disease, or other disasters. The death of each person is a real loss in and of itself, but it might serve to make the larger whole, such as the society, more intrinsically worthy as it allows more people to survive and flourish than would otherwise be the case.

The loss of a specific person can have greater or lesser value than the loss of a generic person, depending on the whole one chooses as context and

15. Based on the works of Thomas Robert Malthus.

on the specific person. Recall that the intrinsic value of a specific person is the result of a variety of factors, including but not limited to relationships and abilities the person has, as well as experiences the person is having or has had. Some people are intrinsically far more valuable than other individuals, especially if the latter are specific people who fail to satisfy the conditions that make someone a minimally decent person. Hitler and Stalin are always good examples of individuals whose intrinsic value as specific individuals is overwhelmingly disavaluable, i.e. having more negative than positive intrinsic value. Furthermore, their deaths could very well increase the overall intrinsic value of the societies to which they belong and of the world as a whole if we use those larger contexts to understand their value. At the same time, we must acknowledge that the loss of their value as a person in general is the same as the loss of any other person in general.

Additional loss occurs when people have disavaluable mental states about the loss of the individual. For example, if Sally mourns her husband's death for the rest of her long life and that action causes her not to flourish as she could have otherwise done, then mourning as she does must count as part of the loss generated by his death. If other people have similar negative feelings, then those would also be part of the accumulated overall disvalue resulting from Sally's husband's death. In general, we can find a rule that the more people who care for another individual and the more they care about that individual's death, then the greater the loss. A person for whom no one cares would not be as great a loss as one for whom many care. If the death is mourned by the survivors in a very minor way, then it is not as large a harm as it would be had the same survivors grieved deeply. Of course, this rule does not imply that we should minimize positive relationships and feelings people have toward us so that the loss suffered by our deaths is reduced—we and they need these for our flourishing. It merely states how to evaluate the death of specific people based on their relevant relationships.

The destruction of relationships because of the death of one of the entities in the relationship is also a harm suffered to intrinsic value overall and to the surviving entities. Since some relationships are intrinsically good, then not having those anymore will affect the survivor's intrinsic worth as a result of the mere fact that the relationship is nonexistent. There are other moral factors as well, such as sorrow from the loss and inability to interact with the deceased in any meaningful way, but we cannot ignore the loss of the relationship that is part of both individuals' identities in the relationship. Sally is no longer married to Peter when Peter dies. They are no longer a couple, which gave them enhanced value from the positive, caring relationship of which they were both part. Sally's worth, hence, is less than it was before the death. A general rule here would be that the greater the number of positive relationships a person has at the time of her death, the greater the loss overall suffered through her death. The more negative relationships the person has, the greater the gain from her death.

What might seem odd about these rules is that a very young child with lots of potential will have less intrinsic worth through his relationships than an elderly person who has lived well and created many meaningful, deeply caring relationships with others. Generally, when a very elderly person dies, we tend not to be as upset over it as when a child perishes. In fact, we do value things this way. If we are considering who should get scarce medical resources, then we generally believe that the younger moral subject should receive more than the elderly person.

However, given the theory of value, the less-integrated youngster is less valuable based on the value that is lost when considering the two entities side-by-side. The greater upset we feel should be mirrored in the greater loss, which should be for the elderly person in a web of concrete, nurturing relationships. Given this way of thinking about it, the very elderly person has to have more intrinsic worth than the child. Although this goes against much of what many may believe, I think this conclusion is correct. Comparing the two organic, embedded person wholes that are the child and the elderly person has to end in this result.

However, if we broaden the context by considering larger wholes, such as the communities to which each belong and the world as a whole, then we can account for the evaluation that the child is more intrinsically valuable than the elderly person in such a way that the child should receive the scarce medical resources. Once again, we have the feelings involved in the deaths, relationships ended, and so on, but we also must consider what it means to the community and the world as a whole. A person who has lived a long and rich life has flourished and can continue to flourish, but for a much more limited time than the child. The child has a potential that offers the community and society the same rich and long life of flourishing the other has already lived. So, giving resources to the young could be considered to be favoring the well-being of the community and society for great intrinsic value that will come over intrinsic value that exists but does not have the same long-term durability. This sounds terribly cruel, but making life-and-death decisions of this sort is necessary for the sustainability of societies and other large organic wholes, and it is done in a large number of cases. Since these tragic decisions have to be made, they should be something reasonable people can understand, although such people might not agree with the results or that the reasoning is sufficient to justify the conclusion.

Now that the value theory and normative principles have been identified and explained, we can begin to apply them to moral issues surrounding death and dying.

COMMENTARY

COOLEY:

My question is rather simple and difficult at the same time, but here goes. Which theory or theories do you think are most valuable in issues about death and dying? Why?

STEFFEN:

The question you ask about death and dying is—you are right—both simple and complex. The simple answer—in light of what we have both said above about allowing for the possibility of a hybrid ethic, one that includes duties, consequences, and virtues—is that all have a role to play. We shortchange moral reflection by discounting or excluding an assist from other theoretical resources because we want to play out our own commitment to an ethical perspective. We can become ideological about ethical perspectives—and all I mean by "ideological" is concluding a matter without pondering the meaning of relevant evidence. So I think there is reason to appeal to all of these ethical resources in situations of death and dying. I think that natural law ethics actually includes significant features of all three of these perspectives. I know not everyone would agree with me on that, and there is the tendency to equate natural law ethics with Roman Catholic moral theology, which is based on natural law. But I do not accept all that has been done in the name of natural law in the religious realm, and my reading of Cicero and others who have worked as natural law ethicists convinces me that this is an ethical resource that addresses the complexity of the moral life by opening ethical deliberation to duties, consequences, and virtues.[16] All of these play a part when confronting issues of death and dying.

---

16. For a discussion of this inclusive view of natural law ethics, and in particular a discussion of Cicero's ethics, see Lloyd Steffen, *Ethics and Experience: Moral Theory for Just War to Abortion* (Lanham, MD: Rowman and Littlefield, 2012).

The difficult part of your question has to do with something other than what role these theories might play as we consider death and dying. The problem is with the actual death-and-dying situation—one's own or those of others—and the pressure people are under to make decisions they do not want to make even if they think they understand the morally good and ethically right thing to do. People of course want to do the right thing—they want to respect the dying person, they want to provide a cure or deliver care, they want to extend life and do what is in the dying person's best interest or that of society or of themselves. We rely a lot on assumptions and ideological commitments in confronting ethics: Is there any factual basis for knowing the death of the condemned prisoner is salutary for a crime victim's family or that it enhances the value of life in society, given that we are willing to exact a life for one who takes a life? Or is there any factual basis for holding, as in Roman Catholicism, that fetal life is more valuable than the pregnant mother's life because the fetus is innocent? Ideology, religious teachings, relationships, assumptions (many of them unexamined), and empirical realities all play a huge role in our decision making—and our theories sometimes do not or cannot deal with all of these factors. I know what I mean when I say a prisoner on death row has been exonerated because he or she is innocent, but does the Roman Catholic ethicist mean the same thing by "innocent" when saying that the innocent fetus ought not be killed and that because of its innocence its life has value above that of its mother?

We have these theoretical resources and they are helpful and we need to use them. But the fact is that we do experience disagreement with other people over moral meaning. And I think much moral controversy is actually a disagreement over what the facts of the case are, which facts are relevant, how we are to assign weight to factual variables, which of our assumptions we are willing to examine as assumptions, and how those assumptions play a role in our relationships with one another and in our ideological stances. We don't know all the facts and certainly not all the relevant facts when we are confronted with moral quandaries. If there is humility required in ethics, I think it is in the area of trying to discern and establish facts, and that difficulty is what makes the application of theories difficult.

That is a general response to your question, and let me ask you a question or two. A moral theory has to apply to everyone—I place a lot of weight on the idea of universalizability—and in running a calculus to figure out consequences it is important not to fall into an egoism that would put one's own self-interest at the heart of the calculus. It may be that the right thing to do is something that brings me no personal benefit at all.

On your comment that virtues are universal I would suggest that virtues are cultivated in and even determined by social contexts, so virtues—more so than deontology or consequentialism—seem to open to the charge of "relativism." That is, if my group holds, say, that greed is a virtue—isn't the Wall Street debacle our great example of this?—then greed will be cultivated *as a virtue*. Virtues are vital to moral deliberation and development, but they need to be checked by ideas of goodness that extend beyond and outside of what group members might fashion for themselves as the excellence they want to see instilled in character.

COOLEY:

Utilitarianism is basically cost-benefit analysis that compares the overall value of doing one thing against that of another. Unlike ethical egoism, or Ayn Rand's objectivism, which focuses solely on the cost and benefits to the agent of the action, utilitarianism considers all people affected by the action, no matter how distant the effect is. So I think that utilitarianism as I have described it would take care of most of your concerns about the principle becoming too narrowly focused on the individual.

As for virtues, I agree that a virtue theory needs to be developed in light of normative principles dealing with right and wrong actions. Having theories about character without a theory about right action is rather odd given that character develops from doing right actions enough times to inculcate the virtue in the first place. But, action theories need normative theories of right actions as well. Some of the theories, such as Kantianism, are cold, rational deliberations that miss the point of why and how we are ethical creatures. We need both to be virtuous people while doing the right thing and to do the right thing while being virtuous. It is a high standard but one that we readily obtain in everyday life without thinking about it.

2

Abortion

INTRODUCTION

It would be trite but true to say that abortion is a contentious moral issue in the United States, although it seems less of a problem in other areas of the world. Many people's feelings run deep on the issue, which makes it a very personal thing for them because it challenges who they think they are as moral agents. An unfortunate consequence is that both sides have done considerable demonizing of those holding opposing viewpoints. Of course, once demonization happens, or is even a live option, then it is obvious that people are failing to see each other as persons. Instead, opponents consider those who hold contrary views more as objects or evil forces, which often leads to conflict, violent behavior, and thoughts unfitting mature individuals. After all, we might not agree on something, and the other person might be morally wrong in what he or she is doing, but that never gives us permission to act as if the other person is not a person. It certainly never grants permission to harm those with whom we disagree.

In what follows, we consider various moral and religious views and arguments on abortion and then try to provide more insight into what reasonable people could develop as arguments.

STEFFEN

The issue of abortion is an unusual "ethics" issue for several reasons. It is, first of all, notoriously divisive. Many moral controversies involve disagreements and lead people to differing conclusions, and ethical disputes can sometimes become heated. This issue, however, has led to a breakdown in societal civility. Abortion opponents and supporters of abortion rights have expressed more than strident words with one another. They have at times adopted extremist views, which have led to fanaticism and even outbreaks of violence. Abortion providers have been threatened, even murdered, and women's health clinics where abortions and other women's gynecological services are provided have been targeted for bombing. An abortion provider, Dr. George Tiller, was shot and killed one Sunday morning while attending worship services in his Lutheran Church in Wichita, Kansas, and in Pensacola, Florida, where a physician and his volunteer escort were gunned down entering the women's clinic that had been twice bombed by anti-abortion activists. President Bill Clinton described the first Pensacola bombing as an act of "domestic terrorism."[1]

If divisiveness to the extreme is one unusual characteristic of the abortion issue, another is the way abortion has come to play a critical role in American politics. A candidate's position on abortion may very well determine victory or defeat in an election, and abortion is a touchstone issue in political campaigns from the local level all the way up to the presidency. Ronald Reagan was the first presidential candidate to place abortion front and center in a political campaign—a previous Republican presidential nominee, Senator Barry Goldwater, believed abortion was a question best left to a woman to decide with her doctor, and in keeping true to his vision of conservatism he opted to keep government out of the issue. There is no question that abortion is a charged political issue. Its continued presence at the forefront of political and legal debate for the past forty years has led people to weary of further discussion, but further discussion goes on, sometimes in a different, even sublimated form. For example, abortion is at the crux of the whole debate over embryonic stem cell research, for many oppose such research for the same reason they oppose abortion—a fertilized egg, which is often described as an innocent human being, is intentionally destroyed. Embryonic stem cell research continues to be a controversial issue involving politics and decisions about the extent of government regulation.

The great ethics issues of our time concern the beginning of life and the end of life, and abortion involves both beginning and end. Is the killing that takes place in abortion justified? Ever? Always? Never? If the answer is "sometimes," then how do we distinguish abortions that are justified from those that are not? Abortion brings together ethical concerns about both beginning of life and end of life, and few other ethical issues present such serious challenges.

In the following discussion, I shall lay out what I think are the critical moral issues in abortion and consider some influential responses to those issues. And I shall describe how I think the abortion issue is best treated as a moral issue. That

---

1. Christopher B. Daly, "Gunman Kills 2, Wounds 5 in Attack on Abortion Clinics," *Washington Post*, December 31, 1994, http://www.washingtonpost.com/wp-srv/national/longterm/abortviolence/stories/salvi.htm.

discussion about moral meaning, however, will then turn to some reflections on religious contributions to the abortion debate, and I will defend the claim that much of what goes on in our so-called ethics debates over abortion is really inspired by religious beliefs and religious claims. That may help to clarify some issues. What I want to show is how important religion is to the abortion debate, for this very fact may help to provide a way out of what is otherwise an intractable problem. The depth of the religious contribution to the abortion controversy will not be apparent at this point, but I shall argue that abortion as a moral controversy may actually be more a dispute over religious beliefs about fetal humanity. Those views are quite varied and involve a pluralism of religious perspectives that we ought not to settle as long as we have a commitment to the free exercise of religion. It may be that our "solution" to the abortion issue is to acknowledge that people are and must be free to believe what they want about an issue like fetal humanity when religion is informing their moral views. Let us begin by looking at four perspectives on the ethics of abortion and the "solutions" they offer.

ETHICS

To begin we must be clear about what is at stake in abortion from a moral point of view. Abortion is the direct and intentional killing of a developing form of human life. Ethics is interested in any act of killing, but particularly where human life is concerned. Human beings value human life above other forms of life, and the destruction of human life constitutes, from the moral point of view, a presumptive evil. I say "presumptive" because that identifies a starting place of common agreement for moral evaluation but does not commit one to saying anything in particular about particular situations where that presumptive view might be overruled for good and justifiable reasons.

Life is itself the great precondition not only for ethics but for everything human. It is also a preeminent good on which all other goods of life depend—one cannot enjoy aesthetic experiences, or friendships, or freedom without the good of life. Killing, then, especially the killing of human beings, is deemed wrong because it destroys the possibility of realizing or enjoying anything else in life we would consider good. And while the good of life is something we want to enjoy, promote, and recommend to others—that in essence defines a core of anything we would call "good"— the good of life is a preeminent though not absolute good, not if one believes there can be justifiable reasons for killing, say, in self-defense or to prevent a greater evil. The moral community recognizes prohibitions on killing—it is presumptively a wrongful act so that any act of killing from a moral point of view requires justification. Killing is as serious as things get in ethics.

The abortion debate begins here—with a killing. Any killing is presumptively wrong, but not every killing is wrong or even morally consequential. We excise tumors, rinse with mouthwash, cut fingernails. These inconsequential acts lead to death. An individual who slaps on deodorant in the morning kills more bacteria than all the people killed in all the wars in human history. And not only do we think that such killing is good, but the reason for the killing is trivial—to smell nicer. We know that killing things can sometimes be inconsequential, sometimes good, and sometimes evil. In ethics we make judgments about such things after evaluating a variety of factors relevant to the killing—the intentions and motives for the killing, the status of that which is killed, the consequences of the killing, the principles that help us preserve our shared moral view that ordinarily killing is a wrongful act. It is not wrong however, if it can be justified, and the issue in abortion is whether the killing that takes place can be justified. When we treat abortion as we would any other moral issue involving life and death, we approach the issue with the viewpoint that some abortions are justifiable and others are not. The ethics chore is to tell which are which.

The ethical literature on abortion is blessed with some notable and deservedly influential perspectives, and I will discuss in short compass three of them before offering my own moral analysis of the ethics question.

Four Ethics Positions

"Killing Is Wrong"

In an important article, "Why Abortion Is Immoral," Don Marquis begins with the obvious ethics issue involved in abortion—the killing that takes place.[2] Marquis argues that killing is wrong, so abortion, which is a killing, is also wrong—presumptively wrong, he says, because he does make some exceptions. He does not focus on a fetus's right to life but on the idea that killing is wrong because "the loss of one's life deprives one of the all the experiences, activities, projects and enjoyments that would otherwise have constituted one's future." "When I am killed," he writes, "I am deprived of all of the value of my future. Inflicting this loss on me is ultimately what makes killing me wrong. . . . [W]hat

---

2. Don Marquis, "Why Abortion Is Immoral," *Journal of Philosophy* 86, no. 4 (April 1989), reprinted in Thomas A. Mappes and David DeGrazia, eds., *Biomedical Ethics*, 6th ed. (New York: McGraw-Hill, 2006): 477–71.

makes killing *any* adult human being life prima facie seriously wrong is the loss of his or her future."[3]

Extrapolating from this analysis of what is wrong with killing in general—again, presumptively—the move to abortion is easily made. Abortion is wrong for the same reason any killing is wrong—it deprives a developing form of human life of "a future like ours." A logical syllogism is at play: Killing is wrong because it inflicts a premature death that deprives an individual of its future. A fetus has a future. Abortion is a killing that inflicts a premature death on a fetus with a future. Therefore, the killing involved in abortion is morally wrong.

Marquis's argument is focused not on whether or at what point in fetal development a fetus is or can be recognized as a person with the attendant rights of personhood including the "right to life." Abortion is wrong because it deprives the fetus of its future, "a future like ours," which is what makes any act of killing morally wrong. The argument holds open the possibility of certain kinds of abortion being permitted: "Morally permissible abortions could be justified in some circumstances, only if the loss consequent on failing to abort would be at least as great."[4] Morally permissible abortions would be rare but would include fetuses so handicapped that they would lack the awareness to enjoy life experiences if born, and those prospective newborns with defects that would cause such pain and trauma that they would never have a future to enjoy. Marquis concedes that his argument would allow for actively euthanizing permanently comatose patients: "Killing does not necessarily wrong some persons who are sick and dying."[5]

"A Woman and Her Body"

In what may be the most anthologized article on abortion, "A Defense of Abortion," Judith Jarvis Thompson uses vivid illustrations to make a case that a woman's body is her own and that as an autonomous individual the pregnant woman can make a justifiable decision to abort a fetus even if we grant that the fetus has standing as a person with a right to life. Thomson does not actually hold that latter view but accepts it for the sake of argument. So her position proceeds on the supposition that even if we grant the debatable belief that a fetus is a person, a woman can still be morally justified in aborting it.

3. Ibid., 467.
4. Ibid., 470.
5. Ibid., 468.

To make her case, Thomson uses a now-famous illustration. A woman wakes up connected bodily to a famous but unconscious violin player who is using her kidneys and circulatory system to stay alive. The woman has been kidnapped and the violin player will require use of her body for nine months. Thomson asks whether the woman has a right to disconnect from the violin player even if doing so causes his death. She says yes:

> The fact that for continued life that violinist needs the continued use of your kidneys does not establish that he has a right to be given the continued use of your kidneys. He certainly has no right against you that *you* should give him continued use of your kidneys. For nobody has any right to use your kidneys unless you give him such a right; and nobody has the right against you that you shall give him this right—if you do allow him to go on using your kidneys, this is a kindness on your part.[6]

The argument here is that no one, not even a fetus accepted to be a person, has a right to use the body of another without the other's consent. To wake up connected to a violin player without having given such consent violates the woman's bodily integrity and her right to make decisions about how she will use her body. She can exercise her decision-making capabilities as an autonomous person to detach herself from the violin player without any moral violation. Moral violation, in fact, comes from the attaching of the violin player without the woman's consent, for what reasonable person would agree to that? The woman in this case has a right to make decisions about her body free of any moral obligation to save the violin player. To save the life, she would have to surrender her autonomy and accede to the injustice of those who violated her autonomy in the first place by attaching the violin player to her without her consent.

In her discussion, which goes into many subsidiary but related questions, Thomson restates the issues about whose rights are in play and whose rights are being violated. The issue is not that the violin player's right to life establishes an insurmountable claim to which the woman must accede. The issue, rather, is that the violin player in the first instance has no right to use the woman's body. Therefore, disconnecting the violin player is not violating the violin player's right to life but denying, rather, a use of the woman's body to which he has

---

6. Judith Thomson, "A Defense of Abortion," *Philosophy and Public Affairs* 1 (Winter 1971), reprinted in *The Ethics of Abortion*, ed. Robert M. Baird and Stuart E. Rosenbaum (Buffalo, NY: Prometheus Books, 1989), 35.

no right. He has no right to use her body, and she has no duty to oblige him though her decision would cost the violin player his life.

The right to life, in Thomson's view, entails a right not to be killed unjustly but does not also include the right to use another person's body. Thomson then draws the parallel: when a woman finds herself with an unwanted pregnancy and has not willingly offered the use of her body to a developing form of human life—rape is an especially egregious example but the argument seems to extend to all unwanted pregnancies—no violation of the right to life occurs.

Abortion, according to Thomson, deprives the fetal intruder not of a right to life but to the use of something it has no right to use because it is the woman's and not the fetus's—the woman's body. The woman who would allow herself to continue to be connected to the violinist for nine months—and by this we extrapolate to say the woman who would carry an unwanted pregnancy to term—is, as an autonomous person, free to make that decision. But there is no moral obligation to do so and no moral violation if she decides to detach, even if it would cost the violinist (fetus) its life. The woman's act to remain connected or to carry the pregnancy to term in such a situation would be altruistic, an act of kindness

Thomson, by arguing for the moral permissibility of abortion "in some cases," does not think every abortion or reason for abortion is justifiable. An abortion late in pregnancy for the reason that a ski trip is coming up and a pregnant woman does not want to suffer the cosmetic indelicacies of being pregnant would not withstand moral scrutiny. Moreover, for a woman to opt for abortion does not also entail "a right to secure the death of the unborn child."[7] In general, Thomson's position holds that the question about a fetus being a person with a right to life is separate from the question about a woman's right to make decisions about how she will use her own body. What she decides to do will depend on the burdens of the pregnancy and the potential sacrifices it would ask of her, but even if the fetus is a person, the woman, as an autonomous agent and a fully endowed member of the moral community, possesses the right to make the decision about her life and her pregnancy. As she has a right to make decisions about her body, she has a right to deflect claims to use her body that proceed without her consent and so she also has a right to abortion.

7. Ibid., 44.

"The Characteristics of Personhood"

Mary Anne Warren argues that abortions are permissible because the fetus is not a person and therefore cannot claim a right to life. In her article, "On the Moral and Legal Status of Abortion," she inquires into the characteristics of personhood and asks when in development those attributes are actualized so that a right to life is in place and should be recognized.[8]

Warren's claim is that abortion is permissible if the developing form of human life does not actually possess the developmental attributes necessary for personhood. Those attributes are moral, psychological, and even physical. In her thought experiment, Warren imagines an interplanetary space traveler having to make a decision about an alien being. How is the alien to be treated? Is it to be treated as a person, an end in itself with a right to life, and as such does it impose a corresponding duty on others not to kill it or eat it? The argument proceeds to identify five characteristics that would settle the issue. The alien would be a person if it possessed the following characteristics:

1. Consciousness and the capacity to feel pain.
2. Reasoning (the developed capacity to solve new and relatively complex problems).
3. Self-motivated activity.
4. The capacity to communicate messages of an indefinite variety of types.
5. The presence of self-concepts and self-awareness[9]

These are the criteria of personhood, and according to these criteria, "Some human beings are not people [persons in the moral sense], and there may well be people who are not human beings."[10] All of these characteristics must be in place before we can acknowledge any entity as a person, and to "ascribe full moral rights to an entity which is not a person is," according to Warren, "absurd."[11] Warren goes on to challenge the ideas that a fetus's resemblance to a person and its potential for personhood provide a sound basis for a claim that it has a right to life.

The arguments of Marquis, Thomson, and Warren all have commendable aspects and all have problems. Abortion is a difficult topic. Marquis can be

---

8. Mary Anne Warren, "On the Moral and Legal Status of Abortion," *Monist*, January 1973, reprinted in *The Ethics of Abortion*, ed. Robert M. Baird and Stuart E. Rosenbaum (Buffalo, NY: Prometheus Books, 1989), 35.

9. Ibid., 77–78.

10. Ibid., 79.

11. Ibid.

criticized for failing to recognize our intuition that because of some developmental issues the value of all life may not be equal, so that it makes sense to say that killing, say, an eight-year-old child or a mother or husband and father is intuitively worse, morally speaking, than killing a zygote or embryo. Furthermore, Marquis does not distinguish *having a future* from *having an interest in one's future*. That Marquis allows for the possibility of justifiable active euthanasia could in some cases be related not only to an individual not having a future but, more precisely, to the individual not having an interest in a future—the biological life of a permanently comatose patient could be said to have no interest in a future just as a zygote or embryo has no interest in a future. Why would we allow the death of the comatose patient but not an embryo? The distinction between future and interest in a future would seem relevant to discussions involving an embryonic form of human life, which has a future but no realized ability to have an interest in the future.

Thomson's article provides ample support for a woman's right to claim justification for abortion in the case of rape and in the case of contraceptive failure, but if a woman should engage in sex without using contraception, is she giving tacit consent to becoming pregnant so that in that kind of situation abortion would not be justifiable? And Warren's case allows for the possibility of infanticide, for if personhood depends on the actual realization of developmental criteria of personhood, then we must acknowledge, as Warren does, that these are not in place until up to two years after birth. She overlooks the social reality that personhood is something a moral community confers. It is simply a fact that her criteria of personhood are more realized in dolphins than newborns, yet the moral community acknowledges newborns as persons with a right to life that must be protected while dolphins do not enjoy personhood status. This may reflect speciesism, but only if one grants that personhood must be actually realized in the particulars of Warren's criteria rather than by means of social conferral. Warren does not approve of infanticide, but her position is such that killing an infant who is not a person is not a terrible moral wrong. In the moral community, killing a dolphin with realized personhood criteria would not be as morally wrong as killing an eighteen-month-old child.

Just Abortion

A less well-known approach to the abortion question, "just abortion," starts with the premise that from the moral point of view some abortions are permissible and others are not.[12] Taking as its procedural model the "just war" theory rooted in natural law, this perspective argues that the moral community shares a common agreement that ordinarily abortions should not be permitted. Life is a good of life, reason recognizes it as such, and that good is advanced and preserved through pregnancy. Pregnancy is therefore ingredient in promoting the good of life, and as such it should be welcomed. And, empirically, it is. Sometimes abortion discussions overlook how deeply people do want families—women do want to become mothers and men fathers—and how bearing and raising children is one of life's most longed-for, fulfilling, and joy-filled tasks. How wonderful it would be if every pregnancy were a wanted pregnancy, and every child a wanted child.

The just abortion theory, however, also holds that just as life itself is complicated, unpredictable, and messy, so are many pregnancies. Some pregnancies are unwanted, and only unwanted pregnancies are candidates for abortion. The moral chore according to the "just abortion" theory is to establish moral grounds for abortion, doing so by identifying some reasonable justice-related guidelines that would allow one to overrule the moral presumption or common agreement that ordinarily pregnancies should not be terminated. Just abortion seeks to evaluate whether an unwanted pregnancy can be aborted as a justified exception to this agreement. "Just war," when it is configured as an ethic, is premised on the idea that conflicts should be settled in some other way than using force, and various justice-related criteria (legitimate authority, just cause, right intention, last resort, and others) are advanced to guide consideration of empirical particulars in the effort to determine whether an exception to the agreement against using force is possible.[13] Just abortion, as an ethic, follows the same tack. It begins by acknowledging a moral presumption against abortion but then allows for the possibility of an exception on the moderate ethical idea that some abortions are permitted and others not.

In working the "just abortion" approach to the ethics of abortion, the first step is to acknowledge the moral agreement or presumption that reasonable people, both pro-life and pro-choice, could be expected to acknowledge—namely, that because the good of life is promoted through pregnancy, pregnancies ought ordinarily not be terminated through abortion. But because the theory avoids moral extremes, it then proceeds to guide reflection on the possibility of a justified abortion. Several criteria are then advanced to guide that moral reflection over empirical particulars:

12. The theory of just abortion here is taken from Lloyd Steffen, *Life/Choice: The Theory of Just Abortion* (Eugene: OR: Wipf and Stock, 1999).

13. For a discussion about just war "as an ethic," which it is not in many presentations, see Steffen, *Ethics and Experience*.

1. *Competent authority.* The pregnant woman herself is ordinarily to be identified as the competent authority for making a decision about abortion because she is in a unique position to establish in the first instance whether a pregnancy is wanted or unwanted. This should be neither the government's role nor that of the biological father, though a woman might be expected to consult others, including the father, in determining the desirability of ending a pregnancy. This is not a hard-and-fast rule, however, since rape, incest, and abuse situations may seriously affect the feasibility of such consultation.

2. *Just cause.* Rape, incest, and the saving of a mother's life were at one time widely held to be justifications—just cause—for abortion, even among pro-life advocates.[14] The teaching of the Roman Catholic Church hierarchy has, since the late nineteenth century, been an exception because it does not acknowledge the legitimacy of abortion in any circumstance, even to save a mother's life. Just cause can be reasonably extended to include other reasons for abortion, including denial of access to contraceptives and inadequate information about pregnancy and contraceptives due to social injustices, lack of economic and educational resources, and poverty.

3. *Last resort.* It would seem reasonable for pregnant women with unwanted pregnancies to consider the possibility of bringing the fetus to term and giving it up for adoption or keeping it, with abortion a last resort. Women who have unwanted pregnancies typically do reflect on the options available to them. This theory acknowledges that giving a child up for adoption is itself morally problematic and challenging, and it therefore does not consider adoption a simple or even morally preferable solution, only one that it would seem reasonable to consider.

4. *Medical success.* There is a point in pregnancy when proceeding with the pregnancy is actually safer than having an abortion, so prior to this point, which must be medically determined in individual cases, abortion would be deemed a permissible option. If the medical determination is that proceeding with an abortion poses a greater risk to the mother's life or health than continued pregnancy, abortion should not be the medically recommended option.

5. *Preserving values and preventing subversion of the value of life.* Abortions involve a loss of life, and when they are performed they should be done in

---

14. The Republican Party Platforms in 2004 and 2008 eliminated any reasons for granting a woman a right to choose abortion in cases of rape or incest, and "to save a mother's life" was dropped in 2012. The platform in 2012 said that "the unborn child has a fundamental individual right to life which cannot be infringed." Michael Cooper, "G.O.P. Approves Strict Anti-abortion Language in Party Platform," *New York Times,* August 21, 2012, http://thecaucus.blogs.nytimes.com/2012/08/21/g-o-p-approves-strict-anti-abortion-language-in-party-platform/.

the interests of preserving other goods of life, such as a woman's life and health, her relational integrity, and her well-being. Abortions can become a form of birth control, as happened in the last years of the Soviet Union, with the number of abortions of women of child-bearing years averaging between five and seven.[15] This might lead to subverting the value of life, although it did not in the Soviet Union. Published evidence indicates that women who had numerous abortions did so only because of economic hardships that kept more noninvasive methods of birth control scarce or impossible to find, and pregnant women who had not desired to become pregnant deplored having to go through abortion procedures that contraception could otherwise have prevented. This criterion focuses attention on the value of the good of life and the desire to continue to preserve and promote that good.

6. *Prior to promise criterion.* This, the most difficult criterion of the theory, responds to theories such as Warren's that look to biological or psychological developmental criteria to establish a point in gestation beyond which abortions should no longer be permitted. Just abortion offers this perspective: Abortion is a moral issue, and the status of the fetus is a moral determination. Therefore, the decision about the point when abortions are no longer permissible ought to be decided by a moral criterion. This just abortion approach states that the moral criterion for establishing a cut off point beyond which abortions should not be performed is this: when a pregnant woman makes the promise to her fetus to bring it to term. Promise keeping is a moral act, and if a woman promises to bring the fetus to term, whenever that promise is made—it could be the moment she finds out she is pregnant—it ought to be kept and honored. If the pregnant woman does not make that promise, then the developing form of human life is not protected morally, for it is not in the category of "wanted pregnancy" and is thus eligible for abortion consideration. It is reasonable to accept that a woman who has not made a decision by midpregnancy—twenty weeks—has made an implicit promise to bring the fetus to term. The moral community can reasonably make this inference because the fetus is moving toward viability and already has a 10 percent chance of surviving out of the womb. The more important point, however, is that the woman has been given ample time to decide whether the pregnancy is wanted or unwanted, and allowing a fetus to continue to move toward viability becomes more problematic morally speaking as it comes closer to resembling a newborn. Resemblance to the newborn is a relevant consideration because as a matter of empirical and sociological fact,

15. Steffen, *Life/Choice*, 101, 154n14.

newborns are granted the status of person with a right to life in and by the moral community.

In order for an abortion to be considered a "just abortion," all the criteria identified above must be satisfied, not just a select few.

The just abortion approach has strengths we have seen in other perspectives. For instance, it acknowledges a presumption against abortion as does Marquis. Like Thomson it supports the moral validity of the abortion option and insists that the pregnant woman be recognized as an autonomous agent with the responsibility to establish whether a pregnancy is wanted or unwanted. And it recognizes, as does Warren, the importance of the moral community, disagreeing with Warren that biologically based characteristics rather than moral relationships should determine personhood yet affirming Warren's argument that there must be a cutoff point for establishing when a fetus should be treated as a person.

Just abortion theory does not emphasize or even draw on rights talk but is focused on goods, especially the good of life. The theory acknowledges that the good of life can come into conflict with, and even be overridden by, other goods. It is my opinion that this theory of just abortion is the preferable means for establishing an ethic of abortion. It avoids absolutism and offers, in the spirit of moderation, that some abortions are permissible while others are not. On the level of moral theory, it brings together theoretical matters that are usually kept separate and are even seen as antagonistic toward one another—duties, consequences, and virtues. Just abortion attends to consequences (such as medical success and nonsubversion of the good of life) and to duties (acknowledging, for instance, the presumptive common agreement against abortion), and it is operationalized when persons bring such virtues as courage, honesty, wisdom, and justice into conversations about difficult and often divisive issues. The theory itself provides justice-related guidelines for determining whether any particular consideration of abortion can satisfy the requirements of justice, not directing that an abortion proceed but establishing the moral warrants for the decision that individual women should be free to make. It places the responsibility for decision making on human persons and the moral community to the end that the value of life is preserved. It emphasizes in the first instance the presumption that pregnancy promotes the good of life, and it could be said to endorse societal actions, such as the increase of education and the elimination of poverty, that would inevitably render abortion a rarer and, ideally, an unneeded medical procedure. It seems reasonable that if abortions can be avoided, it would be good to avoid them, but just abortion recognizes that there will always be problematic pregnancies and complex reasons for that problematic status. Abortion can provide a justified means for addressing health problems and social injustices while promoting the goods of life, including the good of life itself.

RELIGIOUS RESPONSES AND PERSPECTIVES ON ABORTION

What has just been presented is a moral analysis of abortion. Abortion has been addressed as a topic in ethics, and the approach to this particular life-and-death moral issue has proceeded as it would with any other life-and-death moral issue. I hold that an ethics of abortion will develop on the understanding that some abortions are justifiable and others are not—the moral issue is to distinguish which are which. This is an important point to reiterate, since there are other perspectives on the abortion issue that present as moral perspectives but are directed by religion and skew this basic ethics insight.

Religion can of course reflect a moral point of view, and religion as we earlier stated is one of the main transmitters of moral meaning in society and culture. Religious views can be advanced that do transmit a reason-based moral point of view. There are other perspectives, however, that do not express and may actually defy the moral point of view—that some abortions are permissible and others not—and it is important to understand that some of these perspectives advance metaphysically and religiously grounded viewpoints that are not universalizable and thus not reflective of the moral point of view.[16] A religious perspective may yield a moral directive, a "should" or "ought" about human action, but if this is a conclusion based on religious revelation and certainty grounded in the divine will rather than reason, then it may not satisfy the requirements of the moral point of view. A religious "ought" on abortion may appear as a vertically revealed directive rather than as a moral analysis, which would be horizontal and involve human persons in relationship with one another. To make this point clearer and to provide some insight into the differences between religion (or religiously-grounded ethics) and reason-based ethics on the abortion issue, let us consider abortion from the perspective of several religious traditions, then offer a conclusion about what the diversity of religious viewpoints means in and for the moral community. What is offered below does not speak for all who affiliate with a tradition nor does it express all the differences within traditions and among religious people. The diversity of religious viewpoints is vast, and my attempt here will be to sketch some primary affirmations held within a tradition that should be recognizable to members of that tradition.

16. The moral point of view and its requirements are discussed in chapter 1.

Judaism

Judaism is a religion of the rabbis, and the rabbis grounded themselves in scholarly study of the texts of the Tanakh, which includes the Torah, the Prophets, and the Writings. The Tanakh, sometimes referred to the Masoretic Text or the Miqra, refers to the canon of the Hebrew Bible, or what Christians call the Old Testament. A Jewish understanding of abortion would consult the Tanakh for guidance, and only one biblical verse, Exod. 21:22, seems to address the issue of fetal death by killing, although it is not the intentional termination of a pregnancy we define as abortion: "When people who are fighting injure a pregnant woman so that there is a miscarriage, and yet no further harm follows, the one responsible shall be fined what the woman's husband demands, paying as much as the judges determine." Compared to other religions that consider the embryo or fetus protected due to its status as a person or innocent person, and Roman Catholicism is perhaps the best-known example, Judaism, as a general statement, does not acknowledge the fetus as a person, and the talmudic law approaches abortion as a legal issue related to feticide, holding that feticide is not a capital crime.[17]

The legal status of the fetus in rabbinic teaching is as "part of its mother rather than an independent entity," and an embryo is not recognized as a "viable, living thing" (*bar kayyama*) until thirty days after its birth.[18] Thus, if it dies before that thirty-day period expires it is not eligible for treatment under the laws of mourning—it is considered to be of "doubtful viability."[19] Rabbinic teaching holds that only when a fetus comes into the world is it a person, since before that time it is not a *nefesh adam*, a term describing the "human person" that specifically excludes the unborn fetus.[20]

Although that legal status renders abortion something other than the killing of a person, "Jewish law (halakha)," writes Rachel Biale, "has no single coherent position of abortion."[21] Yet some clarity is available despite the many voices. Is the killing of a fetus homicide? In general the answer is no, and

---

17. See David Feldman, "Abortion: The Jewish View," http://www.rabbinicalassembly.org/sites/default/ files/public/halakhah/teshuvot/19861990/feldman_abortion.pdf

18. David M. Feldman, *Marital Relations, Birth Control and Abortion in Jewish Law* (New York: Shocken Books, 1968), 253.

19. Ibid., 254.

20. Ibid., 254–55.

21. Rachel Biale, "Abortion in Jewish Law," in *Abortion: A Reader*, ed. Lloyd Steffen (Eugene, OR: Wipf and Stock, 2009), 190.

rabbis, referencing the Exodus passage, have talked about a *havalah* offense being committed, referring to tort or damages to person or things: "If, now, we maintain with Maimonides and the Shulham Arukh that a person has no right to inflict damage even upon herself, abortion on request would be a punishable offense on those grounds—not to speak of the moral offense of thwarting potential life," which in turn thwarts the duty to procreate.[22]

If abortion is to be considered a crime in any sense, it is not as a murder or capital crime but as a tort-property offense. Therapeutic abortions where the real issue is the mother's welfare are permissible, but they are not permitted if the abortion itself creates some kind of physical hazard to the pregnant woman. In the Mishnah this is written: "If a woman has [life-threatening] difficulty in childbirth, one dismembers the embryo within her, limb by limb, because her life takes precedence over its life. Once its head (or its 'greater parts') has emerged, it may not be touched, for we do not set aside one life for another."[23]

Traditional Jewish teaching, then, holds that the fetus is not a "person" in the moral language we are using in this discussion. Abortions are certainly possible, but, more than that, there is a clear distinction between the "value" of the fetus and that of the mother. The mother's life takes precedence. If her life were in danger from a pregnancy, a fetus is considered, morally speaking, a material aggressor threatening the woman's life, and it is then the woman's duty to abort the fetus even if she does not want to. If the woman took the view, "Let me die but save my baby," a Judaic perspective would hold that that community must overrule her choice and not allow her to risk death. The life of the pregnant woman clearly is more important than that of the fetus, and if abortion itself poses a danger to the mother, as discussed above in our "just abortion" criterion of medical success, it would be imperative to disallow the abortion, not in the interest of the fetus but in the interests of the mother.

Given the diverse forms of Judaism today, one can find contemporary rabbis who hold that the abortion of "partial life" (prior to crowning) is not in general permitted, but exceptions must be made when the mother's life or welfare is threatened. Conservative Judaism has corporately held that "Jewish law does in fact, in a number of circumstances *sanction* abortion, basing its view of permissibility upon the belief that a foetus is not an autonomous person."[24] More liberal forms of Judaism—Reform and Reconstructionist—generally hold

---

22. Feldman, *Marital Relations*, 256–57.

23. Ibid., 275, quoting *Mishnah, Oholot* 7, 6.

24. "Conservative Judaism Statement for the Rabbinical Assembly and the Women's League for Conservative Judaism (1990)," in Steffen, *Abortion: A Reader*, 194.

that a woman must be recognized as an autonomous agent capable of making decisions about reproductive health questions, including that of abortion.

Buddhism

Buddhism instructs its followers to protect and promote the value of life, and the first Buddhist precept requires that all persons refrain from destroying living creatures. Because abortion destroys the life of the embryo or fetus, Buddhism in general opposes abortion. Yet "there are varying opinions amongst Buddhists, especially Western Buddhists, concerning abortion," and the practice of abortion among Buddhists varies in differing cultural settings.[25] Important to the Buddhist understanding of abortion is the belief that consciousness enters the embryo at conception, so Buddhist teaching is that conception is the moment to recognize a human being's full humanity. Buddhist teaching in general discourages abortion, although it acknowledges that abortions are justified in certain circumstances. Buddhism furthermore recognizes that the legitimate authority for making a decision about abortion should rest with the pregnant woman.

There are three issues to discuss when considering the Buddhist understanding of abortion: the Buddhist cosmological belief in birth and rebirth; the meaning of conception, embryonic life, and consciousness; and the abortion practice.

In Buddhist cosmology, all sentient life is subject to a constant cycle of birth and rebirth. The origins of life are set back in a timeless beginning obscure to human understanding; individual lives are lived consecutively until enlightenment brings about an end to suffering. Despite this understanding of life beyond the span of a mortal human lifetime, Buddhism nonetheless holds that particular human lives start at conception. An intermediate state precedes a human being's birth—Tibetan Buddhism identifies this as *bardo*—and when semen and blood from the male and female mix in the mother's womb, the "mental continuum enters at the moment of conception and consequently the embryo is felt to be fully human."[26] This continuum of consciousness in the Buddhist sense is independent of human physical development. Consciousness is always whole, and its presence in the conceptus marks the beginning of an individual human life. Theravada Buddhist monastic codes recognize conception as the point from which to measure the twenty-year minimum required for ordination: "When in his mother's womb, the first mind-moment

---

25. Phillip A. Lecso, "A Buddhist View of Abortion," in Steffen, *Abortion: A Reader*, 213.
26. Ibid., 214.

has arisen, the first consciousness appeared, his birth is (to be reckoned from that time). I allow you, monks, to ordain one who is aged twenty from being an embryo."[27]

In the Theravada tradition monks and nuns are prohibited from being involved in abortions: "When a monk is ordained he should not intentionally deprive a living being of life, even if it only an ant."[28] Yet there is also an understanding that the seriousness of abortion corresponds to the growing complexity of the life form. As Buddhist scholar Trevor Ling says, "It is relatively less serious to destroy a mosquito than a dog; less serious to destroy a dog than an elephant; . . . less serious to terminate the life of a month-old foetus than of a child about to be born."[29] And although some Buddhists may hold that abortion is akin to killing an adult, others will hold that not all killings are equally bad—abortion is always *worse* than killing an animal but not always as bad as killing a human life that has developed beyond an embryo or early fetus. Some abortions are understood to be necessary evils.

Because rebirth as a human being is considered "rare, difficult to obtain and to be highly protected,"[30] some authorities hold that pregnancy in the case of rape is not an occasion for abortion. Even so tragic a situation as pregnancy from rape can be, for the Buddhist, an opportunity to express altruistic compassion to others and to benefit life beyond egoistic self-interest: "Concern for the other life and its inherent value and potential may prevent the woman from adding another injustice to the situation."[31] And in situations where physical deformity afflicts a fetus, which might be an occasion for considering abortion, Buddhists may hold that outcomes cannot always be predicted and that if a possibility for meaningful life exists, abortion is not necessarily called for, not even when catastrophic defects such an anencephaly promise a short life: "Buddhism teaches that life and life's events are complex, karmic interactions and undue interference in natural processes is to be avoided."[32] While Buddhists may dispute the justifiability of abortion in situations of rape or fetal defect and disability, there does appear to be consensus that abortion is justified if it is necessary to save a pregnant woman's life.

27. Peter Harvey, *An Introduction to Buddhist Ethics* (Cambridge: Cambridge University Press, 2000), 311.

28. Ibid., 313.

29. Ibid., 316.

30. Lesco, "A Buddhist View of Abortion," 215.

31. Ibid.

32. Ibid,

Buddhism makes a point that we shall return to at the conclusion of this "religion" discussion: the fact that the world is religiously pluralistic and there is room for divergent views. Recognizing such divergence of views is in the interest in harmony and understanding of others. His Holiness, The Dalai Lama, for instance, has stated, "Each person has the right to choose whatever is most suitable. We must openly accept all ideologies and systems as means of solving humanity's problems. One country, one nation, one ideology, one system is not sufficient. It is helpful to have a variety of different approaches on the basis of deep feeling of the basic sameness of humanity."[33]

On the other hand, the Buddhist Churches of America, a Japanese Shin sect, declared that "abortion, the taking of human life, is fundamentally wrong and must be rejected by Buddhists." As strong as that statement is, it is not translated into any kind of call for legislation or governmental action, for the statement goes on to say that "it is the woman carrying the fetus, and no one else, who must in the end make this most difficult decision and live with it the rest of her life. As Buddhists, we can only encourage her to make a decision that is both thoughtful and compassionate."[34] Still, some Buddhists will hold that abortion brings karmic harm to a fetus and also will "sow seeds for more suffering for the mother than she sought to avoid by having an abortion."[35]

We gain greater insight into the Buddhist understanding of abortion by looking at how abortion is practiced in various countries where Buddhism exerts a significant influence on society and in people's religious lives. In the Theravada Buddhist country of Sri Lanka, abortion is prohibited except when a pregnant woman's life is in danger, yet in another Theravadan country, Thailand, legal action expanded the idea of "just causes" for abortion. The Thai Parliament in 1981 liberalized existing laws to allow abortion in the case of danger not only to a pregnant woman's life, but also to her health; the law allows abortion if deformities are expected, for social or financial reasons, and in the case of failed contraception.

Peter Harvey has identified Japan as having "the most permissive abortion system in the world" with abortion a "preferred means of birth control."[36] Yet because of the Buddhist teaching about karma and the harm abortion can do to a fetus's spirit, women in Japan who have had abortions have had emotional problems following abortion. In 1975 Buddhist priests began offering the rites

33. His Holiness, the Fourteenth Dalai Lama, *Kindness, Clarity, Insight*, ed. and trans. Jeffrey Hopkins (Ithaca, NY: Snow Lion Press, 2006), 73.

34. Lecso, "Buddhist View of Abortion," 215–16.

35. Harvey, *Buddhist Ethics*, 324.

36. Ibid., 333.

of the *mizuko kuyō*, memorial service for the spirit of the aborted fetus or stillborn. The service was meant to provide positive karmic transfer from the rite to the fetus's spirit so that it might have a quicker rebirth. These psychologically complex post-abortion rituals have been criticized for catering to irrational fears and also for having spurred crass commercialism.[37] Statistics indicate that the number of abortions in Japan dropped almost by half between 1975 and 1995, but abortion in Japan is still common, with government statistics being unreliable due to physicians protecting confidentiality and underreporting abortions. The most common reason given for abortion in Japan is to protect a mother's health.[38]

In general, we can say abortion is widespread in South Korea and Japan, highly restricted in Sri Lanka, but less restricted in Thailand and elsewhere in Southeast Asia. The practice of abortion in Buddhist countries, then, does not exactly follow Buddhist teaching and interpretation of the First Precept, but Buddhists are concerned about the suffering of women whose health might be endangered by botched abortions, as well as about the injustice of allowing only the wealthy to have abortion access.[39] Buddhists can find themselves advocating liberalized abortion laws while also holding that abortion is a destruction of life to be avoided and criticized, but two things seem to render this apparent paradox sensible: First, Buddhists insists on valuing life and preventing harm or injury to sentient beings so that where abortion is concerned one must confront the harm being done. Buddhism's precept of life directs attention to the wrong in abortion—the destruction of life—insisting that those considering abortion be conscious of the moral seriousness of taking a life. Yet Buddhists are not generally inclined to refer decision making to legal authority. Second, Buddhists strongly affirm that where abortion is concerned women should have choice in the matter. This paradoxical perspective has been identified as the "pro-choice/anti-abortion" position.[40] Again, there are a diversity of Buddhist views on abortion; and although this "pro-choice/anti-abortion" perspective does not govern abortion practice in all Buddhist countries, it reflects Buddhist attitudes in more modernized, industrialized countries.

37. See William LaFleur, *Liquid Life: Abortion and Buddhism in Japan* (Princeton, NJ: Princeton University Press, 1992).

38. Aya Goto, Chihaya Fujiyama-Koriyama, Akira Fukao, and Michael R. Reich, "Abortion Trends in Japan, 1975–95." *Studies in Family Planning* 31, no. 4 (December 2000): 301–8; also available at http://cla.calpoly.edu/~bmori/syll/Hum310japan/AbortionTrends.html.

39. See Harvey, *Buddhist Ethics*, 331–43.

40. Ibid., 343. This represents the view of Helen Tworkov, an American Buddhist.

Christianity

Christianity, the world's largest religion, is also its most variegated with three Christianities (Roman Catholicism, Orthodoxy, and Protestantism), each of which is itself splintered into diverse rites, ethnically-based churches, and, in the case of Protestantism, literally thousands of denominations. Given the diversity of belief perspectives one can find on almost any conceivable issue within the Christian community broadly conceived, it is safe to say that there is no single perspective that expresses "the Christian viewpoint" on abortion. Christian opposition to abortion in the United States may appear to be monolithic, but that is due to the coalition created when conservative evangelical Protestants, sometimes referred to as the "Christian right," joined forces on the abortion issue with the Roman Catholic Church, the largest single Christian denomination in the United States. But the diversity of viewpoints within Christianity is quite real.

Protestantism, for example, includes many abortion opponents but also many individual Christians and mainline church bodies that have collectively spoken out in support of a woman's right to make reproductive health choices, including the right to abortion. The progressive United Church of Christ is one such body, and representatives from diverse American religious bodies, most of them Christian, have organized for action in the Religious Coalition for Reproductive Choice. Roman Catholics who object to the teaching of the church hierarchy on the abortion issue are represented by Catholics for a Free Choice, an organization that affirms the Catholic teaching that believers must be free to follow the dictates of conscience. Noting that the doctrine of infallibility has never been invoked on the abortion question, despite several papal pronouncements, the Catholics for a Free Choice organization has declared: "The teaching of the hierarchical magisterium on moral issues related to human reproduction, while serious, is not infallible. Catholics have the right to dissent from such non-infallible teachings without fear of reprisal from the institutional Church."[41]

Abortion is clearly a divisive issue within the Christian community, and many churches have spoken to the issue in national assemblies, synods, and conventions—even in local congregations—and religious viewpoints on the issue have helped create voting blocs and influenced political direction and the outcomes of elections. Views on abortion can be a singular issue that affects many people's voting decisions in elections from the local level all the way up to the presidency. Abortion has played such a role in national elections since

---

41. "Catholics for a Free Choice," in Steffen, *Abortion: A Reader*, 120–21.

1980 when candidate Ronald Reagan ran for president, having sought and won the support of conservative evangelical Christians with his clear statement of objection to abortion and abortion rights.

We have noted in discussing the transmission of moral views on abortion though religion that we can find diversity of opinion. But on one question there is common agreement. Religious people endorse the moral viewpoint that reasonable people of good will share—namely, that abortion to save a mother's life is justifiable. One major perspective in the Christian community—the view of the Roman Catholic hierarchy—however, does not hold to this view but rather to a more radical view that no abortion is allowed, no fetus can ever be considered a material aggressor, and no intentional and direct killing of a developing form of human life is allowed under any circumstance.

I want to say two things about this perspective. First, this perspective is, from a moral point of view, extreme and unreasonable, and it does not accord with the characteristics we earlier noted about the moral point of view. It cannot be universalized and it does not show beneficence toward the pregnant woman. And, if this teaching is willing to sacrifice a pregnant woman to a fetus in every situation where there is a contest for life between them and only a direct and intentional abortion could save the mother's life, then this teaching elevates fetal life above the woman's life. They are not being treated as equals or with an eye toward equal justice. The Catholic Church's 1974 Declaration on Procured Abortion stated that there could be serious, even grave problems in pregnancy: "It may be a serious question of health, sometimes of life or death, for the mother . . . [but] [w]e proclaim only that none of these reasons can ever objectively confer the right to dispose of another life, even when that life is only beginning."[42]

Pope John Paul II expanded the explanation on this issue saying,

> "The moral gravity of procured abortion is apparent in all its truth if we recognize that we are dealing with murder and, in particular, when we consider the specific elements involved. The one eliminated is a human being at the very beginning of life. No one more absolutely innocent could be imagined. In no way could this human being ever be considered an aggressor, much less an unjust aggressor."

The pope goes on to say that the fetus is to be "respected as a person from the moment of conception; and therefore from that same moment his rights as a

---

42. "1974 Statement on Procured Abortion," in Steffen, *Abortion: A Reader*, 112.

person must be recognized, among which in the first place is the inviolable right of every innocent human being to life."[43]

From a moral point of view we see here both a clarity and a radicality that is not apparent in other religious viewpoints on abortion. Buddhists, like the Roman Catholic hierarchy, avow that a conceptus is a person but they will take a tact different from the papal teaching and allow that a woman facing a decision about an unwanted pregnancy has a right to make that decision and is certainly justified when seeking an abortion to save her own life. Teaching and legal reasoning in Judaism will go further, being open to identifying an unwanted fetus as a material aggressor and *insisting* on abortion if the mother's life is in danger, even overruling a woman who would prefer to die that her newborn might live. There are reasons for this Roman Catholic position and for Pope John Paul's statement, and I believe they are to be found in the idea of "absolute innocence." As the pope said, "No one more absolutely innocent could be imagined." I have discussed the deep logic of this position at length elsewhere, but suffice it to say here that "absolute innocence" points to a kind of religious or metaphysical purity that is outside the realm of human moral relations and thus beyond reason and ethics.[44] The pope denies that an innocent fetus could ever be a material aggressor, but that is exactly how the Buddhist and Jewish perspectives characterize the situation facing a woman whose life is in danger from a pregnancy, and that characterization allows for abortion to be a moral response of reasonable self-defense. The papal perspective denies this situation as involving a right to self-defense—the value of the fetal life is religious and metaphysical, not, strictly speaking, moral. The fetus takes precedence over the woman.

I point out the Roman Catholic hierarchy's perspective on abortion and that of Catholic for a Free Choice to indicate the diversity of Christian viewpoints on the abortion issue. This diversity of viewpoints then leads to important questions: If religion is a major transmitter of moral understanding and a cultural conveyer of ethical understanding, what are we to make of the morality of abortion? What does it mean that we have so many different moral perspectives on abortion—for example, Marquis's, Thomson's, Warren's, and my own—and then find religion also divided, with some perspectives advocating positions that ordinary moral reasoning cannot accept as morally justifiable? What is the right answer to the question about abortion?

43. John Paul II, "The Unspeakable Crime of Abortion," *Evangelium Vitae* (The Gospel of Life), encyclical, March 25, 1995, in *Biomedical Ethics*, 6th ed., ed. Mappes and DeGrazia, 458.

44. See Steffen, *Ethics and Experience,* 173ff.

My response is this: the answer is in the diversity of answers. That is to say, there exists no consensus in the moral (or religious) community about the meaning of fetal humanity. Reasonable people of good will understand that a conceptus from its earliest moment is human, a member of the *Homo sapiens* species, but to say it is a *person* endowed with the rights of a person and that it ought to be protected at all costs is a particular belief. Beliefs about fetal humanity are quite divergent, as we have seen. These differing beliefs are not objective in the sense that they are confirmable and must—or even can—command assent from all reasonable persons of good will. They are actually beliefs about fetal humanity akin to religious beliefs. Thus, Buddhists and Roman Catholics affirm "personhood" from conception, although for quite different metaphysical reasons. Jews affirm it from the time of appearance outside the womb—"crowning." Many others, progressive Protestants for instance, find themselves somewhere in the middle. If these beliefs are akin to religious beliefs, who is to say who is right and who is wrong? Science cannot adjudicate the issue for the simple reason that fetal humanity is a moral, not a scientific, issue. What is important to keep in mind is that we are left with a diversity of beliefs and that on this issue of fetal humanity people disagree with one another.

The division of belief is actually the most important point to take away from studying the ethics of abortion. The diversity of beliefs grounded in metaphysical ideas enmeshed in sectarian views means that in a society where religious freedom is protected, we must protect the diversity of viewpoints on the question of personhood, which will always be a moral rather than a scientific question.

Some abortions are permissible and others not—following the "just abortion" method of analysis will direct people to a process whereby they can make an informed judgment on that issue as it arises in particular situations where women find themselves facing an unwanted pregnancy. For societal harmony, a political context like the one we currently have under the First Amendment, which guarantees freedom of religion and prohibits any governmental establishment of a religious viewpoint, seems the optimal means to protect society, to restrain radicalism of viewpoints, to protect people and to preserve a social environment that allows for a diversity of viewpoints and beliefs while not subjecting others to oppression or coercion of belief. There is an "ethics" answer to the abortion question: that some abortions are permissible and others not. And there is a political answer as well: in an environment of diverse beliefs over moral questions, the ability to continue to hold those beliefs free of governmental interference—as is the case in some of the Buddhist countries—seems to be the optimal route to take. Abortion thus has a moral and a political response. The moral response is indeterminate because of the diversity of beliefs about fetal humanity. The political response that involves creating, sustaining, and preserving a context for diverse viewpoints is vitally important for so complex an issue as abortion because that context makes it possible for people to argue their diverse points of view in a safe and civil context of free expression.

COOLEY

The controversy over abortion seems to become stronger or weaker depending on the circumstances of a particular society or where people find themselves at the moment. In many areas of the world, it is not that important an issue.[45] In the United States, there is considerable consternation between pro-life and pro-choice groups expressed by laws restricting or liberating abortion access, picketing, verbal confrontations, political maneuvering, and other forms of protest and engagement. In some instances, the controversy has crept into other seemingly unrelated issues, such as federal and private funding to Planned Parenthood for mammograms and other women's health procedures that have nothing at all to do with abortions. In fact, providing abortions accounts for only 3 percent of Planned Parenthood's work.[46] The other 97 percent is generally uncontroversial because it focuses on what the majority of people in the United States find to be acceptable medical advice and assistance, even if that assistance is contraception. Yet when many people think of Planned Parenthood, if they think about it at all, they primarily associate it with abortion services.

Before beginning my individual contribution to thinking about the abortion issue, I will first briefly outline what I consider to be the most prevalent, and sometimes powerful, arguments used for and against abortion. This is not an exhaustive list but provides a good grounding in the debate. Note the elements of justice, Kantianism, and consequentialism threaded through them.

45. Rita J. Simon, *Abortion: Statutes, Policies, and Public Attitudes the World Over* (Westport, CT: Praeger, 1998); Axel Mundigo and Cynthia Indiriso, eds., *Abortion in the Developing World* (New York: St. Martin's, 1999).

46. Planned Parenthood, *Annual Report, 2011–2012*, 4, http://issuu.com/actionfund/docs/ppfa_ar_2012_121812_vf/1.

PRO-LIFE ARGUMENTS AGAINST ABORTION

1. Taking a human life is morally wrong, and abortion takes a human life. Since human life begins at conception, all abortions are morally wrong.
2. Our society says that abortion is morally wrong because it is the taking of a human life.
3. Allowing others to adopt one's unwanted offspring is a good thing, while killing the unwanted offspring is an evil action. Therefore, there is an obligation to continue the pregnancy and then give the child up for adoption.
4. Abortions make women more likely to suffer more physical and psychological problems in the future than if they did not have an abortion.
5. No innocent being should ever be punished for a crime he or she did not commit. Even in the cases of rape and incest, it is morally wrong to abort because so doing will punish the innocent fetus.
6. If women have an unwanted pregnancy because they did not use birth control or were not abstinent, then they have failed in their responsibility to control their body. Therefore, although it makes us a bit squeamish to say it, they deserve to be pregnant.
7. Having an abortion causes intense psychological and physical pain, which might increase the chances of the woman dying and will make the woman's life less valuable than it would have otherwise have been.
8. God prohibits abortion.
9. Some abortions are selected for morally irrelevant reasons, such as sex selection. Losing human life should not be the result of the desire for an infant with a morally irrelevant characteristic.[47]

PRO-CHOICE ARGUMENTS FOR ABORTION

47. M. Das Gupta, "Selective Discrimination against Female Children in Rural Punjab, India," Population and Development Review 4, no. 2 (1987): 257–70.

1. There are many instances in which it is permissible to take a human life. The justification for abortion is the right to make decisions about one's own body and how that body is to be treated.
2. Although the fetus is a human life, it is not a person. The woman is a person. Only persons have rights. Therefore, the fetus has no right that overrides the woman's right to choose.
3. It is unjustifiably cruel and disrespectful to make a woman carry a fetus to term just so that it can be adopted.
4. Abortion is a safe medical procedure, whereas childbirth is more medically dangerous to the woman.
5. A woman who is the victim of rape or incest is innocent. To force her to carry a fetus to term would be to ignore her innocence.
6. The right to control one's own body is one of the most central rights to a person and society. To violate this right to give a fetus—which cannot exercise any rights, if it has them—use of the woman's body is to degrade the value of civil rights for all.
7. If we care about what happens to women, then we should recognize that some women are not ready to have babies. Some women and girls are not mentally or physically mature enough to sustain such a burden.
8. Being pregnant and carrying an unwanted fetus to term can cause psychological and physical suffering on the part of the woman that is equal to or greater than that of having an abortion.
9. There is always a problem making assertions about what a divine entity wants, even if we can show one exists. Sheer faith does not give us sufficient evidence to know what God wants in a particular case.[48]

Clearly, one of the main issues in arguments for or against abortion is the moral status of the various entities involved. That is, one of the biggest questions to figure out is the status of each object in the organic whole making up the situation. To discuss these controversial issues rationally and reasonably, we need to obey the principle that questions of meaning come before questions of truth. We have this obligation because it is impossible to answer a question without knowing what is being asked of us. If we consider whether or not all

48. Linda Lowen, "10 Abortion Arguments: 10 Arguments for Abortion, 10 Arguments against Abortion," About.com Women's issues, http://womensissues.about.com/od/reproductiverights/a/AbortionArgumen.htm.

abortions are morally wrong, then, among other informational items, we would have to know the entities in the situation. This would require that we figure out if the entities are persons, potential persons, or moral subjects and whether they have any other feature that gives them intrinsic value deserving of respect. That will be useful for the Quasi-Categorical Imperative to be used. We also need to know if the entities can experience pain and pleasure, or have some other intrinsically valuable state of affairs that will be used in the cost-benefit analysis of Reasonable Person Consequentialism. So there is an imperative to know the groundwork before making claims about something being right or wrong.

In most cases, the pregnant woman or girl is a person, and is obviously a person to others. That is, other people recognize, with great ease, that the woman is a person. Although recognizing that an individual is a person is not what makes the individual a person—slaves, for instance, were not treated as the persons they were—it is useful to show that there is very little controversy that the woman is a person, which would entail that she be treated as such.

But what is a person? Although it is a rather high standard, Mary Ann Warren's definition of a person is useful here. A person meets the following necessary characteristics: consciousness, the capacity to feel pain, reasoning, self-motivated activity, the capacity to communicate, and a self-concept and self-awareness.[49] Even if an entity met some of the criteria, we would not automatically call that being a person, but we might give it some moral standing. For example, cats, rats, and other sentient creatures have the necessary consciousness to meet the first criterion but would lack others. Therefore, they are not persons. Reasoning at a high enough level to be considered rational would be the biggest deficiency for most nonhuman animals, although there seem to be some indications that the higher primates might be close enough to at least be called an almost-person. However, the ability to communicate would require some abstract terms and thinking to have the sufficient self-concepts and self-awareness to be a person. The way to summarize the distinction between almost-persons and persons is that a person is any entity that has the capability of asking why things are as they are, which requires that the five criteria Warren lists are highly developed beyond merely having them.[50]

Of course, one of the most contentious problems with any definition of personhood is drawing the line between those individuals who are persons and those who are not. For example, is it legitimate to ask if children or severely

49. Warren, "Moral and Legal Status," 77–78.

50. Warren focuses far too much on rights in her argument on the permissibility of abortion. Rights talk can be eliminated in favor of less difficult ontological claims, such as intrinsic value and normative principles.

mentally disabled human beings are persons under this definition? What of the elderly who are undergoing extreme dementia and individuals who are mentally ill? If a person is in a coma—even for a short period of time—then is that entity still a person? We do not want to be inhumane here by making the personhood standard too high and then mistakenly classifying people who are persons as less than what they actually are. That would allow people who deserve respect to be treated in ways that no person should be treated. For example, the mere fact that an individual is mentally disabled does not mean on its own that the individual is not a person.

My solution is to draw a rather gray line that errs on the side of caution because the stakes are too high to get this wrong, even if it is a well-meaning error on our part. I contend that many relatively young children are persons. They have concepts of "me" and "mine," as well as "you" and "yours." They are capable of figuring out right and wrong, even though they might not have the advanced ethical theories, principles, and concepts or moral decision-making processes that we do. I am not going to claim that these persons are moral agents because I do not think they are developed sufficiently to be able to operate at the much higher intellectual standard required of moral agents. Moral agents have to be able to take consequences into account, understand how their actions will affect others, have proper ability to feel empathy for others, and possess other necessary features of moral agency that require much more depth of thinking than can be done by the very young and undeveloped. But children should not be thought of as nonpersons when they have fulfilled the rudimentary requirements. Any other human being who also can have the same claim made about them with legitimacy, such as the mentally disabled or ill would also be classified and treated as persons. We can extend the personhood franchise to those who are temporarily comatose because they are merely on hiatus from these abilities for a small period of time.

On the other hand, there are a number of living human beings—those entities that have the requisite DNA that allows them to be *Homo sapiens*—that would not be persons. Babies and toddlers do not meet the standards because their minds have developed insufficiently to be able to carry out the basic requirements of being a person. Those in a permanent vegetative state would also not be persons. Those who are so mentally deficient that they cannot have a concept of themselves or others would not make the personhood standard. This is not to say that there are no moral duties or values to these kinds of being; in fact, there are many, strong obligations to act for their flourishing, but they will not be based on any notion that such individuals are persons.[51]

Let us now turn to the much more controversial issue of the moral status of the entity that is aborted. For the sake of this discussion I am going to assume a few things about the terms used. First, instead of "unborn," "baby," or "clump of cells," each of which convey an emotive definition—that is, a definition based too greatly on emotive reactions, which will be more about rhetoric rather than reasoning—we should use a term that has a descriptive definition. Since we want to reach a conclusion that all reasonable people should understand, although they might not agree with it, we have to avoid dragging in terms that are used primarily to appeal to emotions rather than to reason. Unfortunately, some people use certain terms so that part of their argument gains force by the way people react emotionally to the term. For instance, no one would want a baby to be killed, and people would be justified in recoiling in horror at the thought of a morally valuable entity such as a baby being aborted. On the other hand, "clump of cells" conveys the impression that there is no more moral value to what is there than in the cells of one's fingertips. Neither term—nor similar ones—does the job we as reasonable people want it to do, which is to find reasonable solutions to complex moral issues. In controversial moral issues, we have to move away from emotionally charged reactions because they make the strife much worse and increase the difficulty of finding solutions. Instead, we have to let reason be primary to promote individual and community flourishing; therefore, I will state that we use the term *fetus* when discussing the entity that might or will be aborted.

After boldly stipulating the terminology, I will express a concern. Using the term *fetus* is incorrect in many instances. The zygote, morula, blastocyst, and other stages of development need to be considered in addition to a fully developed fetus. The former bring unwanted but real complexity to figuring out if abortion is morally permissible or not. For instance, the sooner in the development process the fetus is, then the less likely people will feel as much as when the fetus is near birth. It is rather difficult to get emotionally involved with something that is smaller than the head of a pin and looks like a clump of cells. Although emotions need to be kept in check, we still need them, along with our reason, for ethics and moral decision procedures. These emotional reactions provide important information for recognizing intrinsic moral worth. It seems as if most people would not attribute as high of a moral value to a zygote as they would to a fetus in the eighth month of gestation. The valuation is probably right. If Frans de Waal is correct, an entity might have to resemble

---

51. Frans de Waal argues that we are morally obligated to favor our innermost circles, including our species. Such favor is based on loyalty, which is an evolutionarily selected trait. Frans de Waal, *Primates and Philosophers: How Morality Evolved* (Princeton, NJ: Princeton University Press, 2006), 165.

us sufficiently so that our loyalty to the entity as part of our community is engaged.[52] But in the interest of space, I will not consider the complexities this issue generates, other than stating that early-term abortions will likely be much more acceptable to many people than late-term ones on the grounds of this perception, which might turn out to be wrong. (We always have to worry about not recognizing intrinsic value when we should.)

Returning to the issue, let us employ the most expansive definition of fetus we can so that we do not err in giving it too little intrinsic moral worth. Fetuses are not persons according to the definition of a person; however, fetuses are potential persons and sentient inasmuch as they are capable of feeling pleasure or pain after sufficient development of the nervous system and brain in the twenty-eighth week of gestation. Either of those two features confers intrinsic value to fetuses, and together they add more value. First, anything that is a potential person should be treated with respect because it has that potential.[53] Rocks, cats, and other entities might be conceived to be potential persons if we rearrange reality a great deal, but we can put such implausibilities to the side.[54] Human fetuses, on the other hand, are likely to become people if they undergo the normal gestation period and other requirements of development, whereas cats and so on are capable of being people only in the annals of science fiction. Although thinking about whether something could happen is sometimes fun, it is mostly a waste of time preventing us from trying to find reasonable solutions to these controversial issues. In other words, if it is not likely to help out with individual and community flourishing, then it can be put aside in favor of those things that accomplish our stated goals.

As potential persons, fetuses have intrinsic value. But we should never think that the intrinsic value is equal to or greater than the inherent value of persons. The reason for this should be obvious. While fetuses have potential to be persons—and could actually have intrinsic value for being alive or having

---

52. Ibid.

53. Potential personhood eliminates the worry some philosophers have that if a pro-choice individual claims that the fetus is not a person, agent, or social being, then abortion is not a wrongful killing. Don Marquis, "Why Abortion Is Immoral," in *The Problem of Abortion*, ed. Susan Dwyer and Joel Feinberg, 24–39 (Belmont, CA: Wadsworth, 1997), 25. Killing potential persons would still be wrong if the action is unjustified. There is also an argument that life confers value. I think that is right but do not see it as being much of a benefit in the human abortion debate. If all living things have value—which I think they do—then they have equal value for this particular characteristic. However, we do not think it wrong to abort other living things such as plants. So life alone is not a value on which we can build a complete argument about abortion, or even understand its actual significance.

54. Michael Tooley's kitten-as-potential-person argument is a classic of this type of reasoning. Michael Tooley, *Abortion and Infanticide* (Oxford: Oxford University Press, 1985).

the ability to feel pleasure or pain—persons are capable of using and do use those mental features that make them persons in the first place. That is, they instantiate the value of personhood. The only reason that potential personhood has intrinsic value is because of personhood's value; hence, the actuality is more important than the potentiality. This is why potential persons cannot be as intrinsically valuable as persons. In addition, because persons have the same abilities to feel pleasure or pain and are alive, then potential persons capable of the same merely tie potential persons in intrinsic value on these grounds. When actual personhood is factored in, then the overall value of a person has to far outweigh that of a potential person.

We can consider an example to show that my claim about the value differences between persons and potential persons has some justification. Suppose that a woman is three months pregnant. If she continues her pregnancy, then she will not survive. I am not saying that she might not survive but that she will die if she carries the fetus to term. In this situation, which entity should be saved? The vast majority of people will say that the woman should come first. Not only is she a full person with all the intrinsically valuable features attaching to such, but she also has relationships and other intrinsically valuable properties not found for the fetus. Now I will make it a bit more complicated. Suppose that we are given the power to decide for the woman. Before making the decision, would you ask the woman what she wants to do or would you impose an answer without consulting her? Most people would find that not asking the woman what she wants shows a lack of respect for her autonomy, and we will probably be inclined to follow her wishes. However, no one would consult the fetus because there is no person to consult.

In another example, suppose that a fertility clinic is on fire. Inside are a male technician who has passed out from smoke inhalation and a vat of frozen embryos. The fire is raging, and we have the strength and time only to save one thing. If we left the technician to die so that we could take out the vat, most people would think that we acted unethically. In all likelihood, in a burning building we would not even think to check or worry about the embryos' safety. We would just save the man, although we might regret the loss of the embryos when we learn of it. How we would actually behave and react emotionally shows a bit of what we really think about the value of each entity. We believe that women are people whereas fetuses have some lower moral status. Both have worth, but women as people are so much more valuable than fetuses that allowing fetuses' interests to trump those of women makes us guilty of wrongdoing. A woman's intrinsic value comes not only from being alive and sentient but from being a person, and very likely from the relationships she has with other people that are part of her identity as an individual person.

Speaking of relationships, we cannot forget that in most cases there are many stakeholders involved in an abortion. Stakeholder theory was first developed for business ethics, but the central idea that those affected by the action need to be taken into account in decision making works here as well.[55] For the sake of brevity, let us say that someone is a stakeholder if he or she would be affected by the action and would care about being affected if informed of those effects.[56] For example, the man who fathered the fetus cannot be considered to be morally irrelevant in abortion situations in which he cares about the outcome. That does not mean he has final or primary say in the matter, but his feelings and needs should at least be considered in the decision procedure. If he wanted or would have wanted the fetus, but the woman did not, then he has been harmed when the fetus is aborted. This is not to say that the injury makes the action unethical; there are times when unwanted harm is justified, such as in the case of a person who takes a job, thus injuring the other candidate who needed the job and would have been offered it if the first person had not taken it. But the important point here is that there is some reason to recognize and appreciate the harm of the man who fathered the fetus and to respect him as the person he is.

Others affected by abortions can include family, friends, medical personnel, and the community. The family of the women and other interested parties who care about the situation and will be positively or negatively affected by it need to be recognized and appreciated, and the positives and negatives that happen to them as a result of the abortion should be considered. For example, the family of the male progenitor might have a stake in the fetus being aborted. Since these groups of people are emotionally attached to the primary actors in the tragedy, then how the action affects them is a matter of moral importance.[57] Their benefit or burden, if there is any, matters in evaluating the overall moral situation. The medical personnel are also not cold, heartless individuals. They

---

55. R. Edward Freeman, *Strategic Management: A Stakeholder Approach* (Cambridge: Cambridge University Press, 2010).

56. One of the difficulties with stakeholder theory is defining what a stakeholder is. My definition is a compromise between the extreme views that everyone affected by the action is a stakeholder and that only those who are directly affected by the action are stakeholders.

57. I use the word *tragedy* for a specific reason. No woman who undergoes an abortion or chooses not to undergo one does it lightly. She makes the best of a situation in which there are hard choices and in which the overall situation is not going to be good on balance. That is the tragedy.

recognize the importance of what they are doing. Since they have to be part of the abortion, then they and what happens to them matter as well.

Finally, communities do not and should not have a great say in such affairs—that is, if we respect people enough to allow them to make their own choices—but communities do matter when it comes to evaluating the situation. Some societies need more people in order to continue to function. Russia, for example, is not replacing population at a rate that will allow it to avoid serious complications in the near future. An abortion will help to destabilize them. That result counts. Other societies, with limited resources, might need fewer people because they have too many to take care of as it is. What happens to them also matters. How much each individual and group and the relevant consequences happening to them should count in the decision procedure—that is, how important they are as moral factors—is determined by the strength or weakness of the relationships between them and the woman and fetus. The closer the relationship, the more they deserve to be respected and the more that what happens to them as a result of the decision-making procedure leading up to an abortion and the abortion itself count in determining the alternatives' goodness or badness. A close-knit family would be far more important than a parent who had abandoned the pregnant woman, for example. Although this leaves the issue rather vague, it does help establish that there are a number of moral factors affecting abortion's ethics and sketches a way of evaluating those moral factors using RPC and QCI.

A comprehensive list of arguments for and against the permissibility of abortion have been provided above. I am going to develop one that seems to have been overlooked: the stewardship argument. Given that fetuses are intrinsically valuable on the various grounds already mentioned, including being potential persons, then anyone in possession of one would have to treat it according to the intrinsic value it has. This would require good stewardship in many cases because the fetus cannot ensure that it, on its own, can maintain its intrinsic value. Stewardship also includes the intuitively appealing requirement that the steward freely accept the role of being a steward rather than it being a duty created for the individual by outside forces.

Stewardship plays a very large role in environmental ethics. Instead of people owning land to do with as they like, those who possess it are thought of as stewards who are keeping the land for someone else. That someone in religious circles is God, who merely allows humans to use God's property until the time when it is taken back. But God never gives full title to the land to any person, only lifetime use. Others replace God with current or future generations who will have to make do with what is left to them by us. Just as our ancestors did not own the land because there can be no permanent owner for something that was there before them and will be there long after they are gone, so too we do not own the land. Even though we are obligated to maintain it, pay taxes on it, work it, and so on, there is never an absolute ownership that allows us to destroy, neglect, or fundamentally alter it for the worse. Regardless of the land's true owner, the lack of absolute ownership leads to the same result: we must care for the land so that its initial value is maintained. We can improve the land and we must preserve it if we shoulder the burden of being a steward, but in normal circumstances we are forbidden to make it worse than it was before we took temporary control over it.

When a woman becomes pregnant, she is given the potential role of steward of an intrinsically valuable entity, namely, the fetus. She, of course, is also sole proprietor and domain holder of her own body and person, but we would find it odd if a woman talked about owning her fetus. I think this is one reason why so many people are squeamish about the notion of individuals owning unused, frozen fertilized eggs that were created for artificial insemination. We do not believe that we can own other humans or human life. So, we can think of the fetus as being similar to the land with the understanding that the fetus has far greater intrinsic value than physical assets do. The fetus is the woman's fetus—not as a piece of property but as an intrinsically valuable entity in the woman's care and in intimate relationship with the woman.

In normal circumstances, pregnant women act as good stewards. They exercise, adopt a healthy eating regimen, stop drinking alcohol and smoking, and take other healthful measures for the simple reason that they want the fetus to fulfill its potential. They do it not because they are taking care of their property but because they want what is best for the intrinsically valuable entity in a relationship with them that the women chose for themselves. Pregnant women do what is necessary to protect what they truly believe is intrinsically valuable.

With good reason, we condemn women who are not good stewards. Those who do unhealthy things knowing full well that it might lead to congenital problems for their fetuses are bad stewards of what has been entrusted to them. The fetus is not a particular person's property to do with as she would like. We would think that anyone who destroys or harms anything, even nonsentient objects, through her intentional or negligent actions has some sort of moral failing. For example, if someone destroys a rare painting, then we castigate him for doing something wrong even if he owned the painting. Potential persons deserve at least as much consideration as physical objects that lack intrinsic value. Women who endanger their fetuses have been punished by the courts for their actions, although such decisions have been very controversial, to say the least. However, in the court of public opinion, many feel antipathy or anger for a woman who behaves in ways that would harm her fetus, which is unlike how they would react if the woman damaged a dress or other inconsequential physical object. These common emotional responses seem morally justified to us. Those responses also show that we think that the fetus has some moral standing that needs to be protected. The recognition of the fetus's moral standing demonstrates the strong plausibility of the stewardship argument.

There are, however, limits to stewardship obligations. First, no obligation is created if the intrinsically valuable entity is forced on a person. This is what happens in the case of rape. Again, the land stewardship model is useful for explaining how this works. No person can be forced to accept land to be cared for. We cannot use violence that disrespects people's intrinsic value and seems unlikely to maximize utility to create a moral obligation to care for the land on the part of unwilling agents who were merely going about their lives in a permissible way.

Moreover, if someone is too young to be held accountable for the contracts she signs because she is too immature to understand what they entail, then we cannot hold her accountable in more important circumstances with even greater consequences. If a thirteen-year-old signs a contract to buy a piece of land, for example, then her guardians would be in their rights to nullify the contract. The thirteen-year-old is a person but not sufficiently mature to make such significant decisions, so we should say that she is not a moral agent in this regard. To hold her accountable for her land deal would be to penalize ignorance that is the result not of willfulness or neglect but merely of being permissibly immature. If we cannot hold someone to a contract, then we certainly cannot hold the same person to a pregnancy on the very same grounds. In both cases, the best interests of the non-moral agent who is pregnant should be the primary consideration. Guardians are obligated to do what is best for the flourishing of the person who is not a moral agent; that could very well be refusing to allow her to be a steward to something that is intrinsically valuable.

A second limit to stewardship is that even if the person agreed to be a steward, we cannot hold her accountable if she later gives up her stewardship on the grounds that acting in this role will destroy the steward herself. No one is obligated to kill herself or allow herself to die to take care of another entity. We cannot expect the farmer to die for his land, and we cannot expect the woman to die for a potential person. In fact, since she is so much more intrinsically valuable, her death would cause consequences much worse than if she had an abortion. In general, it might be wrong for an individual to sacrifice herself for a potential person. After all, people are stewards of themselves and their relationships with others. They have an obligation to maintain each of those entities, which is rather difficult to do when dead. However, if the steward wants to sacrifice or risk herself, then that is her decision, but it would be a supererogatory action that goes above and beyond the call of duty.

How would the Pragmatic Principle justify this seeming rejection of doing the best we can and the disrespect to the intrinsically valuable entities affected by the action? First, as an intrinsically valuable moral agent, the woman must have autonomy to make decisions for herself. Because of her worth and autonomy over herself, she gets to write her life narrative—that is, she gets to decide her life story. If sacrificing her life for another is what she wants her final chapter to be, then she respects herself and all others affected by her action. She pays proper honor to herself because she is making her life and her death her own in a very significant way. In addition, a reasonable person could very well reasonably believe that the woman's sacrifice will likely lead to the best outcome. Although a very large amount of intrinsic value is lost by the woman's death, it will be replaced by the former fetus developing into a person with her own relationships and general and individual intrinsic values. Moreover, the sacrifice made by the woman is something that she wants to do. Choosing and carrying out that choice, depending on the circumstances, could bring more value than having to act contrary to her life narrative. That discordant chapter, a reasonable person could reasonably believe, would alter her overall life value in a way that would not create the best possible outcome. So in some very unusual circumstances a woman could permissibly sacrifice her life for that of her fetus, at least according to RPC and QCI.

Reflecting again on the morality of abortions, we consider some abortions to be morally wrong. In some cases, if the woman is having an abortion merely to get into a swimsuit or to take a vacation, then we would say that the woman had an abortion unethically.[58] She was not a good steward taking care of the intrinsically valuable entity in her possession. We can make a rule that abortions are morally wrong on the grounds that they are not good stewardship because an abortion does not preserve the intrinsic value of the entity entrusted to the care of the woman. We can understand that intrinsically valuable things may be sacrificed in order for other intrinsically valuable entities to flourish—that is permitted by RPC and QCI—but even then we rightly expect an emotional reaction appropriate to the situation. Regret, which is felt

---

58. I doubt that there are many, if any, of these cases.

when one has done nothing wrong but wishes that a better alternative had been available, is appropriate when someone has undergone an abortion. To coldly sacrifice an intrinsically valuable entity for an unnecessary and unjustifiable reason shows a moral defect in the person. If one cannot have some negative or painful emotions in this case, then one cannot have the proper empathy to be motivated to do the right thing and be a good person.

Now that the extreme cases on the periphery have been addressed, we can turn to those cases of abortion that are more commonly found. Using the Pragmatic Principle, a woman's stewardship of a fetus can be given up only to save something equally or more intrinsically valuable than the fetus.[59] Since the pregnant woman is a person with relationships that make her life more intrinsically valuable, then it might be the case that the woman's relationships need their own stewarding that having a baby would not allow. She might have to care for her ill parents, a significant other, or the children she already has. Some people are unable to afford another child, so they use abortion as a way of keeping the family at a financially sustainable level, although there are few women who use abortion as family planning.

There are a variety of other ways that the intrinsic values could be balanced. Each individual woman's life, relationships, and all the other relevant moral factors in her existence have to be examined and taken into consideration to see if caring for one or more of them outweighs the stewardship obligation to the fetus. Since this process is so amorphous, there is no hard rule by which we can judge these values and how they fit together. The best we can do is determine if it is a reasonable weighing, which brings us back to our reasonable person standard.

Each pregnant woman also might need to take care of her own intrinsic value by developing her flourishing or that of others—which is good stewardship of herself. There might not be enough resources for her to live her life as a full person and to have a child, even if she gave the child up for adoption. Both RPC and QCI would recognize her stewardship of herself as having greater moral worth and therefore as deserving of protection. First, stewarding herself rather than stewarding a potential person, with its lesser intrinsic value, would be her best alternative based on the notion of good stewardship. Second, she respects all intrinsically valuable things as they should

59. Catriona Mackenzie, "Abortion and Embodiment," in *The Problem of Abortion*, ed. Susan Dwyer and Joel Feinberg, 175–93 (Belmont, CA: Wadsworth, 1997), 180. Mackenzie claims that "the decision to abort is a decision, for whatever reason, that one is not prepared to bring such a child into existence." If a person chooses to continue her pregnancy, then she makes a commitment to parental responsibility for the fetus and, possibly, to the child the fetus will become.

be. When comparing the needs of an intrinsically valuable person to the needs of an intrinsically valuable fetus, the person—because she has greater value as a person—wins the contest. Unless she willingly and knowingly sacrifices herself, she is permitted to do what is best for the most intrinsically valuable entity for which she must care—herself.

As we examine the issue of who gets to decide the balance of comparable moral worth, I would like to remind everyone that the woman is a reasonable person. If she uses the Pragmatic Principle the way that it should be used, then she can act permissibly by having an abortion. First, she would have to treat everything with intrinsic value in the way it deserves because of that value that justifies treating it in that manner. As we have seen in the case of the job applicants, just because something has intrinsic value does not entail that its interests must always be met. Sometimes we have to do what is best even when it harms another. Second, a woman, as a reasonable person and if she reasonably believes that the abortion will lead to the best outcome, has satisfied RPC. Other reasonable people might disagree with her, but she needs only one other reasonable person to have that conclusion, and she can do that for herself as long as she is thinking and acting reasonably.

We should never think that an abortion is something that is entered into lightly or leaves no emotional residue. Abortions can be morally permissible yet are always tragic choices. A good steward recognizes what is being sacrificed in order for her to do better. She realizes that something with intrinsic value has been lost in order for her to be respected as she should be. Any steward would feel the loss of having to destroy even part of the land that is entrusted to him, even if it for the very best of reasons. There will and should always be regret that it had to work out as it did, and one should even hope that the situation never has to be repeated. As a person, this feeling is right and proper, whereas the action is permissible.

COMMENTARY

COOLEY:

What do you think of potential conflicts between the morality and religious beliefs of health care professionals and those women who seek abortions?

STEFFEN:

On the question about health care professionals and their involvement in abortion let me also include pharmacists, who may oppose contraception and who would not want to dispense an oral contraceptive, much less an abortifacient or "morning-after pill." Such views are probably grounded almost exclusively in religion. I support the general principle, which, incidentally, the courts in the United States have upheld, that health care workers and pharmacists have a right not to participate in medical procedures that violate their consciences. I very much affirm the free exercise of religion guaranteed by the First Amendment to the U. S. Constitution, and health care workers and pharmacists should ordinarily be exempt from doing professional work that violates their consciences.

But I say this noting that this right of exemption for reason of conscience has limits. Professional obligations in my view must overrule religiously grounded moral perspectives if the conditions warrant. If a woman needed an emergency therapeutic abortion and a Catholic hospital were the only place she could go to have a procedure to save her life, the physician and nursing obligation should overrule the religious beliefs of medical personnel. Saving the woman's life is the highest moral concern, and medical professionals must save the woman's life even if it requires an abortion to do it. If a woman went to a physician who opposed abortion and the patient insisted on more information, the physician has an obligation to direct the patient to a place and to a professional who can provide the care she wants and needs. No medical professional should lie or in any way mislead the patient into taking a course of action based on false or innacurrate information, for this amounts to coercion and it is wrong to force people to surrender their autonomy.

Despite the fact that in American cities there can be three pharmacies within blocks of one another, there are also rural areas where pharmacies are scarce and separated by great distances. Should a woman seek contraception or an abortifacient and the only place within a reasonable distance were a pharmacy where the staff opposed dispensing such things, I think moral decency and professional obligations call for the pharmacist to dispense what is requested. I do believe that when patient care comes up against conscience claims of medical professionals, the professional obligations must take precedence if there is no reasonable way to provide a safe and convenient alternative for the patient. I would assume situations like this are relatively rare, but they have arisen in court cases, and the invoking of conscience to refuse to provide needed or sought after medical services does fly in the face of autonomy, individual rights, and even public health. Health care professionals have a duty to their professions and to the health care of patients who have a right to direct their own care.

A medical professional can refuse to participate in a procedure or pharmaceutical transaction that violates conscience on the condition that what is sought can be acquired elsewhere without unreasonable obstacles. But conscience should not be allowed to insist on its own way within the professional context past the point where it endangers patients, exposes them to ill health, or violates their rights when, in a religiously pluralistic society, the procedure or transaction is neither illegal nor a violation of conscience for the patient. Medical professionals who invoke conscience protections can harm patients by so doing, and this they ought not be allowed to do. If they do put "private" morality based on sectarian religious views above patient welfare, they should be subject to review and possible expulsion from the profession.

COOLEY:

R. M. Hare uses the Golden Rule to argue that a developing fetus with a serious handicap should, in some circumstances, be aborted.[60] If it is a choice between a fetus with a serious handicap and one without such a long-term problem, then Hare believes that it is wrong to bring the former into existence if it will prevent the latter from being born in turn. Do you think that the Golden Rule can be used in this manner?

STEFFEN:

I believe that there are some fetal medical conditions that are so serious that the condition itself creates "just case" for abortion. Such a determination is often difficult to make. The severity of retardation for a Down Syndrome fetus, for example, cannot be accurately gauged prior to birth, though Down Syndrome can certainly be detected. Some Down Syndrome infants can, if they receive stimulation and intense care early on, have IQs as high as seventy-five and go on to live full lives, limited in some ways but nonetheless capable of flourishing. The problem is that one "defect" is often accompanied by others, so a focus on Down Syndrome may overlook other medical complications. Multiple surgeries may be required for bowel obstructions and other anomalies, some of which could be life-threatening and which may lead parents to wonder if they should treat the other anomalies.

60. R. M. Hare, "Abortion and the Golden Rule," in *Philosophy and Sex*, ed. Robert Baker and Frederick Elliston, 231–248 (New York: Prometheus Books, 1984), 240.

From a moral point of view, it seems to me the Golden Rule question may have to do with "as you would have them do unto you." When genetic disease or abnormalities are determined to be such that they threaten the capacity of an individual to flourish, to enjoy the goods of life in any meaningful way with others, one might reasonably ask, "What would I want were that me?" Life is a good of life, but it is not absolute. Life is a good of life in relationship with other goods, and other goods can override it. The prospect of a newborn life lacking the capacity for meaningful relationship and unable to enjoy the goods of life and thus flourish seems to me to be a tragic situation, one in which the abortion option should become a live option—that is, one worthy of considering.

I find Hare's statement as you put it to me somewhat convoluted since, as I understand it, it rests on the supposition that a severely handicapped infant could prevent a less severely handicapped infant from being born, and if the more severely handicapped infant actually did prevent the birth of the less severely handicapped infant, it would be wrong to allow the more severely handicapped infant to come into existence. I do not see how this is a practical situation—how does a severely handicapped infant prevent a less severely handicapped infant from being born, practically speaking? That is too much speculation for me and not real life.

We have greater and lesser forms of disability and handicaps, and the reality is that every prospective mother and father wants a perfect child. The sad reality is that there are no guarantees—no one can be promised a perfect child. If we can find out about severe disability before birth, handicaps that would prevent flourishing and render life itself a burden for a neonate, or if we find out that a parent is psychologically unable to accept such a child, then abortion seems to me to be a reasonable option to consider. The whole point of prenatal testing is to determine fetal normality, and suppressed in that statement is that if anomalies are found, they might be sufficient to warrant consideration of abortion to terminate the pregnancy. This of course raises other issues, since eliminating certain kinds of anomalies could render abortion a eugenics practice—and in fact it does. But it is in no one's interests—not the interests of the parents or society or even the fetus itself—to be born with no reasonable prospect of enjoying the goods of life.

STEFFEN:

Let me stop here and now ask you a question: Much of the energy for opposing abortion comes from arguments that are grounded in religious affirmations and values. Do you think your stewardship notion would have much currency among religious people as they think about abortion? Part of this question arises for me due to my perception that philosophers often approach abortion as if religious views can be bracketed out—and they can be bracketed out for purposes of making an argument, but in my view they cannot for purposes of thinking about public policy. Any thoughts?

COOLEY:

In your questions and writing, I believe that you have captured the fundamental reason why abortion is, and will continue to be, so controversial an issue—namely, religious belief and personal identity. To think that one's deity commands one to act in one way rather than another is one thing, but it lacks force without the second element. As we know, many folks claim that they belong to a religion, but they often do very little to show that besides attending their religious house on certain holidays and telling those conducting surveys that they are of a religion. Beyond that, the religious tenets and dogma have little impact on their day-to-day life or on most events that matter when they go about doing their business.

It is only when the religious belief becomes part of the individual's identity that the power to motivate emotionally or physically violent actions arises, and this gives rise to a set-in-stone quality to positions that generally make them impossible to change or discuss reasonably. If someone could not imagine being the same person if they were not a member of a particular religion, then we can tell that being a member of that religion is a necessary feature of who the person is at her very heart, at least according to the person who holds that fundamental belief. To change that person's religion is to simultaneously essentially alter who she is.

Of course, when an individual change strikes at the very heart of who the person is, then the person is far more likely to react negatively and aggressively to the threat. He will do what he needs to do to protect himself, which might entail acting in a manner that would harm another or himself physically or psychologically. At the very least, it will cause a great deal of anger and other emotional reaction in the person who feels threatened. This makes conversations on abortion difficult at best when engaging members on both extremes of the issue. No matter how carefully done, by bringing in information that cuts to the person's core, he will feel as if you were saying that there is something wrong with him as a person. Those things he thinks make him who he is are somehow bad things.

The impossibility of being wrong also has a role to play here. If a person's core being appears to be challenged, then it is far less likely that the person will be able to consider that she is wrong in her beliefs. To self-reflect would be to question who she is as a person, thereby internalizing the attack on herself. The self-awareness required for this introspection is beyond many of us, especially given that fact that none of us likes to admit that we might be not only wrong, but wrong in a very significant way that would cause us to have guilt for serious harm caused.

We should also not forget the comfort and pleasure people take in fighting someone they think is evil. It makes life far easier for us to have clearly identifiable demons to fight. It gives us a black-and-white solution that only the worst person would question, while we are on the side of the angels. And when it does happen that others think differently from us, we get the opportunity to be superior to them since we are good, as determined by God, and they are evil, also as determined by God. What a boost to one's self-esteem to think that God or supreme right is on one's side! I'm afraid that is one of the motivations for crusades that may start with a good intention but that cause horrible destructive consequences—all because one thinks one is justified by supreme right to do whatever it takes to achieve one's end.

Hence, I am not hopeful that those on both sides of the issue will be able to come to some sort of compromise in the current situation. It is far too hard to question our core values and beliefs because they are part of who we are. It is also far too easy to have demons that offer us no real harm but are so satisfying to fight to enhance our self-esteem. The only way to overcome these roadblocks to peace is through serious introspection and self-awareness, which can be found when people are able to recognize the value of those who oppose them. That requires familiarity found through positive interaction on other shared values, which can require a mediator to help opponents search for those shared values.

I am interested to know if you think a woman could have an abortion when her intention is directed not at abortion per se but at something else, some other good? And then there are at least two other interesting questions for me that arise from your position. First, if the woman does not make the promise to bring the fetus to term, then, on your account, the fetus does not have personhood. Can another person make this promise and make the fetus into a person?

Second, I am a bit concerned with the need to have a form of social recognition to achieve personhood. Some would argue that being a person is an objective truth that does not require any outside force to confer the status. That personhood status exists because certain internal features exist, such as having a soul or a certain type of DNA or a "human life." What would you say is the greatest advantage to your position that they should accept?

STEFFEN:

You have put a couple of questions to me I had not considered, and I think they are certainly worthy of response.

Your first question asks whether a woman who becomes pregnant and does not want to be could seek to have an abortion with her intention not directed at abortion but rather at something else. What if her intention is to preserve her bodily integrity from invasion by an unwanted outsider or to exercise her right to maintain and protect her body-as-property? Perhaps she wants to act in a way that allows her to exercise self-determination, or she does not want to subject herself to an upset in the stasis of her health with a pregnancy that will cause inevitable changes in health and pose certain risks to physical or mental well-being. What if a pregnant woman articulates these intentions and in pursuit of these intentions an abortion occurs—it is conceivable that she does not intend to have an abortion but intends these other things? Do I have that right?

The question you ask here makes a case for abortion becoming more broadly a "double effect" question. That is, the primary intention is to preserve bodily integrity or health or to exercise self-determination, and in pursuit of the intentions to do these things, a developing form of human life dies. In such a case, the secondary or "double effect"—which is the death of the fetus—is a foreseen but unintended consequence of pursing the articulated primary intention. My short answer to this is that I don't buy it. Can a woman faced with pregnancy want to preserve bodily integrity and health and to exercise self-determination? Yes, of course. But abortion is a direct and intended killing by definition.

I cannot accept that a woman who understands that she is going through a medical procedure to terminate a pregnancy is not intending to do so. Whether she admits it or not, her actions reveal the intention. To go through all the preliminaries and then submit to the voluntary abortion procedure means that she is intending to have an abortion. I can certainly agree that what appears to be one act can be described as several acts, all of which can have specific intentions attached, and we can have more than one intention for any particular thing we do. In this double-effect scenario, however, the idea of a person having an abortion procedure on the claim that her *only* intention is, say, to protect her body-as-property—*and not to have an abortion*—is an unreasonable claim. Of course she intends to have an abortion—the abortion may fit a larger intention she holds relevant to her moral personality, but this individual is either ignorant about the meaning of intentions, or she is being lied to by her physician into thinking she is just having a pelvic exam, or she is self-deceived by holding as her "cover story" that she can subject herself to an abortion without having an intention to do so.

Your other questions go to issues in my "just abortion" theory. On the question about whether another person, someone besides the pregnant woman, can make the promise to the fetus to bring it to term, I would have to say, in general, no. I say "in general" because there are possible exceptions. We can of course imagine coercion scenarios that would present a woman being forced to bring a pregnancy to term, and there have been rare situations in which a brain-dead pregnant woman is kept alive so her fetus can be born. Society, the medical attendants, or the family are making that decision, but someone other than the mother is a surrogate "promise keeper."

Keep in mind with respect to promise keeping that pregnancy is a finite temporal condition—a forty-week experience. Most women who get pregnant and want to be pregnant make the "promise" to bring their fetus to term when they find out they are pregnant (some even before!), and the promise must be seen as implicit or tacit. The pregnant woman's actions subsequent to committing to bring the baby to term show the promise at work: the mother-to-be stops smoking and drinking alcohol, she goes to her physician for prenatal care, she takes vitamins and eats more salad to up her intake of necessary nutrients, and so on. All of those actions show that the pregnant woman wants to bring the baby to term and do so in a healthy way, and all of those actions are evidence that she has promised to take care of herself and the fetus so this relational partner—this fetus—will have every chance for an normal delivery and a healthy start to life. Her promise reveals that she wants her prospective baby to flourish, and it is evident in her actions; her actions allow us to impute the promise and her intention to help the newborn flourish.

Some women may postpone making that "promise," and because of the finite, forty-week nature of the pregnancy term, one cannot allow an abortion decision to go up to the thirty-ninth week when delivery is imminent. There comes a point in pregnancy when the fetus comes to resemble a newborn more than the conceptus, and I think this moment is about twenty weeks. It seems to me reasonable to think that if the woman has not decided by that point to have an abortion, then it is reasonable for society not to impose but to assume that the mother has made a tacit promise to bring the fetus to term. Remember that over 90 percent of abortions take place in the first fourteen weeks, with those that go over this point also being performed prior to the twenty-week cutoff. Abortions that occur past that twenty-week point are pregnancies where there are issues with the mother's life or health or a recognition of a distressful handicap, all of which can be justified on the "just abortion" theory. But when viability starts to become a reality on the medical front—and the *Roe v. Wade* decision took this tack as well—the possibility for justifying abortion lessens except for threats to the woman's life or health. Such threats are always justifications for terminating a pregnancy on the just abortion theory, although a late-term abortion where fetal viability is established does not allow that a viable fetus can or should be killed if the woman's medical situation demands that the fetus be extracted.

So, to answer your second question, I believe society does not and should not *make* a decision to establish personhood during pregnancy and gestation; what it does is recognize that a woman, by inaction and not exercising the abortion option, is herself making a promise, tactily, to bring a fetus to term. I would keep this question focused on the autonomy of the pregnant woman. I hope that helps.

Your question about objective truth and intrinsic value may need some referral to the chapter where we discuss the "objective-subjective" distinction. Let me say this on the particular abortion-related question you ask: personhood is a moral category, not a scientific category. Members of the species *Homo sapiens* can present to us the necessary properties of human beings but not be persons in the moral sense—for they can suffer brain traumas that leave them irretrievably lost to the world of human relationality and beyond any hope of returning to consciousness itself. That is an objective scientific determination that could affect how we think about personhood. On my natural law–based "goods" approach to ethics, I would say that there are situations in which personhood cannot attach to individuals because they have irretrievably lost the capacity for human relationality and consciousness and are therefore incapable of enjoying and pursuing in any meaningful way the goods of life, including the good of life itself. When this is determined in an ICU, families will often give permission to shut down the life-sustaining equipment—the respirator, the feeding tube, the IVs. We make these decisions, and these decisions are all tied up to what you term "social recognition." Doctors and families decide Uncle Vanya is dead and should be removed from life support though his heart is beating on its own. Uncle Vanya is gone. Continuing his biological processes to no good end, not even the possibility of providing transplants, is to fall into the fallacy of vitalism, the fallacy that the very processes of life deserve to be maintained and continued beyond any relation to actual *goods* that can be recognized in those processes.

Likewise at the beginning of life: a mother is in a sense an "outsider" to the fetus, but she is closer to it than anyone else, and that intimacy gives her privileged standing to recognize the fetus as person. Ascribing personhood to a fetus is not objective in the sense that it is scientifically determinable—if personhood is a moral category, then what is important is the fact of recognition. We all recognize newborns as persons even if they cannot talk or reason, and during the period of infancy they are on the receiving end of relationality with not a lot to give back, though smiles and coos suffice for most parents to meet any kind of relationality standard. People who would deny any *conferral* of personhood because of a belief in intrinsic properties of personhood misunderstand the category. We get personhood and species membership all mixed up and we need a little precision—even *Roe v. Wade* confused things by saying that the Supreme Court was not going to decide "when life begins." That was not the question. We would have to say, I think, on the question of when life begins that, biologically speaking, life began a long time ago and it has continued through sexual reproduction over countless eons of natural history, and we know that life continues in a new instance when a sperm fertilizes an ovum. But that is not when personhood begins; personhood begins when someone—the moral community—says it does. The moral community confers this in the promise recognition a mother gives to her developing form of life that cannot reason or speak and may be a clump of poorly differentiated cells; society confers it by offering protection to vulnerable individuals who may not meet all the criteria of personhood as laid out by different philosophers—you mention Mary Anne Warren's criteria of personhood above in your essay here—and through social conventions and legal protections.

However it is accomplished, the conferral of personhood is a moral act and process that issues from the moral community. The answers to our many quandaries and problems about personhood cannot be found in the back of biology textbook. The meaning of personhood is created and constructed—and undergoes critique and analysis—through the deliberations of people of good will as they advance and promote the goods of life so that the moral community and its many members might thrive and flourish.

3

The Death Penalty

INTRODUCTION

Discussions about the death penalty seem fewer and less volatile than in years past. Reasons for this include, but are not limited to, shifting attitudes about the death penalty and more pressing needs demanding attention, such as a continuing focus on abortion in some areas of the world and on war in others.

However, the death penalty remains a critical moral issue, in part because it involves the state's ability to kill its own people as well as visiting citizens from other countries, provided that the latter have transgressed some law that permits capital punishment. There are relatively few countries and states that practice capital punishment, but their scarcity is irrelevant.[1] What matters is the fact that the state, which already wields enormous power over regular folks, can impose the ultimate punishment of death on certain individuals if the state so desires. The fact that the state is entitled to kill individuals should be a matter of moral concern for any reasonable person.

Unlike the other chapters and topics on death—with the notable exception of war—this chapter deals with the state's actions more than it does with what individuals do. Of course, the state is comprised of individuals, but when someone is to be put to death, it is the state that claims authority to do it. Abortion, euthanasia, and other deaths are generally considered to be personal or individual actions with which the state should not interfere or should engage only to help people rather than to intervene intentionally to kill them.

---

1. Depending on whether you count Taiwan, there are either 195 or 196 countries in the world today, and 140 of them have abolished the death penalty. For the death penalty statistic see "The Death Penalty Worldwide," Infoplease, http://www.infoplease.com/ipa/A0777460.html.

STEFFEN

Ethical discussions about state-sponsored execution usually focus on capital punishment. A person who has committed some grave offense is subjected to arrest, trial, and conviction and then sentenced to death, with the actual execution being the end result of a legal process. In a formal sense, then, the death penalty refers to a legalized state-sponsored killing inflicted deliberately and intentionally on human beings as a punishment for some offense. But the execution power claimed by political communities is broader than a reference to "capital punishment" for crime might indicate, for political communities of one sort or another have claimed an execution power from time immemorial to cover all kinds of offenses that by our ordinary moral lights do not merit death. The Hebrew Bible allows that a child who curses a parent may be taken out of the city and stoned, so the capital offense need not be criminal. Hitler authorized the killing of thousands—millions—of persons on what were believed to be "racial" grounds, so there was no "offense" or crime involved except the contingency of individuals belonging to an ethnic-religious group irrationally out of favor with the ruling authority. The execution power, distinct from capital punishment, can creep into such situations.

Capital punishment is actually a more restricted way of talking about the execution power, although it is an instance of it. When we refer to the death penalty or capital punishment, we are focusing attention on a legal process that results in the imposition of a death sentence for crime—the worst crimes, such as murder—under the rule of law. This is important to note because communities have at times assumed the execution power and killed individuals who were believed to pose some threat to their community—think of the thousands of lynchings that occurred in the United States as white vigilantes killed black citizens often for no reason other than to terrorize the black community. This was not capital punishment, but it most certainly was the execution power being exercised against those believed to be threatening to the social order and community values.

Capital punishment is held to be a justified killing inflicted for crimes of such gravity that the offender has forfeited a fundamental right to life. States where executions are permitted hold that law can demand the offender's life on behalf of society as recompense or retribution for the offense. When death sentences are carried out, a society acts through its legal system and by means of an authorized machinery of execution to confront an individual and deliver death by a legalized procedure that is also an act of violence—killing. The person who faces actual execution is, at that point, physically unable to defend him- or herself.

States are free to exercise the execution power or refuse it. More than two-thirds of the countries in the world have now abolished the death penalty in law or practice. Amnesty International reports that capital punishment is retained in 58 countries with 140 countries not using it. Some have abolished it outright (97), others have abolished it for ordinary crimes (8), while others refuse to practice it (35).[2] In the United States, 33 states currently have the death penalty on the books, 17 states have abolished it, and in 2012 only 9 states carried out any death sentences.[3]

The death that results from an execution involves several moral issues. First of all, a killing lies at the heart of the death-penalty debate, and, as we note several times in these pages, any time a human person is killed, that killing is subject to moral scrutiny and analysis. Moral questions attend the issue of justification: Is justice delivered to society and to the victim survivors when executions occur? Is execution justified by retribution? And are there limits to retribution? A question often not asked is whether the result of the execution—death itself—can even be a punishment. Is it more accurate to say that the punishment involves all that leads up to the execution—say, the terror of knowing one will be killed and the psychological distress created by being subjected to a ritualized killing process?

In the following discussion I will note some of the major moral issues involved in the death penalty, describe arguments both for and against execution, and will focus briefly on what a "just execution" theory would look like. I say "theory" because the natural law ethic I am advocating, which depends on "common agreements" in the first instance, must then be tested against the practice. The issue to consider in using the ethic is how closely or how well the actual system of justice that hands people over to execution meets the test of a theoretical "just execution." Following this, I will turn attention to religious issues, commenting on the role of execution in religion and the reasons why religious people may support or oppose a death penalty for religious offense and secular crime.

CLARIFYING THE MORAL ISSUES

The major ethical justifications for a society imposing a death penalty have to do with retribution, deterrence, and the protection of societal values, particularly

2. Amnesty International, "Abolitionist and Retentionist Countries," http://www.amnesty.org/en/death-penalty/abolitionist-and-retentionist-countries.

3. Death Penalty Information Center, "The Death Penalty in 2012: Year End Report," December 2012, http://www.deathpenaltyinfo.org/documents/2012YearEnd.pdf .

the value of life. The retribution idea goes back to one of the traditional ideas of justice itself, retributive justice, which holds that if an individual abuses freedom to inflict harm on another person, the imbalance created by the harm may be redressed by inflicting on the offender an equivalent harm as punishment. The idea of "an eye for an eye," which stretches from Hammurabi's Code up to present-day philosophies of punishment, maintains that if a life is unjustly taken, the individual who unjustly took that life must forfeit his or her own. Society demands this retributive punishment as a *proportional response* to the offense. The idea of proportionality—a life for a life—leads many who support the death penalty to hold that it is a just punishment, that is, a justified act of retributive justice.

Another justification is that society benefits from executing those who transgress against its highest laws and most cherished values. The idea here is that the death penalty is so severe that it acts as a deterrent to prevent others from committing a like crime. The death penalty, according to this defense, saves lives. The loss of life through execution becomes an instrument of societal benefit, this utilitarian argument would go, for it arouses a fear that by killing one puts one's own life at risk, something no reasonable person would want to do. This deterrent effect prevents many unjust deaths, and thus the societal benefit of more lives saved justifies the death penalty as a utilitarian good.

A final justification is that the death penalty is a serious act that exemplifies how far society will go in order to preserve the value of life. This may sound paradoxical—killing to save lives—but what is at stake is the idea that life is precious, and society can act to protect and promote the value of life by imposing a death penalty. Society is upholding what it holds most dear—the value of life.

Arguments against the death penalty are often religious and we shall discuss this momentarily, but the main moral arguments have to do with the contradiction and thus absurdity of claiming that killing saves lives, fair imposition, the protection of society by means other than killing, the possibility of errors that would lead to the execution of the innocent, and the irrevocable nature of execution—that fact that justice systems are fallible, errors are often uncovered long after trials are completed, and injustices cannot be corrected if an individual is dead.

All of these arguments come into play in a theory of "just execution," and let me lay out what that theory would look like. Again, I claim that this way of examining the issue—the natural law "common agreement" ethic—is the best way to analyze the moral meaning of the execution practice.

Just Execution

A theory of just execution does not begin by saying, "Capital punishment is a good thing" or "The death penalty is a bad thing." There is obviously disagreement on that very question. Opinion polls indicate that 63 percent of Americans still support the death penalty although when the death penalty is made one option and life imprisonment without the possibility of parole is another option, support and opposition are equal.[4] In the opening chapter where the natural law "common agreement" ethics option was put forward, we indicated that the ethic required the articulation of an easily agreed upon moral starting place on any particular issue where the ethic would be applied. An actual point of common agreement needed to be articulated, a place where reasonable people of good will could actually acknowledge agreement on a moral position. The common agreement relevant to engaging the issue of capital punishment does not fall directly on the question of capital punishment—again, there is obvious disagreement on the issue, so the common agreement must lie elsewhere. The common agreement underlying the death penalty is rather to be found in a statement like this: "States ought ordinarily not kill their citizens."

This statement articulates a moral presumption against use of the death penalty because, morally speaking, the killing of persons is presumptively wrong and capital punishment is a killing: it is one way states can and actually do kill citizens. But if it is presumptively wrong for the state to kill its citizens, are there ever circumstances or situations that would create an exception to that rule? And is capital punishment a legitimate exception? How would we know?

These questions lead to a distinctive theory of "just execution." Can the state ever kill its citizens justifiably? Although there are some individuals, like Leo Tolstoy, who would deny on religious grounds that the state can legitimately take the life of any citizen, reasonable people of good will can acknowledge that, in the terrible messiness of life, there are occasions when the state is justified in using force—lethal force if need be—to defend the lives of innocent citizens or otherwise to protect society. A bank robber who, holding

---

4. Death Penalty Information Center, "Public Opinion: 2012 Gallup Poll Shows Support for Death Penalty Remains Near 40-Year Low," http://www.deathpenaltyinfo.org/public-opinion-2012-gallup-poll-shows-support-death-penalty-remains-near-40-year-low. A recent Pew Research Center poll shows that those who "strongly support" the death penalty has fallen from 28% to 18% since 2012; 37% of Americans now oppose the death penalty; six states have repealed death penalty statutes over the past six years and the reason for the change are two fold according to the polls: the possibility of error and the increasing belief that execution is simply immoral. M. Lipka, "Support for death penalty drops among Americans," Pew Research Center, February 12, 2014) at http://deathpenaltyinfo.org /national-polls-and-studies#Pew2014.

innocent people hostage, is killed by a police sniper, or a police officer who fires a weapon in self-defense against an armed aggressor—these are just two examples that would present to reasonable people of good will occasions when a use of lethal force would seem justifiable. So the question of whether the state can ever justify killing a citizen in the face of our common agreement that the state should not seems answerable with a yes.

On the basis of that yes, we can open the next questions: Is capital punishment another instance of justified killing by the state? Does the death penalty constitute a legitimate exception to the moral presumption against the use of capital punishment? At this point we can now ask if the death penalty is a legitimate exception to our reasonable agreement that the state ought ordinarily not kill its citizens. While all of us would acknowledge that, in general, killing is wrong, we also want to acknowledge that some state-sponsored killings, like a police officer's self-defense, might be justifiable. But are the killings that the state undertakes in legal execution practices morally justifiable?

A theory of just execution will start off by acknowledging that the moral presumption against the death penalty is in place and acknowledged. Only a small number of persons who commit the "worst of the worst" crimes are ever subjected to execution. In 2011, more than 14,600 murders occurred in the United States.[5] That year, 76 individual were sentenced to death, so the death penalty was handed out to less than half of one percent of all murders and nonnegligent homicides.[6] Why so few capital sentences? The reasons are complex, but we do not impose an "eye for an eye, a life for a life" retribution ethic and demand that every person who kills another person then forfeits—or should forfeit—his or her life. The common agreement that ordinarily the state ought not to kill its citizens, even for the heinous crime of one person killing another, is firmly in place. Those who are subjected to execution, however, become the "exceptions" to the rule, and a just execution theory must be devised to see if those individuals are given death sentences in accordance with the requirements of justice.

I have elsewhere laid out in detail the content of a theory of just execution, and all I shall do here is lay out the structure of the theory. "Just execution" will impose criteria, or justice concerns, that have to be satisfied in meaningful ways in order for reasonable people to agree that an exception to our moral

---

5. Federal Bureau of Investigation, Uniform Crime Statistics, "Crime in the United States 2011," http://www.fbi.gov/about-us/cjis/ucr/crime-in-the-u.s/2011/crime-in-the-u.s.-2011/tables/table-4.

6. Death Penalty Information Center, "The Death Penalty in 2012: Year End Report," http://deathpenaltyinfo. org/documents/2012YearEnd.pdf.

presumption against execution is in fact justified. Those criteria would take into account the following:

1. Just authority. This has to be included to prevent any vigilantism—such as lynching—from ever being deemed morally justifiable.
2. Just cause. Although the death penalty has been expanded in the United States, and some capital crimes, like treason or espionage, do not involve murder or result in a victim's death, in general the death penalty is reserved for aggravated murder, the "worst of the worst" crime to many minds.
3. Motivation should be justice and not vengeance. In practice, the fact that jurors have to weigh both mitigating and aggravating circumstances lends support to the idea that the motivation ought not be vengeance but a concern for justice and just punishment.
4. Fair imposition. The death penalty should not be imposed in any way that is unfair or that shows discrimination for reasons of race, sex, or economic status.
5. The method of execution should not be cruel or torturous.
6. Execution should be a last resort. When deciding to impose a death sentence, all other penalties and punishments that would serve the interests of justice and the protection of society must be considered and rejected as inadequate.
7. Executions must preserve respect for the value of life.
8. The end of execution must be some kind of restoration of an equilibrium upset by the offender's crime. The issue here is that families of aggravated murder victims need to heal, and an execution should contribute to that end and otherwise help restore the balance of justice upset by the loss of life.
9. Proportionality. Execution must be a proportionate response to the injustice of the criminal's act, so no excessive punishment is allowable. Torture should not be allowed, and death should not be demanded for certain crimes, heinous though they be, since death is not a proportionate punishment. Execution for rape, for instance, was at one time a regular occurrence in America's Southern states, usually inflicted on black men accused of raping white women. Aside from issues of discrimination, that

punishment has been deemed excessive and disproportionate in relation to the crime.

This is in brief compass a theory of just execution. To recap: the theory begins by affirming a moral agreement that all people of good will can be expected to affirm without controversy—namely, that the state ought ordinarily not kill its citizens. From this affirmation of common agreement, the theory then moves to consider whether the death penalty is a justifiable exception to that agreement. The nine criteria just listed identify justice requirements that would have to be satisfied in a reasonable way in order for executions to proceed.

Now that we have the theory, the work required by the just execution theory begins. That work is to investigate the details of the execution practice. Concerned citizens must examine the criminal justice system that doles out death sentences and determine the extent to which reasonable people of good will can affirm that the criteria of just execution are actually being met in practice.

My view is that a reasonable examination of the practice of execution provides ample evidence that the criteria are not satisfied—not at the level of practice. On every one of the criteria, I have argued elsewhere, serious questions can be asked about the execution practice, and I hold that the practice of execution fails to meet the reasonable tests of justice required by the theory. For instance, the death penalty is not imposed fairly, and discrimination can be shown with respect to race—especially the race of victim—and on issues of sex and class. Death rows are filled with poor people who could not afford a lawyer, a disproportionately large number of nonwhite racial minorities, and an overwhelming number of males. Racial disparities are visible in who is charged and who becomes eligible for the death penalty. The common idea that the death penalty is reserved for the "worst of the worst" is undermined as prosecutors use the death penalty as a bargaining chip; the truly "worst of the worst" offenders—serial killers—often receive life sentences and avoid the death penalty through a plea bargain. Furthermore, the practice of execution is marred by a horrible statistic. Since 1973, the year executions resumed in the United States, over 140 persons sentenced to death have been exonerated and released from death rows. The criminal justice system has had to acknowledge mistakes and wrongful convictions—and those are just the ones found out. How many were not discovered and how many persons went to a gas chamber or electric chair or a lethal injection gurney for a crime they did not commit? The criminal justice system is broken in significant ways, and it is error prone.

Subjecting an innocent person to execution is a moral horror that points to significant failures in the whole system of prosecution and sentencing.

Using the just execution framework, which requires individuals to investigate the factual and legal issues relevant to each of the just execution criteria, leads, in my opinion, to the conclusion that the death penalty fails the test of justice and that the moral presumption against capital punishment should not be lifted. An exception to the common agreement that the state should not kill its citizens might be allowable in the case of a police officer killing someone in defense of self or other innocent persons, but it does not extend to the death penalty as practiced in the United States. The criteria cannot be satisfied in practice, so the theory structures a conversation about moral issues and practical problems that leads to the conclusion that the death penalty is wrong, unjust, and immoral. To make that case would certainly require more discussion, but readers can look into the issues involved with particular cases and make their own decisions.

Still, people do disagree over the moral appropriateness of the death penalty. The just execution theory acknowledges that people can come to different conclusions using the "common agreement" theory on an issue like the death penalty. While that may appear to be a flaw, it is actually its strength. The theory requires a common starting point, namely, the recognition that there are deep moral agreements that hold a moral community together despite disagreements over particular issues. The theory invites all people of good will to acknowledge that common moral agreement, and then it requires conversation, a discussion of facts and discernment of their meaning, and citizen action and interaction. All of these things are hallmarks of a democratic society functioning as it should, engaging, that is, in reasoned debate about justice issues that are of concern to all people of good will. However one feels about the death penalty, no reasonable person should want such a penalty imposed unfairly or in a way that would show, say, racial or class or gender bias, or would subject an innocent person to death. The theory structures debate and identifies the issues that need to be discussed by citizens informed and concerned about the moral meaning of the actions done in their name and on their authority.

The just execution theory assumes that a "just execution" is at least theoretically possible—another of the theory's strengths if one is concerned to avoid moral absolutism and engage moral issues at the level of practice. But the just execution theory also allows us to ask some even more basic questions. Three come to mind, all of which are worthy of attention.

The first has to do with the idea of death being a punishment. The question is whether the idea that death is a punishment even makes sense. If an offense is committed and an imbalance of justice created, does taking action that puts an individual perpetrator in the same state (of nonbeing) as the victim constitute a punishment? Is a punishment not supposed to be *experienced* in some way? If the punishment is the result of execution—death—and death is not experienced, how can we say a punishment took place? The process leading up to an execution is certainty painful, psychologically cruel, and even torturous, and awaiting execution certainly qualifies as an infliction of pain and suffering—if that is what one wants from a punishment. But is the punishment in capital punishment supposed to be the process leading up to the killing—instilling fear and terror—or the actual result of execution, which is death? If it is death, how is that a punishment, as the individual cannot experience whatever end one hopes for in punishment—continued remorse, a willingness to reform, or even offering oneself in some way to victim survivors to help redress the injustice? This leads to a second question.

Does the idea of "eye for an eye, a life for a life" really embody ideals of justice people of good will want to acknowledge and enshrine in law? Recall that in Iran in 2004 a suitor flung acid in the eyes of a woman who had rejected his marriage proposal. The woman was blinded. This was of course a horrible act, but what extended the horror was that the woman petitioned courts operating under Sharīʿa and committed to literal "eye for an eye" thinking to have her attacker blinded the same way she had been. The courts granted the woman's petition to blind her attacker with acid in the eyes. This is an example—mercifully rare—of literal "eye for an eye" thinking. The civilized world reacted with shock and horror.[7] A "life for a life" may be just as horrible as this example of an "eye for an eye," but we are unable to see it, perhaps because of the medicalization of the execution process itself—lethal injection seems sanitary and nonpainful but could be, and actually has been, for those who look into the question, as barbaric a practice as "acid in the eye for acid in the eye."

Does that "eye for an eye" retribution amount to justice? Should not the attacker have been "punished" in such a way that he would be forced to spend the rest of his days caring for this woman whose life he so grievously injured? Should he not have been allowed to work, thus contributing to her financial upkeep and taking responsibility for the life he damaged? Would that not have been more in line with a notion of justice that seeks to hold individual offenders

---

7. For references to the story see Steffen, *Ethics and Experience*, 223–24.

responsible for their acts and to redress the imbalance in justice created by their unjust act? The blinded woman will be blind her whole life—why should the offender not be involved with helping her for the remainder of her life, thereby taking responsibility for what he had done? What good is served by blinding him? What good is delivered to the victim of his terrible act?

A third moral issue involves the loss of life that occurs when a murder is committed. That loss is irretrievable. Nothing can ever put it right and balance the scales of justice again. Is it not curious that we think the loss of another life creates some kind of justice equity—it just creates another loss of life and leaves in its wake more damage, compounding loss rather than restoring any imbalance. The loss for a loss may look like equity and balance, but that is to miss the point that a true restoration of balance could only be achieved if, in the wake of a murder, killing the criminal restored the victim to life. If this were possible, that would constitute a reasonable rebalancing and rectification of a grievous harm. As we all know, this is not what happens when a murder is committed and a life is lost. If there were in nature some kind of immediate killing reaction, so that a killing of one human being by another resulted in the immediate loss of the offender's life, then we should know that it is in the nature of things that murderers should die for their killings. But this does not happen. As we noted, only a very small percentage of murderers actually face execution, which demonstrates that we do not acknowledge that killing a murderer should be the mandatory response for the injustice of the killing—we exercise reason and make decisions about particular cases and go out of our way to respond to the injustice of killing by taking all kinds of factors into account. On that basis we establish grades of killing, from low levels of homicide and unintentional manslaughter to aggravated murder.

The loss of life cannot be rectified however we respond. The evidence is clear that victims' families are not healed by the execution of the one who killed their loved one—they are, after an execution, plunged into the grief they may have been holding at bay while focused on their desire for vengeance. Nothing good comes of an execution for the simple reason that the imbalance created by the loss of life is irretrievable—nothing can restore the balance when life is lost, not even taking the perpetrator's life. The moral question must finally be, What good is served for society, for the victim's families, and for perpetrators by an execution?

The loss of life resulting from governments or political groups executing political opponents to preserve power or suppress opposition raises a whole different range of issues about the execution power, which also at some point should be considered in tandem with legalized, state-sponsored executions for criminal offense. Our focus here has been on capital punishment and whether killing a killer is just. The execution power, however, has been used throughout history—and is still used today—for purposes that have to do with preserving political power or economic advantage, and such executions are perhaps even more provocative examples of the general idea of execution, of which capital punishment and a legalized death penalty are but a part. The just execution theory can and should be applied to such executions. While doing so would yield a greater consensus that such exercises of power are wrong, it was important to keep focused here on those executions often held to be just because they are legal and in conformity with social traditions. However, we ought not lose sight of the fact that the execution power, whether wielded by the state of Texas or required by der Führer in Hitler's Germany, arises from an exercise of political power and must be subjected to moral analysis however it arises.

These are some of the moral issues important to reflect on when considering the ethics of death brought about by execution.

RELIGIOUS ISSUES

The just execution theory is morally moderate in the sense that it is premised on the idea that some killings by the state or governing authority can be justified and others cannot. The moral task is to decide which are which. In examining capital punishment from a moral point of view, we noted the gap that exists between the moral requirements of justice and how the system of execution is put to work in actual practice. "Just execution" would hold that if the practice does not satisfy the justice requirements, capital punishment is immoral and thus should not be practiced.

The gap between justice values and practice noted in a secular ethics analysis has significant parallels in religious ethics, and how that gap is present to us can be quite curious. For instance, many Christians support the death penalty in practice while adhering to values that would, on their face, appear to oppose it. Judaism, on the other hand, has textual sources that lend rather easy support to the idea of execution, but rabbinic teaching actually throws obstacles in the way. Thus, in Judaism capital punishment receives little support at the level of actual practice. From a religious ethics point of view, the practice of capital punishment must be tested against core values that could support or oppose the execution practice, and it requires investigation of any gap that appears between theory and practice. The following discussion will examine some of the general issues that attend the idea of capital punishment in various religious traditions, with attention given to the gap between core religious values and practice. We shall begin with Buddhism, discuss Islam and Judaism, but reserve most of our attention for Christianity, a religion whose "founder" was himself the victim of state-sponsored execution.

Buddhism

Buddhist views on capital punishment have not received much attention, primarily because the first of the Five Precepts, which apply to all Buddhists, affirms a prohibition on taking life. Since all sentient beings possess a Buddha-nature and are thus capable of achieving enlightenment, the destruction of life constitutes a terrible offense that impedes progress toward enlightenment. Capital punishment is thus, on the face of it, contrary to the first and foremost Buddhist ethical principle. Opposition to the death penalty is in fact so obviously consistent with Buddhist teaching about nonviolence and noninjury toward sentient beings that one standard account of Buddhist ethics, Peter Harvey's *An Introduction to Buddhist Ethics*, simply does not address capital punishment as a major ethics issue, although it talks about governance and the ruler's duty to punish offenders.[8]

A variety of sources could be invoked to link core Buddhist values to death penalty opposition, including these words from the best-known collection of the Buddha's teachings, the *Dhammapada,* which in chapter 10 offers this teaching on punishment:

> 129. All beings tremble at the rod (punishment);
> All are afraid of death. Seeing their likeness to yourself,
> You should neither kill nor cause to kill.
> 130. All beings tremble at the rod (punishment);
> Life is dear to all.
> Seeing their likeness to yourself,
> You should neither ill, nor cause to kill.
> 131. The one who, desiring happiness for himself,
> Harms with the rod
> Beings who desire happiness/
> Will have no happiness hereafter.
> 132. The one who, desiring happiness for himself,
> Does not harm with the rod
> Beings who desire happiness

---

8. Peter Harvey, *An Introduction to Buddhist Ethics.*

Will have happiness hereafter.[9]

These verses enshrine in sacred Scriptures the Buddhist teaching regarding a punishment that causes death, and in chapter 26, the text further comments:

405. One who has laid down the rod
In dealing with beings, moving or still,
Who neither kills nor causes to kill,
Him I call a Brahmin.

These passages articulate core values that could be applied to a Buddhist ethic on the death penalty. Those core values commit the Buddhist to noninjury of others and to lives that neither kill nor "cause" killing. Buddhist ethical teaching appears to be clear on its opposition to the death penalty. What can we make of the Buddhist practice? How well have these core values been put into practice when rulers in jurisdictions affected by Buddhist teachings are faced with the practicalities of governance?

Although Buddhism spread throughout Asia and continues to be a significant religion in various countries with secular governments, four countries today have Buddhism as the official state religion: Bhutan, Cambodia, Sri Lanka, and Thailand.[10] Sri Lanka is a republican government, and the others are constitutional monarchies. Bhutan is distinctive in that it follows a Mahayana tradition, while the others are Theravada. Of these four Buddhist countries, Cambodia eliminated the death penalty in its 1993 constitution, and Bhutan abolished the death penalty in 2004, also by constitutional mandate. Thailand retains a death penalty and averages 50 death sentences a year; no executions took place between 2003 and 2009, and, as of December 2012, 658 individuals had been sentenced to death with fewer than thirty having exhausted appeals and with no women facing execution.[11] Sri Lanka also retains the death penalty with 225 convicts on death row as of October 2012, but no one has been executed since 1976. Recently, in response to popular demand that the death penalty be restored and used for child molesters and rapists, the Sri Lankan prison department made news by advertising for and recruiting two new executioners, who were selected from 145 applicants.[12]

---

9. *The Dhammapada*, ed. and trans. Valerie J. Roebuck (New York: Penguin Books, 2010), ch. 10, "The Rod," p. 28.

10. Damien Horigan, "Of Compassion and Capital Punishment: A Buddhist Perspective on the Death Penalty," *American Journal of Jurisprudence* 41 (1966): 271–88.

11. "Death Penalty—Facts from Figures," *Death Penalty Thailand*, January 13, 2013, http://deathpenaltythailand.blogspot.com/2013/01/death-penalty-facts-from-figures_22.html.

In other Asian countries with historical ties to Buddhism and a significant Buddhist population, the death penalty continues. In Japan, Shinto and Japanese Buddhism have formed an unusual religious system. Many more people practice Shinto rites than would even admit to being religious, but among those who admit to being religious, most would identify with Buddhism. That said, there have been periods in Japanese history when the death penalty had been either abolished—the Nara period (715–795)—or essentially discontinued—the Heian Period (794–1185)—but today it is on the books and used. No executions were carried out in 2011, and three people were executed in 2012.[13] Amnesty International reports that there is some difficulty in ascertaining exact numbers of those sentenced to death in the sixteen countries in Asia that provide for drug-related death sentences. Thailand is a Buddhist country with a complex Hindu influence, and contemporary Thailand reports a high proportion of death sentences for those convicted of drug-related offenses.[14]

This shows that in countries where Buddhism affects the population, Buddhist values have not proven compelling enough to create a firewall that has prevented a death penalty from being used. The record is mixed, but perhaps the important thing to note descriptively is that the death penalty continues, thus indicating, for our purposes, that a disparity exists between core values and practice.

Judaism

An unusual twist on the divide between theory and practice occurs in Judaism. The Hebrew Bible specifies death as a punishment for thirty-six offenses, including religious offenses such as desecrating the Sabbath. We find the retributive notion of "life for a life, eye for an eye, tooth for a tooth" in Exod. 22:23-24, as well as in Gen. 9:6: "Whoever sheds the blood of a human by a human shall that person's blood be shed." However executions may have taken place in ancient Israel when Jewish law functioned as both religious and secular governance, the reality is that the religion of Judaism—the religion of the Rabbis—did not allow the death penalty in practice but actually went out of

---

12. "Sri Lanka Recruits Two Executioners to Implement Capital Punishment," *Death Penalty News*, February 2, 2013, http://deathpenaltynews.blogspot.com/2013/02/sri-lanka-recruits-two-executioners-to.html.

13. Asia-Pacific Human Rights Information Center, "Death Penalty in Japan," *Focus* 68 (June 2012), http://www.hurights.or.jp/archives/focus/section2/2012/06/death-penalty-in-japan.html.

14. "Thailand Caries out First Executions in Six Years," Amnesty International, August 26, 2009, http://www.amnesty.org/en/news-and-updates/news/thailand-first-executions-six-years-20090826

its way to create obstacles to a death penalty. Emphasis was put on "Thou shalt not kill" texts, other rabbinic interpretations sought out alternative penalties for offenses, and the death penalty fell into disuse. Death for various crimes or purity violations were not "excised" from the sacred texts, however, and relevant texts were so interpreted that the rabbis imposed evidential barriers and a narrowness of meaning for specifics related to legal view of offenses, along with so many conditions attached to accusations and trial, that executions became virtually impossible. So, for instance, two witnesses had to be present at a crime for which the death penalty was going to be considered, and the offender had to be informed by those witnesses that the act could lead to execution, and confessions were not sufficient to allow movement toward a death penalty.

The Rabbis imposed many different conditions, thus rendering the death penalty theoretical rather than practical. One interpretation holds that the power to impose a death sentence under Jewish law ended in 70 c.e. when the Temple was destroyed in Jerusalem, and in 1954 the state of Israel abolished the death penalty except for Nazi war criminals. The modern state of Israel has only executed one person, Nazi Adolf Eichmann, confirming that what one sees in Jewish law, in Judaism in general, and even in the laws of Israel, is a death penalty that is on the books but not practiced. The movement within Judaism, unlike that seen in Buddhism and Christianity, is from a scripturally supported "theory" of possible enactment to nonpractice. As Louis Jacobs has written, the Rabbis piled on restrictions "in order to make the death penalty virtually impossible. In practice it became illegal for a Jewish court to impose the death penalty."[15]

Islam

That capital punishment is sanctioned by Islamic law is not disputed, but the perception that capital punishment is unquestioned and enjoys widespread support by Muslim people is at least misleading. Representatives of Muslim states have contributed to that misperception. For instance, when the United Nations conference that formulated the Rome Statute and then created the International Criminal Court was underway in 1998, representatives of Muslim countries asserted a demand for the death penalty. They claimed that a death penalty was essential to their tradition, but Islamic law "in no way mandates capital punishment for the crimes falling within the jurisdiction of the

15. Louis Jacobs, *The Jewish Tradition: A Companion* (New York: Oxford University Press, 1995), 67.

International Criminal Court, namely, genocide, crimes against humanity, and war crimes."[16]

Islam, like other religions, has followers who support a death penalty and others who do not, and the claim that "Islam favors capital punishment" must not be asserted without qualification. Islam affirms a foundational or basic right to life that must be respected, and an execution is deemed an exception to that rule justifiable under only one condition: "Killing is only allowed when a court of law demands it."[17] This exception to the respect-for-life position is akin to a due process requirement, and Islamic law is marked by a spirit of "clemency and sympathy for the oppressed. Punishment is ordered to be free of any spirit of vengeance or torture."[18]

Islamic law draws from the teachings of the Prophet Muhammad. In the seventh century, Islamic law was formalized around two sources of jurisprudence. First and foremost are the instructions of Allah directly communicated to Muhammad in the Islamic sacred book, the Qur'an, together with the Sunnah—texts that relate the actions of the Prophet and how he lived his life. Jointly, the Qur'an and the Sunnah constitute Sharīʿa, which is "a comprehensive body of norms and codes of conduct" that address "every aspect of life, including international, constitutional, administrative, criminal, civil, family and religion."[19] In addition to this first source is *fiqh* ("full comprehension"), "the second important source of guidance of Islamic law," which include legal rulings by Muslim scholars based on Sharīʿa.[20] There are four legal schools of *fiqh* in Sunni Islam and two in Shi'ite Islam, and they address issues of proper practice—rituals, morality and social conduct, and legislation.

Islamic law is divided into four categories; the *haad* or *houdoud* (also *hadd*) category is the most important and the one where capital punishment is addressed. It addresses crimes that are believed to threaten the existence of Islam by threatening social stability. Islamic jurists hold that in this category of law, the Qur'an and Sunnah dictate punishments, leaving jurists and judges with no discretion in sentencing. According to William Schabas, "Houdoud crimes consist of adultery, defamation, theft robbery, rebellion, drunkenness,

---

16. William A. Schabas, "Islam and the Death Penalty," *William and Mary Bill of Rights Journal* 223, no. 9 (2000): 224.

17. Ibid., 230.

18. Ibid.

19. Ibid., 231.

20. Ibid.

and apostasy. Several Houdoud crimes are punishable by death, specifically robbery, adultery, and apostasy."[21]

Punishments proscribed for *houdoud* offenses can be severe because the punishment itself is meant to have a deterrent effect. Although *houdoud* crimes can be punishable by death, death is not demanded as the only option. As the Qur'an relates: "Those that make war against Allah and His apostle and spread their disorders in the land shall be put to death or crucified or have their hands and feet cut off on alternate sides, or be banished from the country" (5:32).[22] The Qur'an permits but does not require a death penalty for intentional murder. Because Islam emphasizes mercy and forgiveness, the families of murder victims are given a choice either to ask for a death penalty or to accept a monetary alternative.[23]

Death for the crime of adultery requires that four witnesses must testify that they saw the penetration and agree on all details, but the Qur'an itself establishes the penalty for adultery, so if all the legal conditions are met the punishment is not easily mitigated. Saudi Arabia, Afghanistan, Nigeria, and Iran have had notorious instances of stoning as punishment for adultery; in contrast, a Muslim country like Malaysia rejects such punishments for this crime. The film *The Stoning of Soraya M.* and the book on which it was based tell the story of an innocent woman stoned to death for adultery in Iran following the deposition of the Shah; many Americans are familiar with a stoning for adultery in the novel *The Kite Runner*, and there is evidence that the Taliban has executed women for adultery.[24] Sakineh Mohammadi Ashtiani, a woman convicted in Iran of adultery in 2006 and whose mandatory sentence of death by stoning was upheld by the Iranian Supreme Court, is still alive and in prison today. This case was reported in the world press. Amnesty International made appeals for the woman's life, and clearly the influence of human rights groups has significantly diminished any possibility of executions for adultery even in Muslim countries where strict obedience to Shari'a would dictate a mandatory sentence. There is confusion in Shari'a between definitions of adultery and fornication for purposes of punishment. The Qur'an requires flogging (Qur'an 24:2) while various hadith—texts similar to the Sunnah but including a narration

21. Ibid.

22. Qur'an 5:32, *The Koran*, trans. N. J. Dawood (New York: Penguin Books, 1981), 391.

23. Clemens Neumann Nathan, *The Changing Faces of Religion and Human Rights: A Personal Reflection* (Leiden, Netherlands: Brill, 2009), 128.

24. Hamid Shalizi and Amie Ferris-Rotman, "Taliban Execute Woman Accused of Adultery, Officials Say," *World Post*, July 7, 2012 (updated July 9, 2012), http://www.huffingtonpost.com/2012/07/07/taliban-execute-woman_n_1656253.html.

about the life of the Prophet and his instucitons—reflect Muhammad's judgment that adultery requires death. Islamic opinion on this subject may be traceable to the more ancient Hebrew teaching, which prescribed death for adultery: "If a man commits adultery with the wife of his neighbor, both the adulterer and the adulteress shall be put to death" (Lev. 20:10).

Sharī'a is subject to many differing interpretations, even on the question of the death penalty. In his call for a progressive Islam, Imam Fiesel Abdul Rauf, the controversial Muslim leader who had planned the mosque in New York City near "Ground Zero," the site of the September 11, 2001 attacks, has written that the Qur'an says:

> whoever kills a person without his having killed or for his act of evil on earth, it is as if he has killed all of humankind; and whoever saves a life [literally 'gives life to a soul'], it is as if he has saved [or 'given life to'] all of humankind" (Quran 5:32). While the passage is usually cited as justification for killing a person—for having killed or for evil doing—the second half of the passage goes in quite a different direction.[25]

Imam Rauf goes on to note that the Prophet Muhammad forgave the individual who killed his own uncle in battle, he forgave those who had killed Muslims in war, he did not retaliate when he returned to Mecca as a conqueror, and he banned blood revenge in his farewell address.[26] Rauf is a Muslim who calls for the end of the death penalty, citing the Prophet's example, but the reality is that capital punishment is still practiced in many Muslim countries today where Sharī'a influences legal codes and is "incorporated into legal systems relatively easily." The great issue facing Islam is how well Sharī'a can prove compatible with democracy. As Ali Mazuri of the Institute of Global Cultural Studies has said, "In reality, most Muslim countries do not use traditional classical Islamic punishment"—although it must also be admitted that when such punishments are used, they receive heightened international media attention.[27] The present reality worldwide is that, in general, *houdoud* punishments are not usually officially sanctioned in Islamic countries, although in countries moving toward

---

25. Imam Fiesal Abdul Rauf, *Moving the Mountain: Beyond Ground Zero to a New Vision of America* (New York: Free Press, 2012), 68.

26. Ibid., 69.

27. Toni Johnson and Lauren Vriens, "Islam, Governing under Sharia," Council on Foreign Relations, Backgrounder, January 9, 2013, http://www.cfr.org/religion/islam-governing-under-sharia/p8034#p3. Previous quote in paragraph from this source as well.

greater incorporation of Sharī'a in the wake of the 2011 uprisings (the Arab Spring), this could change. And vigilantism in Islamic countries, especially related to honor killings, is an acknowledged worldwide problem.[28]

The death penalty is a recognized feature of Islamic law and punishment. How it is used in practice is enormously variable; public executions—public to emphasize deterrence—are still prominent in some countries and the practice seems to be rising. Amnesty International reported that in 2011, "Saudi Arabia executed at least 82 people, which was 55 more than the minimum known figure for the previous year. Iraq, which had acknowledged only one execution in 2010, used the death penalty at least 68 times in 2011. Yemen executed at least 41." The report commented that the increase in use of the death penalty has been a means by which officials have tried to discourage dissidents from participating in prodemocracy movements.[29]

Islamic texts, tradition, and teaching support the death penalty, and while use is variable country to country where Sharī'a influences governance, it is still used and very much a part of Muslim legal practice.

Christianity

We come now to Christianity, the religion that incorporates an execution into the core of its theology. For that reason alone, Christianity is arguably the most interesting religion when it comes to capital punishment.

The religion of Christianity centers on Jesus of Nazareth, whom Christians believe had a special status and relationship with God. But Jesus was killed—executed—and the fact of his execution is critically important to theological developments. Jesus' death on a cross is foundational to basic tenets of faith professed by Christians, and reflection on Jesus' death was critically important to the creation of the religion of Christianity, which, in significant ways, was the work of St. Paul, also a victim of state execution according to tradition. Christians will ground their positions on the death penalty in religious convictions; some Christians oppose capital punishment while others support it.

As on many other issues, no consistent ethic affirmed by all Christians is available on this matter. Those who support it do so believing that they are upholding the order of the state and that God has put this legitimate, divinely ordained power into the hands of those who govern. Those who oppose it

---

28. Ibid.

29. Saeed Kamali Dehghan and Ed Pilkington, "Arab Spring Leads to Wave of Middle East State Executions," *Guardian*, March 26, 2012, http://www.guardian.co.uk/world/2012/mar/27/arab-spring-middle-east-executions.

would argue that, in light of the Christ event, such punishments are contrary to the core values of Christian faith. Despite disagreements, Christians are not silent about their ethical viewpoints on the issue, and a review of certain salient factors related to Christian perspectives on capital punishment is therefore in order.

The first prominent concern in developing a Christian perspective on capital punishment involves the crucifixion of Jesus itself. What does it mean morally and ethically—maybe even legally—that he was put to death by the Roman state by means of an extraordinarily cruel mode of execution designed to deter other potential offenders?

The case is usually made that Jesus of Nazareth was an innocent man unjustly put to death, and in the tradition—this appears in the Gospels—blame for his execution is directed against the Jews. But that anti-Jewishness in the Gospel stories cannot obscure the fact that Jesus' death by execution was a rather ordinary dispensing of Roman justice. The point may be asserted with historical confidence that the Romans killed Jesus—the role of the Jews, if any, is lost to history and obscured by anti-Jewish polemics. Attributions of Jewish responsibility for the death of Jesus in the Gospels must be viewed with the utmost skepticism. Visible through the Gospel narratives that cover Jesus' passion, trial, and death is the simple fact that Jesus was accused and tried under Roman law and sentenced to a specifically Roman means of death—crucifixion—for a specific crime that concerned the Romans—sedition. Had Jesus been found guilty under the Jewish law of blasphemy, as the Gospels report (Matt. 26:65), Jesus could have died the death prescribed under Hebrew law—death by stoning. Jesus was not stoned. The Gospels show Jesus being taken at the Roman procurator's command to Israel's king, Herod, for judgment, but Herod had no power to inflict death because Israel was occupied by Rome and the death penalty was Rome's exclusively. The Romans killed Jesus.

Jesus is often portrayed as a pacifist and a nonviolent innocent. Given what happened to Jesus, however, scholars acknowledge—and perhaps other Christians should also consider—the possibility that Jesus of Nazareth did pose some kind of threat to the established order of his day and that he was in fact guilty of sedition.[30] Jesus caused some public commotion, according to the Gospels, resorting to violence in the temple to chase out moneychangers and merchants, and when he says to the Roman procurator, "My kingdom is not from this world," for if it were, "my followers would be fighting to keep me

---

30. For a discussion of "the guilty Jesus," see Lloyd Steffen, *Executing Justice: The Moral Meaning of the Death Penalty* (Eugene, OR: Wipf and Stock, 2003).

from being handed over to the Jews" (John 18:36), he here imagines a justifiable uses of force.

So even Jesus' pacifism may be overstated.

The critical question for religious ethics to ask about Jesus' death in the context of Christian teaching is this: how dos this particular instance of capital punishment become a redemptive act in Christian theology? In Christianity, the state killing of Jesus is actually suppressed as an ethics issue while, in the foreground of theology, the cross is transformed into a sacrificial and life-saving event for all of humanity, even for the cosmos itself according to Ephesians and Colossians. While Christians will acknowledge that the crucifixion was horrifying, they also have constructed a theology that transforms this ghastly event into an atoning act for human sin that appeases God's very own demands for justice, so that the death by crucifixion becomes a positive event—the most positive event imaginable. Jesus' willingness to submit to death is interpreted as a sacrificial act, and the cross becomes a symbol of salvation. In other words, the capital punishment inflicted on Jesus is ultimately understood theologically—not ethically—to be a good thing. The cross is the means for human salvation—the cross is transformed from an ethical symbol of the power of the state to crush offenders into a positive theological symbol of life, not death.

Jesus as he appears in the Gospel narratives is not recognizable as an ethicist, and we do not have any argument from him laying out his ethical perspective on capital punishment. One story in John 8:1-11 shows him encountering an adulteress about to be stoned by a crowd, and Jesus explicitly repudiates the "life for a life, eye for an eye" thinking so often connected to retributive justice and the ethic that justifies capital punishment. Furthermore, in this story he actually interferes with what would have been an apparently lawful execution. A reasonable interpreter could conclude from this story that Jesus did not endorse a death penalty, but this story may be as close as we come to an expression of opposition to state execution from Jesus.

When looking at Christian attitudes toward the death penalty, the salvific work wrought by Jesus' execution cannot be denied. His followers held that his death was indeed salvific. The death of Jesus by means of a state execution provides backing for Christians who hold that good things can come of the death penalty and that Jesus' unjust death on the cross opened a doorway to eternal life for all of humanity. So for some Christians there is no prejudice against the death penalty to be gleaned from the story of Jesus' own execution, and that story then poses no challenge to the idea that states can legitimately use a death penalty to maintain social order.

St. Paul's writings developed much of the theology vital to the creation of the religion of Christianity, and he is often cited by Christians as a reason for support of capital punishment. Paul's writings, the earliest we have in the Christian Scriptures, include ethical imperatives charging the faithful to love one another, to extend hospitality to the stranger, to bless one's persecutors, to live in harmony, and to refuse to repay evil for evil but to overcome evil with good. He advocated not coercive force in response to persecution but returning kindness to one's enemies, for in that "you will heap burning coals on their head" (Rom. 12:20). Specifically, Christians who support capital punishment and look to St. Paul for guidance on the issue often point to Rom. 13:1-7a (NRSV):

> Let every person be subject to the governing authorities; for there is no authority except from God, and those authorities that exit have been instituted by God. Therefore whoever resists authority resists what God has appointed, and those who resist will incur judgment. For rulers are not a terror to good conduct but to bad . . . if you do wrong you should be afraid, for the authority does not bear the sword in vain! It is the servant of God to execute wrath on the wrongdoer. Therefore one must be subject, not only because of wrath but because of conscience. For the same reason you are also to pay taxes, for the authorities are God's servants.

Paul in this passage acknowledges the right of government to use coercive force to maintain the social and political order. He acknowledges the "power of the sword," an image of lethal power, but adds that Christians should recognize and accede to this power not out of fear of wrath or terror but out of conscience—because all authority comes from God. Christians will, then, meet their obligations to the state because the state wields power on authority from God who sanctions the state's activities, including the coercive power to tax and even the power of the sword itself. The sword appears to be a justified power of the state, and it is even a reference to capital punishment—or is it?

Some Christians understand this appeal to the "power of the sword" to be nothing more than a general reference to state power and the necessity of the state to use its power to provide for a general ordering of civic affairs. In other words, as Mennonite theologian John Howard Yoder put it, government may have a legitimate ordering function to perform, but the power of the state is restricted and akin to that of the librarian who puts the books on the shelves in an orderly way so that they might be readily found and used effectively.[31]

Government has such an ordering function, but many Christians will argue that the state receives no blessing from God for the use of violence or coercive force. Christian interpreters are not agreed about the meaning of Paul's invocation of "the power of the sword." But those Christians who support capital punishment will appeal to the passage cited above to show St. Paul supporting use of a deadly instrument—a sword—to maintain order, and that would include the legal process of state sponsored execution. Often overlooked in this kind of analysis is the fact that the book of Romans from which this passage is extracted was written while St. Paul was in prison and himself awaiting execution. If that tradition is true, some very practical questions can be asked: Would St. Paul be concerned to provide the Roman authorities with a Christian justification for their brutal and tyrannical rule? More specifically, knowing he was to be executed by the state, would he be spending his last days providing Rome with theological support for his own execution? This strains credulity and is more than far-fetched. It is stepping into the realm of preposterous interpretation.

The widespread support for capital punishment that can be found among Christians may be not the result of an interpretation of Jesus' crucifixion or a peculiar interpretation of St. Paul's writings, but rather a legacy from historical developments. The most cataclysmic events in the history of Christianity—Western civilization is still reeling from their effects—were Emperor Constantine's conversion to Christianity in 312 ce, which legitimized the faith, and the declaration of Emperor Theodosius I in 391 that Christianity was to be the official state church of the Roman Empire to the exclusion of all others. This rise in the status of Christianity as an official religion of the state entangled temporal and ecclesiastical powers, and one of those powers was the execution power. When the church came to have access to temporal powers, including the execution power, a religious or theological offense could be deemed an offense against the state. As the story of Christianity unfolds in Western culture, we see church authorities giving sanction to the death penalty and even using it directly in ecclesiastical matters, such as in the Inquisition and for offenses such as heresy or blasphemy. These are both ecclesiastical and state offenses. This entanglement of church authority with state power has led some Christians to create actual theocracies or wish for them as the optimal way to maintain a Christian social order, and this entanglement also brings capital punishment into the foreground as a power the church can both justify and ask the state to use on its behalf for very specific offenses, such as heresy, blasphemy, and witchcraft. Likewise, the state has also called on ecclesiastical

31. John Howard Yoder, *The Politics of Jesus*, 2nd ed. (Grand Rapids, MI: Wm. B. Eerdmans, 1972, 1983), 204.

authority to sanction its use of the execution power, which it does by providing theological justification for capital punishment and even by having clergy present at executions to send the condemned on their way, hopefully, if they are repentant, to life with God.

The execution power—capital punishment—is embedded in the history of a Western culture dominated by Christianity. The church has had institutional influence on the state and provided sanction for the exercise of that power. Differentiating the religious from the civic realms allows Christians to repudiate the state's execution power as a legitimate religious function. Again, there are Christians who do believe in the divine sanctioning of governmental authority. Separating church authority from state power, however, moves in the direction of withholding from the state explicitly religious sanctions for the execution power. American historian Edmund Morgan writes this about the views of separationist Roger Williams, who believed religion was corrupted by involvement with government:

> Moses could wield the sword for God with righteousness. Israel could send forth its armies to smite the heathen. But no body of men who now employed force in defense of religion, whether at home or abroad, could claim the name of Christian. Force could be successfully exercised in religion only in support of false, unchristian religions. Any religion that could benefit from the use of force was by definition not Christian.[32]

For Christians, then, the death penalty is a call—either legitimate or illegitimate—for a use of lethal force by the state sanctioned by the divine will. For Roger Williams, Christians are called to deny the state any power to encroach into religious and ecclesiastical matters. Even more significantly, entangling matters of faith with the exercise of governmental power calls into question one's identity as a "true" Christian. The problem, of course, is that identity can be established and supported on either side of the question of entanglement; at issue are interpretations of core Christian values and beliefs and how Christians should witness to them in the world of temporal power.

In the end, what religious ethics requires in the examination of the death penalty is some application of core religious values to a use of the execution power and a determination of how a transcendent authority legitimizes—or delegitimizes—that use in pursuit of temporal order. Theological viewpoints about how such power is to be used or not used are also ethical views that must

32. Edmund Morgan, *Roger Williams: The Church and the State* (New York: W. W. Norton, 2006), 94.

be tested against actual practice, and actual practice leads even religious people who support the death penalty to examine and assess the way a death penalty is operationalized. The death penalty will always call on people of good will to determine if the power to put people to death is being used in a way that conforms to moral goals, such as nondiscrimination and the preservation of the value of life, and religious people will want to know whether a death penalty system, even if held to be formally legitimate, is so constructed that it conforms to action directives grounded in transcendent sources.

COOLEY

The death penalty is another moral issue involving death that has received considerable attention from philosophers since the time that civilization first began. From the moment in which the first moral agent sprang, or more likely, developed, into existence, there have always been crimes and wrongs done. The question, of course, is what, if anything, the state should do about such wrongs and why it should act in this manner. Moreover, we should always question whether any state should be given the power to execute its citizens or those foreigners who are visiting the country.[33]

I think that the "why" part might be the more important question of the two because it is primary. If we do not know why we should be getting ourselves involved with other's wrongful actions, then it is virtually impossible for us to know how we should act toward them. If, for example, the unethical action plus other moral considerations require us to make the wrongdoer pay a debt, then we need to know what the debt is, which entails we know why doing the action was wrong in the first place.

ARGUMENTS FOR THE DEATH PENALTY

1. Retributive justice demands death for cases in which the person has committed a sufficiently heinous crime by taking another person's life. That action creates such a debt on the criminal's part that only his death can eliminate or begin to pay what he owes.[34]

---

33. Although the statistics are dated, an excellent introduction to the death penalty is Hugo Bedau's edited volume *The Death Penalty in America: Current Controversies* (New York: Oxford University Press, 1997).

2. The aim of executing someone is to prevent similar crimes from being committed in the future. To prevent the individual from committing the crime again—or committing crimes while he is incarcerated—it is better to kill him in a state-sanctioned event rather than to allow him to remain a threat.

3. The second and more important deterrence argument involves preventing other citizens from being harmed in ways similar to that of the victim of the executed person. A state execution serves as a threat large enough to create a moral hazard that no rational person would risk.[35] If the state does its job well, then no person would be foolish enough to engage in the behavior, thereby creating a safer society.

4. In many cases, justifications of capital punishment contain elements of both deterrent and deontological principles, such as justice, as well as moral values of respecting life.

ARGUMENTS AGAINST THE DEATH PENALTY

1. By engaging in executions, the state fosters violence, rather than safety, in its communities. After all, if the state is permitted to kill, then some might think that other people should be allowed to do likewise.

2. The death penalty does not deter murders and other capital crimes. Countries with the death penalty tend to have higher murder rates than those without it.[36]

34. Immanuel Kant, *The Metaphysics of Morals*, trans. Mary Gregor (New York: Cambridge University Press, 1996).

35. Moral hazard is the risk one takes for which the person is responsible when doing any sort of activity. Generally, the higher the risk involved and the greater the share of burden the person has for whatever injury occurs, then the less likely the person is to engage in the behavior and, simultaneously, the greater efforts the person will make in trying to avoid the injury by taking precautions, attempting to mitigate risk, or avoiding the activity altogether.

36. States without the death penalty tend to have lower murder rates than states with the death penalty: 3.1/100,000 versus 4.7/100,000 in 2011. Death Penalty Information Center, "Nationwide Murder Rates," 2013, http://www.deathpenaltyinfo.org/murder-rates-nationally-and-state. This empirical fact might be attributed to a more cohesive society, lack of guns or other efficient killing devices, and other social forces, though that question cannot be answered here.

3. The death penalty is more expensive than imprisonment for life. Life imprisonment provides taxpayers with reduced taxes while simultaneously generating the same benefit of the person being removed from society.[37]

4. Innocent people have been executed.[38]

5. The death penalty is applied in a way contrary to equality and fairness.[39] Those who are on death row tend to be members of certain groups and not of others. First, women convicted of murder are far less likely than men to receive the death penalty.[40] Men, therefore, are at a distinct disadvantage because of gender and sex stereotypes.

Second, and possibly more disturbingly, people of color, especially men who have committed crimes against whites and women, are far more likely to be sentenced to death than whites are.[41] Given the other social burdens placed on these classes, it seems unfair to make them more likely to die than people whose advantage is to be born white.

Third, age plays a factor that it should not if people are being fair in making their decisions about life and death. "Jurors' age and gender significantly influenced sentencing. Men, with the exception of the youngest men, were more likely than women to choose the death penalty. Additionally, young women were more likely than older women to select the death penalty."[42]

37. Death Penalty Information Center, "Costs of the Death Penalty," 2013, http://www.deathpenaltyinfo.org/costs-death-penalty.

38. Cameron Todd Willingham was executed for the deaths of his three children in a house fire, which experts could prove, before he was executed, was not the result of arson, much less arson committed by Willingham. David Grann, "Death by Fire," New Yorker, September 7, 2009, http://www.newyorker.com/reporting/2009/09/07/090907fa_fact_grann.

39. Richard C. Dieter, "The Death Penalty in Black and White: Who Lives, Who Dies, Who Decides," Death Penalty Information Center, June 1998, http://www.deathpenaltyinfo.org/death-penalty-black-and-white-who-lives-who-dies-who-decides.

40. Steven F. Shatz and Naomi R. Shatz, "Chivalry Is Not Dead: Murder, Gender, and the Death Penalty," Berkeley Journal of Gender, Law and Justice 27, no. 1 (2012): 1–49.

41. Mona Lynch and Craig Haney, "Looking across the Empathic Divide: Racialized Decision Making on the Capital Jury," Michigan State Law Review (2011): 573–607.

42. C. M. Beckham, B. J. Spray, and C. A. Pietz, "Jurors' Locus of Control and Defendants' Attractiveness in Death Penalty Sentencing," Journal of Social Psychology 147, no. 3 (2007): 285–98.

Finally, there are very few wealthy people who are facing the death penalty, whereas most of those convicted and executed are poor. It might be that wealthy individuals receive a better education and those with such learning do not tend to commit such crimes of violence because it does not make rational sense to them. However, being able to afford the best legal defense must have some impact on the outcome of trials. Just as in any situation, quality, which is a function of how much one can afford, helps decides the verdict. Since the poor must rely on overstressed, underpaid, and overworked free legal counsel provided by the state, the accused poor are at a severe disadvantage to those with more financial resources readily at hand.

Given this inequality in treatment and other biases based on accent, appearance, and so on, the state using the death penalty is acting in a sexist, racist, and classist way, which it should not do.

6. Finally, the state generally has enormous resources available to prove its case—the police, a prosecutor's office with a large number of people, people's perceptions that the state only charges those it thinks are guilty, and so forth—which the defendant does not and generally can neither have nor overcome. This imbalance in resources makes it much more likely that the state will prevail.

There can be a strong theoretical case made—which requires a great deal of abstraction to the purely rational and necessitates perfect processes—for the morality of the state using the death penalty.[43] Suppose that each element of the case meets at least the bare minimum required by a reasonable person to think that the overall process is fair and equitable. The defense lawyer is good at her job, has all the resources needed to effect the best possible defense, and produces a flawless defense of the accused. The prosecutor uses only those resources matching those of the defense and never does anything that is not fair and equitable in the judicial process. Furthermore, assume that all the jury members are reasonable people who follow the law, make decisions based solely on the evidence available to them and their rational decision-making procedures,

43. Hugo Bedau is considered, with excellent reason, to be the leading authority on death penalty arguments on both sides of the issue, although he is clearly against the death penalty. H. A. Bedau, *Killing as Punishment: Reflections on the Death Penalty in America* (Boston, MA: Northeastern University Press, 2004).

and never use any illicit biases or guesses based on ignorance. The judge, who is neutral, wise, and knowledgeable, also must have run the trial without irrationality and judicial error. Finally, the physical evidence is overwhelmingly against the defendant and there is little material in favor of his innocence, even though due diligence has been performed to find exculpatory evidence. The crimes he has committed for which there is the overwhelming proof are morally and legally repulsive, involving the murder of children and other innocents. The murderer has also obliged us by saying he would continue his crime spree if he were not given the death penalty. Even incarcerated, he tells us that he will do his best to make sure that others are harmed to whatever degree he can injure them. This would be an excellent case for the death penalty, but it could be made stronger with a few other assumptions.

Although this pseudocase might seem a bit silly because it is causally impossible, let us make this the best case conceivable. I believe that a lot more people would be in favor of the death penalty if its implementation on a criminal could restore the lives of those who had been killed by the convicted. To make the death penalty pseudocase more appealing, some additional stipulations would have to be put into place. First, the murder victim would have to be returned to both psychological and physical states that are at least as good as the states he or she was in before being murdered by the defendant—that is, he or she would not come back as some horribly maimed individual whose life would not be worth living. Second, the death of the convicted would be a direct cause in the reanimation of the deceased. One life is surrendered for at least one other, and if there are many lives to be restored, then that makes this argument all the stronger. Taking the life of one murderer to bring back his many murder victims' lives appeals to our consequentialist leanings and respect for human life. Third, the reanimated people would not be worse people than the convicted person. We do not want to bring back to life people who are even more dangerous than the person to be executed. Fourth, the reanimated people have to have a better existence alive in this world than they would if they continued in a different world to which they went after their death. The final criterion incorporates an afterlife familiar to many religions. If the person is flourishing in that afterlife and would not be able to meet that flourishing level here, then it would be wrong to bring that person back to life in the physical realm. In fact, we would do more injury to the murder victim than the murderer did if the afterlife was significantly better than life in the physical world.

Of course, this is an idealized case, but I have incorporated it to show that much thinking about the death penalty deals with ideal worlds that cannot come into existence, as I will show below. That is, we are not being realistic about capital punishment; therefore, we make considerable errors in our reasoning about it. It would be far better for us to limit ourselves to what makes practical sense in the actual world in which we live rather than designing arguments that work merely in idealized worlds.

Even with this most perfect of cases in the most perfect of worlds, how many people would find the death penalty justified? I believe that the number of people who would believe this case persuasive would be reduced drastically if they actually had to impose the death penalty themselves. That is, although in theory they would think that the death penalty is morally justified, they would not think the same in an actual court situation in which they were a jury member. Deciding that the living person you see in front of you should die is much more difficult than putting to death a nonexisting entity from a theoretical thought experiment. As in the case of war, it is difficult to greatly harm an entity that we consider to be part of our community. Such action would be tantamount to harming ourselves or our ideas about ourselves because if a person is a member of our community, then we must share basic values, even if the value is merely looking like us.

In addition, I contend that the willing number would decrease again if we asked the jury members to push a switch that would terminate the convicted person's life. After all, if a jury member really believes that a person should die, it seems appropriate that the jury member should be willing to carry out the sentence. When the actual case is removed from the theoretical world or any undue abstraction created by placing emotional distance between the decision and carrying out the jury's verdict, very few people would be willing to apply a death penalty. Although juries are comprised of people who must attest that they are willing to impose capital punishment, the clean, sanitary distance the jury deliberation room and courtroom provide from the actual execution precludes people from understanding the true, full consequences of what they are doing. By requiring a more hands-on experience, the emotional buffer created for them is stripped away so that they can understand and appreciate the stark reality of what they are deciding.[44] Once the situation's reality is grasped

---

44. To make thought into deed, I would recommend that each jury member have to push a button that sends a charge into a capacitor. When the convicted is executed, then the capacitor drains the charge to create a circuit that will start the procedure that kills the convicted person. Without each jury member pushing the button, the capacitor would have an insufficient charge to start the process. In this manner, the jury members will know that they did something that will directly cause the convicted person's death. Without each of them doing what they did, they would not have killed him, and it is only with their actions that they kill him. Moreover, they should be willing to see what it is to die in this manner.

more fully—namely, that one of our community members will be killed at our hand—most people would be very reluctant to kill another person, even if that person is a confessed murderer.

We should begin seeing two other major problems for the death penalty. First, as already has been mentioned, application of the death penalty is difficult to justify because of illicit biases and imperfect processes, such as inadequate resources to put on the best defense for the accused. For example, a problem can be seen with the process when 49.2 percent of jurors in capital punishment cases have already decided sentencing before the trial's sentencing phase.[45] This means that jurors have not listened to the mitigating and aggravating evidence that they would need to take into account in producing a fair sentence. In addition, in order to be selected to be on a capital punishment case, a potential juror cannot express misgivings about the death penalty. Hence, a bias is built-in because only people in favor of using the death penalty can be selected.[46]

Most people think they are not biased, but how do they know that they are rational and neutral evaluators of the appropriate evidence and use only that evidence and neutral decision-making processes in their choices? Consider a study done by Bertrand and Mullainathan in which the researchers produced phony résumés for job applications. Each résumé had virtually identical qualifications, but the names were made to represent different racial groups—in this case black- and white-sounding names. Those with white-sounding names had a callback rate 50 percent higher than those that had black-sounding names.[47] If people were truly unbiased, then the percentages would have been the same.

Of course, overt, extrinsic racism is something that most people recognize and abhor. When someone is called a "nigger," "wetback," or "gook," we know that the racist name-calling is morally wrong and should not be done. If possible, the person saying such hateful things should be made to account for it. Other obvious racism is also easily identified, and people are taught to watch out for racism in any of its forms and not to follow such morally repulsive ways. That is as it should be.

---

45. William J. Bowers and Wanda D. Foglia, "Still Singularly Agonizing: Law's Failure to Purge Arbitrariness from Capital Sentencing," *Criminal Law Bulletin* 39 (2003): 51–86, at 56.

46. Clay S. Conrad, "'Death-Qualification' Leads to Biased Juries," *USA Today* 129, no. 2670 (March 2001), http://www.questia.com/library/1G1-72272563/death-qualification-leads-to-biased-juries.

47. Marianne Bertrand and Sendhil Mullainathan, "Are Emily and Greg More Employable than Lakisha and Jamal? A Field Experiment on Labor Market Discrimination," *American Economic Review* 94, no. 4 (2003): 991–1013.

But the more insidious bias is intrinsic and unintentional, and people are unaware they have it. This might explain, in part, why a higher percentage of blacks than whites are convicted of violent crimes, especially for interracial crimes, and why there were differences in the job callbacks. It might also give insight into why more men than women are given the death penalty and why in situations with basically the same court case, some can be convicted whereas others walk free.

Given the unconscious racial bias—as well as prejudices based on age, gender, sex, class, and so on—there is excellent reason to believe that the judicial system, including murder trials, is too morally defective to use death as punishment. Since death is the ultimate penalty the state can impose, it can only be justified if the system can do its work with perfect equity and fairness. That is, we never, ever want to risk someone's life on the basis of a prejudice we or others might have but can neither identify nor control—if it could be controlled. Given human failings in reason and virtue, this is not causally possible, even though it might occur in some perfect world in which people are able to know all the facts and process them appropriately.

Of greater moment is the irrationality of revenge on which the death penalty is based. When something really wicked is done to the innocent, especially those for whom we care deeply or with whom we deeply empathize, we often get very angry and seek to satisfy our desire for revenge by hurting the person who injured the innocent. Assume for the moment that the victim of the crime looks a lot like a loved one, or like us, for that matter. We would have much greater grounds to be empathetic with the victim because of the shared bond we create by putting ourselves in the victim's position. If the victim does not share sufficient empathy-creating characteristics with us, then we will not unconsciously weigh the evidence in the same way as we do for someone for whom we feel empathy. This is one of the reasons that prosecutors try to get a jury filled with people like the victim whereas the defense tries to place as many people like the defendant in the jury. If such identification is successful, it unconsciously biases the jury members in favor of the party with whom they identify and against the other party.

Although we try to dress the feeling of revenge in the respectable clothes of doing one's duty to punish in a way demanded by impartial justice, it can be shown for what it is by an example John Helgeland developed in connection with his work on religion and war. Helgeland asks us to imagine that we are attending an action-adventure movie along the lines of those featuring John Wayne, Clint Eastwood, Bruce Willis, Jason Statham, or any of the comic-book sort of heroes in which there is a cartoonish, unredeemable villain for whom we have no empathy. The villain in this movie does his usual evil deeds including but not limited to murdering the innocent (who look a lot like us), injuring them in inventive and horrible ways, endangering others, and generally being a totally despicable person. The film's hero is able to overcome all the evil machinations of the villain until, in the end, the hero has managed to corner the villain in a situation in which the hero can easily kill him. Basically, this is the plot for all movies of this genre.

Now here is the interesting bit that twists the movie out of shape for us: let us suppose that the villain has a true change of heart. He realizes that what he has done is evil and despicable, and repents wholeheartedly. Let us also suppose that this epiphany and alteration in character are legitimate. The former villain really is remorseful and wants to make amends as far as he can with his remaining resources, including his life and talents. Moreover, we have more than adequate evidence to believe that this change has occurred and that the person will not go back to his evil ways. Basically, we have someone seeking redemption that we can prove is seeking redemption. The hero, being a hero who can know this, lets the villain go so that the latter can put right as far as he is able what he put wrong. As a result, the former villain lives a long, simple life of saintlike devotion to the good. He helps those whom he has harmed to pursue a similar life of flourishing and serves as a role model for how people can change their lives for the good.

At this point, Helgeland asks how we would feel about this ending rather than the one in which the action hero kills his opponent. Would we feel as if something good and right occurred, and be satisfied with what the hero did? On one hand, we have been primed for the villain's punishment to be as horrific as the actions that he performed earlier. On the other hand, if we believe in redemption and people trying to make amends for their wickedness, then we should be in favor of what happens. The world would be a far better place if the latter would occur. More importantly, it appeals to our better angels—that is, the values to respect life and goodness that we say that we possess.

Professor Helgeland, however, says that we would ask the theater management for our money back because the happy ending does not satisfy our need for revenge in the way that killing the villain in a fantastic manner would have. Many people, for instance, would be very angry to think that Hitler, Stalin, and the other moral monsters from history are in a divine state because they repented at the moment of death and God in God's infinite grace gave them salvation.[48] Even though a divine entity created and endorsed the forgiveness, it would still be hard for many to accept this outcome. Why?

---

48. I have no evidence that this happened; this is merely a thought experiment.

Because we want our pound of flesh from evildoers in movies and in real life. They have to suffer for us to think that the world is a good and fair place to be. The positive ending leaving us dissatisfied means that there is something wrong with our beliefs about redemption, punishment, and value and the impact they have in moral decision making. Either we do not have such beliefs or we have those beliefs but they are overridden by our desire for revenge and punishment.[49] The latter seems most likely.

The death penalty should not be based on revenge, which is an emotion that does not lead to our flourishing or that of others. As Gandhi and others have said, revenge is self-indulgence. It is the self-indulgence of a person who has power and should use that power only in its proper channels but instead employs it to satisfy some base desire to hurt another person. To be justified, the death penalty must be based on a purer desire for justice or something like it, which should make the world a better place than it would otherwise have been. Such a desire would be based on the further desire to prevent bad things from happening or to give someone their just desert so that those who need reward get it or those who have a debt to pay have to pay it. If the punishment stems more from the desire to harm the individual wrongdoer so that we feel satisfaction at their pain and suffering, then justice was ancillary to the revenge and now we have a debt to pay and amends to make. We cannot behave ethically if we act primarily or significantly out of evil desires; therefore, we incur whatever debt our wrongdoing creates for us.

To drive home the problem of eliminating revenge, anger, or some other illicit motivation from decisions about capital punishment, another thought experiment is helpful. With the advent of drugs and other medical devices that can alter mental activity, we can begin to imagine a world in which we could take criminals and change them into someone better than they are. That is, we could alter how we think about chronic criminal tendencies by treating them as mental illnesses to be controlled with drugs and therapy. Suppose that we have a person who has been a Mafia member for his entire adulthood of forty-five years. He is now sixty-three years old. He has committed murders, been in racketeering, and performed other associated acts of violence. He is now on trial for his life on murder charges.

Assume we have a drug that will alter the Mafia member's character to such a degree that he becomes a new person. Instead of being able to perform

49. George W. Bush was forced to make this choice as governor of Texas. A woman who had killed her children was on death row but claimed that she had been saved by Jesus after her crimes. Many people begged the then governor to commute her sentence to life in prison because of the significant change in her personality. Instead, he chose no clemency.

violence without much thought to the real nature of the crimes, he becomes like us. We cannot imagine wanting to kill another person or being able to look another person in the face and then injure her in horrible ways. Part of not being able to act or think in this way requires a certain kind of character, which we have. Our empathy for those in our community is such that we could never knowingly do this to them.

If we used our own character and mental states, we can try to imagine what would be necessary to desire to murder another person in cold blood. We would need to form the intention to do it and create the motivation—or the understanding of it—to act in this manner. We would also have to overcome the empathy any normal human being has with other human beings and sentient beings—that is, the feeling of repulsion we have when thinking about the innocent being harmed in serious ways. Although we might be able to say that we can think in this manner, we cannot. Most people cannot imagine what this would be like because they do not have the character capable of having the necessary mental states of a murderer. When another person is murdered, they cannot understand how someone could do such a thing.

As we return to the issue of how people can intentionally kill others or hurt them to a great psychological or physical degree, it is useful to point out the extreme oddness of such activity. We cannot imagine framing the actual desire to do such actions—in fact, twisting a child's arm enough to cause it to break, thrusting a knife into living flesh, and so on should and does nauseate us if we think about how it would actually look and feel to do them. Not to be too morbid or gruesome, but it is important to think really hard about what this would be like and to move this sort of analysis from the theoretical domain into the real world. Understanding how someone can harm others in such disgusting ways is alien to the way our minds work, provided we are capable of empathy. If we have been in severe pain, then we do not want to have that happen to other beings, especially those we know and who feel the way we do. If we have had a broken bone, been cut, or had some other injury, then we cannot comprehend why anyone else could do this intentionally, or even in the heat of the moment, to another person.

The extreme alienation of human empathy required to harm someone to the degree justifying the death penalty should make us wonder how we are to explain why people intentionally kill other people. How can they do something we can never really understand because we cannot place ourselves in their situation to the degree required to feel empathy? I contend the reason for our inability to place ourselves in their situation is that desiring to kill or severely injure people is a sign of mental illness. That is, people who can severely harm or kill others have a mental disorder, at least according to Jerome Wakefield's definition of an internal disorder.

> A condition is a disorder if and only if (a) the condition causes some harm or deprivation of benefit to the person as judged by the standards of the person's culture (the value criterion), and (b) the condition results from the inability of some internal mechanism to perform its natural function, wherein a natural function is an effect that is part of the evolutionary explanation of the existence and structure of the mechanism (the explanatory criterion).[50]

Being able to commit a murder and actually doing it show a condition that is likely to cause harm or deprivation in the society.[51] First, most people disfavor those who commit murders. Social condemnation makes it far harder for a person to function in the society and therefore reduces his ability to flourish. Many of the murderer's fellow citizens will not want to create nurturing and sustaining relationships with him, for example, because they are afraid of him or dislike him because he has harmed the community. Second, since the murderer lives in a state that practices capital punishment, he greatly reduces his ability to survive, especially if the state has a competent police force and justice system in place.

Murderers also can fulfill Wakefield's explanatory criterion. The vast majority of human beings do not commit murder. There are likely many more who allow the thought of murdering another person to cross their minds, but the important thing to note is that they do nothing to carry out the unjustifiable killing of another person. They would not do it even if they could get away with their crime. The absence of large numbers of murders in society—that is, large enough so that murder becomes the norm rather than the exception—might well show something about an evolutionary mechanism that functions to keep people from murdering each other. If there is such a natural, internal mechanism to not unjustifiably kill another, then a murderer's mechanism can be considered defective.

If murderers are mentally ill, then several conclusions follow that go against any argument establishing the death penalty's moral permissibility. If murderers are not mentally competent in this particular aspect of their reasoning processes,

---

50. Jerome Wakefield, "The Concept of Mental Disorder: On the Boundary between Biological Facts and Social Values," *American Psychologist* 47 (1992): 373–88, at 384.

51. I am putting to one side those killings that can be justified. They will not be liable to capital punishment. Instead, the focus is on killings that are unjustifiable—namely, most murders.

then they cannot be moral agents in this aspect, which, in turn, eliminates their moral responsibility. That is, if they could not help doing what they were doing because they could not make a rational choice, then the action is not an action at all. It is merely an event caused by a nonagent in these particular circumstances. Hence, we should not execute murderers because they are not morally responsible for what they have done.

In fact, we have a moral obligation to place murderers, along with other people who would greatly harm others, in mental institutions to treat or manage their conditions and even, if we ever get such mind-altering drugs, change them into functioning, flourishing members of society. It might not be something that we are emotionally drawn to, but if we take RPC and QCI seriously, then we should see our duty. We would respect and increase the intrinsic value of all those affected by the action while simultaneously making the world the best place it can be, at least according to a reasonable person thinking reasonably.

This argument about treating murderers as mentally ill rather than as entities worthy of punishment might raise some ire, but why should that be the case? The Mafia member example can be helpful to answer the question.

Recall that the drug-treated Mafia member is now sufficiently similar to us that he no longer lacks empathy and other mental components that make good people good and no longer has those mental states that allowed him to harm others willingly that we do not have. I contend we would have to go so far as to erase memories of what he did so that he would not be filled with overwhelming guilt and horror, which in turn might make his life not as good as it could be. He has to be able to flourish as we flourish. With all these essential alterations, we would be justified in saying that the person who was a criminal no longer exists, whereas a new entity that has the same body but a different personality has come into being. Where we had an evil person we now have a good person with necessarily different traits.

The issue now is whether we should execute such a person, given that he is no longer identical to the former person—that is, the murderer—in essential ways. Clearly he is not the same person; hence, we cannot punish him for the actions of the person he once was. It would be just as wrong as punishing someone for her parent's wrongdoing before she was born. The child had no role in the matter, so there is no legitimate ability to claim that the child created a debt owed to another by what her parents did. Similarly, the new man created from the murderer is not the murderer who was; therefore, we cannot make the new person liable for the former man's debts since that person no longer exists.

Changing the Mafia member to a good, upstanding community member also offers a lot of deterrence. First, the person will no longer act as he did because he is incapable, as any decent person is, of behaving in individually and socially evil ways. Therefore, he will not commit crimes that his former self performed without moral qualms. Second, if capital punishment deters people from murder, then other people in society would have as much motivation not to commit death-penalty worthy crimes. Since the person has ceased to exist as a Mafia member and the person he was, then any benefit from the fear of being put to death—and therefore being caused to cease to exist—still is in existence for any potential murderer. If people are afraid of dying—which is a type of ceasing to exist—then they would have to be afraid of being made into a new person. Finally, there are a number of other benefits that would outweigh the costs and also make the treatment option the best thing that we can do, at least according to one or more reasonable people. There is the enormous benefit of not having the expense of incarceration or execution added to the tax burdens of society's citizens, there is now another good member of society working for his flourishing and the social good, and the government is not involved in creating cycles of violence.

How should we feel about treatment rather than execution as punishment? We should be happy that the world is a better place and that intrinsic value is respected as it should be. However, there will be those that have a lingering anger or other inappropriate emotional reaction to the fact that the individual will not have to undergo punishment. They do not like the fact that he managed to get away with vicious acts that no one should do. But there is no reason to feel dissatisfied with this nonpunishment outcome. If we do feel punishment is still merited, then we see that punishment is based too greatly on a desire for revenge, anger, or another emotion rather than on a desire for justice. It is unsatisfying not have the punishment even though there is no longer any reason to impose it because the new person does not have the former person's debts. But this is obviously not a rational emotional reaction to have because it serves no purpose other than to satisfy our irrational desire to hurt the person who harmed others.

So, individually, many people have a problem filtering out revenge and other inappropriate emotions. What does that say about state-sanctioned takings of life as punishment? Again, the death penalty must be grounded in reason and appropriate emotional states rather than self-indulgent revenge if we are to take it seriously as a morally legitimate state action. It must be done on the grounds of deterrence or punishment. Since punishment is unwarranted in this case because of the change in identity, and deterrence is accomplished as well as being maximized, then the state has no business imposing harm on the new entity. Moreover, we should treat the new person with all the consideration we would give to another decent person of the same sort even though it might not seem fitting to our emotional reactions.

COMMENTARY

COOLEY:

I have several questions for you. First, most religions have the view that there is life after death. This means that if a person is wrongly convicted and executed by the state, then he or she will still have a chance to have things set right in the afterlife. God, for example, would know that capital punishment was not deserved and would therefore rectify the situation. But what happens if there is no afterlife and an innocent person has been killed? Is there a religious view that would make sense of such a situation?

STEFFEN:

Many religious people the world over hold beliefs about the afterlife, and you are correct that many see it as a place where compensation will be had for the sufferings endured in this life. Heaven is often referred to in American slave spirituals, for example, as a home where suffering is ended, but these are complex ideas. Heaven may indeed point to a supernatural afterlife that provides recompense for suffering and injustice, but scholars point out that in slave culture heaven was also a metaphor for freedom and the very practical idea of escape to a free country. In Thailand, where young women from the countryside are unwittingly sold into sex slavery by poor and gullible parents, slavers tell the women that if they accept their sufferings without complaint, they will be assured a better rebirth in their next lifetime.[52] The idea of something better to come after death takes many different forms, and the heaven idea accepted by many Christians does seem to hold open the possibility that injustices endured in life will be offset by life with God (heaven), where all suffering will cease, where "Death will be no more, mourning and crying and pain will be no more" (Rev. 21:4).

---

52. Kevin Bales, *Disposable People: New Slavery in the Global Economy* (Berkeley: University of California Press, 2004).

Of course any kind of afterlife is purely a matter of speculation: if there is such a thing, we can be certain we know nothing about it. People in different religious traditions hold different ideas about what it might be, and although many religious people understand the afterlife as a reward for their faith or a place of punishment for disbelief or wrongdoing, many others believe that the teachings of their faith tradition call them to live a certain way in this life, which is the only life we know, and the rest is nothing we need to worry about. In addition, for every person who believes that he or she will maintain a sense of personal identity in the afterlife, there are others who believe that the individual self will be subsumed or incorporated in the ultimate reality that awaits. This is the difference between thinking of the post-death self as being akin to a grain of sand on the beach versus a drop of water in the ocean. In Buddhism, the ultimate state of attainment, nirvana, is the final liberation where the individual ego is actually extinguished.

So if someone is caused suffering due to injustice or even unjustly killed, will God compensate for it? Religious people may very well believe so. "What if there is no afterlife?" you ask. Even if there is no afterlife, religion is a transmitter of moral values, and while religions can be enmeshed in cultures where injustices occur and even contribute to those injustices, moral ideals cannot and ought not be strangers to religious life and thought. If they are strangers, then one may offer up a moral critique of the ways individuals are using religion to endorse injustice and promote human suffering. That is the point of mentioning the slavery songs and the Thai sex slaves—religion is always what people believe it to be. When people enact their religion in publically observable ways, we discern that people can do anything in the name of religion: endorse slavery, tell indigent sex slaves in Bangkok to grin and bear it because they will get a better rebirth, or even kill themselves by flying planes into New York skyscrapers believing that God is honored by their doing so. If there is no heaven—or even if there is—religious people are also restrained and directed by moral guides and frameworks, and when those moral guidelines encounter religion defying basic notions of goodness and respect for persons, then the way religion is being used and practiced needs to undergo moral assessment and critique. If ultimate reality is good—if God is good—then the responsibility to act justly and to take responsibility for improving the world, as you say, has the endorsement of a divine vision. But if that vision is destructive, we are entitled to talk about demonic religion and even about the possibility of God being what Melville's Ahab thought God to be—evil or mad. The call to justice can come through religious revelation, whatever particular beliefs one might hold about an afterlife, or it can come from outside religion through reason and the call of conscience to take others into account, to act benevolently toward others, to abide by principles that apply to us all. From the moral point of view, religious people need to be moral even more than they need to be religious.

COOLEY:

You argue that there can be just executions if nine conditions are met. I think those conditions provide a strong case for the permissibility of capital punishment, but my worry is that these might only work in theoretical worlds instead of actual ones. For example, it might be impossible to have those involved in the system have the right motivations and intentions. Human persons' thinking about morality is too complicated by interdependent and interconnected beliefs, desires, and other mental states to allow any individual to do something with totally pure intentions and motivations. The same would apply to fair imposition, which also might carry its morally suspect baggage of unintentional but actual biases based on morally irrelevant features such as race and sex. Can we overcome these practical concerns? Or could we build a case that incorporates them?

STEFFEN:

On the question of "just execution," what I have offered is a framework—an ethical structure—for the kinds of justice issues that people of good will should take into account in thinking through the moral meaning of the death penalty. There is really no content in it. The discussions about what is to be done with those justice concerns—those criteria—await the involvement of citizens who will investigate the death penalty and discover how it is actually practiced. I myself have investigated the death penalty, and I am convinced that the death penalty—and the execution power human beings claim through governments—is unjust and cannot be made just, given the way the criminal justice system is infected with racism, sexism, and classism.[53] I believe the death penalty will never rise to the level of "justified killing of citizens by the state" and therefore I hold that it ought to be abolished.

I disagree, however, with the poke in your question that what I offer is impractical or ideal—it is, to the contrary, so practical that invoking the

---

53. Steffen, *Executing Justice*. See Michele Norris, *The New Jim Crow: Mass Incarceration in the Age of Colorblindness* (New York: New Press, 2012).

specifics of the "theory" is inescapable even if we do not name it a theory of "just execution," as I have. Not only do our courts implicitly appeal to the criteria of "just execution" every time they place a new restriction on the death penalty due to some issue of injustice or unjust discrimination, but your own presentation appeals to it in its critique of the injustice of selecting who gets executed. In your consideration of such things as the need to eliminate revenge (criterion 3), your focus on only the crime of murder (a just cause, criterion 2), your discussion of societal indebtedness, which invokes equilibrium and proportionality (criteria 8 and 9), and other matters in your essay, you enter into the framework of "just execution."[54] In your discussion you bring relevant information to bear on justice issues—for instance, how women are less likely than men to receive a death sentence for a similar crime—and from that information you start to draw some conclusions about fair imposition. That is how this theory actually works. If someone can refute the claim you bring from investigative social science literature, then let that person be heard as well—that is how the theory works. I think it inconceivable to have a discussion about the death penalty without proceeding this way. The theory is simply proposing that we identify the justice concerns entailed in the idea of a just execution and test these criteria against the reality of the practice. My claim is that this ethical framework is eminently practical, a good place to voice disagreements, and a structure of moral reasoning within which we can fashion moral meaning and justification for particular actions. And I will reiterate that the Supreme Court and other federal courts go through a similar process in deliberating discrimination issues or other challenges coming up on appeal from death row inmates.[55]

STEFFEN:

I found your points about mental illness quite fascinating and worthy of reflection. Mentally ill individuals who commit murder are in a sense ignorant of what they are doing. The Greeks believed that knowledge of the good was irresistible on the will so that if one *knew* the good, one would *do* it. Evil then is "ignorance," as Socrates said, and education is needed as a corrective

---

54. There are over sixty crimes in the United States that are death-penalty eligible, including desertion from the army, treason, and espionage at the federal level, and certain states have such crimes as aggravated kidnapping, rape of a victim younger than eleven by a repeat offender, perjury that leads to execution, and many others. All executions since 1976 have involved murder or conspiracy to murder. See http://www.antideathpenalty.org/crimes.html.

55. I actually discuss this at some length in Steffen, *Ethics and Experience*, 145ff.

when wrongdoing occurs. That is, in a sense, what the "institutionalizing" of a murderer would be—education. You are certainly aware that an attorney who presents a court of law with a "not guilty by reason of insanity" plea is today tossing a "hail Mary" pass not likely to receive much sympathy from a jury.[56] And, for the record, the Greek "evil is ignorance" perspective received its greatest challenge from Christianity, which opened up in new ways in Greek society the idea that evil is "perversity." That is, evil results from knowing what is good to do but willfully and perversely refusing to do it. St. Paul said as much in Rom. 7:15: "I do not understand my own actions. For I do not do what I want, but I do the very thing I hate." Most people who commit murder do so against persons they know, they are under great duress with frustration and rage, and most people who commit murder are terribly ashamed of what they have done. You raise an issue about murderers being mentally ill—I think they are in the moment they kill, but there are some murders that seem embedded in human perversity. Let me ask you, just so I am clear: Do you accept the idea of a perverse will or are you convinced the "evil as ignorance" view adequately covers horrendous deeds and that moral equilibrium requires a death for a death? Do you think an execution could ever be justified, given the realities you mention about inequities and revenge?

COOLEY:

I am going to take the controversial step of claiming that state-sponsored and other types of execution cannot be justified because of the practical inability to adequately remove inequality and illicit motivations from the decision-making process in which a person's life is ended. Even if these factors were eliminated, which is unlikely, there will be other biases that will take their place and produce the same result of killing another person on the basis of unethical motivations.

One idea I have not introduced before is an obligation to ourselves when considering the death penalty's morality. Basically, the kind of person we want to be should be a primary question for this issue as well as for others. We

---

56. This is traceable to the trial of John Hinkley, the would-be assassin of President Ronald Reagan. When Hinkley was found not guilty by reason of insanity, the verdict ignited a firestorm of protest and "by reason of insanity" has not had much cachet in the criminal justice system since then, although it can still sometimes work. A judge accepted an "insanity plea" from James Holmes, the gunman who opened fire in a crowded theater in Aurora, Colorado, in July 2012, killing twelve and wounding fifty-eight people. He awaits trial as of this writing in a Colorado psychiatric institution and will probably be sentenced to a care facility rather than prison.

should want to flourish because thriving is our ultimate end; therefore, we have an obligation not to harm our own flourishing if doing so is easily avoidable. Given that incarceration is a viable moral alternative that produces justice and because of the great intrinsic value people have merely from being a person, which should not be eliminated unless ethically necessary, and our obligation to do the right thing in the right way for the right reasons, we owe it to ourselves not to use or allow the death penalty to exist. That is, it is unacceptable for us to be or to become the type of person who would sentence or kill another person if that decision could be illicitly biased.

First, if one truly respects the intrinsic worth of people, then it is very hard for one to eliminate it wherever it occurs. Even a murderer has value, although we can safely say that it is less than that of an innocent person. But we should never lose sight that there is a unique entity that we will eliminate from the world if we execute him, and that value can never be replaced. When we can keep the person alive at the same time we punish him, then killing him seems more an indulgence than a necessity of justice. It feeds a need for revenge or other negative emotions while simultaneously making us more callous to intrinsic value—albeit less than that of the innocent—that deserves some form of respect.

In addition, rejecting the death penalty improves us by making us more caring people who want to improve the lot of others and the world. We recognize that there is always a hope that the murderer can improve his or value as a person, as well as of the world as a whole. By going to jail, he begins to lessen the individual debt that he has taken on himself, even though he can never remove it fully. By paying off portions of it, he makes himself better, and the world is a better place when those who owe a debt pay it. Even if it occurs against his will, his incarceration or punishment is enough to remove some of the bad in the world and act as an example so that others do not behave in similar ways. Moreover, as I argued above, there is good reason to believe that those who commit murders might be mentally unbalanced. If so, then we should not treat them as if they were acting as fully autonomous agents would act. Finally, there is always hope that the murderer will take responsibility for his evil conduct. Incarceration could be a learning experience that will make him wise enough to understand and appreciate what he has done. This will be part of his self-improvement performed through his own actions, which is rendered moot if he is dead.

If we are decent people and do not have revenge or other negative emotions in our hearts, then we cannot be motivated to kill another person for the state.[57] It just does not fit with our attempts to improve ourselves morally speaking. And that is one reason why state executions are not performed by those who care for the person being executed. It is not an easy task even for those who are not in caring relationships with the condemned. In fact, for their mental health and safety, those officials involved in executions should be as detached as possible so that they do not feel guilt or other harmful emotions caused by killing another person. For example, Utah's firing squad uses five police officer marksmen but only four live rounds to prevent any one marksman from knowing if he fired a fatal shot.[58] Hence, even in the best-case scenario, it is thought that those most likely to be able to administer justice require some device to protect their conscience or mental health.

Let us also consider what has to happen in the jury room. When the defendant is sentenced to death, he must become more an object than a person. First, we have the endemic problems with bias in jury members of which they are unaware. The decisions might not be based on outright racism, sexism, or any other "ism," but the choice is not made in the interests of pure justice or benefit to the state, which needs to be the high standard when considering killing a human person. Second, there are the negative motivations, such as anger and revenge, which destroy actual justice being done. To be permissible, state justice must be as pure as it can be; otherwise, it is merely a wrong done to a wrongdoer. In addition, in too many cases, the defendant is thought to be some kind of monster. Because he is a dangerous, evil object rather than a person, it is much easier to take his life.

Since each agent's life is so precious and incarceration is a clear, appropriate alternative to execution, then choosing death reduces each jury member's flourishing or ability to flourish, as well as that of those who support such a sentence. We should not treat any human beings as objects, no matter how morally disgusting they are, because they remain persons, which we, as morally adult individuals, must acknowledge.

If there are times when taking another person's life is warranted, which seems to be the case, then that individual may still not be treated as a mere means. For example, euthanasia cases must respect the dying person in a manner appropriate to who she is as a person. Even self-defense cases demand that the agent acting to save her own worthy life recognize that the person she is killing is a person. Self-defense has to be a last resort because each person's life has such high moral worth, although some lives are clearly better than others. In addition, as argued above, the death penalty cannot satisfy the Pragmatic Principle because it cannot respect everyone affected by the action. To harm

57. I leave it an open possibility that we might kill out of a positive emotion, such as love.

58. The firing squad is an option only for those people convicted of a capital crime before 2004.

oneself needlessly is not to respect oneself. A long prison sentence, on the other hand, respects everyone involved in the action and helps us make the world a better place. Don't we owe it to ourselves to reject the death penalty on these grounds?

4

War

Although we generally begin each chapter by sketching out the arguments for or against a position, war does not lend itself as easily to this approach. This difference is likely caused by how bad wars are and the resulting destruction of life, relationships, stability, property, and other goods on which individuals and societies depend. Because of what it is and what it does, war needs to be justified in each and every situation in which someone claims it is a viable option.

STEFFEN

War is a major cause of death in the world today, mainly because it is the leading cause of hunger and a source of massive and traumatic social dislocation, impoverishment, and disease. War is a conflict resolution project that employs organized fighting aimed at meeting objectives by means of killing and destruction; and it is at least an unwelcome and unfortunate state of affairs if not an outright evil. The extreme human experience of war can indeed provide the occasion for people to exhibit virtues like courage, wisdom, and self-sacrifice, but people of good will are averse to war and the killing war inevitably entails. No reflection on war can avoid confronting the reality that it inevitably brings out the worst in people. War involves life-and-death decision making, it raises profound issues about what to do and what is allowable to do, and it involves activities that call for moral analysis and ethical justification. War is, in short, a prime ethics topic for any discussion of the ethics of death.

Any discussion of the ethics of war must include attention to the view—and it is an ethical view—that war should admit no moral constraints. The Prussian author of *On War* (1832), Carl von Clausewitz, held the "realist" view that it was dangerous for a nation to limit war by involving moral concerns. War, according to Clausewitz, identified the process whereby a nation organized to use violence to force an opponent to submit to its political will. The American Civil War general William Tecumseh Sherman held a similar view. His famous "war is hell" comment speaks to the irrationality, chaos, and general loss of moral meaning in war, a position that endorses a Machiavellian perspective that because in war winning is everything, everything in pursuit of winning is permitted. If war is hell, then everything necessary and expedient to defeat one's enemy is permissible, and ethical protocols that are extraneous to the bloody realities of the battlefield should be put aside and victory secured as quickly as possible by whatever means possible. If "war is hell" is the "realist" view of war, then war should not be thought about as a human activity governed by moral rules and ethical conscientiousness.

This "realist" viewpoint may reflect a common perception about war. Although it may appear to be an "anti-ethical" view, it clearly articulates a normative view about war, even if, as Clausewitz says, it represents the "the continuation of policy by other means," and "in such dangerous things as war, the errors which proceed from a spirit of benevolence are just the worst [while] he who uses force unsparingly, without reference to the quantity of bloodshed, must obtain a superiority if his adversary does not act likewise."[1] If one is going to engage in the "duel" or "game" of war—Clausewitz's characterizations—then using the "utmost force" "unsparingly" constitutes the prudent and justified policy that will lead successfully to the objective of war—namely, the subordination of the enemy's will.

This realist perspective may reduce to a "do what it takes to win" ethic, but it is an ethic nonetheless, and war, it turns out, is a topic that cannot possibly escape ethical analysis. Ethics is vitally concerned with the problems created by the violence and destructiveness of war, and warfare deaths are critically important to thinking about the morality of war. From an ethical point of view, war raises a variety of questions, and in this discussion I will address some of those questions.

We can ask, for instance, about the justification for going to war and also address how justifications are established for particular kinds of practices and activities that go on during war. Ethical concerns arise about alternatives to war and to the modes of force that rely on violence rather than nonviolence. Whether there could ever be a just war is both a theoretical and an empirical question. These are all "ethics of war" questions, and addressing the ethics of death in war requires that we make mention of several ethical perspectives—the realist viewpoint just mentioned, which need detain us no longer, and three

---

1. Carl von Clausewitz, *On War*, trans. J. J. Graham (London, 1873), Statement 24, http://www.clausewitz.com/readings/OnWar1873/BK1ch01.html.

others: pacifism and nonviolent resistance, just war, and holy war—an explicitly religious idea of war. All of these approaches to the ethics of war have advantages and problems. As we consider each in turn, we shall attend to the way religious ethics addresses the very same problems that are of such concern in secular ethics.

PACIFISM AND NONVIOLENT RESISTANCE

War is a coping mechanism for conflict. It is a way that organized corporate bodies—nation-states primarily—choose to resolve conflict by means of destruction and violence. War is the result of a decision to pursue various identifiable objectives, which may be related to politics, to honor, to justice, or to the distribution of power.

An ethics of war will include attention to *pacifism*, a term that indicates, in general, a philosophically or religiously grounded opposition to war and to the use of violent, coercive force to settle conflicts. The term can be employed to indicate opposition to the use of military force and to the institution of war. In extreme forms, pacifism will oppose any use of force whatsoever. Pacifism admits of varieties, so it always appropriate to inquire into the particular form of pacifism at issue. Pacifism can refer to the renunciation of any use of force at all in conflict situations, or, as is usually the case, it can identify a commitment to nonviolence as an alternative application of force to achieve political, social, or justice-related objectives. Some find grounding for pacifism in religion while others rely on nonreligious philosophical perspectives. Some people associate Henry David Thoreau with philosophical pacifism, while Mohandas Gandhi, the Rev. Dr. Martin Luther King Jr., Leo Tolstoy, Jesus, and the Buddha are often associated with religiously grounded pacifism. Pacifism can be associated with religion or religious perspectives like Buddhism, Christianity, Jainism, Quakerism, or Sikhism, but there are diverse views within religious traditions. Many Christians, for example, would object strenuously to a claim that their religion commanded them to be pacifists. Moreover, pacifists can be absolutist pacifists or practical-but-not-theoretical pacifists or, like the late Paul Goodman, self-described "fist-fighting" pacifists. And there are lots of places in between.

Let us clarify some important ideas about pacifism by contrasting two perspectives, the first being an absolutist pacifism, represented by Leo Tolstoy, and the other being nonviolent resistance, exemplified by Gandhi and King. First, an absolute pacifist—Leo Tolstoy.

TOLSTOY—NONRESISTANCE AS ABSOLUTIST PACIFISM

Arguably Russia's greatest novelist and certainly one of the most important writers of all time, Leo Tolstoy, author of *War and Peace* and *Anna Karenina*, experienced a spiritual crisis in his life that never quite resolved completely. A member of the Russian Orthodox Church, Tolstoy came to believe that the organized institutional religion he knew had missed the central teachings of Jesus and had affiliated itself with what he called the "law of violence." Jesus, on the contrary, gathered the faithful in obedience under the "law of love." As he came to revere the life and teachings of Jesus as the model for how to live a life of total nonviolence and nonparticipation in violence in conformity with the law of love, Tolstoy came to hold an absolutist perspective on nonviolence. Inspired by the Sermon on the Mount and Jesus' instruction "Do not resist an evildoer" (Matt. 5:35), Tolstoy came to reject any authority that did not express the law of love.

> [In the Christian Gospels] it is clearly and definitively stated that there are, and can be, no circumstance when it is permissible to deviate from the very simple and vital requirement of love: not to do to others which you would not have them do to you. . . . In other words, violence performed against you can never justify violence on your part. . . . [T]he true Christian teaching in its true meaning, recognizing the law of love as supreme, and permitting no exceptions in its application to life, ruled out any form of violence and consequently could not but condemn the whole structure of the world founded on violence.[2]

Tolstoy's absolutism rejected not only such obvious applications of the law of violence as military service and conscription, but also any governmental function whatsoever since government functioned by a threat of coercive force, which is the heart of the law of violence. So Tolstoy's invective targeted everything from police protection to using stamps to using government vehicles to convey food to Russians starving because of drought.[3] Tolstoy was

---

2. Leo Tolstoy, "The Law of Love and the Law of Violence," in *A Confession and Other Religious Writings*, ed. and intro. Jane Kentish (London: Penguin Books, 1987), 173–75.

3. Like all absolutists, Tolstoy contradicted himself and did finally relent and use his influence to help those suffering from draught, but the relevant point is that he felt guilty about involving himself in such activity because government ("the law of violence") was involved as well. These comments on Tolstoy as exemplar of pacifist extremism draws on a more extended discussion of Tolstoy to be found in Lloyd Steffen, *Holy War, Just War: Exploring the Moral Meaning of Religious Violence* (Lanham, MD: Roman and Littlefield, 1987), 143-165.

a "nonresister"—that is, one who would not oppose evil by resisting it with the powers claimed by those who operate according to the "law of violence"—he would respond to evil only by using love. His commitment to nonviolence was extreme and uncompromising, absolute and "without exception" as he said repeatedly, leading not only to his excommunication by the Russian Orthodox Church but to a break with anything having to do with "violence"—namely, government and governmental authority. Nonresistance is an extreme form of pacifism and nonviolence, a radical rejection of government and a call for anarchy vis-à-vis the state. In Tolstoy's eyes, however, nonresistance identified nothing more than a simple commitment to the literal teachings of the Sermon on the Mount, which, as he noted, many followers of Christ, including members of the Russian Orthodox Church, affirmed as a divine message but then failed to observe or even defend as a practical way of life. Tolstoy did defend nonresistance as a way of life and tried to practice it consistently, even literally.

NONVIOLENT RESISTANCE

Gandhi and King both advocated a different understanding of pacifism. Although Gandhi would early on talk about "passive resistance," he acknowledged that what he endorsed was described "less accurately" as passive resistance: "Non-co-operation is not a passive state. It is an intensely active state—more active than physical resistance or violence. Passive resistance is a misnomer."[4] Gandhi would come to identify nonviolent resistance with *Satyagraha*, a term that means soul force, love force, truth force. The term in all of its synonyms refers to an application of *force,* an active spiritual force that can be employed to advance justice while opposing and resisting injustice. Nonviolent resistance is not a weapon of the weak, he would write, but a spiritually grounded weapon superior to any available in the arsenals of adversaries: "The only weapon of the Satyagrahi is God, by whatsoever name one knows him. Without Him the Satyagrahi is devoid of strength."[5] This idea led Gandhi to say nonviolent resistance wields a power—a sword—that can defeat violence and "convert" those who rely on violence. King will reiterate the Gandhian perspective. In *Stride toward Freedom* he writes:

First, it must be emphasized that nonviolent resistance is not a method for cowards; it does resist. If one uses this method because he

4. Mahatma Gandhi, *Satyagraha (Non-Violent Resistance)* (New York: Shocken Books, 1951), 161.
5. Gandhi, *Satyagraha*, 14, 95.

is afraid or merely because he lacks the instruments of violence, he is not truly nonviolent. This is why Gandhi often said that if cowardice is the only alternative to violence, it is better to fight. . . . [W]hile the nonviolent resister is passive in the sense that he is not physically aggressive toward his opponent, his mind and emotions are always active, constantly seeking to persuade his opponent that he is wrong. The method is passive physically, but strongly active spiritually. It is not passive nonresistance to evil, it is active nonviolent resistance to evil.[6]

Active nonviolent resistance to evil easily distinguishes Gandhi and from Tolstoy's nonresistance absolutism. Nonviolent resistance as a form of pacifism intends neither to inflict injury nor endorse any act of killing, so such pacifists are not involved in any warfare deaths. Yet this pacifism does aim to convert and transform adversaries, calling nonviolent resisters to self-sacrifice, which includes a willingness to accept the suffering that might be inflicted on them. This leads to questions about how the conversion of the oppressor—that change of heart—is to take place. If it is by evoking guilt in the oppressor who inflicts violence on nonviolent resisters with impunity—the violence toward the nonviolent resister leads to guilt and the guilt then leads to the conversion sought—then it could be said that such a form of pacifism might depend on inciting the oppressor to inflict violence so that the process of conversion can get underway. Whether this accurately teases out some of the deeper logic of both Gandhi and King, it is clear that both understood nonviolence to be an actual use of force that provided a powerful weapon for accomplishing the ends of justice.

Gandhi and King, both victims of assassination, eschewed killing and sought to address injustices in ways that avoided bringing about anyone's death, even the death of the oppressor. Their perspectives were formulated in the religious realm where nonviolence is grounded in transcendent reality. The training that each of these leaders insisted their followers go through was spiritual preparation designed to steel the resolve of nonviolent resisters so that they could receive the suffering that their oppressors would inflict and not resort to violent retaliation. In the ethics of war, the nonviolent resistance of Gandhi and King presents a religiously grounded ethic of "fighting" for justice and resisting injustices actively but nonviolently. While there is much here to associate with a holy war idea, given the transcendent sources each calls upon,

6. Martin Luther King Jr., *Stride toward Freedom: The Montgomery Story* (New York: Harper and Brothers, 1958).

there is also much in their approach that conforms to the basic structure of "just war" thinking, as we shall make clear shortly.

JUST WAR

The predominant ethic of war in the West involves a tradition of thought called "just war." The idea may seem repugnant or nonsensical, perhaps even oxymoronic: if war is terrible and inevitably provokes the horror of killing innocent people, how can we talk or think ethically about a "just war"? Can such a thing exist? Isn't it more likely that just war a "myth"?[7]

When discussing "just war" we have to be clear what we are talking about. There is a tradition of just war thinking in the West that articulates a set of criteria, which, if met, allows one to assert moral justification for a use of force. The criteria involve what are called *jus ad bellum* criteria, that is, criteria that must be satisfied if one is going to justify going to war, and *jus in bello* criteria, which govern the conduct of war itself. Here is what I believe to be the best formulation of the criteria for just war:

- The war or use of coercive force must be sanctioned by a legitimate and competent authority.
- The cause must be just.
- There must be a right intention and announcement of that intention (that is, achieving a just settlement of the conflict and restoring peace).
- The results of using force and going to war must yield results proportionate to the end of peace, meaning more good than ill must result—a proportionality requirement.
- Combat or use of force must always be a last resort.
- The war must be undertaken with a reasonable hope of success.
- By resorting to force or going to war one must preserve values that otherwise could not be preserved.

These are a contemporary formulation of the *jus ad bellum* criteria that can be used to establish whether a war or use of coercive force is itself morally justifiable. In addition, two other criteria, reflecting the *jus in bello* tradition, articulate constraints on the actual conduct of a war, guiding action with respect to the means of warfare:

7. See Andrew Fiala, *The Just War Myth* (Lanham, MD: Roman and Littlefield, 2008).

- Noncombatants must be protected from harm (noncombatant immunity).
- The use of force cannot resort to means (that is, weaponry) that are disproportionate to the end of restoring peace (proportionality).

These criteria begin in a secular philosophical tradition of natural law thinking. Cicero is the earliest originator of a principled, rule-governed approach to the ethics of war, and he drew the distinction between *jus ad bellum* and *jus in bello* in his writings on the state. Cicero's basic appeal to criteria of a justified use of force influenced other Roman philosophers, such as Seneca, and it was then picked up by the Christian thinker, St. Augustine, who was living at the time of the fall of the Roman Empire and who faced the problem of what the Christian is to do when confronting invasion and chaos. Augustine asserted that the end of war must be the restoration of peace, and a justified use of force must not sanction the deliberate and direct intention to destroy life. Thus did Augustine's idea of "just war" include an idea of legitimate authority and right intention (that is, action consistent with Christian charity), and his ideas about the just causes for war included punishment for sin unaccompanied by hatred. In the thirteenth century, Thomas Aquinas supported the idea of limiting a just war to military engagements between sovereign princes who were protecting their communities. War was an enterprise involved with defending the common good, and Aquinas abided by criteria of legitimate authority, right intention, and just cause. Aquinas addressed the question whether killing in self-defense was permissible and introduced the idea of "double effect." This idea was invoked to justify killing an aggressor as a foreseen but unwanted consequence (secondary effect) of pursuing a good intention—namely, the good end of self-defense. Self-defense has been a major idea of just cause in just war theory ever since.

The history of the development of just war theory is long and involved, but we can note for our purposes here that just war thinking did evolve over the centuries. The Spanish Scholastic Vitoria held that just cause for war could include self-defense, punishing wrongdoers, and securing peace, and he opened up the idea of a justified war to the realm of international relations. The Dutch Protestant theologian Hugo Grotius identified war as being consistent with the laws of nature, thus identifying self-defense as a natural right that not even God could abrogate or countermand. Suarez, another of the Spanish philosophers addressing the problem of war, opened up discussion of the just war criteria to include a "reasonable hope of success" criterion plus two additional ones: proportionality (the idea that no more force should be used than is necessary to accomplish the aim of war) and the idea of going to war only as a last resort. With these philosophers, just war thinking expanded and secularized.

Today, just war thinking has full currency in the realm of international relations, and nations are said under international agreements to be justified in going to war to defend their sovereignty. Just war thinking actually is present in international law as a means of restricting war, restraining force, containing conflicts, and governing the allowable limits of what can and cannot be done in warfare. Just war thinking is present even when it is not explicitly identified as such. The Nuremberg trials of Nazi war criminals, for example, which appealed for authorization to The Hague Convention of 1907 and the Geneva Convention of 1929, asserted the right of international tribunals to prosecute those who commit war crimes in violation of the "law or customs of war," and the idea of a war crime points to warfare acts that violate the protections afforded noncombatants.[8] Just war thinking has shaped the moral framework of warfare by requiring restraint in the use of force and imposing limits that prevent murder, killing of hostages, enslavement, and wanton destruction not justified by military necessity, all criminal war practices proscribed under just war provisions. (Incidentally, the United States, which was party to the creation of the International Tribunal that prosecuted Nazi war criminals at Nuremberg, does not by domestic law allow its citizens to be prosecuted for war crimes by a non-U.S. court.)

Just war theory provides a framework for restraining the use of force to the end of restoring peace, and it is invoked to determine whether going to war can be morally justified. As a position on the ethics of war, it stands opposed to a realist approach to war as well as to pacifist absolutism, which would say no use of force is ever justified.

Yet just war has problems. The structure and criteria of just war say nothing about any particular conflict and contain no content with respect to specifics, yet the criteria must be applied to real-world situations of conflict. Those criteria can be manipulated by sometimes untruthful or unscrupulous leaders to advance self-serving political goals or nationalist policy agendas, and it is simply a fact that political leaders have over the centuries appealed to just war ideas to establish the moral warrants for all kinds of military adventures that never rise to the level of a "just war." Political Machiavellians or realists have invoked just war ideas to create a claim to moral righteousness for a war policy, the aim being to garner public support for a prospective war. Just war ideas, then, are subject to abuse, and this leads to the major criticism of just

---

8. Charter of the International Military Tribunal, Nuremberg Trial Proceedings, vol. 1, Article 6a, available as part of the Avalon Project at Yale Law School, http://avalon.law.yale.edu/imt/imtconst.asp.

war—namely, that it is too permissive and does not actually yield the restraint the tradition of just war thinking promises. Leaders can and have appealed to just war ideas to claim moral justification for military action, and they can spin messages and even distort facts to make sure that the actions they are seeking to pursue "satisfy" just war criteria and render what they are doing "moral."

There are three major points I would offer about just war thinking as we consider warfare deaths. The first is that just war ideas carve out a morally moderate space for reflection and for democratic deliberation. Avoiding realist absolutism on the one hand and pacifist absolutism on the other, just war stands in the middle, offering this proposition: some wars may be morally justified and others not. The chore is to determine which are which, and the criteria require persons of good will and leaders averse to killing to come together to establish the facts of a conflict and to deliberate questions of authority, intention, just cause, last resort, and so on. Just war serves democratic values by requiring assessment of facts, shared deliberation, hard question asking, and citizen engagement. No war is on the face of it just—justice-related criteria must be invoked and applied, and the facts of a conflict must be honestly and fully presented so that deliberation can proceed with integrity and with due attention given to the many ways conflicts can be settled short of using force.

The second issue has to do with the status of just war theory, just war thinking, and just war ideas as they pertain to ethics. Just war theory, as a set of criteria, does not, in my view, constitute an ethic. The criteria are justice-related abbreviations that require some ethical foundation to make the criteria themselves morally relevant, and this foundation is rarely if ever articulated. Just war as we typically use it does not establish a reasoned ethical foundation or normative principle acceptable to all reasonable people of good will. It is in relation to such a foundation of principle that the criteria of just war come to command strict moral attention.

This problem can be corrected. What is required to turn just war ideas into a just war ethic is the articulation of a common moral agreement that proposes something like this: War is understood by reasonable persons to be an evil that should be avoided. Our common moral agreement is that *war should be avoided and that conflicts should be settled in some way other than war or a use of force.* Yet we understand that life is messy. Some situations arise that are so horrendous that a use of force is actually the lesser evil, for some situations—Hitler's genocidal regime, for instance—present evils even worse than war. When that occurs, a use of force is the most reasonable and effective way to settle such a conflict. Using force is an option in conflicts where people are being subjected to terrorism, murder, genocide, enslavement, and injustices that violate values central to human decency, particularly human rights.

The just war criteria guide our reflection and deliberation on the facts of a conflict, allowing us to consider whether an exception can be made to our governing moral understanding that we should not ordinarily use force to settle conflicts. All of the justice-related criteria, not just some of them, have to be satisfied if an exception to the moral presumption against war is to be lifted and a use of force authorized. If they are not satisfied, then an action consequence follows from the application of the ethic: a use of force not justified must not proceed. Just war, then, as an ethic, affirms not simply nine criteria but also a common agreement—a moral presumption against war and even against the use of force to settle conflicts. The criteria serve a secondary role to guide reasonable people as they consider whether a particular conflict rises to the level of a justified exception. That is what a just war ethic would look like.

Moving from just war ideas and structure to a just war ethic makes just war something other than a justification for using force. Just war as an ethic actually stands as an impediment to using force so that the restraint originally associated with just war is restored. Just war is transformed into a normative presumptive commitment *against the use of force* rather than a justification for using force. The ethic promotes settling conflicts through the nonviolent means of negotiation, conflict arbitration, and even a war alternative like coexistence.[9] War, and resorting to force, must always be a last resort.

Just war *as an ethic* grounds and supports a common moral agreement shared by all good people of good will that force ought ordinarily not be used to settle conflicts. The just war ethic is so deeply grounded in a *moral commitment against the use of force* that it can even be thought of as supporting a practical—although not theoretical—pacifism.

The third issue I wish to raise pertains to warfare deaths.[10] I would point here to the noncombatant immunity provision of the *jus in bello* criteria of just war, which says noncombatants—those not involved in the war or fighting—must be preserved from harm and must never be made targets of warfare violence. The killing of noncombatant civilians is undoubtedly the greatest injustice in war. The noncombatant immunity provision of just war acknowledges that civilians are by definition not armed or equipped for self-defense and should to be exempt from involvement in the violence of war. By

---

9. David Chan, *Beyond Just War: A Virtue Ethics Approach* (New York: Palgrave Macmillan, 2012). Discussion of coexistence as alternative to war occurs throughout the book.

10. Much of this discussion relies on chapter 9 of Steffen, *Ethics and Experience*, 195–202.

any empirical analysis, however, they constitute the group most subjected to violence, suffering, and death as the victims of war. Over thirty million of the estimated fifty-five million casualties suffered in World War II were civilians. China, Russia, Poland, and Germany accounted for the vast majority—estimates are up to 85 percent—of those noncombatant deaths and injuries. The British journal *Lancet* had estimated "excess deaths" in Iraq from 2003 to June 2006 at more than 650,000, a figure that would include death from lawlessness, degraded infrastructure, and poor health care.[11] The Opinion Research Business poll, which interviewed Iraqis in August 2007 about deaths in their families, put the estimates of civilian deaths at over one million since the start of the war.[12] Figures about Iraq casualties are estimates and have been disputed.

No controversy, however, attaches to the idea that civilians die in war and sometimes in horrendous numbers. The World War II numbers would suggest that civilians can expect to make up more than half—a good majority—of the number of war casualties. And any in-depth analysis of a war zone would show what the *Lancet* estimators did: excess deaths. Excess deaths are those that noncombatant civilians suffer beyond actual combat and that linger on in hunger, disease, poverty, homelessness, and social and economic dislocation. Warfare technologies have been designed to produce just such deaths beyond assault: antipersonnel, chemical, biological, and nuclear weapons generate suffering and death beyond the moment of engaged conflict. Noncombatant civilians not only bear the effects of such weapons but are, as in the case of strategic nuclear weapons, the actual targets of the weapons. Over seventy thousand died in Hiroshima from the direct atomic blast, but over two hundred thousand died up to five years after the bombing, victims of radiation poisoning.[13]

Just war theory allows us to say that the deaths of civilians are unjust. Civilians are possessed of a status that exempts them in war from direct and intentional harm. The adversaries in war are not permitted under just war

11. Gilbert Burnham, Riyadh Lafta, Shannon Doocy, and Les Roberts, "Mortality after the 2003 Invasion of Iraq: A Cross-Sectional Cluster Sample Survey," *The Lancet*, Volume 368, Issue 9545, Pages 1421-1428, 21 October 2006, doi:10.1016/S0140-6736(06)69491-9. See a web article by Les Roberts, professor of public health at Columbia University, defending the *Lancet* findings in "Death Toll is Far Worse than Our Leaders Admit," http://www.informationclearinghouse.info/article17059.htm

12. Opinion Research Business, "More than 1,000,000 Iraqis Murdered since 2003 Invasion," press release, September 16, 2007, http://zcomm.org/znetarticle/more-than-1-000-000-iraqis-murdered-since-2003-invasion-by-orb/, cited at http://en.wikipedia.org/wiki/ORB_survey_of_Iraq_War_casualties, where a report on the ORB report is available.

13. Department of Energy, "The Atomic Bombing of Hiroshima. August 6, 1945," http://www.osti.gov/manhattan-project-history/Events/1945/hiroshima.htm.

to directly harm civilians, and civilian deaths in war constitute a profound evil. Failure to prevent the deaths of civilians in war can deprive even an apparently justified war of its claim to justification. And while the case can be made that new wars are different—that in the contemporary geopolitical situation terrorism is a tool of conflict and distinctions between combatant and noncombatant are blurred as agents of war hide in the civilian populations—even then, the moral idea holds that civilians hold a presumptive moral right not to be harmed in war and that the killing of civilians is wrong.

The reason we need restraint on uses of force and even agreements as to what is a permissible weapon to end violence is that the heaviest burdens in war fall on those not directly involved in it—civilian populations. Civilian vulnerabilities inspire the moral presumption against using force to settle conflicts; they direct moral attention to restraints that are needed to prevent unjust breeches of human rights, especially the violation of unjust killing. A just war ethic will attend to the reality of war and its horrors, and no horror is greater than the "slaughter of innocents" that is the largest category of war casualties. A just war ethic will require observance of the criteria of just war and refuse to grant approbation to any use of force that does not observe the restraint of the ethic; it will require people of good will to deliberate on issues of justice before using force and demand that they recognize and serve the common moral agreement that force ought not to be used to settle conflicts.[14]

Just war thinking arose from secular sources. Historically, it has been preserved and transmitted through religious traditions in the West—the previous discussion focused on Christianity, but Islam also abides by a rule-constrained use of force in what amounts to a just war theory.[15] The case can even be made that Gandhi and King, both of whom understood nonviolent resistance to be a use of force, were reluctant to use force and thus observed the common agreement against using it. The nonviolent activities of boycotts and strikes could bring harm to those not involved in the action, and both worried about those harms, thus showing concern for "noncombatant immunity." In fact, all of the criteria of just war are applicable to the kinds of nonviolent force Gandhi and King advocated, so when nonviolence is conceived of as resistance to injustice and an application of force, even Gandhi and King are subject to analysis under just war rubrics.

14. I discuss the application of the just war ethic and the presumption against the use of force in an analysis of Gandhi and King in Steffen, *Ethics and Experience*, 51–72.

15. See James Turner Johnson points out the features of "just war" thinking in Islam in *The Holy War Idea in Western and Islamic Traditions* (University Park: Pennsylvania State University Press, 1997).

Just war thinking survives today in international law and the just war ethic. Because it starts from the assumption that some wars and uses of force are permissible, morally speaking, and others are not, it asserts a morally moderate perspective that avoids the absolutes of both realism and pacifism. The moral task is to tell the difference, and the just war ethic is to my mind the best ethics resource available for undertaking a moral analysis of war.

HOLY WAR

A third major ethical perspective on the question of war and the use of force is "holy war." This term is commonly associated today with Islam and specifically with the idea of jihad, but there are some misunderstandings about the meaning of jihad. While it is true that some extremist militant Muslim organizations have become associated with "Jihadism," now a synonym for global international Islamic networks like al-Qaeda that use terrorism and armed force to advance their goals, the term *jihad* has a broader significance than any association with "holy war." Jihad identifies "struggle" or "striving" and originally connoted spiritual struggle—so that getting out of bed to greet the world and live a life pleasing to Allah could be jihad. The jihad of the pen could mean the struggle to overcome writer's block. This spiritual meaning was the "greater jihad" to be contrasted with the "lesser jihad" of struggle against the enemies of Islam, and this "lesser jihad" identifies the meaning that has been at times translated as "holy war" and used so much in the contemporary media as an indicator of Islamic justification for uses of force.

Use of "holy war" to translate jihad is thus somewhat misleading, given the association of the term with Islamic spirituality. The fact remains, however, that the use to which jihad has been put, not only by outside observers but even by Muslim extremists who want to reclaim divine sanction for acts of violence, does point to the very real phenomenon of language use—language comes to serve the purposes of those who use it. Jihad has been associated with holy war not only by observers of Islam who may not grasp the spiritual supremacy of the term in the Islamic tradition but also by Muslims themselves, some of whom have called for jihad to become a sixth pillar of the faith.

If we can exclude jihad as a synonym for holy war, we can note that in a generic sense "holy war" simply refers to a war undertaken on authorization from transcendent sources. If an ethics of war requires a moral framework—a moral theory, if you will—then holy war provides a kind of "divine command" ethic of war. The appeal to such an ethical resource ought not be dismissed lightly. If one believes in a transcendent reality, and if one believes that such a reality can communicate its will to human beings, and if one believes that transcendent reality knows in the perfection of its being what is right and wrong, and if one believes that communication from the transcendent source can be received without being obstructed by the fallibility that marks human knowledge and insight, and if one believes that the transcendent reality has issued an order for war against another people, then one has a very solid justification for going to war. The rightness or wrongness of war is deferred to the divine will—the war is God's desire. What gives this logic such power is the assumption that God does not suffer imperfections in knowledge or understanding, so if one is clear that the divine will desires a war to proceed, the justification for using force against an adversary is secure. The ethical justification for war could not be more secure. To have God as one's justification for war is to possess the highest, the tightest, and the most authoritative source for sanctioning a war imaginable. If such a war is by definition holy because it is directed by the will of God, then "holy war" must be taken with the utmost seriousness as an ethical support for justifying war.

There are of course problems with this perspective, not least of which is disagreement about whether such a transcendent source even exists or, if it does, whether it is of such a character as to sponsor the killing and slaughter so common to war. If one believes in a creator God, then holy war would require a belief that God is endorsing the destruction of the very beings who are the triumph of the divine creative activity. Another problem is that, given religious affirmation of human fallibility, holy war would require that human beings have received the divine message for war clearly and without the obstruction of egotism, nationalism, or other impediments that could make war look self-serving to individuals or nations. Holy war entails powerful and logical supports for going to war; the logic may be valid, but it can issue in an ethic of war that is not sound, philosophically speaking.

Classic questions arise when contemplating holy war. If God is all-knowing and all-powerful, why would God entrust the divine will to fallible human beings and not simply act in such a way that the divine will is realized? Why depend on human beings, who are notorious for misunderstanding and misinterpreting? In the Hebrew Bible, Yahweh was the warrior for the people of Israel, and if enemies threatened, Yahweh defeated them and preserved the people of Israel. Yahweh slaughtered the Egyptians following the crossing of the Red Sea—Moses just stood with an outstretched arm but undertook no violence toward the pursuers. Yahweh was quite capable of protecting the people of Israel and dispatching the enemies of those in covenant with Yahweh. Jericho was razed with shouts and trumpets. Once defeated, however, the

Israelites "devoted to destruction by the end of the sword all in the city, both men and women, young and old, oxen, sheep and donkeys" (Josh. 6:21). Was that destruction a "holy war"? The trumpets bringing city walls down looks like Yahweh's activity. But what about all the slaughter of the city inhabitants including children and donkeys? The Israelites did that, not the "commander of the army of the Lord" who appeared to Joshua just before the "battle"—the marching and trumpet blowing—began (Josh. 5:14). Distinguishing where the divine will in using force against a divine enemy ends and the human will to subdue and conquer begins is very difficult, which is to say that any claim about a "holy war" needs to sort out the divine will, the limitations of that divine will on human action, and the actual ability of human beings to receive the message clearly and without obstruction.

Religions can provide inducements to violence and destruction, and generic holy war has been a blight on human history. We know this from the outstanding example of holy war—the Christian Crusades—which took place between the eleventh and thirteenth centuries. Pope Urban II called Christians to join the march toward Jerusalem to fight the enemy of God—the Muslims—and those who joined were absolved of sin before setting off. This "holy war," however, was not a clear and unfiltered communication from God to the pope. The First Crusade is remembered historically as a practical effort to heal the rift between Eastern and Western Christianity that had broken open in the Great Schism of 1054.

No religion seems to escape involvement in military adventures, and the designation of "holy war" in the generic sense of war authorized by transcendent sources seems to leave no religious tradition unaffected. Buddhism has not undertaken organized religious war with other religions, but this "does not mean that Buddhists have always been peaceful," according to ethicist of Buddhism Peter Harvey, who writes,

> Buddhists countries have had their fair share of war and conflict, for most of the reasons that wars have occurred elsewhere. Yet it is difficult to find any plausible "Buddhist" rationales for violence, and Buddhism has some particularly rich resources for use in dissolving conflict. Overall, it can be observed that Buddhism has had a general humanizing effect throughout much of Asia. It has tempered the excesses of rulers and martial people, helped large empires (for example China) to exist without much internal conflict, and rarely, if at all incited wars against non-Buddhists. Moreover, in the midst of wars, Buddhist monasteries have often been havens of peace.[16]

The world's religions all contain "rich resources for dissolving conflict," and who knows how much worse the historical terrors of war might have been without the "humanizing effect" of religion. But the fact remains that human beings, in their desire to subordinate or eliminate enemies, have shunned coexistence as a legitimate and acceptable mode of political life, and they have involved religion in war and in statecraft. What makes holy war efforts so terrible is the appeal to absolutist certainty that accompanies a "God is with us" attitude, which then issues in a sense of moral superiority and certainty about the divine will that can seriously upset any hope for a just peace. Abraham Lincoln's second inaugural address is singular in calling such certainty into question and leaving the question about God's will open to human speculation. Beyond that, going even further, Lincoln actually opined that God's will is beyond the ability of human beings to grasp. That insight calls "God is on our side" holy war into question and challenges its ethical foundation. Humility in the face of the divine will, which was Lincoln's posture, exposed the foundation of holy war to be something other than a perfectly received communication of the divine will. What was received was not a clear revelation from God but a reason to ponder the spilled blood and the catastrophic destruction that render claims about God's approval of war the self-deceptive assertions of fallible people gripped by delusion and wishful thinking.

COOLEY

There are different types of wars. Some may be justified, whereas the vast majority cannot be. One of the reasons why morality is generally against war is because of the failure to satisfy the right intention or purpose clause of just war theory. In order for a war to be ethical, the war needs to be fought for a right intention or purpose, or a set of right intentions and purposes. Although it might seem easy to figure out a right intention and then focus all of our energy to make it our primary intention, this mental gymnastics is very difficult to do for a number of reasons. First, right intention does not seem to capture the moral standard being used. Of course, intentions are important because they are the goals or plans for what we are trying to do—for example, I have to intend to murder in order for a killing to be a murder—but intentions are only part of the bigger story. Included in this clause must also be motives, or what causes us to try to bring about what we intend to do. The murder above, for instance, could be a revenge killing, an attempt at self-defense, or a killing caused by some

16. Peter Harvey, *An Introduction to Buddhist Ethics*, 239.

other emotional driver. Wars, then, must be declared with the right intentions and motives, such as to protect one's citizens from being conquered; otherwise, the declaration cannot be ethical.

Second, we have little control over our fundamental beliefs and ideologies. They can influence our decisions without us even noticing. For example, many people would feel uncomfortable with men wearing dresses because it challenges social conventions and deep beliefs we have about how men should dress. However, few people question women wearing pants. There are no second, puzzled looks when a woman walks by wearing slacks, shorts, or any other form of pants. But at one time, this was an outrageous thing for women to do. Many people thought it showed that women wanted to be men, which would disturb the natural order. Over time, as we all know, this social convention changed. So why should we find men wearing dresses a matter of concern and not of indifference? We respond with concern because of an unconscious bias about how things should go when it comes to men's interaction with society and how men should be. If we respond in this way for rather unimportant sartorial matters, then it is possible and probable that we will make unconsciously biased decisions about war and have intentions affected too much by basic beliefs and ideologies rather than by reason.

Perhaps of greater concern are our natural emotional reactions to threats. We already know that one cannot go to war merely because one illicitly hates one's opponents or for gain or for any of the other vice-driven reasons that cause us to do what we should not do. Nor are wars permissible if the main motivating force is one or more of the vices. But we should ask ourselves why most wars are fought in the first place. I think we will find that underlying motivations are driven by vice or negative desires, which we then rationalize to show that going to war is ethically sound. To decide to begin a war in which we know that innocent people, our opponents, and our own troops will be maimed and killed, and that other suffering and misery will be caused, there have to be very strong motivational forces acting on us, such as the negative emotions of fear and hate.

The odds are always against a war being just. We know that only one side, at most, can be ethically permitted to declare and fight a war and that the other side has to be unjustified in its actions. In addition, both sides may be unjustified. For the latter, a war fought with both sides having vicious intentions is, by definition, an unjustified war. One side, for example, might be fighting out of irrational hatred for the other side, a hatred that is the result of many years of strife over boundaries, theft, and revenge. The other side may have the same hatred, only directed toward their opponent. If this is the case, then much as in the Hatfield and McCoy debacle in the southern United States, the killings and destruction cannot be justified on either side, thereby making the war unethical. There are many other causes that would make each side act unethically either in the declaration of war or the prosecution of it.

Because it is impossible for both parties to act in self-defense, for example, we do not have any situations in which both sides are justified in their actions. Therefore, the odds are stacked against wars being just.

IDEAL WAR

Philosophy often uses thought experiments to illustrate a point or to make people begin to think more clearly about an issue. The first type of war that I want to consider is the ideal war to see if perfect circumstances can make a war incontrovertibly the right thing to do. The ideal conflict fulfills every one of the moral conditions found in just war theory—and more. One side of the conflict has satisfied the conditions of *jus in bello* and *jus ad bellum*; that is, we have right intention, proportionality is maintained, and so on. The "more" condition is an elimination of many of the negatives associated with war, such as the killing of noncombatants.

What makes this war an ideal one is that it involves only people who freely and autonomously choose to be part of the war. There are no definitional issues of what a noncombatant or innocent person is because there will be no noncombatants or innocent persons. Everyone who is in danger has placed himself in that situation as the result of his autonomous decision-making procedure; therefore, he cannot be said to have made an irrational selection. Moreover, the person was not coerced into making the decision by some force greater than one can allow for individual freedom. He did not go to war because he needed the soldier's pay to keep his family from starving. He did not choose his role because someone threatened his life or those of his loved ones. He was not drafted against his will.

There were, of course, some internal and external influences on him to make the decision because there are always those sorts of influences in our lives. Our decision about what to do is influenced by the type of person we have chosen to be, social norms, our loved one's expectations of us, and so on, but we still have meaningful, real options from which we can select as autonomous agents. In the war situation, we can say that the agent choosing to go to war had a meaningful option not to go to war. The only reason he chose one over the other was because of his decision procedure and free will.

Trickier than the exclusion of noncombatants is the requirement that there are no unjustified damages, injuries, or costs caused to outside parties in an ideal war. Let us stipulate in our thought experiment that there is no destruction of any good that is owned by any external party to the war. Somehow these folks can keep all the explosions and other war-related phenomena confined solely to those who have chosen to be part of war. Moreover, the costs of war, such as paying for rehabilitation of injured soldiers, funerals, survivor benefits, guns, armored vehicles, other required war material, and the bureaucracy for carrying on a war are borne only by those who chose war. Social relations between nations and other large groups are not interfered with by the war. For example, if a country is a friend and good trading partner to both countries at war, then those relationships are not harmed. Finally, there is no psychological harm to those who do not choose to be engaged in the war. They are not bothered by pictures of the slain, news report of casualty figures, or any of the other detritus of war we can easily see by examining what has happened in Afghanistan, Iraq, the Republic of Congo, and other war-torn countries.

It should be clear by now that the ideal war is an impossible war. There is no practical, plausible way to conduct such a massive event so that it does not adversely affect people who have not chosen to be part of it. However, there is still something of interest to think about for this fictionalized situation. If we can show that even the ideal war is not a morally justified war, then it will go a long way in our thinking about whether other wars can be justified.

Let us focus on the question of whether wars can be reasonable and rational choices for any moral agent to make. We have set aside the war costs to noncombatants and others, costs that should bother morally decent individuals so much. We have settled the losses squarely on those who have chosen to bear them. The possible costs include the following:

1. Being severely emotionally, physically, financially, or otherwise injured so that one's life is not worth living.
2. Being severely injured in a way that allows for a life worth living but that is significantly less good than it would have been.
3. Being injured in a way that will make life less worth living than it would have been but not to a significant degree.
4. Being injured so that one has greater suffering than would have been the case without going to war, but in a way that one's overall life is worth living to the same qualifiable, although not quantifiable, degree.

Each of these injuries makes one's life less good overall, whereas some of them make one's life worse than being dead.

Even if a person does not have the misfortune to suffer one of the four harms, she still increases her risk of them by agreeing to be part of the war. After all, if she is fighting, then she is much more likely to be hurt than if she is one of the noncombatants who have chosen not to engage in our ideal war. Her increased risk can be considered an injury because she has lost something of value to her— namely, not being in so much danger.

But does increasing risk for oneself pass the test of being rational? If we assume, as I have argued elsewhere, that we are to pursue our own flourishing, then increasing risk makes little sense unless it can be shown to increase either flourishing or our chance to flourish.

The risk of the more significant harms (1 and 2 above) is not acceptable, though there is a difference between the harm and the chance of that harm occurring. The worse the injury is, then the lower the acceptability of the risk of the harm, even if the risk is minimal. The less damaging the potential injury, the more acceptable the risk becomes. If the agent is in a position that is generally not exposed to the worst dangers of war, then there is a low risk of experiencing a life not worth living, which might allow the choice of involving oneself in a war to be rational, if certain conditions were met. If one is merely chancing a graze from a bullet, the higher probability risks are permissible if the agent freely chooses to take them on.

So what are the conditions to justify the risk to an individual's flourishing? What would not illicitly harm that ultimate goal and allow the person to make a rational, autonomous choice to engage in war? Patriotism of the right sort could do it. That is, the person's flourishing is tied to the flourishing of her country; fighting would then achieve both goals to thrive. A justified belief in the purpose of the war is another one. If doing the right thing is necessary to flourish, then fighting an ethical war in an ethical way would help the person to thrive. Using the military to have a job and advance one's career is another. The first two address the individual risking her own flourishing for the flourishing of her society though the two are intimately intertwined, whereas the third deals more with individual flourishing.

To make rational sense of the third, the work of being a combatant would need to be less risky than the other alternatives open to the agent at the time of the choice. Perhaps she is employed in a very dangerous job that has a higher probability of affecting her thriving than being a combatant that could be killed in a war would have. For instance, fishing has a fatality rate of 116 per 100,000 workers.[17] If there is a smaller chance than that of her dying in combat, then pursuing combat would be a rational action designed to increase her chances of thriving.

What might be more interesting to some is the altruism of service as a combatant for one's country in the time of war. In this instance, the individual sacrifices his or her own safety and potential to try to improve the flourishing of the society as a whole. Of course, motives for all of our actions can be mixed, and this is especially the case for dangerous, complex actions in which fundamental values are in contradiction with each other: self-flourishing versus social flourishing. However, the heroic nature of the sacrifice is understandable as a rational and reasonable action, especially if the flourishing of both is linked in the manner defended here. This is why the vast majority of people laud those who fight for their country and justifiably believe that these actions are accurate indications of good people who have put the country's flourishing at a higher priority than their individual thriving.

Those who autonomously agree to go to war on the basis of patriotism or a justified belief in the purpose of the war create a larger moral problem for those in charge of the war and society than they do for themselves when they risk their flourishing. That is, it is much easier to show the moral permissibility of an individual placing himself in danger than it is to show that a country can risk its citizens, especially the ones who seek the thriving of their society. We will consider the rationality and irrationality of the state exposing these people to danger in a moment.

A practical problem is getting universal agreement on what is an acceptable risk for someone who willingly places himself into danger. The soldier on the front line of action has the greatest probability of being harmed. His opponent is not justified in going to war, as we have already seen, which might make it more likely for his opponent to resort to measures that are more destructive than just war theory would allow. That is, since the opponent's cause is a bad one, the opponent's methods might also be bad, such as bombing soldiers who are off duty or not actively engaged in combat. The lowered moral standards and tactics will increase the risk to the agent who is fighting for the just cause. At some point in these chaotic circumstances, most reasonable people would say that fighting is too much like Russian roulette and the good reasons a soldier has for what she is doing are insufficient to justify the danger to which she is exposing herself. If there were little chance of surviving because the other side had superior tactics, forces, material, and position, then many would say that

17. Les Christie, "America's Most Dangerous Jobs: The 10 Most Dangerous Jobs in America," CNNMoney, August 26, 2011, http://money.cnn.com/galleries/2011/pf/jobs/1108/ gallery.dangerous_jobs/index.html.

it is irrational to continue to defend one's country because defeat and death are almost certain. However, here is the complication: at the very same time, those who hold out based on their honor would be considered heroes while those who ran away to fight another day would be labeled cowards. Our minds produce contradictory intuitions that will make general agreement virtually impossible.

Let us return to the question of whether it is rational or irrational to endanger those who are autonomously willing to sacrifice themselves for the good of the society. What should the state do in these circumstances? If the war is justified to preserve a good society, then it should be rational for those who make the decision to go to war and those who prosecute it to endanger those who have freely made the informed decision to fight. Assuming that the war appears to be winnable and the society is worthy of preservation, then acting in that way seems designed to promote the society's flourishing. In this case, the good of the many will outweigh the good of the few.

This situation needs closer examination for its long-term effects. If the society is sacrificing those who have an altruistic drive to help the society, then what are the likely results of engaging in a war? Putting aside those who lack the mental and physical capacities to be voluntary, informed combatants, those who choose not to be engaged in the war could be a varied lot. I am assuming that those who do not go to war either do not have the altruistic bent favoring society or might think that their individual flourishing is more important than that of the state. Of those who remain, some might think—rationally I might add—that their individual flourishing as noncombatants is necessary for the state's flourishing as they engage in those activities that made the state a good one in the first place. These are the individual citizens who face no greater risk than their normal life because they are not engaged in the war.

Whichever way we separate combatants from noncombatants, the truth of the matter is that the state is risking those members who place the state's flourishing above their own. These individuals are central to the state's existence because they are part of the social glue that keeps the state functioning as a state. There have to be enough people in the society to act in this manner or there would never be any sacrifice for the common good in the form of taxes and charity. Although Ayn Rand thought differently, the state cannot exist if it is merely a bunch of people who are pursuing their own individual thriving without reference to what those pursuits do to the state. Each person would be looking out for what is best for himself, which entails that each is trying to find a weakness in the others that can be exploited for personal profit, all the while not realizing that the society will become worse as each person views the others only in the way a vulture views a weakening member of the herd.

Social flourishing is a necessary component to a state and its society because without it there is no cohesive force that allows the state to represent the people it governs. When there are fewer people who are willing to sacrifice themselves for the state, there are, as a result, more people who are focused on their own self-interest and fewer willing to pursue the state's flourishing over their own. Hence, even in an ideal war, the state is weakened, which will negatively affect its ability to remain a good state that is flourishing. Therefore, the state weakens itself by endangering those who give the state the social cohesion it needs in order to survive. The end result is that even ideal wars are irrational for the leaders of the state unless they can guarantee that the state can flourish without being diminished. This would be impossible unless the state were able to protect its most altruistic people through supremacy in materials, tactics, or some other device. When the United Kingdom fought in World War I, for example, it was said to have lost an entire generation of men who could have well served the country. Imagine losing those who put the society first and what negative impact it would have on whether the society was better off than it would otherwise have been.

Given that I am trying to show that, even in the ideal war situation, the ethics involved are not intuitive or easy to understand, I am not going to try to sort this all out. There seems to be a conflict between different moral values we hold especially dear to us. I am unsure whether there is a solution to the quandary. Perhaps one value overrides another, or the person choosing one over the other makes the one value more important than the other. At the very least, there is good reason to think that risking a society's most committed members to the public good is not an action conducive to the society's flourishing.

OBLIGATORY WAR

Is it ever the case that countries and people have a moral duty to go to war? One justification for obligatory war rests on divine command theory. If God commands that a person or country go to war, then it is a moral duty to do so. God's command, according to this theory, is sufficient to make the command a moral obligation that no human may override. Therefore, if God states that war is necessary, then it is necessary.

I will not spend much time with this justification because it has several obvious problems that render it impractical, including the problem that we can never know with any reliable degree of certainty what God wants us to do.

Although religious belief is all well and good if it does not interfere with a flourishing life, too many wars have been caused by religious difference, either between religions or within a religion, as in the cases of conflict between Muslims and Jews, Jews and Christians, Christians and Muslims, and Christian Protestants and Christian Roman Catholics. The very faith that underlies the combatants' thinking might make these wars proliferate. If each person thinks that God is on her side and is not on the side of her opponent, then there is very strong reason to believe that fighting the nonbelievers is the morally right and obligatory thing to do. Moreover, since opponents do not believe the right thing and are therefore against God, it is permissible to do horrible things to them that would not be permitted in a conflict between believers on the same side. For example, terrorists use extreme violence against noncombatants to bring about some social change, such as toppling a government or making military or police forces leave the place in which the terrorist actions occurred. Terrorist actions are thought to be justified by those committing them because the victims are hated by God, whereas the groups performing the actions are loved by God. If one is loved by God, then what one does has to be right, at least if it is punishing those God has taken a dislike to. So, anything can be done, including killing innocents because they are not really innocent according to the belief that God permits punishing God's enemies.

Given the horrific consequences of religious wars, we can say there is no obligation for countries or individuals to fight in such until there is sufficient evidence—in these cases we would need extraordinary evidence—that God has made any such demand. Those interpreting a passage, reading a book, or telling us of dreams they take as prophetic are not going to be reliable and sufficient sources of information. Their information could have easily been caused by ignorance, an inadequate interpretation, or some other mistake on the part of the believer.

Douglas Lackey has a more realistic way to justify war based on moral obligations to protect others.[18] If a person or country gives a solemn promise to another country to provide defense for it, then the entity that made the promise has a duty to go to war if all the conditions of *jus ad bellum* are met. For example, if an agent agreed to provide protection to someone who is under threat, then the agent would have to give that protection, much as Secret Service agents have a duty to sacrifice their lives to preserve those whom they guard. Promises are contracts in which one party willingly gives up something that is his or to which he is entitled to the other party in the contract. Unlike most contracts,

---

18. Douglas Lackey, *The Ethics of War and Peace* (Englewood Cliffs, NJ: Prentice Hall, 1989).

there is no need for a quid pro quo, although that usually happens. Through treaties and other means, countries can create alliance contracts with other countries for mutual benefit or for the benefit of one.

The crux of Lackey's argument is based not merely on promise keeping—which is, of course, an important thing for us to do in general—but on the resulting weakness of the promise recipient caused when the promise is made. If someone accepts a promise, then that person must think that the promise will be kept, else there is no reason to accept the promise. If there will be no fidelity, then it is irrational to believe that someone will carry out the contract's terms because contracts rest on trust. No one, for example, would rationally sign a contract with someone who has never honored a contract in her long life. Hence, the person must think that the promise will be kept based on the promise giver's integrity and past performance or on some other reliable evidence that will allow her to believe rationally that the promise giver will act in the manner promised.

The weakness of dependency is a consequence of the belief that the promise will be fulfilled. Strategic plans are made and actions taken based on that belief. If a country believes the pledge of an ally, then the country's weapons systems, military strategy, and other means of defense will be structured around the other country coming to its aid when it needs help. That is, after all, why the North Atlantic Treaty Organization and other alliances exist as a deterrent for wrongful offensives against member states. If one member is attacked, then the other members respond as if they had been attacked.

If a country does not fulfill its pledge, then the plans of the other nation that believed the promise are defective. The unsupported country cannot offer its best defense because that defense was built, in part, on the promise of assistance. The betrayed country can try to cobble together a new strategy, but remember that it is already under hostile actions from the aggressor. Even if the defending nation can stave off destruction and even win the conflict, it will be a far more difficult process than if the promise to defend it had been upheld. In fact, given the disruption, it would have been far better and kinder not to have given a lying promise at all than to make one and let the trusting country put itself into a far more precarious position than otherwise would have been the case. There may be other reasons that wars through alliances are mandatory beyond the fact that a promise has been given and now needs to be honored, that the promise created a special dependency relationship between the contract's parties, and that the war is just, but these three are sufficient to make the war obligatory.

I think that Lackey's argument can be compelling if we limit ourselves to considering only the promise to go to war and the dependency caused by the promise, but perhaps we should expand our scope a bit to consider mitigating factors. Perhaps we should consider whether giving a promise to go to war on behalf of another country is ethically justified. If not, then a country may be obligated to go to war but the country did the wrong thing by creating such an obligation.

Binding treaties to go to war are morally permissible to sign or fulfill only if they are likely to maintain or increase the flourishing of those signing the treaty. Actually, since we might not know whether it would have this beneficial result, let us weaken the condition a bit to say that the treaty is permissible if the majority of reasonable people would reasonably believe that the treaty will maintain or increase the signees' flourishing. Given the destructive nature of war, we need to have a higher standard than that of a reasonable person or even a plurality of reasonable people thinking this way: it has to be the majority of reasonable people to commit a country to such a devastating course of action. After all, if one signs such an agreement, then one is locked into coming to the defense of one's allies. Since this will cost a great deal of pain, suffering, other misfortunes, and goods, then one should never go into war without the strongest evidentiary justification. If less than half of the population believes the treaty will increase flourishing, then there are clear competing perspectives regarding its success. While the actual outcome cannot be determined by a poll, having a majority of reasonable people come to agreement about the treaty assures us that it is a reasonable conclusion to draw.

In order to fill out the argument regarding which wars are required and which ones are not, we must first assume a few conditions. First, the war is justified and the country that will fulfill the contract is on the right side. Second, the majority of reasonable people reasonably believe that fighting the war will not interfere with the country's flourishing. That is, there has to be evidence that choosing not to fight will lead to much worse circumstances than if the country engages in war. For example, the country might be fighting a delaying action to allow its people to flee, and those people will be able to return to set the country back in order after the conflict is over. It might be that the power of the two countries combined is sufficient to force the aggressor states to capitulate or cease hostilities. If the country is going to be destroyed anyway, then fighting a war will not harm it more than is already in store.

Honoring a contract that requires the country to go to war is irrational unless that undertaking is likely to lead to the country's thriving. If there is an option open to the country that makes it more likely to flourish, then alliances may be permissibly broken. Suppose, for instance, that a country is bound by a common defense treaty with another country, but the aggressor has no interest in the former country. Let us say that two countries—A and B—have entered into an alliance. If one is attacked, then the other must come to its aid. A far superior force of a third country—C—is ready to invade A. C has discovered that A has a valuable resource that C needs. B does not have the resource, and C views B as unworthy of being invaded or attacked. If C conquers A without any interference from B, then C will leave B alone. However, if B attacks in response to C's aggression to A, then C will respond to force in kind. Although it might appear to be cowardly, B's abrogation of its treaty is not necessarily a wrongful action. B has a duty to A, but its primary duty is to itself. Therefore, even if A is weakened, there is no obligation for B to go to war to protect A. This conclusion is reinforced if A and B together cannot defeat C's might. B would have no duty to risk itself since doing so would be clearly destructive to B's long-term thriving.

If we bring back the insight from the ideal argument—namely, that nations generally act irrationally by risking the citizens who give their society social cohesion—then it becomes harder to understand why nations could be obligated to go to war. A nation cannot risk its more valuable entities unless it is the best thing they can do out of all their alternatives. Since wars are rarely, if ever, the best alternative, then a nation should not sign a contract that would risk its citizens who best promote social cohesion.

COMMENTARY

STEFFEN:

1. Your focus on intentions and the influence of ideologies is important because our motives for going to war—our stated intentions—are usually articulated broadly while we are usually unaware of ideological influences. We operate *out of* ideologies if I may put it that way; that is, we do not think our way to our ideological perspectives then figure out ways to apply the lessons or implications that flow from them. If that observation has truth in it, then can we say that, on your account, wars are fought from what are, in a very practical sense, "unconscious" motives? (How does that square with a Realpolitik view of the world where wars are fought for specific objectives that leaders go to great lengths to articulate in order to gain support for the war? Could the criticism be made that you have gone "too psychological"?)

2. You argue that a state willing to risk the lives of those altruistic enough to put the good of the society above self-interest weakens itself by risking the lives of the very people the society (state) needs for social cohesion. Do you consider this an argument for pacifism? It strikes me you are articulating a contradiction that makes war itself so irrational an enterprise that it cannot be justified, which then moves us to a position of avoiding contradiction, which would support pacifism. If it is an argument for pacifism, how far does your pacifism go?

3. Your argument poking holes in mutual aid—at least showing its limitations and how national self-interest could lead a nation to renege on a promise to aid another for reasons of its own self-interest—leads me to ask a question about obligations to provide aid and use force to settle a conflict. What does one do in a situation of genocide where the question of war is one of intervening not for narrow nationalistic reasons but for the humanitarian reason of helping to stop genocide and prevent people from being unjustly killed? In examining intentionality in going to war, do you think moral obligations to stop genocide constitute just cause for using force to settle a conflict?

COOLEY:

These are all interesting questions that you raise, and they are difficult as well. To answer them requires that I avoid the trap of being too idealistic, especially since I advocate a very pragmatic way to think about solving real-world problems. The theoretical is nice for those who can afford it, but actual life is often not in keeping with the abstract theory. Therefore, I need to find solutions that not only work but work well enough to achieve the ultimate goal that people and societies have to thrive.

Let me begin by saying that I am not advocating for Tolstoy's type of pacifism because it seems contrary to the human need to alter things for the better. Although it is a nice idea, and might work well if people were saints rather than human persons, it merely seems a form of passivism that allows things to happen no matter what they are. However, to thrive we need to actively engage others and our environment, which requires something with more power to it.

King and Gandhi have a much more appealing position. As you noted, King and Gandhi are pacifists of sorts, but ones who are far more practical. They know that their methods involve the use of power that can alter events in ways that outright violence can never do. The goal was to end violence by convincing enough people that it made no sense to continue as they had been.

Moreover, they would want to avoid violence based on the basic recognition that all involved are people deserving of the respect and emotional ties we should feel to all other fellow beings. Among other admirable features, Gandhi and King's methods should only be used after everything else has failed, which makes their methods a sort of just war thinking, only without the actual war. I see this as an approach that actively engages without resorting to self-defeating behavior—that is to say, if we want to end violence we cannot use violence.

For situations in which genocide happens, it seems to me that we assume that direct violence against those who are committing it will end that violence. That is, if we use force, then we will be successful and everything will set to rights quickly, efficiently, and for the long term. In other words, we see violence, and then believe that using a lot more violence or force in just the right way will stop things going awry.

But what do we actually perceive when examining military conflicts? We relearn the powerful lesson that it is easy to defeat an inferior force with a more powerful one, but it is impossible to conquer a country if it does not want to be conquered. The conflict in Afghanistan, for example, was intended to be a war against terrorism that would be easily won by the far superior force of the United States. If we could just remove this repressive regime and kill the leadership of the terrorist organization that attacked the homeland, then we could be safe from future attacks. More than twelve years later and at the cost of enormous treasure and, far more importantly, of life and limb, Afghanistan has shown why it was labeled the "Graveyard of Empires." The Taliban was thrown out of the government, but it remains a lethal and powerful force in that dysfunctional nation that looks to return to even worse conditions when the United States leaves it. Iraq is another example of the "violence to end violence" error. Vietnam is another, and so on.

It might be merely wishful thinking to believe that force can actually solve problems in the way portrayed through television and films. John Wayne was able to kill all the bad guys, and no new bad guys ever took their places in the power vacuums. But in reality, there is always someone there to keep the feud going for however long they can receive sufficient resources to do it. We should not be surprised by this fact; if a country invaded the United States, then we would be sure to do anything in our power to repel the invaders so that we could return to our own autonomy.

So what would I do about genocides that are horrific to watch unfold? My goal is to break the cycle of violence early on in one of three ways. First is prevention. Since any country may be involved in wars, and likely so, then it is imperative for every country to be involved actively in world events. The goal here is to know what is happening and be able to prevent the worst excesses from beginning in the first place. For example, it should have been clear that tensions were building in Rwanda between the Tutsis and the Hutus. Diplomacy at that time attacking the core of the problem might have been enough to ease those tensions. We could also have used police or covert intelligence agencies to infiltrate and break up groups bent on using extreme actions to make their case. By taking these precautions, we tend not to have situations that would cause us to go to war in the first place. In fact, it is morally reckless to act otherwise.

Second, nonviolent resistance has been shown to be effective. Since it has a good track record, why not use it for international conflicts? It will cost lives, and that is an ugly truth that we cannot ignore or minimize, but it will also be more successful in the long run to achieve the aims we seek. By rejecting the idea that we should be conquerors who can come in and use violence to solve a problem, we avoid creating a situation in which one side demonizes the other.

Third, often when outside entities become involved in a conflict, they make the situation much worse than it needs to be. By giving aid to a group picked by the outside entity, outsiders cause resentment from all other stakeholders involved in the situation. Those who were not favored now have to find an outside force to take their side, which draws in more and more people and creates greater chances of disaster for all. If the disfavored group cannot find such an outside party, they will still hate those who are benefited by the outsiders and the outsiders themselves.

By intervening militarily, the outside entity also prevents the immediate stakeholders from solving their own problems. The resources the outside entities provide do not allow the immediate stakeholders to become exhausted from the conflict in their own time. Exhaustion is a very good thing in these situations because it forces the stakeholders to step back and consider their actual options rather than blindly pursuing a path of destruction financed by others. The United States' exhaustion in the Vietnam War led the United States to leave the Vietnamese to work out their own problems, for instance. The Vietnamese did a terrible job in some instances, but no one would now consider Vietnam to be an evil place to live nor the Vietnamese government to be equivalent to some Orwellian horror story. It might not be what we want, but it is working for those who actually live there. Overall, the point here is that even if people are killing each other, if left alone, they will become exhausted and then begin the process of peace. Outsiders should remain engaged only to the extent that they are helping those involved to create their own peace on their own terms.

You have recognized that I think that war is always an impractical enterprise if one has the flourishing of the society as the primary responsibility of the government. As can be seen above, war is thought to be something that can solve problems, but it actually makes them far worse than a more involved, preventative method would achieve. In addition, I think that our ideologies make it impossible for our intentions and motives to be pure enough to justify going to war. As in the case of capital punishment, there always seems to be an underlying negative emotion or desire driving the entire enterprise. After all, when we see the atrocity of genocide, we become very angry at those who have done it. We want to harm them as much as they have harmed the innocent. Possibly, we want to harm them more.

But is this the type of people we want to be? Do we want to be driven by hate, anger, or whatever is making us think about committing the lives of our finest citizens and the treasure of an entire nation to a war that is likely to destroy both while not accomplishing the goals we have set for ourselves or for the war itself? Or do we want to be better people than that even though it hurts us emotionally to use slower, less-satisfying processes? Ethically speaking, the latter should be our course because it leads to our flourishing and our country's flourishing, so I think you are correct in identifying virtue as a significant component in my argument. We should act virtuously by doing what virtuous people do. If we think that the major religious figures are virtuous, then we should act on their example, as long as that is conducive to flourishing individually and socially.

My question to you deals with what I perceive as an inconsistency between the tenets of religions and how their adherents pursue them. Jesus and Mohammed, for example, eschewed violence against the innocent, but many Christians and Muslims do not seem to have a problem killing the innocent. In some cases, members of these religions use the concept of collective guilt to justify their actions: although the innocent are innocent, they belong to a group that is guilty; therefore, it is permissible to kill them. At other times, the innocent are merely means to a bigger end required by the god of that religion. So is it possible to get believers in religions that are generally against violence to see the error of their ways when it comes to pursuing war of any kind? What prevents them from seeing the contradiction?

Second, my grandfather used to say that the dirtiest word in the world was "religion" because religion had led to so much war and strife. Do you think that religious belief actually contributes to more war and violence than if people were agnostics or atheists?

STEFFEN:

Your question about religion and violence is actually a tricky one. You are right in saying that religious leaders can present a nonviolent vision for the resolution of conflict, but their followers may not follow the vision, resulting in inconsistency. The reason I mentioned Buddhism above is that it is generally perceived that this religion eschews warfare in ways that the Western theistic religions do not, and while in many ways that may be true, religious people will resort to war and uses of violence despite the teachings of their leaders and their traditions.

We need to be clear about the relation of a religious teaching to religious practice, and we should reflect again on the relationship of religion and morality.

Let me begin by observing that human beings are prone to engage in "reification," which is sometimes referred to as *the fallacy of misplaced concreteness*. The fallacy is that we can treat an idea or an abstraction as if it were concrete. When we take a concrete action that is clearly a human action and attribute it to cosmic interventions or the divine will, I think we engage in reification—that is, we mistake something that is not concrete (the idea) for something that is (the action).

War and using violence as a means to settle conflict are concrete human actions. When people and nations go to war, they of course want to believe they are justified in doing so. Justification is necessary because war is an evil involving killing and destruction, and to kill or destroy without justification is by ordinary moral lights a great moral evil. So we seek out moral justifications. Just war thinking guides the process of thinking about the moral meaning of using force, and in my view it will almost always lead to the conclusion that using violence as a means to settle the conflict cannot be justified—that "last resort" criterion of just war thinking alone should keep people from using violence for a very long time. When religion enters the context of justifying war and appeal is made to a divine sanction for violence, justification moves to a new and higher level—it goes "beyond the moral," so to speak. If God or some cosmic law or ultimate reality is believed to be providing justification for a use of violence or for a war, the messy and difficult and sometimes ambiguous work of providing moral justification can be fast-tracked. The just war criteria can be bypassed and people will believe themselves authorized to head directly to the bayonets and grenades.

What are we to say to justifications for uses of force when they are grounded in an appeal to "an idea"—the idea of God, Allah, the Buddha, or even democracy. From the moral point of view, what I think is going on when this happens is reification—people want to justify terrible things and they want to know that "ultimate reality" is allowing and even endorsing their violent actions. The concrete actions of human beings are being referred to an abstraction—the divine will—and the divine will is then the true agent of what is occurring. This is not too difficult to analyze morally; when "the fallacy of misplaced concreteness" is offered to justify uses of force, we can say that resorting to God's will as the reason for action allows human beings to abdicate responsibility—moral responsibility—and place it all on God, where questions about justification then do not even need to arise. Human violence and warfare for which humans are responsible are justified in the cleansing wash of the biggest and most comprehensive justification the human mind can conceive—that of the divine will. That is a moral analysis.

Theologically, a believer who holds that "God is on our side" will rest in the assurance of a divine justification. It covers all the bases, including the moral bases, since a justification for using violence and going to war that comes from God simply trumps any other kind of justification—this is why I said in my remarks in the first chapter that a divine command ethic can be extraordinarily powerful. How can a puny ethical evaluation of the good, right, and fitting stand up against a claim for justification vested in God—God, the arbiter of good and evil who is omniscient and thus knows perfectly all that is needed to know in matters of right and wrong?

So let me answer your question by reasserting the obvious—namely, that people will justify killing and destruction in the name of God. This is an empirical observation that is part of the historical record. You point out the contradiction between religious teaching and destruction undertaken in the name of religion, and you do this by comparing violent actions against teachings and texts that offer an alternative to violence. One problem to note, parenthetically, is that there are lots of texts and narratives sacred to traditions that actually do connect the divine to justifications of violence. Just in the Western theistic religions: Yahweh commands or endorses over one thousand acts of violence in the Hebrew Bible, human beings a mere six hundred. Muhammad was a military leader who led troops, was actually wounded in war, and authorized by an appeal to heaven the beheading of seven hundred captured Jews of Qurayzah in the town square, an event that religion scholar Karen Armstrong compares to a Nazi atrocity. Jesus used violence in driving merchants out of the Jerusalem temple and Christian Scriptures end with an apocalyptic vision of the end time—Christianity is, as you recognize, a religion that has a sad history of virulent and murderous anti-Semitism, crusading, witch-hunting, inquisitions, and all kinds of violent events for which sanction was found in an appeal to divine justice dispensed through the church and God's representatives.[19] I just want to acknowledge this history to make sure you understand that I think your question has standing and ought not to be dismissed or made subject to "apology."

You ask what it would take for people to see the contradiction between a leader's teaching and the practices of violence contrary to the teaching. Part of the answer is that the contradiction lies in the traditions themselves—they are imbued with violence and violent images and visions. Those visions can only be countered by a moral sense that evaluates such violence as wrong—even if texts say it is endorsed or commanded by God. The issue, then, is not so much to point out the contradiction but to point out the abdication of responsibility—these are human actions. By pushing such violence off onto God's will as the justification for the violence, an incredible action of reification is occurring—very concrete actions of killing and destruction, of violence toward women and children and nature and indigenous and marginalized peoples, are being denied as human actions for which human beings are responsible. Human beings are relegated to servants faithfully obeying what they believe is "the divine will." The thing people need to remember about religion is that it can be about anything—and is. Religion can be used to justify anything—and has been. It is only our moral sense, our natural and dare I say God-given sense of right and wrong that can lucidly point out our moral violations and our failures of human decency.

In thinking about ethics and the connection of religion to ethics, it is helpful to remember that through religion human persons find and construct answers to perplexing problems and, furthermore, that religious people can reify ideas about God and the divine will so that they can do unpleasant things—violent, destructive, and even murderous things—in order to avoid taking responsibility for them. That is not, of course, what religion always does or what all religious people do, but reification is a part of the inner dynamics of religion considered as a cultural force that serves human needs and aspirations. And people have a need to justify actions that are understood to be morally wrong—religion can be used to cover morally wrong actions with justifications that "pass human understanding," as the Christian Scriptures put it. Religion can certainly be involved in wonderfully creative and life-affirming things as well, but this involvement of religious people in violence where religion is made to

---

19. For the number of violent acts by God in the Hebrew Bible, see Eric A. Seibert, *The Violence of Scripture: Overcoming the Old Testament's Troubling Legacy* (Minneapolis: Fortress Press, 2012). For Karen Armstrong's reflection on the slaughter of the Jews of Qurayzah, see *Muhammad: A Biography of the Prophet* (San Francisco: HarperSanFrancisco, 1992), 207.

serve as the justification for morally wrong actions is the reification process that I think helps to respond to your question. Knowing this, the moral challenge for religious people is to confront the possibilities religion lays open to them and to be aware that they have to decide how they will be religious. This moral decision is profoundly important and is even more important—more basic—in some ways than religion itself.

On the question you ask in light of your grandfather's remark—the question of whether there has been more war and violence because people are religious—I want to say that the violence that goes on in the name of religion would, in many if not most instances, go on without it. Religion is an easy way to justify destructive actions, but I think people intent on destructive actions would do them with or without religion. I am tempted to ask whether the presence of religion might have lessened the number of violent acts over the ages, but of course there is no way to know either way. What we do know is that people will often appeal to religion to justify and sanction their actions. That does not make religion prone to violence or inherently violent—that misses the point of what religion is and how it functions. The significant point is that religion is something people do, and it can be used by people who act violently to justify their violence and that is, if I might make this generalization, a bad thing, morally speaking. We see this in other arenas of human experience. There are patriots who use their allegiance to their country to justify attitudes of hatred toward outsiders; there are people of one race who justify violence against others in the name of racial superiority. There is nothing inherently violent or hate-filled in being white or black, or in being a Belgian or an American or a Russian.

The great moral question for religious people is, as I just said above, how they will choose to be religious, and the options are wide open. Religion is often thought of as a "given," but from a moral point of view it is a *project:* it is something people decide to do, and people actually make decisions about how to be religious. Religion can inspire creative and beautiful things, and it can be used to justify all kinds of indecencies against other people. In the end, it is a decision about what to value, how to act, and who to be. Religion, as I understand it, is one more *moral project.* Understanding religion as a moral project—religion is more than that but it is also that—may help people become more aware that they *ought* to decide to be religious in creative and life-affirming ways because that is what the moral point of view, reasonableness, and human decency commend.

5

Suicide

INTRODUCTION

Anyone thinking about the issue of suicide generally begins with negative attitudes and conclusions on the subject, although there is a clear distinction between suicides done for purely bad reasons and those done as sacrifices for others.[1] Suicide is just an evil thing and wrong to do, as the vast majority of folks will tell us. That is why we have major programs in place to prevent people from taking their lives, one of which is the It Gets Better Project founded by Dan Savage.[2] The goal is to help lesbian, gay, bisexual, and transgender teenagers deal with suicidal thoughts that too often cause them to take their own lives. Our society also allows for individuals to lose their rights of self-governance if they are suicidal. In fact, if a person exhibits such signs they can be committed against their will by the state to mental institutions.

But we should always be wary of placing too much credence in what society does or how society feels about an issue, and we should also be careful about how our individual biases create unwarranted intuitions. Although these facts can be relevant moral factors, we have to remember that they are often not the sole or primary evidence justifying a conclusion. In too many situations, individual intuitions and social conventions are merely reflections of bias or tradition that have not been examined for their evidentiary weight. We have learned that such conventions are wrong, such as in the case of allowing slavery or keeping women subservient to men.

So, we cannot assume that suicide is always morally wrong or that it is forbidden merely because it is something that we individually or as a majority of the population would not do and think is morally wrong or bad when others

---

1. Tom L. Beauchamp and James F. Childress, *Principles of Biomedical Ethics*, 2nd ed. (New York: Oxford University Press, 1983), 93–94.

2. It Gets Better Project, http://www.itgetsbetter.org/.

do it. To see if our and society's views capture the moral view, we should first consider the most powerful arguments for and against suicide.

COOLEY

As always, I will begin with the standard philosophical arguments for and against the death-and-dying issue under consideration, in this case suicide, and then develop what I believe to be the most relevant issues in my own arguments.

ARGUMENTS AGAINST SUICIDE

Some important arguments for the standard moral view of suicide have been around for a number of years. Perhaps the most powerful philosophical argument is that of Immanuel Kant, who believed people are intrinsically valuable because they possess a good will. Most people interpret Kant as a philosopher who prohibited all forms of suicide because a person's taking his own life entailed that the person did not treat himself as an end in himself. That is, rather than respecting his value as a person with the good will that makes him a person, the suicidal individual degrades himself by acting in a way that his intrinsic value was used as a mere means to the end of taking his own life. In fact, Kant explicitly takes up several of the most common reasons people commit suicide—for example, avoidance of a life that is more painful than pleasurable—and then argues that those who want to commit suicide on these grounds cannot rationally act to kill themselves.

> A human being cannot renounce his personality as long as he is a subject of duty, hence as long as he lives; and it is a contradiction that he should be authorized to withdraw from this obligation, that is, freely act as if no authorization were needed for this action. To annihilate the subject of morality in one's person is to root out the existence of morality itself from the world as far as one can, even though morality is an end in itself. Consequently, disposing of oneself as a mere means to some discretionary end is debasing humanity in one's person.[3]

---

3. Immanuel Kant, *Metaphysics of Morals*, trans. Mary Gregor (Cambridge: Cambridge University Press, 1996), 177.

A suicidal person cannot rationally reject the very thing that made him a moral agent capable of choosing and acting as a moral agent in the first place. Basically, there is a contradiction in a suicidal person's thinking that must be resolved by eliminating the contradiction. Because people have self-love, which is the drive to stay alive no matter what the burden of continued life puts on a person, an individual cannot rationally take his own life based on what he thinks is self-love's dictate to avoid an existence of pain and suffering or some other state of affairs that makes his life not worth living. Given that preservation of personhood is far more important than destroying it to achieve some unworthy goal that cannot respect who he is as a person, suicide cannot be morally right.

Closely related to Kant's argument is the one based on the sacredness of human life. One of the main differences between Kant's argument and this one is the fact that Kant focuses on human persons, whereas the sacredness of human life argument concerns itself with life. Kant believes that human persons have the good will, which allows them to do what is right even though they might not succeed—thereby rejecting consequentialism's demand that the person acts because the action is right and each action must always be the very best that one can do. After all, it is irrational to expect an agent to be morally obligated to do the very best she can when she cannot control her action's consequences, which may be illicitly interfered with by other agents or forces. Having a good will entails that the entity with it is a person who is capable of being rational. Among rationality's necessary conditions are being able to choose freely and to have free will, giving evidence available to the person its proper weight, formulating efficient decision procedures and using them, changing one's beliefs and activities when adequate evidence becomes available to justify such an alteration, drawing inferences, and generalizing. Of course, such high-order mental activities require a brain that is capable of performing such tasks. For Kant, only mature humans could fulfill the requirements of rationality, which means that infants and severely mentally disabled adults, among others, cannot be moral agents and therefore do not have the good will. Nonhuman animals are also unable to have the good will because they lack the actualized potentialities of the necessary mental activities required to be a moral agent. Someone who is so irrational when it comes to suicide that she has lost her ability to control herself so that she can avoid the compulsion to kill herself may not be a moral agent relative to suicide decisions. If she kills herself, then it is not a suicide because it is not an action at all. Although she might be a moral agent relative to other decisions, she is not in suicidal instances because she cannot control herself. Free will has been lost through the compulsion; therefore, the event of her death is not an act performed by the entity killing herself.

However, if we think that life has sanctity, which is generally appealing to both religious and nonreligious individuals, then we can more efficiently explain why suicide and other takings of life are morally wrong.[4] Many people regard life as intrinsically valuable and, as a result, that it is morally wrong to destroy such worth for inadequate reasons. To intentionally and unnecessarily crush underfoot a worm that could be easily avoided produces in others a feeling of puzzlement, at the very least, about why the killer did his deed. It makes no sense to destroy the living when there is no need to do so. In fact, if we see such a person being pleased with his action, then we begin to wonder about the killer's mental stability.

The details of the sanctity-of-life argument can be filled out in different ways that yield different results, but two ways in particular will be examined here. First, let us assume that being alive is intrinsically valuable. That is, if something is living, then it has worth in and of itself because it has this property. Those things that are similar but do not have the property of being alive do not have intrinsic value. For example, a living worm and a dead worm are similar in their genetic material and appearance, but the living worm has a moral status that the dead worm lacks. If we stepped on the dead worm, then we might be repulsed on aesthetic grounds, but we would not have done anything that could be considered morally wrong or bad. However, if we step on the living worm and thereby kill it, then we can honestly say that something of moral significance was lost. It might not be morally wrong to do what we did, but it will be bad in that we took life value out of the world. In general, anything living that dies will reduce the value of the world.[5]

Suicides and all other takings of life with inadequate justification would be morally wrong and bad because their very nature ends an intrinsically valuable entity. If we add that the intrinsic value of life is incommensurable or so great that any ending of it could never be justified, then it follows that all suicides have to be morally wrong and therefore forbidden. On these same grounds, all takings of life, such as murder and abortion, will be prohibited.

Although I have argued previously that being alive should be assumed to have intrinsic value until it can be shown not to have such worth, basing the moral permissibility or impermissibility of suicide and other killings on this

---

4. See Ronald Dworkin, *Life's Dominion: An Argument about Abortion, Euthanasia, and Individual Freedom* (New York: Knopf, 1993).

5. At times, the death might actually improve the world's value. Suppose that the world has too many people and not enough food. If a person dies, then we can say that value has been lost from the person's demise but also that the world is a better place because the remaining people have enough food to have flourishing lives.

one moral factor alone is too problematic to adopt. First, life's intrinsic value is insufficient to justify the conclusion that all takings of life are morally wrong. If we allow that some self-defense killings are morally permissible, then we cannot simultaneously hold that all takings of lives are unethical. They might be bad, and in most cases are, but being bad does not mean that the action is also wrong. Wrongness requires additional or different criteria to be fulfilled, whereas badness merely means that something has reduced some good to the neutral or bad, or some neutral to the bad.

Second, and more importantly, in order for human beings to survive, certain other organisms have to die. Even a devoted vegan who never eats or uses an animal product still directly or indirectly causes death. The vegan has to survive by taking in a sufficient amount of nutrients, generally in the form of plants that are harvested and then eaten. The plants die so that the vegan may live, and no one would seriously consider that the vegan has done something wrong by preserving her life. In fact, if she decides that killing vegetables is morally wrong and decides not to continue killing them to sustain herself, we would be justified in trying to prevent her starvation. We might even be justified in institutionalizing her until she realizes the true value of plants in comparison to herself. If all takings of life, even if they are acts of omission, are morally wrong, then no moral agent who needs food can do anything that is morally permissible. The problem, of course, is making all life possess the same value and being unable to make distinctions between more and less valuable entities.

The sacredness-of-life argument can be developed in a different way that would give higher value to human lives than to the lives of other entities, eliminating the issue of uniform value based on possessing one property. That is, what is actually sacred is human life. If an entity is able to fulfill the conditions for being a member of *Homo sapiens* and being alive, then it has intrinsic value merely from possessing those two properties. Being alive and not a member of *Homo sapiens* would have either no intrinsic worth at all or a value that could neither equal nor exceed that of being a living human being.

Both value-ranking options have their advantages. If being alive has no value in and of itself, then we need not worry about the takings of life of any entities other than human beings. The death of animals would be neither morally good nor morally bad on the grounds of their being an end in and of themselves. Humans, then, would be permitted to use animals to eat, wear, employ in medical testing, or kill for any reason the humans see fit. The advantage of this option is that living humans are always the most important entities, and all of the troublesome gray cases in which animal and human interests conflict could be readily solved without difficulty.

Of course, a rejection of animal lives being of moral worth flies in the face of the general view that life is sacred and should not be wasted unnecessarily. As stated earlier, in the normal course of events it makes no sense to squander life when doing so is unrequired or produces little benefit at the tremendous cost. If we have a theory that incorporates the way we actually think about ethics and value and such a theory works well to help us achieve the ultimate goals of individual and social flourishing, then we should assume that life has value until it is shown conclusively not to have such worth.

The hierarchical ranking of lives based on the possession of the property of being alive and other properties conferring intrinsic value appeals more to common views about what is good in and of itself. Human lives are the most valuable because of their potential or actual rationality, nonhuman animals are second, and plants are third. The taking of a life should always be given proper moral weight and consideration when making decisions about what to believe and how to act, but not all lives have the same weight. If a human being needs to kill an animal in order for the human to preserve his life, then killing the animal is morally permissible. The same will apply to the killing of plants. At the same time, the life of any entity should not be ended without good moral reason. Under this interpretation, human life would be so valuable that to take it would always be morally wrong; therefore, suicide could never be morally permissible or right.

There are two objections that can be immediately raised to this position. First, when we talk about human life, many of us do not think about the quantity of life but its quality. It is not important to merely be alive; what matters is how good the life actually is. A life that is flourishing has intrinsic worth; being alive is merely a necessary means to be able to flourish. Being alive and being human are, by themselves, insufficient to generate this type of value because we can imagine human beings who undergo the worst sort of horrors that make their lives not worth living. In fact, taking a human life so that it can avoid descending into such a disvaluable, permanent condition may show respect for the sanctity of human life.[6] Suicide might actually be morally required in these situations.

Second, the valuing of life in this manner exposes us to the charge of speciesism. Peter Singer argues that if we value human being's pleasure or pain more highly than that of animals, without being able to find or explain a unique

6. Dworkin, *Life's Dominion*, 238.

feature of human pleasure or pain that sets it apart from nonhuman pleasure or pain, then we are being speciesist in about the same manner that racists are racist.[7] Much the same argument Singer makes about pain and pleasure can be made for life. If we cannot find some value in human life that is different from animal and plant life, then we cannot be rationally justified in ranking one above another. Of course, we could add other intrinsically valuable properties to the evaluation process, such as being rational, but that is not a property of being alive. After all, one can be alive and not be rational, as in the case of plants. And, in fact, there is nothing that separates and privileges human life above the life of any living thing. Every living thing is an organism and member of a species in the same way that any other living thing is an organism and member of a species. There is nothing special or even interesting about that. Therefore, if we want to create a hierarchy of value, we cannot do it with being alive alone, which we saw earlier.

The third argument against suicide is based on religion. Western religions prohibit suicide, even though many of their main religious texts say nothing about the taking of one's own life. One oft-employed argument focuses on the book of Genesis to argue for stewardship. God creates man and woman in God's image and then allows them to use the earth that God has also created. However, the text never states that God did all of this to make people totally free to do whatever they like with God's creation, including with themselves. In addition,

> [L]ife is God's gift to man, and is subject to His power, Who kills and makes to live. Hence whoever takes his own life, sins against God, even as he who kills another's slave, sins against that slave's master, and as he who usurps to himself judgment of a matter not entrusted to him. For it belongs to God alone to pronounce sentence of death and life, according to Deuteronomy 32:39, "I will kill and I will make to live."[8]

A divine entity created man and woman with a purpose in the divine entity's mind. After all, such a being would not do things randomly, so there has to

---

7. Peter Singer, *Animal Liberation* (New York: Harper Perennial, 2009).

8. St. Thomas Aquinas, *Summa Theologica*, in *Basic Writings of Saint Thomas Aquinas*, ed. Anton Pegis (New York: Random House, 1945), part II, Q64, A5. Aquinas uses the same type of argument, substituting Community for God: "Secondly, because every part, as such, belongs to the whole. Now every man is part of the community, and so, as such, he belongs to the community. Hence by killing himself he injures the community, as [Aristotle] declares" (ibid.).

be some sort of purpose to the creation of humanity. This position is further strengthened by claiming that the creation confers upon God property rights because each entity is created by God. Even if there is no individual creation, there is still an overall plan by God for the universe. Since people are part of the overall universe that is owned by God, they are owned as well. This is similar to owning the engine of a car. We own our car, therefore we own all the parts of our car, including its engine. If someone owns the whole, then it follows that the same person owns each of the whole's parts.

Since we are God's property, we do not have the authority to do with ourselves as we please. In fact, we have stewardship obligations to our bodies the way that we have duties to others whose property we have borrowed. For example, if we use our neighbor's lawn mower, then we must take due care of it. We cannot run it over large rocks, leave it without oil, or do other things that would make the lawnmower worse than when we received it from our generous benefactor. Our bodies, which are created by God, are far more important than an object such as a lawn mower. God has given us a special role to fill in creation, and that requires we take care of ourselves because we are God's property with a duty to do as God sees fit. Suicide cannot be permissible: if people do not own their individual lives, then people killing themselves robs the proper owner, God, of God's due property. Moreover, since the divine entity is likely to be angered by this theft of what is only on loan to us, it is prudent not to kill oneself.

St. Thomas Aquinas argued against suicide for the justification just described and for two more reasons involving natural law. Natural law theory, which represents divine order, states that whatever happens in nature is morally right and good, while those things that violate the natural order are morally wrong and bad. Suicide goes against the natural order: "First, because everything naturally loves itself, the result being that everything naturally keeps itself in being, and resists corruptions so far as it can. Wherefore suicide is contrary to the inclination of nature, and to charity whereby every man should love himself. Hence suicide is always a mortal sin, as being contrary to the natural law and to charity."[9] If we look to the animal world, we never see animals committing suicide. They can behave recklessly inasmuch as what they can shorten their lives below the average for their species, but animals cannot form the intention to take their own lives because they do not have the mental capacities to do so.[10] In fact, when we observe how humans and other animals behave in nature, we are sure to notice that each tries to preserve its life. The

9. Ibid.

10. We will leave aside whether the greater primates, such as some chimps, can pull this off.

lamb does not lie down with the lion, people do not step in front of cars bearing down on them, and no human or nonhuman animal seeks self-destruction in normal circumstances. In fact, animals fight for survival no matter how terrible conditions are, as we can notice from even the most minimal exposure to wildlife documentaries. If suicide is unnatural in the animal kingdom, of which human beings are part as animals themselves, then it must be the case that suicide is unnatural for humans. If we add that charity as a virtue is part of our human nature, although it is not part of nonhuman animal nature, and that charity requires that we love ourselves so much that we cannot kill ourselves and still be charitable, then the argument from natural law is supposed to become stronger. As in the case of using our moral agency to subvert our moral agency, we cannot use charity and self-love to subvert ourselves. Hence, suicide is morally wrong and bad for human beings, regardless of the reasons it is performed.

Not surprisingly, natural law theory arguments on suicide have their critics. David Hume uses natural law theory to prove that suicides do not violate natural law. Hume states that "all events in one sense, may be pronounced the action of the Almighty, they all proceed from those powers with which he has endowed his creatures."[11] By giving human beings the power of altering their environment through their actions, anything done with those divinely gifted forces has to be natural because those actions are caused by the powers that Hume states are God's workmanship to the same degree that the laws of motion and gravitation are God's.[12] If this is true, then it would be impossible for us to ever violate natural laws because everything we do is natural by its very definition.

Moreover, God expects us to take care of ourselves since nothing else in the universe has been given that charge save for us. "Men are entrusted to their own judgment and discretion, in the various shocks of matter, and may employ every faculty with which they are endowed, in order to provide for their ease, happiness, or preservation."[13] In other words, we are responsible for our own lives, which gives us enormous power in deciding how our actions should go. In normal circumstances, we and other persons are to be preserved and helped to flourish. But there might be other situations in which this is impossible or highly unlikely.

Given the two conditions of natural law theory, in certain situations suicide is not only permissible but might be the only rational action to take. If the

---

11. David Hume, *An Essay on Suicide* (Yellow Springs, OH: Kahoe and Company, 1929), 6.
12. Ibid.
13. Ibid., 7.

evidence is overwhelming that a person may no longer be able to preserve herself or have sufficient ease or happiness to justify continuing on with her life, then her faculties might tell her to end her life. The reasonable probability of being able to flourish makes it rational to see that end, but the high probability of a life not being worth living makes it irrational to remain alive. After all, if a person is unable to function as God intended, then it might be a sign to her that God wants her to no longer be among the living. Her faculties tell her the unfortunate but clear natural truth. On the grounds of natural law, she would be acting unnaturally by attempting to stay alive and fulfill her functions when there is no real probability of her being able to do so.[14] By clinging to a life not worth living, she is defying her constitution as God gave it to her and the situation that God created.

There are many who claim that suicide cannot be rational because suicide is the act of an individual who is not acting as a rational person would. In fact, although it is technically possible for a suicide to be rational, the vast majority of them are not, which entails that all suicides should be prevented because they are generally not based on the rational beliefs of rational people.[15] Of course, the definition of rational is vital in this argument. For many psychologists, "rational beliefs refer to beliefs that are logical, and/or have empirical support, and/or are pragmatic. Other terms, used interchangeably for these beliefs, are: adaptive, healthy, positive, and functional."[16] Although this definition is related to rationality as found in philosophy, there is a far greater emphasis within psychology on observable behavior and how minds work, which should not surprise us as these folks are psychologists. A rational belief has all of the following necessary factors:

1. Humans are constructivists and have a considerable degree of choice or free will. However, free will is constrained by the fact that individuals are also limited by strong innate or biological

14. Hume also argues against duties to others and oneself to stay alive. First, in situations in which staying alive produces only trivial benefits for society at great costs to the individual, then there cannot be a duty to the community (Hume, *Essay on Suicide*, 16). Second, when our continuing to live is too great a burden on ourselves and we have deliberated to a thoughtful, careful conclusion that things will remain this grave with no reasonable hope of change for the positive, then there is no obligation to suffer (18).

15. Peter V. Rabins, "Can Suicide Be a Rational and Ethical Act in Persons with Early or Pre-Dementia?," *American Journal of Bioethics* 7 no. 6 (2007): 47–49.

16. Albert Ellis, Daniel David, and Steven J. Lynn, "Rational and Irrational Beliefs: A Historical and Conceptual Perspective," in *Rational and Irrational Beliefs*, ed. Daniel David, Steven J. Lynn, and Albert Ellis (Oxford: Oxford University Press, 2010), 3–4.

tendencies, their community living context, and how they have learned from society to think, feel, and behave.

2. People have many goals and purposes—especially the goals of continuing to live, being reasonably free from pain, and being happy.

3. People's beliefs or cognitions are strong and influential in selecting their goals and values, but they are rarely, if ever, pure. Beliefs, goals, and values are interdependent and interrelated.

4. People's desires include, first, wishes and preferences.

5. People's desires also may include absolutistic shoulds, oughts, musts, and demands.

6. Human desires and preferences are usually healthy and productive, but absolute musts and demands are often unhealthy and destructive.

7. When people wish for something and don't achieve it, they usually have healthy feelings, thoughts, and behaviors of sorrow, regret, and frustration. These are healthy because they motivate people to get what they want and avoid what they do not want next time.

8. When people's desires escalate to arrogant demands, they often have unhealthy feelings, thoughts, and behaviors of severe anxiety, rage, and depression.

9. When people who wish to perform well and be approved by others, instead perform badly and are not approved by others, they often make themselves sorry and regretful and also make themselves severely anxious, raging, and depressed. They frequently feel sorry about their sorrow

10. When people demand of themselves that they perform well and be approved by others and they instead perform badly and are disapproved, they not only often are anxious, raging, and depressed but also make themselves anxious about their anxiety, enraged about their raging, and depressed about their depression. They have primary symptoms of emotional disturbance but they also have secondary symptoms—disturbance about their disturbance.[17]

So given the psychological requirements for a rational belief and action, is suicide rational? The answer would have to be uniformly negative. First, there is an acknowledgment that free will exists but is severely constrained by objective

17. Ibid., 6–7.

forces that help determine what is normal and therefore rational. Second, and perhaps most importantly, people have the goals of continuing to live, being reasonably free from pain, and being happy. Suicide is counter to two of those fundamental goals. Finally, depression and other emotions are unhealthy. Left unchecked, they spiral into greater depth and cause other unhealthy feelings, which can further rob people in such a state of their free will. Given that up to 90 percent of suicides have some form of mental disorder, which we have seen is intimately linked with other unhealthy feelings, it is clear why many psychologists would argue that suicides cannot be rational.[18] If more than half of suicides are committed by people who are depressed—a state that makes it more likely that a person will commit suicide—then those who take their own lives might not be acting as a moral agent should act.[19] As Michael Cholbi points out, those who commit suicide are very psychologically vulnerable, which seriously casts doubt their ability to rationally choose and carry out their self-killing.[20] Given that hopelessness and problem-solving deficits are the two best predictors of suicide attempts, we should be skeptical of merely accepting that suicide is a rational alternative for any person.[21]

It is, however, unclear if irrational behavior is even an action because if a person is not acting rationally, then we cannot say that he is acting at all. Actions require that the individual performing it can be held accountable for the action, which in turn requires that the agent have rational control. Since suicide is not a rational action, according to those who claim that the person's unhealthy feelings have unbalanced her mind, then it is neither right nor wrong for the person to kill herself. But just as we have a duty to prevent a child from wandering into a busy street, we have a moral obligation to prevent individuals from harming themselves in this way.

---

18. John Mann, "The neurobiology of suicide," *Nature Medicine* 4 (1998): 25–30.

19. M. M. Henrickson, H. M. Aro, M. J. Marttunen, M. E. Heikkinenen, E. T. Isometsa, K. I. Kuoppasalmi, and J. K. Lonnqvist, "Mental Disorders and Comorbidity in Suicide," *American Journal of Psychiatry* 150, no. 6 (1993): 935–40. F. Angst, H. H. Stassen, P. J. Clayton, and J. Angst, "Mortality in Patients with Mood Disorders: Follow-Up over 34–48 Years," *Journal of Affective Disorders* 68, nos. 2–3 (2002): 167–81.

20. Michael Cholbi, "Suicide Intervention and Non-Ideal Kantian Theory," *Journal of Applied Philosophy* 19 (2002): 245–59.

21. G. K. Brown, A. T. Beck, R. A. Steer, and J. R. Grisham, "Risk Factors for Suicide in Psychiatric Outpatients: A 20-Year Prospective Study," *Journal of Consulting and Clinical Psychology* 68, no. 3 (2000): 371–77. G. Dieserud, E. Roysamb, M. T. Braverman, O. S. Dalgrud, and O. Ekeberg, "Predicting Repetition of Suicide Attempt: A Prospective Study of 50 Suicide Attempters," *Archives of Suicide Research* 7, no. 1 (2003): 1–15.

There is considerable room for reasonable disagreement with the position that suicide is not rational. First, although useful, the definition of the term *rational* utilized by psychologists might not necessarily capture what it means for a choice or belief to be rational or for a person to act rationally. C. G. Prado combines definitions of *rational* from the *Oxford Companion of Philosophy* and *The Cambridge Dictionary of Philosophy* to produce an amalgam definition: the decision to end life is based on "sound reasoning and ... the act of ending life is for the best."[22] As can easily be discerned, Prado is not interested in a definition based on function per se but on a rational evaluation of whether continuing to live is better than dying. Margaret Pabst Battin provides a fuller set of criteria for rational suicide by joining together interest and cognitive conditions. An interest condition basically deals with how well the suicide fits with the individual's considered interests, and a cognitive condition focuses on whether the particular individual's assessment of her situation is satisfactorily rational and well-informed. Battin argues the following:

X is a rational suicide if

1. The facility for causal and inferential reasoning is adequately working.
2. The person possesses a realistic world view.
3. The information available to the individual is relevant to the decision
4. The suicide enables the person to avoid future harms, and
5. The suicide is consistent with the person's most fundamental interests and commitments.[23]

Criteria 1, 2, and 3 are cognitive conditions, whereas 4 and 5 are interest conditions. I would also add that time has a role to play in rationality in these situations. There are instances in which time is very limited, and the agent must make a rapid decision. This choice might not be rational had there been more time to analyze the situation, collect data, evaluate it, use the data in a rational decision procedure, assess the result, and do what must be done to satisfy

22. C. G. Prado, *Choosing to Die* (Cambridge: Cambridge University Press, 2008), 2.

23. Margaret Pabst Battin, *The Death Debate: Ethical Issues in Suicide* (Upper Saddle River, NJ: Prentice-Hall, 1996), 105. I have made Battin's conditions merely a sufficient set rather than a necessary and sufficient set. The reason is that there might well be other sets considered to be rational that do not have all five conditions or contain different criteria. For example, this set says very little about the interests and commitments of those in relationship with people contemplating suicide.

Battin's conditions. For example, a person might commit sacrificial suicide to save another person, but if the suicide had been able to know the person she saved, then she might not have done it. If the saved individual was a serial killer who would continue his crimes indefinitely, then it would not be rational to sacrifice the life of the potential hero for that of the killer. Hence, the amount of time, as well as other relevant resources, such as information, can have an effect on whether a decision or action is rational.

Clearly, rational suicide would apply only to a limited group of people. Those who are too depressed or have some other mental condition that prevents them from satisfying all five conditions can neither rationally choose nor commit rational suicide. Their takings of their lives would have to be classified as irrational. Although a suicide being rational carries no guarantee that others should not prevent it, an irrational suicide has at least prima facie justification for others to interfere in the decision on the grounds of its irrationality. The agent is not entitled to the presumption of being left alone because the proper use of his autonomy is lacking when he thinks or acts irrationally. Moreover, his irrational behavior will result in the loss of a great deal of intrinsic value when there is no reason for it to be destroyed.

ARGUMENTS FOR SUICIDE

There are a number of arguments in favor of suicide; some might make us more squeamish than others. Jeremy Bentham's quantitative utilitarianism states that at times it might not only be morally right but also a duty to take one's own life. Since utilitarianism is interested in maximizing utility, an individual person is not privileged as in Kant's theory. Act utilitarianism allows individuals to be treated as a mere means—whatever action produces the greatest amount of utility, or is tied for the greatest amount, is what the agent must do. Suppose that there are seven people awaiting organ transplants in a nearby hospital. Sam, who is a healthy person with all his organs intact, lives in the vicinity. If Sam's organs were harvested, then the seven people would live good, beneficial lives. Sam, of course, would die from the procedure. If Sam's organs stay in place, which he prefers, then he would live a good, beneficial life, but the other seven would die. If we merely consider the number of lives saved and the value of each life, then a quantitative value utilitarian would state that it is morally right for Sam's organs to be used to save the seven. After all, doing it will result in a net gain of six people surviving. On the other hand, not taking Sam's organs produces seven people dying, with one survival. That is a net negative of six people lost. Hence, on the mere grounds of cost-benefit analysis, Sam must die.

But it becomes worse if one is already worried about someone being obligated to die. If the very best action Sam can do is to die in a way that maximizes the potential for successful organ donations, then that is required of him. If we have a moral duty always to do the right thing and this action is the only permissible thing Sam can perform in the situation, then he would have to donate his organs, even though he really does not want to do it.

Libertarianism would never argue that there is a duty to die unless there is a legitimate contract requiring it, but based on the fact that freedom is the ultimate right, there always must be an entitlement to take one's life. Of course, as we have seen before, rights can be positive or negative. In the former case, if we have a right to suicide, then others would have to help us commit it. If it is a negative right, and this seems the most likely because it does not force others to help do something that might be abhorrent to them, then no one may legitimately interfere when someone is trying to kill himself. That is, they may not prevent the suicide as long as the person has chosen this course in an appropriate way, which would require that the action be a mere exercise of the right to take one's own life rather than the result of an irresistible internal or external force compelling the person. For example, if the person is severely depressed, then she might not be able to exercise her right in the proper way because she has lost her freedom through the mental compulsion. Even if she would act in the same way if she were not too depressed, the mental condition transforms what she does from an action to a morally neutral event similar to that of a dog biting the hand of a stranger. The dog's fear caused it to lash out; we cannot hold the animal accountable because it was not an action. For certain individuals, suicide is performed in the throes of an overwhelming emotion. Suicide done out of desperation, because of depression, or primarily as a result of some other overly coercive emotional force would not be an action at all, much less an action justified on the grounds of a free agent freely exercising her freedom to choose and act.

Not all libertarians think that this moral principle is capable of justifying suicide. John Locke, for example, has an argument against suicide that is similar to the one Kant employs: namely, that the grounds of the suicide are inherently contradictory. For Kant, one cannot use that which makes one a moral agent to justify ending one's life as a moral agent. For Locke, liberty can justify quite a few actions but not one in which the free agent freely chooses to take her own life. Basically, one cannot use freedom to justify destroying freedom. Freedom, at most, may maintain the freedom we have or even increase it, but it can never permit itself to be destroyed.[24] Locke argues something similar when he contends that free men can never enslave themselves.[25] To become a slave requires that the person freely choose to be a slave. However, by becoming a slave, the person has rejected the very freedom that allows him to be a person who can choose and whose choice should be respected. Since this is an impossible position, we can conclude that people are free and they can never act in a manner that would harm their freedom.

The position of virtue ethics on suicide is extremely difficult to ascertain with any certainty, although there is historical precedent found in philosophy in favor of suicide.[26] According to one interpretation of Hume, "there are cases where suicide not only promotes the interest of the individual but in fact honors and shows respect for the person's family."[27] In addition, suicide can be a "generous, charitable, or kindly act."[28]

The Stoics are perhaps the strongest example of a virtue ethics used to justify the taking of one's own life. In regard to becoming elderly and being in danger of losing one's reason through physical infirmities or pain, Seneca stated:

> The man who awaits his doom inertly is all but afraid, just as the man who swigs off the bottle and drains even the lees is over-given to his liquor. In this case, however, we shall try to find out whether the last part of life is really lees, or something extraordinarily bright and clear if only the mind's uninjured and the senses come unimpaired to the aid of the spirit. . . . I shall make my exit, not because of the actual pain, but because it's likely to prove a bar to everything that makes life worthwhile. The man who dies because of pain is weak and craven; the man who lives to suffer is a fool.[29]

There are two primary virtue-vice pairs in this decision. First, courage and cowardice are exhibited; second, foolishness and wisdom. A wise and courageous person chooses death when she knows that her life will no longer be worth living, given the near onset of the degradation of her mind through pain or loss of mental acuity to a point at which the person no longer remains as

---

24. John Locke, *Second Treatise of Government*, ed. R. H. Cox (Arlington Heights, IL: Harland Davidson, 1982), ch. 2, para. 6.

25. Ibid., para. 4.

26. Aristotle is against suicide. Aristotle, *Nicomachean Ethics*, trans. Roger Crisp (Cambridge: Cambridge University Press, 2000).

27. Thomas Beauchamp, "Suicide," in *Matters of Life and Death*, ed. Tom Regan (New York: McGraw-Hill, 1992), 101.

28. James Bogen, "Suicide and Virtue," in *Virtuous Persons, Vicious Deeds*, ed. Alexander E. Hooke, 645–50 (Mountain View, CA: Mayfield, 1999), 648.

29. Seneca, *Seneca's Letter to Lucilius*, trans. E. Phillips Barker (Oxford: Clarendon, 1932), 189–91.

a person. Cowardice and foolishness drive the individual who clings to life as a drunkard excessively drinks. In the latter case, clinging to life is self-destructive in that it destroys the person's virtue while trying to save it, in much the same way that Kant argues that suicide destroys the moral life in an attempt to preserve it. For Kant, the concern is the undervaluing of the life, whereas for the Stoics it is the overvaluing of the life.

Given the nature of the beast—virtue ethics is about character rather than action—a case can be made for suicide being morally wrong in certain circumstances and morally right in others. If we understand virtue ethics as a theory that promotes being virtuous, then it can be a virtuous person who commits suicide just as long as her action exhibits a virtue in the proper way. For example, Captain Oakes left the tent on a disastrous expedition to Antarctica in order to improve his friends' chances of surviving. His suicide is thought to be noble and courageous because it is one of sacrifice for those one holds dear. If he was doing it merely to get back at someone for not being nice to him, then it would not be virtuous and we would not be as interested in it as a tragic situation.

The difficulty with virtue ethics is figuring out what a virtuous person would do in a particular situation. One virtuous person might commit suicide while another heroically struggles to stay alive out of respect for himself or others. Perhaps, he continues to suffer so that others who rely on him can become virtuous or maintain the virtues that they have. The best we can do with virtue ethics is to say that in some clear cases, it is virtuous to commit suicide, but there cannot be an obligation to do so as long as there is an alternative that is also virtuous that does not entail the taking of one's own life.

Narrative philosophy is a combination of existentialism and feminist philosophy. First, it is existential in that it encourages people to create meaning in their own life on the grounds that no meaning exists until a person chooses it for herself. That is, the values and way we view things in this world are not real in any sense of being eternal, universal, or objective. Rather, the truth is nonexistent until a person selects it for herself. If she decides that a common practice in society is unethical, then, in her world and for her, it is unethical. If she wants to make it ethical, all she needs to do is choose it for herself.

Narrative philosophy is feminist in that it challenges the notion that ethics is a set of objective, universal, eternal, rational, and cold principles. Deontological theories, such as that of Kant, and consequentialist theories, such as those of Bentham and Mill, have been criticized because they reduce each individual person to an abstract entity that looks at ethics from a cold, rational viewpoint. In Kant's world, emotions are bad if they interfere with pure reason.

In Bentham's quantitative and Mill's qualitative worlds, cost-benefit analysis is the only thing that matters in the end, as poor Sam discovered.

But there is more to ethics than pure, abstract reason. Emotions and relationships matter as well, as anyone who functions in a society will tell you. For instance, I should privilege my own children over those of other people because my kids are vulnerable and dependent on me and *because I care for them*. I do not have to use reason or create an argument for that conclusion; I know it as a brute fact. Care is the primary motivator of my actions, and that care, rather than some abstract legalistic principle, determines whether they are right or wrong.

A purely rational person would not take such a parent-child relationship into moral consideration unless it somehow was dependent on utility or was something a purely rational person would do. That is, the relationship has to have some sort of bearing on ethics by having moral value that should be part of a decision process or having some other effect on the morality of the situation. But a purely rational approach to ethics makes little sense because of the inability to be ethical if we are coldly rational people. In order to do what we must, we must care about it in some way. That is, we naturally desire to be ethical beings and this provides the motivation for us to be moral in our persons and actions. We cannot get this motivation through pure reason alone; emotions provide the motivating force to move us internally to make decisions to act or not to act, and to be a certain way or not to be that way.

The operating question of narrative ethics is what kind of life narrative we want to write for ourselves. Basically, we have power as a result of the subjective nature of existence. Our lives are not fully determined by forces outside of ourselves, such as genetics, how we were nurtured, and the society and environment around us, although those have a significant impact on who we are. Instead, we have the ability to help mold our identity in ways that can create part of our essential personality as individuals. If we want to have a life narrative in which we are courageous, then we have to act courageously. By choosing and acting in this manner, we have created a life narrative for ourselves that would have been essentially different had we taken another path. Many of our end goals are objective and universally shared with all people, such as flourishing for as long as we can thrive. Many others, perhaps more than the objective, universal goals, are decided by us. What sort of career we select, with whom we share our lives, and so on are within our power and therefore become part of the story of who we are—first, by making the choice itself, and, second, by how well we fulfill that choice.

A person's life narrative helps determine what ending a person's life should have. Suppose Dorothea has lived a life of rich and satisfying independence. She does not want to lose her mental faculties or end her life in a nursing home as a burden to her family. Nor can she stand the thought of being helpless so that other people have to feed, clean, and help her do the normal things that keep her alive and physically in good condition. Any of those outcomes would be discordant with whom she has chosen to be—it would be the wrong note in an otherwise perfect life concerto. If she decides to commit suicide, then she is being consistent with her life story and how she wants her final narrative to end. She would die as authentically as she lived.

On the other hand, if someone has lived a life in which death is avoided at all costs, then suicide would not be consistent with her life narrative. That is, it would not be authentic given the choices she has made and lived that shaped her life. For this individual, suicide would be the discordant note in her life story. However, we have to remember the subjective nature of narratives that make them tend toward relativism. Because there is no value until it is created by the person living the life, taking her own life could only be justified if she wanted her narrative to end in a way that was vastly different from the rest of her life. Therefore, it will often be difficult for others to judge if a suicide is authentic or not; however, given people's tendency to act in character, an action that "fits" the person's character is more likely to be authentic than one that does not.

STEFFEN

"There is but one truly serious philosophical problem, and that is suicide." So asserted Albert Camus in his famous and very short essay, "The Myth of Sisyphus."[30] This may seem an unduly provocative comment, but Camus was beholding this truth: if suicide is connected philosophically to the question about the meaning of life, suicide is an option for the person who believes that life has no meaning. For Camus, believing that life is meaningless is not the same as believing that life is not worth living, and in this essay he actually takes the meaninglessness of life as his starting point. He faces the absurdity of living in a universe without meaning, shunning on the one side suicide, which is an admission that life is not worth living, and on the other hope, which generates faith in values, including religious values, that prevent us from seeing the absurd. Clearly Camus is not advocating suicide, but he is saying, in effect,

---

30. Albert Camus, *The Myth of Sisyphus and Other Essays*, trans. Justin O'Brien (New York: Vintage Books, Random House, 1955), 3.

"If life is meaningless and you are choosing to live, then why—what is your reason?" This is an unusual place to start a philosophical inquiry, and many would disagree with Camus's premise about the meaninglessness of life, but it is a great question and does place before us the task of creating meaning, which is a life project that falls to all of us.

Camus connects suicide to questions of meaning and discusses it not in a moralizing tone where the point is to condemn suicide, but from a perspective in which suicide can be seen as a reasonable response to a certain way of viewing life itself. Because suicide is fraught with overwhelmingly negative moral connotations, we are rarely able to talk about suicide in this "reasonable" way, and that, too, is understandable. For a suicide emotionally disrupts people and shocks communities, and it never fails to leave behind grief-stricken families and friends. Suicide causes enormous pain.

In this chapter I actually want to spend more of my effort on religious viewpoints, which I think are assumed to be more absolutist in opposing suicide than I think they actually are, but I do not want to forgo a brief ethics discussion. The natural law ethical perspective I have advocated as the best method to discern and construct moral meaning would approach suicide as a moral issue by articulating a common moral agreement. Without controversy, that common moral agreement asserts opposition to suicide. Establishing suicide as a wrongful act can be accomplished by various ethical approaches, including Kantianism and consequentialism. The Cooley essay opening this chapter has presented these various ethical approaches and I see no need to revisit that discussion.

My task will be to see if we can reason our way to an idea of "just suicide" in the face of moral attitudes that strongly oppose such a possibility. I think it is important to keep in mind that 90 percent of all suicides involve mental illness (depression or disorders like dysthymia, bipolar disorder, or schizophrenia) or substance abuse.[31] This raises the specter of diminished capacity in the suicide victim who is thus to be regarded not as a fully competent rational agent but as a person afflicted with a mental disorder beyond the agent's control, whose judgment is negatively affected and whose decision-making capabilities are impaired. This background will affect my claim that a suicide committed for morally justifiable reasons will be an extremely rare occurrence.

Life is a good of life, even a "preeminent good," as I have argued, because all the others depend on it for their enjoyment and realization. But as one good among many others, it is in relationship to other goods, and the moral

31. "Fact Sheet: Facts about Mental Illness and Suicide," University of Washington, School of Social Work, 2013, http://depts.washington.edu/mhreport/facts_suicide.php.

question would be whether there could ever be a situation that would allow us to overrule the good of life and justifiably lift our agreed-upon prohibition on suicide. One of the problems here is to devise illustrative cases for consideration. If the overwhelming majority of suicides—90 percent—are committed by persons whose capacity for rational decision making is in some way impaired, then what kinds of cases would make up the remaining 10 percent in which persons are making a rational, unimpaired decision for suicide? I would have to assume that most of those in that 10-percent category involve serious medical conditions where the decision to end one's life is made to avoid pain, to unburden families, and to assert some control over life in the effort to preserve "dignity" at the end of life. (We deal with medically related suicides in a later chapter on physician-assisted suicide.)

So if we exclude all those suicides that are the result of impaired judgment due to mental illness or drug abuse—and there are in the United States about thirty thousand a year—and the probably large proportion of the remaining 10 percent that are a result of people making decisions to end their lives due to terminal illness, what is left?[32] The impaired judgment suicides would come under the heading of "human tragedy" but from an ethics perspective ought not be seen as the actions of rational agents making reasoned decisions in their own and others' best interests. Recognizing that people with terminal illnesses actually do commit suicide (even without the legal protections afforded citizens of states that have physician-assisted suicide laws), I would say that decisions for suicide related to terminal illness can be classified in one of two ways: either they could be seen as acts motivated by depression, in which case we could put them in the larger 90-percent category of nonrational, diminished capacity suicides—human tragedies—or they could be deemed rational suicides. Rational suicide is controversial as a concept, especially in light of ethical perspectives, such as Kantianism, that deny such a possibility. Kant, however, is a moral absolutist, and the ethically moderate perspective I am advocating in these pages holds open the possibility of a rational suicide—namely, a suicide committed in a particular instance for good reasons sufficient to overcome our common moral agreement against suicide. The ethics task is to articulate those conditions or criteria that would uphold the moral presumption against suicide yet make a decision for suicide morally possible if the decision is reasonable and addresses our concerns for the goods of life, including the good of life itself, and our concerns for justice.

---

32. "Suicide Facts," Suicide Awareness Voices of Education (SAVE), http://www.save.org/index.cfm?fuseaction=home.viewPage&page_id=705D5DF4-055B-F1EC-3F66462866FCB4E6.

Particular cases that would qualify as "just suicide" would be rare because we are dealing with fully endowed members of the moral community, persons possessed of reason and committed to respecting persons, including themselves, and killing oneself or another is presumptively disrespectful. Yet for the relatively small number of cases we would be considering, persons would be committed to adopting the moral point of view. They would show respect for persons, including themselves; they would be committed to including others in their deliberations; they would seek to avoid harming others; and they would be acting within the given circumstances to realize the goods of life even to the point of allowing the particular good of life itself to be overruled by the weight of other goods. This identifies the process by which moral grounds would be established for a justified suicide.

A theory of "just suicide" would pertain only to fully endowed members of the moral community. It would affirm a strong moral presumption against suicide, although it would hold open the possibility of a justified suicide if the following conditions were met:

1. The individual contemplating suicide is not suffering from mental illness or defect that which would impair judgment and present diminished capacity to the moral community.
2. By contemplating suicide the individual must not be expressing contempt for the good of life but continue to regard life as a good that ordinarily ought to be promoted.
3. Some issue of "just cause" has arisen that has made suicide a live option for consideration. The cause must be such that suicide appears to be the best way to affirm the value of the good of life beyond the life of the person contemplating suicide.
4. A conflict has arisen in which a person experiences a conflict between the good of life and other goods, and it may be resolved, as Dennis Cooley has written above, by an action that can only preserve one's moral life and commitments at the expense of physical life.
5. The suicide must be a last resort. Every option short of suicide must be explored before allowing suicide to become the preferred action.
6. The decision for suicide must be directed to advancing the good of others and not be done solely for one's own benefit.
7. The decision for suicide, while being forced on one by the press of circumstances, must not obscure a role for autonomy, and the

decision for suicide may involve a desire to take action prior to a foreseen loss of autonomy, say, though torture or the onset of dementia.

8. The decision for suicide must appear reasonable in light of circumstances that are depriving the person of a future in which he or she may pursue and enjoy the goods of life.

There may be other criteria to involve in this picture of "just suicide," but this provides the kind of moral framework I would advocate in order to establish that a suicide is in fact justified from a moral point of view.

So what would be an example of a justified suicide? Let's imagine an individual, Jules, who is captured by a ruthless aggressor enemy in a warfare scenario. Jules has knowledge of the location of many innocent persons who are in hiding from the enemy. Jules fears that if he were subjected to torture, which now that he is captured seems likely, he will disclose the locations of these individuals. In fact, Jules fears that his interrogators are likely to use drugs that would glean information from him without his consent or knowledge and undermine his ability to control a refusal to disclose—some kind of truth serum like sodium thiopental. Subjected to such a drug, Jules would be putting many innocent lives at stake. He considers suicide to protect the innocent from becoming victims of unjustified killing. I would think this kind of situation would provide grounds for a "just suicide."

The problem with this situation is that if we also consider that the war in which this conflict arises is prompted by unjust aggression, then Jules is being coerced into this situation because of injustices larger than his situation and over which he has no control. So what looks to be a possible case of just suicide is provoked by the dynamics of an unjust war, and that could and should affect how we understand the course of action Jules is considering. We could hold the view that suicide is wrong even in this situation and that Jules is not responsible for other acts of evil over which he has no control. My own view is that however unjust the context for decision making, we face moral quandaries always in contexts that require deliberation, and the details of the situation will determine how a decision is to be made. We can understand other contexts of enormous injustice, such as those patriarchal societies in Europe and in America that burned witches—would women in those situations have been justified in killing themselves rather than face trial and execution for witchcraft? What about the woman who is raped and deemed no longer pure in a social context where any hope for a future depends upon her purity? Would we morally condemn her decision for suicide in that context, as tragic as it would be? Do contexts of injustice that rob persons of their futures or force them into being unwilling contributors to evil also rob them of autonomy, and can people ethically and autonomously address injustices by engaging in acts of resistance or noncooperation with evil, including possibly, in certain situations, suicide? In a context of injustice, can suicide be an act of defiance that deprives the perpetrators of injustice of one's unwilling assistance in their wrongdoing? Can resistance to evil justify suicide as an act of political noncooperation that is, morally speaking, also aimed at preserving the goods of life and advancing values that together may be more important than the good of life itself, as was demonstrated in the suicides of Theravada monks in Vietnam in the 1960s and more recently in the suicides of Buddhist monks in Tibet?

The point I would emphasize is that a justified suicide—a suicide not involving mental illness, drug use, or terminal illness—would be rare, and that is as it should be. The ethics perspective being used here is modeled on the formal features of just war thinking, and one parallel between just war and just suicide must be noted: lifting the presumption against using force to settle conflicts by meeting the criteria for a justified use of force in just war thinking should be an extremely rare occurrence, and so should it be in justified suicide.

This perspective on just suicide avoids an absolutist prohibition on suicide while holding open the possibility for suicide being justified from the moral point of view in certain peculiar and difficult circumstances. I find the idea of an "obligation to die" or a "duty to die" via suicide pushing way past the most serious ethics chore, which is simply to provide a possible justification for suicide in certain kinds of unusual situations. I think a theory of just suicide could direct an individual to consider suicide as a justifiable act if it accords with both the moral presumption against suicide and the criteria required to lift the suicide prohibition, but the idea of moving from justification to an "obligation" raises what I think are insurmountable difficulties. Let me say a little more on this issue.

"Just suicide" creates a framework for decision making, but it does not propose to make the decision for an individual. The idea is that suicide could be justified and thus rendered a viable option, but it requires nothing obligatory. The individual is still free to make a decision. The theory of just suicide holds that if the criteria are met, the decision to proceed to suicide can be considered a responsible and morally permissible act in the particular circumstance. In the case described above, Jules is of the opinion that he could not withstand torture and could be the unwilling cause of innocent lives being unjustly lost, but another individual also captured and also possessing the same knowledge about innocent people might think otherwise. Suicide is not for everyone. Even in the just suicide perspective, it could be justified in only a very small number of peculiar situations.

We have difficulty invoking the important moral principle of universalizability because that principle holds that persons in similar situations should act similarly. The practical reality, however, is that everyone is not similarly situated—even if it by outward appearance it seems so—because of the subjective aspects of individual moral personalities. If we have an obligation or duty, it is, as Kant would say to us, to do what is good, right, and fitting as reason commends us to obey the moral law. We are not obligated to take on the responsibility of an unjust act committed by others who want to involve us in a wrongful act or injustice, especially when we can never really know the consequences. One's decision-making autonomy should not be held captive to a formal principle like universalizability when a deeper analysis shows that the idea of "like actions in like situations" does not apply because the ostensibly "like situations" differ as a result of individual moral personalities and the variable of conscience. If it were an obligation to commit suicide in a particular circumstance, then one's autonomy would not be exercised in deciding about the appropriateness of suicide since it could be construed that suicide was rationally required of anyone who was in this situation. That would be to advance universalizability over autonomous decision making, and, furthermore, it would actually suppress the importance of the individual moral personality.

Some persons who might face a "just suicide" situation would oppose suicide not out of cowardice but because the violation against the good of life would be unconscionable. For persons with a moral personality so constituted and so burdened, the idea of acting in a way that jeopardized their moral personality (or their soul) would not allow them to proceed, and criterion 4 above, which pertains to resolving a conflict by preserving values at the expense of physical life, would support them in not proceeding. The just suicide theory takes this reason for not proceeding into account. I think this criterion actually prevents suicide from ever rising to the level of an obligation, and I therefore do not believe there is any "duty to die" via suicide. Creating a structure for moral thinking that renders suicide a morally permissible and ethically sanctioned *possibility* is hard enough, and it is as far as I think we can go—and that is far indeed.

Let me now turn to some religious perspectives on suicide. Religious traditions oppose suicide in teachings, scriptures, and practices, but I wish to show in a brief space here that there is actually some "play" in how suicide is approached and talked about in the various religious traditions. That religions endorse general prohibitions against suicide is easy enough to assert, for this is a true statement. Yet there are some cracks in the prohibitions that are worth considering. There are some religious defenses of suicide that could be deemed morally acceptable (and not religiously condemned), given that they meet the criteria set forth in the just suicide position laid out above.

Judaism's traditions oppose suicide for a theological reason: since God holds ownership rights to everything God has created, including the human body, our bodies belong to God and not to ourselves. Human beings have no right to destroy what God has entrusted to them, and God's rules and guidelines are designed to preserve life. Self-injury is proscribed, and certainly suicide is forbidden. Only in the case of martyrdom is suicide given a pass, as in the case of being forced to convert to another religion or facing torture. (Judaic thinkers acknowledge that the value of life can be overruled in coercive situations, one being the prospect of extreme suffering, another being to prevent committing a cardinal sin which would include idolatry—that is, denigrating or defiling God's name—murder, or sexual immorality.)[33] Eliott Dorff relates the story of Rabbi Ephriam Oshry, who permitted a man about to be tortured by the Nazis to commit suicide rather than betray the location of other Jews, "but Rabbi Oshry did not permit this ruling to be published for fear that it would undermine the commitment to life of the other Jews of the Kovno ghetto, and, other authors . . . have taken pride in the small number of Eastern European Jews who committed suicide in the midst of the Nazi terror."[34]

The Hebrew Bible contains stories in which suicide—an act of intentional self-killing—occurs, and subsequent reflection does not lay censure on the act. In the book of Judges, the story is told of Samson, famed for using the jawbone of an ass to kill one thousand Philistines and defeat them (Judg. 15:15-17). Samson's marriage to Delilah led to the discovery of the secret of his great strength, his uncut hair, which was then cut and his strength was lost. The Philistines gouged out Samson's eyes and he was imprisoned. Brought before his enemies to entertain them, Samson prayed for strength, grabbed the pillars in the house where three thousand Philistines were gathered, and pulled them down. "Let me die with the Philistines," were his last words (Judg. 16:30). Samson knew he would die by his act of destruction and he intended to die this way; nevertheless he is remembered in the tradition as both a flawed and failed judge of Israel and a great leader because he began to rescue Israel from its enemies.

King Saul committed suicide by falling on his sword and not allowing his body to be defiled by the uncircumcised enemies of Israel (1 Sam. 31:3-5)—and

---

33. See the discussion of Jewish exceptions for suicide in the chapter on physician-assisted suicide.

34. Elliot Dorf, "Assisted Suicide," *Journal of Law and Religion* 13, no. 2 (1998–99): 267–68.

the biblical commentators do not object. Neither does the Talmud object to the decision of children to commit suicide rather than submit to sexual violation.[35] It seems that the Rabbis in their reflection and commentary on Jewish law confined suicide to the act of self-killing committed by persons who were possessed of free will and mentally competent. Those suffering from mental illness or temporary insanity were not considered to be ending their own lives by a free exercise of the will and thus could be granted a normal Jewish burial.[36] Judaism allows that some situations may allow a justified exception to the prohibition on suicide, but Judaism takes a strong stand against the voluntary and freely chosen act of suicide.

Josephus tells the story of the Jews of Masada, the mountain fortress in the southern Israeli desert near the Dead Sea to which Jews fled near the end of the First Jewish-Roman War. During the siege, which took place in 73, perhaps even 74 C.E., the Jews of Masada, rather than submit to capture and enslavement by the Romans, committed mass suicide. So far is such a prospect from core Jewish affirmations about life that the story of the Masada suicides may be deemed apocryphal. On the other hand, surrender to the Romans could have been considered a desecration of God's name, and a possible justification could be attached to the cardinal sin of idolatry. In any event, the historical record about this incident is not thoroughly reliable, and the Masada story of mass suicide may have more "mythic" value in inspiring resistance to the enemies of Israel than in presenting an unbiased account of an historical event in which a Jewish community preferred death over slavery. There are more reliable stories of Jews committing communal suicide in Europe during the Black Plague (fourteenth century), when suicide was preferred to submitting to the murderous rampages of frightened Christians who were blaming the Jews for the plague and who tortured and killed Jewish men, women, and children indiscriminately.

Although a few ambiguities (ambiguities rather than qualifications) attend the moral meaning of suicide in Islam (these are medically related and mentioned in more detail in the chapter on physician-assisted suicide), the prohibition on suicide in Islam appears to be strict. Suicide "trades a transient, unbearable life in this world for an even more horrible, eternal one beyond," which is to say that suicide is an offense against Allah that will earn hell and damnation for the person who commits suicide.[37] There is a dispute in Islam

35. Ibid., 266.

36. Ibid.

37. Abdulaziz Sachedina, *Islamic Biomedical Ethics: Principles and Application* (Oxford: Oxford University Press, 2009), 168.

over what constitutes an act of suicide versus what can be legitimately regarded as an act of martyrdom. Suicide is condemned, but martyrdom, which can entail willful self-killing as it did for the Islamic radicals who hijacked planes on September 11, 2001, transforms the self-killing into an act of high spiritual meaning pleasing to Allah. All the Western religions praise the person who loses his or her life through the sacrifice of life—voluntary or involuntary—that defines martyrdom.

The Christian Scriptures only relate one instance of suicide, that of Judas, a disciple of Jesus, who is remembered in the tradition for having betrayed Christ to the Romans who then subsequently executed him. In the story told in only one Gospel, Judas, obviously guilty and regretful for what he had done, says, "I have sinned by betraying innocent blood," and then, throwing away the thirty pieces of silver he received, Judas "departed; and he went and hanged himself" (Matt. 27:5-6). The story seems intent on showing that by this blood money a prophecy from the Hebrew Bible (Jeremiah) was being fulfilled. Judas's "suicide" is also mentioned in Acts 1:18, but in that version Judas used his betraying fee to buy a field into which he falls forward and bursts open—the text does not say that he fell voluntarily, only that he fell. In neither story is the suicide, if the second story is a suicide at all, specifically condemned—it is Judas's betrayal of Jesus, rather than the suicide, that is remembered and censured. Dante will put Judas at the very bottom of hell, condemning him for having done the worst thing any human being has ever done—betraying Christ. His suicide does not come under any specific moral analysis, except that the writer of Matthew suggests it was motivated by guilt, which, for the Christian writer, was probably an indication that Judas had not lost his moral lights but had, to the contrary, discerned the absolute wrongness of his deed and his need for self-punishment. All four Gospels record Judas's betrayal, but only one, Matthew, includes any detail about Judas's suicide and that for reasons of showing prophecy fulfilled, which is a particular interest in Matthew since it is a Gospel addressed to a Jewish audience.

Jesus' own death could be seen as a suicide, a version of "suicide by cop," if in fact Jesus knew he would be arrested, tried, and crucified by going to Jerusalem and, knowing this, then deliberately pursued a course of action leading to this exact outcome. The Christian tradition remembers his story as one of sacrifice, however, with Jesus playing the central role in a divine drama that would lead to the reconciliation of humanity with God over the issue of human sin and unfaithfulness. The divine drama raises its own questions: why would a good and gracious God ask of anyone a blood sacrifice such as the one Jesus is supposed to have made voluntarily on behalf of humanity? We shall leave this and turn to another kind of comment about suicide in the Christian tradition.

Christians, be they Roman Catholic, Orthodox, or Protestant, oppose suicide and regard it as a sinful act, although many Christians take a nonjudgmental stance against persons who commit suicide for reasons of mental illness or medically related end-of-life concerns. But the opposition to suicide in general is clear. Thomas Aquinas argued that suicide, being an act contrary to nature, was a sin against self, neighbor, and God. Moreover, Thomas insists that suicide defies our social obligations and arrogantly denies God the exclusive right to decide when a person's life is over. "To bring death upon oneself in order to escape the other afflictions of this life," Thomas wrote, "is to adopt a greater evil in order to avoid a lesser. . . . Suicide is the most fatal of sins because it cannot be repented of," which is why suicide is a mortal sin that would exclude a person from eternal life with God.[38] The 1997 *Catechism of the Roman Catholic Church* captures the heart of this Thomistic understanding and addresses suicide in its section on the Fifth Commandment (or sixth, by other readings of the Hebrew Bible), the "thou shalt not kill" commandment. After making the case that we are stewards of the life God has given us as a gift and noting the obligation "to accept life gratefully and preserve it" as the appropriate way to honor God, the *Catechism* goes on to say:

> 2281. Suicide contradicts the natural inclination of the human being to preserve and perpetuate his life. It is gravely contrary to the just love of self. It likewise offends love of neighbor because it unjustly breaks the ties of solidarity with family, nation, and other human societies to which we continue to have obligations. Suicide is contrary to love for the living God.
>
> 2282. If suicide is committed with the intention of setting an example, especially to the young, it also takes on the gravity of scandal. Voluntary co-operation in suicide is contrary to the moral law.

By this last statement the *Catechism* explains Roman Catholic opposition to physician-assisted suicide, or assisted suicide in any other form, but account is taken of the psychological dynamics that could lead a person to pursue the suicide course due to circumstances and psychological conditions beyond an individual's control. The *Catechism* acknowledges that those who commit

---

38. Thomas Aquinas, *Summa Theologica*, Part II-II q. 64, A5. http://www.newadvent.org/summa/3064.htm#article5.

suicide may be suffering "grave psychological disturbances, anguish, or grave fear of hardship, suffering, or torture," which create the condition of diminished responsibility, and thus the stance of the church is one of compassion: "2283. We should not despair of the eternal salvation of persons who have taken their own lives. By ways known to him alone, God can provide the opportunity for salutary repentance. The Church prays for persons who have taken their own lives."[39]

Christian opposition to suicide would in general follow these views—the act is in general wrongful and a grave, mortal sin, except that allowance must be made for the conditions of psychological distress, suffering, and torture that can lead a person involuntarily to suicide. Modern approaches to suicide among Christians will include those who think of suicide as equivalent to murder as well as those who would hold that suicide reflects diminished capacity in most cases and thus those who commit suicide should receive nonjudgmental compassion and a Christian burial. There are suggestions, some going back to Emile Durkeim, that Protestants are more likely to kill themselves than Catholics, but the reasons for that are not clear despite theorizing about differences between Protestant individualism and Catholic communalism and the success that the Roman Catholic community has had in reinforcing its teachings.[40]

Buddhism recognizes that persons may choose to commit suicide as a way to resolve problems and escape suffering, but "the state of mind which prompts suicide will be a crucial cause of yet another rebirth, along with its problems." Buddhist scholar Peter Harvey concludes that, "as an attempt to escape from the sufferings of life, suicide is, according to Buddhist principles, totally ineffective."[41] Dying with a mind unsettled and burdened with bad karma not only negatively affects one's own rebirth but also negatively affects others, depriving them of "the benefits one may bring to them."[42] The refusal to interrupt suffering with suicide can be thought of in Buddhist terms as a way of allowing suffering to cultivate the Buddhist path toward enlightenment.

---

39. All quotations in this paragraph are from "Suicide" in the *Catechism of the Roman Catholic Church*, para. 2280–83, http://www.vatican.va/archive/ccc_css/archive/catechism/p3s2c2a5.htm.

40. Benno Torgler and Christoph A. Schaltegger, "Suicide and Religion: New Evidence on the Differences between Protestantism and Catholicism," Working Paper No. 2012-12, Center for Research in Economics, Management and the Arts (CREMA), Basel, Switzerland, 2012, http://www.crema-research.ch/papers/2012-12.pdf.

41. Peter Harvey, *An Introduction to Buddhist Ethics*, 286.

42. Ibid., 287.

There do seem to be some possible allowances for suicide in the Buddhist tradition. Certain bodhisattvas gave up their lives for others; this was not called suicide but altruism, an act worthy of praise.[43] Passive self-starvation is acceptable when a monk is terminally ill and seeks to act so as not to be a burden on those who would have to attend him, and it is also permitted in the terminal situation where the person is clearly dying from illness and has realized the meditative state that has been the person's goal: "Here self-starvation is seen as acceptable when it is because it is an unintended side-effect of a more important task, when it is part of a compassionate act, or when death is already imminent and further eating would be futile, not even allowing the completion of the meditative task."[44]

Self-starvation is allowed in Jainism, a religion that developed in India in the sixth century B.C.E. and is related to both Hinduism and Buddhism. Jainism affirms respect for life and, like Hinduism and Buddhism, puts ahimsa (noninjury) at the center of the tradition while also affirming the law of karma and deep commitment to nonviolence. Jainism allows for the end-of-life practice of self-starvation, or *sallekhana*, a passive form of suicide. According to Dena Davis, *sallekhana* is "the perfect end of a Jain because it allows one to control the transition from one's current life to the next. *Sallekhana* prevents old age and senility from destroying the hard won control over act and impulse that characterizes the pious Jain."[45]

Davis notes the conditions under which *sallekhana* can be undertaken: it must be under the direction of a holy teacher; there must be physical decline and a context of terminal illness or advanced age with the approach of senility; the fast is characterized by gradual withdrawal of food leading to the withdrawal of water; it is performed in the home or in a public place set aside for this ritual; the whole community of the *sallekhani*, or self-starver, is aware of the self-starvation dying process; and the person dies in a peaceful state with mantras being chanted to the end. Davis comments, "The *sallekhani* wants to end her life as she lived it, without subverting at the last the values that she has adhered to for decades."[46] Jainism integrates *sallekhana* into its religious practice, and it is

43. Ibid., 291.

44. Ibid.

45. Dena Davis, "Old and Thin," *Second Opinion* 15 (November 1990): 26–32, at 30–31. I owe this example from the Jain tradition to Dena Davis.

46. Davis, "Old and Thin," 31. Other information about the practice conditions Davis offers are from this page as well, and to my mind this offers a picture of "just passive suicide" in the Jain tradition—a prohibition on suicide but an exception made in special cases so long as various conditions are met.

honored as a ritual of high spiritual meaning and even personal attainment for those who undertake its discipline.

Three other points about Asian religions, Buddhism particularly, are worthy of note. First, the Buddha himself died as the result of eating either tainted pork (or boar) or poisonous mushrooms, and some accounts indicate that the Buddha was aware that his end was coming from this meal since he said to Cunda, the blacksmith who served him this food, "This is a very special dish. . . . Serve (the Buddha) . . . and then bury the rest in the ground, serving my bhikkhus and yourself only such fruits and vegetables as you have on hand today." An attack of dysentery followed the meal and the Buddha relieved Cunda of any burden of moral guilt for his unintended error, saying that Cunda should "feel no remorse" and that a meal "when he passes away and attains perfect insight" is equivalent in meaning to the one taken at the time enlightenment is achieved and thus surpasses all others in value.[47] The case could be made from this story that if the Buddha perceived a problem with the food and ate it anyway, knowing its lethal effect, this could be construed as "suicidal" in the same way some might use that term to interpret Jesus' decision to go to Jerusalem knowing that death awaited him. I am not pushing this interpretation except to ask whether it is unreasonable to conclude that the concept of suicide is entailed to some degree in describing acts that are undertaken knowing that they will in all likelihood lead to one's own death.

Second, under a Confucian influence, Chinese Buddhism allows that a person who protests injustice and does so out of compassion and with an eye toward improving society, as did Theravada monks who self-immolated in Vietnam in the 1960s, would be deemed morally permissible. I would note, however, that this is not considered relevant to "normal suicide scenarios."[48] Buddhist monks have self-immolated today in Tibet to protest Chinese occupation in that country.

And third, in the broader Asian context, the Japanese religion of Shinto, while not approving of suicide, seems to condone it through seppuku, a form of ritual suicide by disembowelment, which had originally been a prerogative of samurai warriors. Japan is a society that has upheld over its history the basic features of an honor culture, and samurai warriors believed it better to die with honor than surrender or become a prisoner of one's enemy:

47. George N. Marshall, introduction to *Buddha: The Quest for Serenity*, by Huston Smith (Boston: Beacon, 1978), 212–14.

48. Ibid., 291–92.

The most famous form of seppuku is also colloquially known as hara-kiri. This form, consisting of a deep knife stab in the abdomen followed by a stab in the head, was a ceremonial act committed by warriors for displaying failure (in which death was preferred to bringing disgrace on the Emperor). Jigai is a suicidal method consisting of cutting of the jugular vein, used by females for penitence of sins. More recently, there has been kamakizi (the intentional suicide mission), the well-known method employed by Japanese soldiers and pilots during the Second World War, which can also be seen as reflecting cultural attitudes: suicide rather than surrender was the honourable act of the Japanese soldier.[49]

In Asian religions, the prohibitions against suicide stand firmly rooted in what I have termed our common agreement or moral presumption against suicide, but in Asia, as in the West, the prohibitions do not rest on moral absolutes that would prevent extenuating circumstances in rare situations from allowing a morally or religiously justified suicide. The suicide may not be accompanied by a positive and explicit moral justification, or it could be translated into the religiously acceptable category of martyrdom, but explicit condemnation in some cases is withheld. Recall that even Judas's suicide, the only one mentioned in the Christian Scriptures, was not condemned by the writers who told the story.

COMMENTARY

COOLEY:

What is the definition of suicide? The question is very important to answer because it will have a considerable impact on how we think about the morality of taking one's own life, and it will allow us to separate suicide from deaths that are very similar but might not bear the same stigma. If we make the definition very narrow, then it will apply to very few cases. Of course, the fewer cases there are, the easier it is to deal with those individuals whose actions satisfy the conditions for being a suicide. However, the definition might be a lot broader if our common intuitions or practical consistency are taken into account.

49. Yoshihiro Kaneko, Akiko Yamasaki, and Kiminori Arai, "The Shinto Religion and Suicide in Japan," in *Oxford Textbook of Suicidology and Suicide Prevention*, ed. Danuta Wasserman and Camilla Wasserman (Oxford: Oxford University Press, 2009), doi:10.1093/med/9780198570059.001.00012009.

My initial thinking is that suicide requires some form of intention to take one's own life, otherwise actions that end in the death of the person might merely be negligence. Psychologists Silverman et al. state that suicides exist only "when there was a self-inflicted death with evidence (either explicit or implicit) of intent to die."[50] Suppose that a person drives drunk, knowing fully that acting in such an irresponsible manner will likely lead to his death. This does not appear to be a suicide, although it is imprudent and wrong for the driver to do. The same lack of intention to die by his own hand is true for someone who throws himself onto a live hand grenade to save his friends. The intention is to save his friends but not to kill himself.

So intentions play a vital role in the definition of a suicide.[51] I would even state something stronger than that by claiming that the intentions underlying a suicide make the action fall under three classifications: as a suicide (which is the general class of action), as a particular type of suicide (which is a subset of suicides containing fewer members than suicide in general), and as the specific act of self-killing that qualifies as a suicide (which is a subset containing one member). Emile Durkheim, for example, states that there are three types of suicide that would create the second subset: egoistic, altruistic, and anomic.[52] Setting aside Durkheim's controversial claim that suicide is mostly the result of social causes, his taxonomy is illustrative if we make egoistic suicides those focused primarily on the self, altruistic those focused primarily on others, and anomic those in which the basic needs of the person cannot be met. The mental states of the person committing suicide would make a specific taking of one's own life fall under one of these three categories. Those mental states also are what make the action the particular, individual suicide it is.

Although the sole or primary intention to take one's own life definitively makes an action a suicide, any intention to kill oneself that is part of the overall set of intentions involved in acting is sufficient to make an action an attempt at

---

50. M. M. Silverman, A. L. Berman, N. D. Sanddal, P. W. O'Carroll, and T. E. Joiner Jr., "Rebuilding the Tower of Babel: A Revised Nomenclature for the Study of Suicide and Suicidal Behaviors. Part 2: Suicide-Related Ideations, Communications, and Behaviors," *Suicide and Life-Threatening Behavior* 37, no. 3 (2007): 264–77, at 273. G. K. Brown, E. Jeglic, G. R. Henriques, and A. T. Beck argue that it is difficult to determine if the action is a suicide or self-injurious behavior. "Cognitive Therapy, Cognition, and Suicidal Behavior," in *Cognition and Suicide: Theory, Research, and Therapy*, ed. Thomas E. Ellis (Washington, DC: American Psychological Association, 2006), 53–74.

51. Michael Cholbi, *Suicide: The Philosophical Dimensions* (Peterborough, Ontario: Broadview, 2011). Jeff McMahan, *The Ethics of Killing: Problems at the Margins of Life* (Oxford: Oxford University Press, 2002).

52. Emile Durkheim, *Suicide: A Study in Sociology*, ed. G. Simpson and trans. J. A. Spaulding and G. Simpson (Glencoe, IL: Free Press, 1951).

suicide. Provoking police officers to shoot oneself because one wants to die is a taking of one's own life even though the bullets are not from the gun one holds. The agent has created a situation in which others act as his cat's paw to kill him, just as someone who steps from a curb with the intention of being killed by the bus makes the driver the suicide's unwitting accomplice. If the drunk driver gets drunk with the intention of dying in an accident, then that is also a suicide.

But we should be very careful here. No one intends to commit suicide for its own sake. Rather, the intention is to act to kill oneself in order to achieve a different end or goal, which has as an unavoidable result the death of the person. The primary or ultimate intention of suicide, therefore, is to achieve some other state, such as not being in pain, escaping punishment by another, sacrificing oneself to benefit another or the community, or harming another. The action of suiciding is the means to the end that produces the person's death and the intended state of affairs that is the primary intention of the person's action. An intention to do something can be defined for our purposes as follows:

S intends X = df.[53]
1. X is a state of affairs that S desires to bring about.
2. S believes that X is possible.
3. S has a plan to bring about X.
4. And S is committed to bringing X about if given the opportunity to do so.

When a person commits suicide to prevent her life from becoming unbearable, then her intention is to prevent her life from becoming unbearable. Being dead is not something that S desires in and of itself because no one, no matter how mentally disturbed, wants to die just for death's own sake. People want their deaths because that event simultaneously results in the state of affairs they actually intend, and both are caused by their dying.

The question that arises is whether, since the person's death is not intended, the self-killing counts as a suicide at all, as in the cases of the reckless driver and hero who throws himself upon a hand grenade to save the lives of his companions. The answer is yes and no. No if we require that suicides must intend their death as the ultimate goal of the action, but yes if we introduce the notion of an intentional action. According to Cholbi, "Suicide is intentional self-killing: a person's act is suicidal if and only if the person believes that the act, or some causal consequence of that act, would make her death likely and she engaged in the behavior to intentionally bring about her death."[54] Moreover,

---

53. "Df." is a philosopher's way of stating that a term is being defined.

a person can intentionally kill herself yet not intend that she die. "A person's self-killing is intentional just in case her death has her rational endorsement in the circumstances in which she acts so as to bring about her death."[55] To have a rational endorsement of one's own death requires three conditions be met. First, the person must foresee that his action will be a significant cause of his death. Here we also see that the death need not be intended by the person. Second, the person must put the situation into some form of context he understands. Finally, there is a weighing of the evidence, although it might be very brief, for the two alternative actions of remaining alive and dying. From these two alternates, the suicide chooses the latter, which implies that he accepts that particular action with its foreseeable and intended consequences.

Although I think that Cholbi's rational endorsement is what happens in many cases of suicide, such as those in most assisted suicide cases, my concern is that it does not capture all of them. At times, an endorsement is much too strong a requirement; the agent does not do it but still commits suicide. In other instances, there might be too little time to form a rational endorsement, which requires more evidence than a weaker commitment entails.[56] The hero sacrificing himself for another is an example of a suicide that is unlikely to meet either condition.

My suggestion to fix this problem is to use rational acquiescence in place of rational endorsement. The rational part is still the same in that the individual understands the situation and makes a rational decision in his given time frame. However, the agent merely tacitly accepts that his death will be a result of his action to achieve his intended goal; he understands his situation but is not committed to it in the way one is when one endorses something. Endorsing is a very strong commitment that entails that the person thinks that other people should endorse it for themselves as well. The agent might well want others to endorse the action, but in altruistic suicides it is hard to see where the person taking her own life wants others to endorse what she is doing because she might not want them to do the same thing. In fact, keeping them alive might be the primary reason she has to kill herself.

Moreover, there has to be a commitment on the agent's part that goes beyond merely foreseeing the consequences of her action. Foreseeing is

---

54. Cholbi, *Suicide*, 21.

55. Ibid., 28.

56. Five percent of people attempting suicide reported that they spent less than one second forming the intention to kill themselves before they made the attempt. T. R. Simon, A. C. Swann, K. E. Powell, L. B. Potter, M-J. Kresnow, and P. W. O'Carroll, "Characteristics of Impulsive Suicide Attempts and Attempters," *Suicide and Life-Threatening Behavior* 31, Suppl. (2001): 49–59.

knowing or reasonably believing that a consequence will result, but there is no necessary acceptance on the part of the agent that makes the consequence part of her action. Foreseen consequences merely happen, and the agent need not feel responsible for those consequences by foreseeing them. She does make herself responsible for the foreseen consequences when she commits herself to them, which can be done with acquiescence or tacit consent. Her agreement to her action's effects shows what the action is and her self-acknowledged responsibility for it. A suicide would be a suicide, in part, because the person rationally acquiesced to her death that was caused by the action of suiciding that she was using to achieve her ultimate goal of no longer being in pain or for some other understandable reason.

The main difference between the two examples given initially in this section—the drunk driver and the hand grenade hero—is whether either rationally acquiesced to the outcome that included their deaths. For the drunk driver, there seems to be no acquiescence because he is not trying to drive drunk as a way to suicide and he is not tacitly agreeing to his death.

The hero is a different story. In order for his action to be as heroic as it actually is, then he must tacitly agree to his death as an effect of his throwing himself on the grenade. He does not intend the death—and does not really want it—but he does intend to save his friends, which he knows entails his likely demise from being blown to bits by the grenade. His taking responsibility for his death consequence means that his action is a true sacrifice instead of merely a bungling. If he thought he could survive the blast, then he would not be as heroic because he was not sacrificing his entire intrinsic value as a person for others. He would think that he could get away with it, which makes it an action that is heroic but not as heroic as one in which he truly understands the situation. It is only with true understanding of the situation and acceptance of it that we see how noble the person actually was. He knows the sacrifice he is making, and yet he still jumps on the grenade to save his friends.

STEFFEN:

Suicide is a self-killing grounded, I believe, in intentionality. I appreciate your helpful comments about suicide, especially that it is not chosen for itself, that death is not the ultimate goal inasmuch as suicide occurs in pursuit of some other end. However, when you write in support of this claim, "When a person commits suicide to prevent her life from becoming unbearable, then her intention is to prevent her life from becoming unbearable," it seems to me that we should look at this a little more closely. The person who believes that his or her life is unbearable is not going to kill herself to "prevent" future unbearability but to put an end to *a present experience* that is excruciatingly painful. What seems to me to be critical is that it is to stop a particular experience *now* rather than prevent an experience in the future.

I do not doubt that suicides can be directed to anticipated events in the future: "When they find out I embezzled that money, I will be ruined, go to prison, disgrace myself and my loved ones, and I kill myself now to prevent such a horrendous experience, which I anticipate." I think a person with a highly developed super-ego might make such a move (though how such a person would become an embezzler in the first place eludes me somewhat), but I think the suicide decision is a "now" decision, and that is what makes prevention of suicide so tricky. The person who contemplates suicide or is experiencing suicidal ideation is looking at suicide itself as a future possibility, looking ahead to a future but doing so now, for now the decision is at hand, real, and at a moment of crisis. Suicide prevention is involved in keeping that possibility in the future while intervening to help individuals deal with the problems giving rise to the ideation in the first place. The Columbia University Suicide Severity Scale rates suicidal ideation from "wish to die" (low end) to "active suicidal ideation with specific plan and intent" (high end, realistic prospect of suicidal action).[57] The "wish to die" points to a future state of affairs; life problems or psychological states give rise to thoughts of a possible future suicide. In contrast, the move into "specific plan and intent" is decision making in the "now." This leads me also to conclude that some people who commit suicide do intend to become dead by self-directed action; that intention may accompany other intentions—can we not do things with more than one intention?—such as pain elimination or the desire to be free of life's burdens.

I do not know if putting an emphasis on "temporality" affects your reflections above. I think your distinction between rational endorsement and rational acquiescence allows for a deeper appreciation of the complexity of issues that would be encompassed in an examination of the mental states involved in suicide. And, of course, qualifying both acquiescence and endorsement as "rational" brackets the suicides that are typically not rational, by which I mean the 90 percent of suicides marked by impaired judgment due to mental illness or drug use. While endorsement may satisfy many rational suicides for medical end-of-life reasons (the larger part of the remaining 10 percent of suicides), your view is that some suicides simply acquiesce to their own deaths, and you use altruism as your example—the hero who intends his

57. Columbia-Suicide Severity Rating Scale, http://www.cssrs.columbia.edu. See other links for baseline determinations and further information.

or her own death but only tacitly, which then defines the idea of "acquiescing" in that death. The tacit idea here is that if there were some other way to solve the problem in this situation—like throwing the live hand grenade out of the foxhole—that would be preferable and the hero would of course do that. The hero does not want to die but acquiesces in his or her own death in the circumstances. The intention is to save others, and only in a very weak sense is intentionality involved in the prospect of dying from a self-directed action that can be described as a self-killing.

In the chapters addressing end-of-life issues, I raise a concern about our moral language and wonder if we have an adequate awareness of the language we actually use to describe events such as suicide. We obviously draw distinctions between a young person who commits suicide because of mental illness or severe psychological distress and the soldier who saves others by falling on a hand grenade, and both of those we distinguish from the kamikaze pilot who crashes into a ship to win the battle for the homeland and the terminally ill patient whose bone cancer is not being controlled successfully with morphine and who is seeking a level of pain medication that will lead to a permanent loss of consciousness.

I think we draw these distinctions. The language we use can allow that all of these situations are self-killings. "Suicide" is the broad category that encompasses them all, and we could include other things, such as the person who arrives at death's door by smoking, knowing full well it could lead to a terminal situation, but I also think the addictive properties of nicotine might push a death from smoking into the 90-percent category to be included with nonrational suicide from drug use. A great deal of moral weight hangs on the term *suicide*, so much so that we are ourselves often uncomfortable employing the term to describe certain self-killings. We approach the person suffering from mental illness with sorrow and compassion, and the grief we feel in the wake of a suicide death is tied in part to our failure to understand all that was going on in the subjective reality of the person—we wonder what we might have done to prevent this from happening. The hero we actually extract from the "suicide" category altogether (or so it seems) and move to positive, virtue-catching moral categories like altruism and supererogation. The individual who in some way "lays down his life for his friends" exemplifies virtuously the ultimate in self-sacrifice for others. The kamikaze pilot (or let's consider the suicide bomber who claims religious or political reasons for his suicide) is subject to a certain kind of *cultural* relativism because the move is made in some cultures to transform the suicide into another positive moral category or description, such as martyrdom. The suicide is morally wrong, but it can be honored in one setting and deplored in another by a redescription. It seems to me that we do not refrain from using "suicide" to describe these acts, but the moral meaning is attached to descriptions that derive their meaning from political or religious contexts. If we agree with the politics, we can move to employ appreciative language like that of "martyr." If we disapprove, we seem to move toward all kinds of negative moral terms, including "evil," "demonic," and even "fanatical," which implies not simply a loss of reasoning ability but a kind of willful irrationality caused by moral perversity or abject evil.

Now, getting back to the altruistic hero who endorses or acquiesces in his or her death, let me offer that the difference between the kamikaze pilot and the soldier who dies on the grenade is that the kamikaze pilot fully grasps the death to come and is ideologically clear about what interests the death will serve; the soldier who covers the grenade lacks reflective time to grasp what interests will be served except the immediate one of saving comrades in the foxhole. It is closer to an instinctive reaction than a reflective thought, and you may be right—there is only the weakest kind of intentionality involved in thinking about this action being the cause of the soldier's own death.

What I take from this discussion is not only that we now have a greater understanding of intentionality, though I think we do, but that we have a language that serves to draw distinctions. Even when we refer actions to the broad category of "suicide" as a way to direct us to moral meaning, communication, and interpretation, we are vitally interested in evaluating the particulars of cases and do so for reasons related to the contexts of politics, religion, and moral understanding. Intentionality plays a role in that evaluation process. I can make my point by muddying the waters with the example of the soldier who leaps on the live grenade having been diagnosed with a terminal disease that will prove fatal but only after a long and painfully slow dying. The diseased soldier chooses the death of a hero and saves the lives of others, yes, but now it looks like there is a bit of the "death by cop" involved; it looks a little more self-interested and not quite so altruistic.

The process of looking at cases and evaluating them so we understand their moral meaning is what I think is most important in examining instances of suicide. The distinction you draw and the case you make for "acquiescence" does allow us to include altruistic cases of weak intentionality, but, in the end, it seems to me the most important question in suicide is why. We always want to know why a person takes his or her own life. One of the problems with the language of suicide and the heavy burden of moral disapproval it carries is that that valence of negative moral meaning can interfere with getting at the reasons. This question about the adequacy of our language and our ability to pay attention to the language we actually use is one I also raise in the chapter on physician-assisted suicide, and there I note that some disapprove of employing the term *suicide* for the very reasons I mention here. I also suggest there that were we to look at "rational suicides" at the end of life in terms of sacrifice rather than suicide, we might create a context within which social attitudes toward physician aid in dying would change more quickly. We are prisoners of our language, but we are also the creators and users of language, and how we use it can affect everything from social policy to legal regulations to how we go about offering compassion to suffering people.

COOLEY:

What do various religions say about the permissibility of suicide?

Do any religions say it is, at times, required to commit suicide? For example, under divine command theory, whatever the morality-creating divine entity commands is not only morally right, it is a duty to do. If God, let us say, told an individual to kill himself, then it has to be an obligation for the person. If Abraham had killed his son Isaac, as God commanded, then the mere fact God commanded Abraham to kill this child on whom Abraham's line depended would make the murder a morally obligatory action. If infanticide can be an obligation, then suicides, which are not discussed in the Bible, could be something God commands.

The problem is that we have no evidence of God's specific view of suicide for guidance. Since we do not know what God does and why God is doing it, we could never say that God would prohibit all taking of one's own life, even in circumstances that might seem unreasonable or irrational to us.

What, if anything, makes you squeamish about any of the above positions for and against suicide? Why do you have this reaction?

STEFFEN:

I think, as I said above, there is a little gray around the edges with respect to religion and the permissibility of suicide. In formal religious teachings suicide is, of course and in general, prohibited, but that is to reiterate ordinary moral thinking, which would likewise oppose suicide. Suicide in general is to be opposed and for very good moral reasons, which we have both acknowledged. The gray around the edges in religion may not amount to anything more than having compassion for the suicide victim, who is now almost universally recognized, even in religious discussions, as mentally ill or otherwise incapacitated to control the pressure to commit suicide. This was not always the case, and compassion toward the person with mental illness who commits suicide represents a step in moral evolution and deeper understanding of human psychology. That said, I did not address the specific question you ask about a requirement to commit suicide in a theistic divine command context.

My response is similar to the one I have elsewhere given in discussing the death penalty: if God wants someone dead, then let God do the killing.[58] Why involve human agency when human beings would be suspicious of such a command, when such a command would conflict with ordinary moral understanding, when the person who received such a command would inevitably experience uncertainty about the source of the command and ought to be suspicious as to why God would ask such a thing? If 90 percent of persons who commit suicide are not acting rationally at the time of their suicides because of mental illness or drug effects, the command to kill oneself as coming from God should, in my view, be interrogated and the person claiming God as the source of the directive should be calmly quarantined to determine if the person is reasonable or in the 90 percent—I would assume the latter. Why? If one believed in a God who was good and the source of goodness itself—and also was all-knowing and all-powerful, as most theists believe—how could one in good faith accept that a command to kill oneself was coming from God?

You can respond by saying, as you do in your question, that a self-killing directed by God would be right and permissible because God commanded it, and anything God would command should be obeyed. But if you had a student who was going to commit suicide for the reason that God was commanding it, would you accede to this claim and allow things to proceed? Of course not. The command itself, its mode of transmission, and the clarity with which it was interpreted would all be subject to critical inquiry, reasoned interpretation, and extensive consultations with others. God is for many religious people the guarantor of goodness and the ground or foundation of moral thinking, and on the supposition that God is good it follows that what God wills is good because it is good. Suicide is not good—it denies the good of life and offends against practical reason. As you have argued, reasonable persons would not kill themselves for the sake of killing themselves but only for some other reason: what kind of reason would propel God to require a human being to self-destruct because God wanted that person to? If God wanted such a thing so badly, God has the power and authority to take that life without human assistance, and that would be better than asking a person to do what by ordinary

---

58. See Steffen, *Executing Justice*, 155ff.

moral lights is not rational, moral, or something one would expect the God-who-is-good to sanction—much less endorse, incite, or motivate.

If a religious believer held that God doesn't act directly to actually kill a person God wanted dead, then one could ask whether God has the power to act directly this way. If God lacks power to intervene to take a life directly, then we are not talking about suicide or murder anymore but about the power and nature of God. On the other hand, if one assumes God is not good but instead mad or evil, then all bets are off as to what God would or would not do, but such an affirmation would then provoke an important moral response from reasonable people, which is this: reasonable people ought not follow commands from one known to be mad or evil.

6

End of Life I: Physician-Assisted Suicide

INTRODUCTION

We continue with an analysis of end-of-life issues, focusing in this chapter specifically on physician-assisted suicide, or PAS. PAS clearly falls under the heading of euthanasia, but because of the ethical commitment health care professionals make to work diligently toward the well-being of their patients (beneficence), it poses unique problems that need to be drawn out in their own way. In what follows, what is said about PAS applies equally well to anyone in the health care field who would play a role in active or passive voluntary euthanasia.[1]

COOLEY

I will begin as always with the main philosophical arguments for and against the position. These are not developed in any detail, but they show how people are thinking about the issue. I will then develop some ideas that are relevant to any in-depth discussion of physician-assisted suicide.

ARGUMENTS AGAINST PHYSICIAN-ASSISTED SUICIDES

1. The slippery-slope argument states that we might start with a morally permissible action, but if we do that action, then we will act unethically in an increasingly egregious way.[2] In the case of PAS, if we legally or morally permit some suicides, then morally

---

1. Among others, Robert Young and Nigel Biggar have excellent overviews of the arguments for and against medically assisted euthanasia. See Nigel Biggar, *Aiming to Kill: The Ethics of Suicide and Euthanasia* (London: Darton, Longman and Todd, 2004); and Robert Young, *Medically Assisted Death* (Cambridge: Cambridge University Press, 2007).

unacceptable consequences will inevitably occur. Included in the results are that the following outcomes: Physicians will become callous toward life in general and might begin taking the lives of people who do not want to die.

    a. Physicians will help people commit suicide who are suffering but do not have an incurable condition and are not in the end stages of life.

    b. If PAS is an acceptable option, then doctors and others might not fight hard enough to save the lives of those who could be saved.

    c. The problem of making a mistake about a prognosis or diagnosis would increase with the additional number of people turning to PAS.

    d. There might be a cure for an individual's medical problem that would benefit him had the person stayed alive long enough for it to be introduced into the market.

    e. If PAS becomes the standard, then because of the prestige of physicians and the medical field, families and the community will pressure ill people to commit suicide even though they would not otherwise want to kill themselves.

    f. Since PAS prevents the patient from receiving health care services, revenue-strapped governments and profit-hungry insurance companies may illicitly pressure physicians into choosing PAS too soon.

2. There are a number of physicians who do not want to be obligated to help people end their lives. PAS forces conscientiously objecting physicians to violate their deeply held moral or religious beliefs.

3. PAS treats human life without the respect it deserves, especially by those who should revere it the most. Medical professionals are prohibited from ending life.[3]

4. PAS violates doctors' Hippocratic Oath to do no harm.

5. Desiring to commit suicide and killing oneself is irrational, which all physicians should know, and no physician should aid another in

2. Wesley J. Smith, *Forced Exit: The Slippery Slope from Assisted Suicide to Legalized Murder* (New York: Random House, 1997).

3. James Rachels argues persuasively against this argument and its foundational belief in the role of medical professionals in *The End of Life: Euthanasia and Morality* (Oxford: Oxford University Press, 1986).

pursuit of some irrational end; therefore, no physician should help another person commit suicide.

6. Palliative care can replace killing a person.

7. Assisting in someone's suicide violates the person's right to life.

ARGUMENTS IN FAVOR OF PHYSICIAN-ASSISTED SUICIDES

1. There are two alternatives in PAS cases: either to keep the person alive even though the person's life is not worth living, according to the person or others, or to help the person to take his own life. A utilitarian would do what is best, which would be to end the person's life and allow him to die with dignity because doing so maximizes utility and produces the best overall result. An added utilitarian consideration would be that PAS would reduce health care costs for the government, insurance companies, and the estate of the deceased.

2. People have autonomy—that is, the right to make choices that affect their lives. If they decide that their lives are no longer worth living, then their autonomy needs to be respected by the medical community. To help them to commit suicide would allow them to die with dignity.

3. PAS allows people to plan for their deaths. By knowing when and how one's death is going to happen, the person can make amends with those she needs to, and then say goodbye to family, friends, and others. If she is not allowed PAS, then the death is more haphazard and might not result in the same closure.

4. People are going to commit or try to commit suicide anyway, which can lead to horrific results, such as botched suicides that keep the person alive but in a worse state than if he had died. With PAS, suicide can be done more humanely for the person committing suicide and those affected by the action.

5. Abuse of the system is not a necessary result of PAS. With proper training and regulation, horror cases of physicians killing people who should not be killed will not happen or will be no greater than those that occur in the current health system.[4]

4. John Griffiths, Alex Bood, and Heleen Weyers, *Euthanasia and Law in The Netherlands* (Amsterdam, Netherlands: Amsterdam University Press, 1998).

RIGHT-TO-LIFE ARGUMENT AGAINST ASSISTED SUICIDE

The right-to-life argument appears to be based on the belief that rights are inalienable even in situations in which the person with the right freely chooses to waive it.[5] Basically, the argument begins by stating that each person has a right to life. This right is an entitlement that is either negative—people are obligated to leave the individual alone to enjoy her right—or positive—people are obligated to help the person to enjoy her right. If it is the former, then no one may ever help another person commit suicide because that would not be leaving the person alone. Helping another to die would be illicit interference. For the positive right, physician-assisted suicide is wrong because the right requires everyone who can do so to help the individual who wants to commit suicide to stay alive, regardless of his actual choice and desire. Assisting the potential suicide to die is antithetical to keeping him living.

Another key component of the right-to-life argument is the assertion that no individual may waive his right to life because doing so would violate his right to life in some way. We can understand this limitation in different ways. First, the right might be inalienable on the brute fact that it cannot be waived. That is, if one is a person, then the right is a necessary possession of the person that must remain as long as the person exists. Second, the right might be so vital—in fact, some argue that it is the primary right on which all other rights depend—that waiving it would be inconsistent with having the right to life. In one argument, Kant, for example, thought that agents cannot consistently will the suicide maxim because it contradicts the more vital self-love that each person has. The natural and fundamental function and purpose of self-love is to keep the person alive, which makes it impossible for anyone to act rationally in a way that is intended to take the person's life. Since the right to life is vital or primary, then the right to self-determination cannot override it, whereas the right to life can override the right to self-determination.

In a similar fashion, according to John Locke, we cannot sell our liberty to become slaves because such a contract is possible only is if it is signed and fulfilled by two autonomous agents who act freely. However, one agent cannot act freely when he is enslaved; hence, he cannot waive his liberty in order to act freely. On the same grounds, the right to life prohibits suicide; the person committing suicide cannot reject the primary right he has as an autonomous agent deserving respect and yet remain an autonomous agent deserving respect.

5. The right to life argument against assisted suicide works equally well for any instance in which the right to life is used to justify a position.

The right-to-life argument continues by claiming that even if the right to life could be waived for the person committing suicide, it cannot be waived by physicians and other medical professionals who might be willing to help people take their own lives. In order to fulfill the demands of the entitlement to life, everyone who can affect the agent must either leave the agent alone or help the agent to live. In the former case, the doctor would not be permitted to assist the patient by giving advice on the most efficient way to kill oneself, providing prescriptions for life-ending drugs, or acting in any manner that would help the person commit suicide. If the right is positive, then the physician would have to try to prevent the person from killing herself. If she is unable to make autonomous decisions in this realm without fatally harming herself, then the physician can act paternalistically by having her sedated or committed to some facility that will keep her alive. If the patient is competent, then the physician must work to convince her to keep her life. Perhaps he could place her in a program of counseling and pain management—palliative care—that will assist her in seeing that she should not kill herself. Perhaps mental therapy is in order for her. Whatever is the best solution for her, the physician would need to help her to change her mind, which entails that he cannot assist her in the taking of her life.

Although it is intuitively appealing at first glance, I am not sure how successful an argument can be made from the notion of inalienable moral rights. Granted that the assumption that rights exist and cannot be waived has a long history in Western culture stemming from the Enlightenment, there is a tendency to begin thinking that Jeremy Bentham's claim that moral rights are "nonsense on stilts" might have some truth to it.

The first oddness about inalienable moral rights is that they reduce the autonomy agents have to direct their lives. For example, when people are talking about alienation, they seem to be generally speaking of one person or group taking a right away from another person. That is, the focus is on the claim that a person's right cannot be alienated by another agent. This distinction leaves open the question as to whether the person who has the right can willfully alienate it by her autonomous choice. If we assume that a person cannot alienate a right she possesses, even though she autonomously chooses to do so based on reason and the evidence available to her, then we encounter a rather peculiar result. The right is an entitlement the person has—that is, something owed to her—but she cannot forgive or waive the debt. That is, she has no power in the matter. An example might help illustrate the point. Suppose that someone has paid good money for a piece of cake for her dessert. By buying the cake, she is now entitled to it. However, she ate a bit too much dinner and now no longer wants her dessert. We would think that she does nothing wrong if she allows the cake to be eaten by another, even though she was entitled to eat it herself. We would never go to the extreme of forcing her to keep the cake because she is entitled to it. She may eat it or not because it is hers, and she has the right to dispose of it at will. This right empowers rather than disenfranchises her.

Lives are far more important than cakes, but the same idea holds here. If someone is entitled to something, then he may waive that entitlement. Moral entitlements or rights are debts that are owed to a person merely because that person is a person. Entitlements are not essential characteristics of a person's identity that the agent must retain in order to be that agent; if they were, they would not be entitlements at all. To be a person, for example, requires that the person be alive; it is a necessary feature that, if lost, would alter the person into a new entity that is not a person. However, *being alive* is not the same thing as an *entitlement to be alive*. One property is a debt owed to the agent, and the other is a necessary characteristic to be an agent. These are two different properties an agent might have, and to classify them as the same sort of characteristic is a category mistake on the level of arguing that oranges are apples. Furthermore, since the properties are different, being alive can have a different moral status as a property from being entitled to be alive. The former is essential to being a moral agent, whereas the latter is not. One can be a moral agent without having a debt owed to oneself. In fact, we can imagine a moral agent existing without rights, but we cannot imagine a moral agent existing without life or the other necessary features of being a moral agent. Therefore, there are no moral or logical quandaries to waiving the right to life, provided that the person does it as a fully informed autonomous moral agent acting as a reasonable person would act in that situation.

Another oddness is that the right to life is a somewhat vague, if not unintelligible right. Although it might seem obvious that everyone is entitled to life, when we start pondering what such a right is and how it works, we begin to see that having such an entitlement is impossible. A right to life, if it exists, cannot be violated because the only way that it could be violated would be if the person exists after the violation happens so that she can be harmed by the violation. If true, then this right is unique among the set of rights.

Consider, for example, the right to liberty. This right entitles the person to as much freedom as is practical for the person to have. If we decide to enslave him, then we have violated his right to freedom. If we leave him alone or help him fulfill his entitlement, depending on what type of right it is, then we have respected his right to freedom. What remains the same in either case is the person with the right. That is, if we enslave him, then it is still *him*, only *an enslaved him*. If we help set him free, then he is still the identical person, only now with his freedom intact. To determine that we did something wrong by enslaving him, we can compare the world in which he is enslaved to that in which he is free. We say that in one world we acted unethically by violating his right, while in the second world we did a right thing by ensuring his freedom.

But the right to life does not have the identical feature to the right to liberty. If someone is killed—her life ceases as the result of another's action—then we cannot say that the person's right has been violated by being killed. The very moment that her right to life is violated is also the very moment in which her life is ended. Her right to life cannot be violated when she is alive because she is alive, although she might be in great pain and suffering. Of course, we might be violating other rights by putting her in a worse state of health and in states of pain and suffering, but her right to life remains intact as long as her living does. In fact, the right to life can only be violated, if it can be violated at all, when she has finished dying.

And here is where the right to life encounters the Epicurean problem: nonexistence of the person necessarily entails nonexistence of the person's rights. In order for an entity to have rights, the entity must exist. Since the person ceases to exist the moment that the person dies, then the person does not have any rights after death. Unlike the argument described earlier about the right to liberty that allows us to compare existing, sufficiently similar entities that have different fates, we cannot similarly compare the living to the dead. Given that the person does not exist in one world, we have nothing to which we could evaluate the living person to see if she is better or worse for being alive and having a right to life. That is, we are comparing a nothing with a something, unlike in the liberty example in which something was compared to something sufficiently similar.

The right to life, if it exists, should be able to show us why it is wrong to take a life, but there is no harm to the person who is killed because she does not exist to be harmed and she has no rights to be violated because she does not exist. If the right to life is an empty concept because it does no actual work, then claiming a right to life for anyone is similar to claiming that men have a right to use their uteruses to bear children. But that is nonsense. Therefore, the right-to-life argument is based on a mistaken notion of what rights are and how they work.

But there is a serious idea behind the right-to-life argument that should not be flippantly dismissed. Composing a line of reasoning that captures the idea behind the right to life—and that can also do the work that those who believe in a right to life want that right to do—will be useful to us.

The right to life cannot merely mean the right to be alive because that is a rather low standard to have for the work people want such a right to do. First, any living thing, including all flora and fauna, would have such an entitlement. When we remove a weed from our lawn or pull a carrot from a carefully tended garden, we violate the plant's right to life if being alive is all that is necessary to create a right. But this seems to cheapen what a right to life is supposed to mean. A person's right to life should not be the same as a plant's right to life.

Second, suppose that someone intentionally placed in constant pain is not allowed to receive the bare minimum for a subsistence existence, or someone's life is made not worth living by being physically and psychologically abused. We could also imagine that a person intentionally harmed another so that the latter's potential was destroyed. For example, the person would have been a great athlete except that our evil wrongdoer, with malicious forethought, struck her with his car in order to injure her. We know that anyone who treated another person in this manner is doing something that is atrociously wrong, but we could not make our finding based on the right to be alive. If the person is kept alive, then no matter how terrible her life has been made for her, her right has not been violated. Yet, there is something about a right to life that should apply in these situations even though the person is not dead and, hence, has not had her right to life technically violated.

The right to life must be an entitlement to some type of life rather than to life itself. More precisely, the significance of the right to life is not the difference between being alive and being dead, but about living a superior type of life rather than an inferior type of life. If we think about the right to life in this manner, then we avoid the problem of trying to compare an existent being with a nonexistent being because we are, instead, comparing a significantly identical being in two different settings. For example, we can imagine a sixteen-year-old boy who is raised in a world that allows him to pursue his potential in a way that fosters his flourishing. We can imagine the same boy in a world in which he is raised the same way until his fifteenth birthday, but then the resources supporting him are withdrawn. The elimination of the means to flourish in one world can be considered to harm the boy because the resources did not have to be withdrawn, as we can see by comparing the two worlds in which there are sufficiently similar entities. Depending on why the resources were withdrawn, we could very well say that in one world the boy's entitlement to a particular type of life was fulfilled while in the other it was not. For the moment, then, let us say that the right to life is actually the right to a flourishing life. This interpretation of the right to life shows respect for life, makes common sense, and allows the right to be violated, thereby permitting it to do the work it is desired to do.

How the right can be violated and how that fits into morality can be shown by continuing with the example of the fifteen-year-old boy. The resource withdrawal might be the result of moral agency at work or some other cause. If it is not moral agency that produced the loss, then the right to a flourishing life has not been violated. The entitlement is only a debt owed to an agent by one or more other people. Nonagents, such as plants and nonhuman animals, cannot be said to owe a moral agent in the proper way. That is, the nonagent has no duty to leave the moral agent alone or to assist her in obtaining that to which she is entitled. A lion, for example, does not violate a tourist's right to a flourishing life when it hunts and kills him. On the other hand, a moral agent can violate another agent's right by preventing or not helping the person get that which the person is owed. By intentionally withdrawing the necessary resources, the fifteen-year-old boy has had his right to a flourishing life violated by the person doing the withdrawing. The same result holds for any morally identical situation. When one person harms another by making the latter's life not worth living, the right to a flourishing life is violated.

The right to a flourishing life can be used to build an argument against a physician or anyone else acting in a way that causes premature death. In our fifteen-year-old-boy case, the suffering he would experience in the life without adequate resources to allow him to thrive would reduce not only his ability to flourish but the longevity of his flourishing. We know that inadequate food, clean water, health care, and other necessities will shorten a person's life, especially if those resources are in such limited supply that the person starves in some way as a result. Because the boy's life was made less worth living for no justifiable reason, then his right must have been infringed by any agent's action that caused him to suffer.

Moreover, the right to a flourishing life requires that a person not be handicapped in his pursuit of having a more flourishing life when the person has a legitimate choice between better and worse lives. Consider what we would think if someone allowed another person to flourish but then, for morally illegitimate reasons, retarded her ability to make her life even better. When comparing this life to one in which the person was not illicitly interfered with, we would say that the interloper did something wrong by reducing the person's opportunities without just cause. If we cling to rights talk, then there has to be something in the right to a flourishing life that would allow us to make this claim. Therefore, the right to a flourishing life entails not only that someone is entitled to a flourishing life but also that she has an inherent entitlement—at the very least—not to be interfered with if she wants to take an opportunity to improve her life beyond the mere baseline level of flourishing.

The right to a flourishing life is a rather complex entitlement. It might be considered a positive right inasmuch as each person should be given what she needs to meet the minimum required to flourish. That is, each person, provided that she cannot attain them for herself, must be given the bare essentials required for thriving, but no more. Simultaneously, it is a negative right when it comes to illicit interference. After her basic needs are met, no one is obligated to help her make her life better, but everyone has the duty not to interfere illicitly with her attempts to improve her lot in life, as long as those attempts do not interfere with others trying to obtain the minimum required to have a flourishing life.

We should now see the moral work that can be done by a right to a flourishing life. If someone intentionally or recklessly violated the right in either of its two aspects, we would rightly condemn him for his action. The individual who takes away the goods necessary for the minimum of flourishing acts unethically by making someone's life not worth living. A person who prevents another from improving her thriving also does a wrongful thing. A person treated in either manner would understandably say that his right had been violated.

Let us now apply this understanding to PAS. When a physician helps someone commit suicide, the right to a flourishing life might be violated. In order for it to be transgressed, the suicidal person must have had a life that was thriving and could thrive in the future. Of course, if the person did not and could not have such a beneficial life, then it makes little sense to say that the physician did anything wrong by helping the person take her own life. Once again, it is a matter of a right that is impossible to satisfy. If a person cannot have a thriving life because of circumstances that are morally unnecessary and virtually impossible to change, then there is no right to a flourishing life that can be violated.

However, we can assume some situations in which a person does or can have a flourishing life. In these cases, there is a very small window of time in which the physician can violate the person's right. From the moment of the physician's interaction that begins her death process to the moment of her death, it can be argued that the patient's entitlement to a flourishing life is intruded upon by PAS. The patient cannot be flourishing because she is dying, and the physician's hand helped create this situation. In this scenario, we are considering a case in two possible worlds, one in which the person is not dying as a physician-assisted suicide and another in which the person is dying as a result of an intentional act to take her own life through PAS. Therefore, we can compare the two to see if her right to a flourishing life is respected in one world and not respected in the other. If we assume that rights are entitlements that cannot be alienated, even by the person making an autonomous decision to act in such a manner, then the physician acts unethically in the PAS world. In that world, for the time she is dying, her right to a flourishing life is violated; she can have a flourishing life but someone has helped her not to have one.

Although somewhat contrived, this argument seems to be the most plausible case against PAS that we can make using the right-to-life concept. What makes it unsatisfying is that it will apply only to cases in which the potential suicide could have a flourishing life but chooses for whatever reasons not to continue her existence. These types of suicide are generally agreed upon as being morally wrong. The vast majority of PAS cases, however, deal with moral agents who cannot have flourishing lives for one reason or another; thus, it is futile to keep them alive. Thus, the argument against PAS on the basis of a right to a flourishing life has very limited use, which those who want an argument against PAS might find unsatisfying.

I think that there is a far more powerful argument that can be given against physicians becoming involved in assisted suicide cases; the argument will take a bit of building before I present it. Throughout this work, I have been arguing that each life has intrinsic value, which means that a loss of life is the loss of intrinsic value. When a physician helps a person commit suicide, the former is destroying value that deserves the highest type of respect, albeit in a way that does not immediately and directly connect the doctor's action to the death itself. This loss should never be taken lightly. It is a tremendous harm that impacts not only the value of the person herself but the value of the world as a whole. The world, in general, is not as intrinsically valuable as it was before the patient's death.

However, it is still permissible for physicians to help others to commit suicide. Although there is a loss of intrinsic value, we have to put that harm into its proper context. Suppose that five people are shipwrecked on a deserted island. There are enough supplies for only four to survive, and one of them decides to sacrifice himself for the others by walking out into the sea until he drowns. In this case, there is a loss of intrinsic value from the man's death, which is exacerbated by the fact that the group lost a person who is noble and willing to place the interests of the others over his own, but the suicide actually improves the overall intrinsic value in the situation's context. Had the man decided to continue to live with the four others, they would all have starved to death when their supplies failed them. So the overall situation is much more intrinsically valuable than if everyone had died. I am not arguing that the man had a duty to kill himself in this situation, only that the value of his doing so is far greater than his remaining alive and five people dying as a result.

The same sort of thinking can explain why it is permissible for physicians to help others commit suicide. First, if those physicians help would have had lives that did not and could not flourish, then even though intrinsic value is lost by their deaths, overall the world is a better place as a result of their assisted suicides. As stated above, we cannot say that the person is better or worse off because he no longer exists to be better or worse off, but we can say something plausible about the world before and after the person's death. Sometimes the loss of intrinsic value can make the overall situation far more valuable than it would have been had the intrinsic worth been maintained.

Second, if the life that was ended was an especially horrific one of unending emotional and physical pain and suffering, then the "before" and "after" worlds will have a significant difference in their values. The latter is more intrinsically valuable overall because it no longer contains a life that was not worth living, although it also has an actual intrinsic loss of a person. Again, the overall context is important. One of our duties is to make the world a better place. That generally should be helping ourselves and others live a flourishing life, but in some cases that is not possible. In these tragic circumstances, an immediate loss of intrinsic worth can enhance the overall intrinsic value of the organic whole called the world in which we live. Each potential case of physician-assisted suicide would have to be evaluated in the same way before anyone could claim that the physician should help.

We now arrive at the strong argument against PAS. Whether or not a physician should assist in a suicide is not merely a matter of whether a person wants to commit suicide and if his death would make the world or organic whole in which he lives a better place. We have to consider the person who is being asked to assist and what her duties and freedoms are in such cases. Clearly, if we take physician's autonomy as seriously as we take the request for assistance in killing oneself, then we cannot state that the physician has a duty to assist in all cases.

I will consider the moral obligations a physician—one who does not want to help because of her personal moral beliefs—has in these situations. Let us assume that the physician's beliefs are permissibly held on the grounds of rationality or nonrationality, whichever one is appropriate for the situation. In the first case, she has reasonable arguments against PAS. In the second, she has nonrational moral beliefs stemming from religious beliefs that are not opposed to the evidence available to any reasonable person in her situation. Unethically held beliefs would be irrational ones; for example, her beliefs and actions would be irrational if she were a religious bigot of some type. But in this situation, her beliefs are based on permissible faith rather than nonexisting evidence.

It is apparent that a physician does not have a duty to help another person commit suicide unless certain conditions are fulfilled. First, the person who wants to kill herself has come to that decision as a moral agent reasonably and autonomously using the evidence available to her and a rational decision procedure. Second, the potential suicide's life is not one that currently or in the near future will allow her to flourish. Third, the sorry state of the potential suicide's existence is highly unlikely to change. Fourth, there are no laws or other means of harm that will make the physician's life significantly worse than it would have otherwise have been. Fifth, all legal requirements have been fulfilled. These conditions are necessary but not sufficient to form a duty for any physician.

Adding a sixth condition to the moral obligation will help resolve clashes between the autonomy of the patient and that of medical professionals. We must always remember that, in some significant areas, the patient is the weaker member in the doctor-patient relationship. First, the patient does not have the ability to obtain the drugs she may need to carry out her plans efficiently and successfully. Second, she has to rely on the physician to help her obtain what she needs. Third, the physician has taken a responsibility to help others by becoming a physician and practicing in the area. That is the choice he made, and with it come both benefits and burdens. Sometimes, those burdens mean taking care of people one does not like or doing procedures one finds distasteful, but they are obligatory because others expect that the physician as a physician will do those things for which he has been trained and which they, as nonphysicians, cannot do for themselves. That is, a professional by becoming a professional has certain duties based on his adopting a role that has necessary duties. Physicians have especially stringent obligations as doctors because their skills and the medical system give them enormous power that is denied to those who are not physicians.

Let us consider an autonomy conflict between patient and doctor. Suppose that the physician does not want to assist a suicide but the patient wants the physician to help. If there are no other available physicians to whom the person contemplating taking her own life can turn without imposing too great of a burden on herself, then the physician's autonomous decision not to help is overridden by the patient's need for the physician's assistance. That is, the physician's autonomy is trumped by that of the patient. For example, the physician must help if there is no other physician geographically close enough to the patient to would allow her to use that physician without too great a cost to herself. Of course, if the cost makes it impossible for her to carry out her wishes, then it is too high. Also too high is any expenditure on her part that would alter her decision merely because she cannot afford to pay that cost. In these cases, since the patient is the weaker partner in the relationship, her needs should be put before those of the physician, who has greater power. If the potential suicide has no meaningful option other than the objecting physician, then the physician must assist even though doing so may violate his moral beliefs.

In summary, I have made four contentious conclusions. First, there are different types of euthanasia and each requires different moral thinking. In certain situations, it is possible for some types of euthanasia to be permissible while others are not. Second, voluntary euthanasia of whatever type is merely a form of suicide. Third, there is no right to life, but, at best, there is a right to a flourishing life and a right to increase flourishing as long as doing so does not limit the ability of others to thrive. Finally, a medical professional can have a duty to help a patient commit suicide even when the professional has moral objections to doing so.

STEFFEN

Physician-assisted suicide (PAS)—some working on this issue prefer to avoid all the negative moral connotations associated with the term *suicide* and talk instead of "physician aid (or assistance) in dying"—has presented a challenge to our moral thinking about end-of-life issues. What has propelled PAS into our moral discussions is neither that we are now trying to think of new roles for physicians nor that we have evolved into a new moral realm where deep-seated prohibitions against suicide are undergoing a sea change. What changes have taken place have been caused by advances in medicine and medical technology, which can today extend life long beyond the medical norms in place one hundred years ago. Recall that Terri Schiavo was kept alive in a persistent vegetative state for fifteen years with no hope of her returning to consciousness. Without the technological interventions available to those who defibrillated her and stabilized her with various medications she would have simply died the night of her collapse. Today, people can suffer enduring illnesses. Once lethal conditions have become chronic illnesses, and medical treatments and therapeutic interventions do an amazing job of keeping death at bay. But extending life can exact a high cost beyond the expenditure of dollars and medical resources—it can threaten to rob patients of their dignity, their autonomy, and their sense of bodily integrity and psychological control. Extending life can also deny physicians the opportunity to act beneficently and in the best interest of their patients, even leading physicians to harm their patients by extending length of life as quality of life decreases. In large part, the movement toward public discussion of PAS has been a response to the medical and technological successes that have extended life beyond what many patients wish to endure.

PAS, even if it is called "physician assistance in dying," is suicide. Where legal, a physician is authorized to write a prescription and advise a patient about how a lethal dose of a medication can and should be taken if the patient chooses to end his or her own life, but the physician is not permitted to administer a lethal injection or be an agent for the actual dispatching of the patient. Dr. Jack Kevorkian personally administered lethal dosages of drugs to patients who requested it—he was tried and convicted of murder and spent eight years in a Michigan prison.

Because the patient must self-administer the lethal drug and understands that by this action death will result, it is reasonable to call what happens a self-killing, a suicide. Using this language affects ordinary moral perceptions about the acceptability of the practice, for "suicide" bears the moral imprint of an unacceptable act expressly forbidden in our cherished ethical views, including Kantianism, and in many if not most religious ethical perspectives as well. Accordingly, physician-assisted suicide is not a common practice. In America, it is not even common in the states where it is permitted. Where such a practice has been legalized, the law imposes numerous conditions and serious constraints on the process whereby a patient moves toward securing a necessary dose of medication. PAS is a highly regulated process.

I would approach PAS through the natural law ethical perspective I have been advocating and using throughout these pages. This ethical approach can be applied to PAS and, more importantly, actually has been. I argued that this ethical approach is one that people actually use—and this commends it to our attention—and I now want to say that we can fashion a morally justified instance of PAS. The Oregon Death with Dignity Act, which first legalized PAS in the United States, actually exemplifies in law the very model of moral thinking I have been advocating. In what follows I will discuss PAS as a rule-governed activity and defend the permissibility of the act if it meets the criteria that would justify overruling our ordinary moral prohibitions on suicide. I will conclude with some remarks about religious viewpoints on this issue.

Involving physicians in the dying process is in some senses a very common and ordinary activity, for doctors attend the dying, make them comfortable, address pain issues, and provide the reassurance of professional care. Yet the idea that physicians could actively euthanize a patient, or even provide medical counsel and then write a prescription that could be used to bring about a desired death, seems to violate common expectations of the physician's professional role. If PAS becomes common medical practice, perceptions of the physician's role will change, and one of the great objections to PAS is that it would transform the physician from a healer into a suicide accessory or even a killer. Objections also focus on the way PAS seems to provide professional assistance, even encouragement, for suicide, a morally and legally prohibited practice, further distorting what a physician is supposed to be doing, which is saving life, extending life, and providing care for the living while keeping death at bay.

That such objections are commonplace helps us ground the necessary first step in a "just PAS" ethic. That is, we can claim that the reluctance to create legal room for PAS actually presents empirical evidence in support of a "common agreement" to the effect that ordinarily physicians ought not be about the business of helping patients die, either by the physician's own involvement in killing or as an agent who makes a patient's desire to end life via suicide possible. That only a few jurisdictions provide legal authorization—for example, Switzerland, Belgium, the Netherlands, and four states in the United States—testifies to its rarity and to the reluctance to alter perceptions of the physician's role as life-preserving healer. We can articulate a common agreement for a theory of "just PAS" thusly:

> Physician involvement in helping patients die ostensibly reflects a conflict between a physician acting in the best interests of the patient and the physician's traditional role as healer dedicated to preserving and enhancing the lives of persons. Since the preservation of life is a preeminent, although not absolute, value for physicians, ordinarily physicians ought not participate in actions that directly lead to the deaths of patients. In other words, the moral presumption involved in physician-assisted suicide is against the practice.[6]

The reasons that the moral presumption articulates opposition to physician-assisted suicide are rather easy to discern. Physician-assisted suicide is, after all, still suicide, an intentional killing that negates the good of life, and we recognize common prohibitions on such actions. Kant pointed out that suicide is undertaken by those who seek to improve their situation but who then act to eliminate any possibility that they can experience the improvement,

---

6. In this discussion I am drawing on material from Steffen, *Ethics and Experience*, 117–31.

thus rendering the act contradictory and irrational. Kant did not consider the possibility of rational suicide. The Kantian perspective would note that a suicide is not an act that can be universalized and that persons of good will concerned to promote the good of life ought to prevent rather than condone or encourage suicide. Consequentialists would note that suicide may create in some situations an overall benefit, but they would also have to weigh the fact that it inflicts pain and suffering on loved ones and even the moral community itself. Clearly, we can grasp why suicide is ordinarily deemed an action deserving of moral condemnation.

Critics of PAS point out that physician involvement undermines the traditional role of the physician and distorts the medical profession's fundamental commitment to preserving life. They worry that if suicide were made an acceptable medical option, pressures could be brought to bear that would encourage people to make PAS a preferred option, which could affect those least able to resist such pressures: the frail, the disabled, and the poor. PAS could thus be used to devalue the lives of disabled or "undesirable" persons, thus offending ordinary standards of patient care. Critics have countered the view that PAS is a reasonable action to take in the face of pain and the prospect of intractable pain with the argument that pain management is highly developed in modern medicine and that it can be made adequate to a patient's need. Furthermore, various medical, psychological, or even spiritual interventions can address some of the mental conditions that might be prompting a terminally ill person to consider suicide. In addition, resorting to PAS could adversely affect a society's resolve to expand palliative care services needed to help gravely ill and dying patients.

Establishing a common agreement or moral presumption as a normative guide is the first step in devising a "just PAS" ethic. The next step is to establish rule-governing action guides, conditions, or criteria to guide the process of making a justified exception to the common agreement. PAS is a step shy of active voluntary euthanasia, but Holland, which holds that euthanasia is a criminal activity, decriminalized physician-involving euthanasia in 2002, making the Netherlands the first country to allow doctors to be involved in direct action to end the lives of terminally ill patients facing unbearable suffering. The criminal sanctions on euthanasia point to the fact that Holland also abides by the common agreement that physicians ought ordinarily not be involved in helping patients die, but the law then provided that physicians are exempt from criminal liability if they strictly abided by all of the following criteria:

a. The physician must be convinced the patient's request is voluntary, well-considered and lasting.

b. The patient's suffering must be determined to be unremitting and unbearable.

c. The patient must be fully informed of the situation and prospects.

d. The patient and physician both conclude that no reasonable alternative is available.

e. Another physician, at least one, must be consulted.

f. The procedure must be carried out in a medical appropriate fashion.[7]

The Dutch Criminal Code constructed a legal authorization for what we could call "just voluntary active euthanasia." From an ethical point of view, these guidelines avoid an absolutist prohibition on physician activity aimed at ending a patient's life while laying out stringent conditions to govern a euthanasia exception. The Netherlands example illustrates how one society generated a public policy on the basis of a moral understanding that reflects the kind of ethics approach I am advocating here for PAS, and at this point we can turn to consider the idea of "just PAS."

In the United States, forty-six states prohibit physician-assisted suicide and only four—Oregon, Vermont, Washington, and Montana—have legalized it either by legislative or judicial act. This overwhelming negative legal stance against allows us to infer that in the United States moral attitudes toward PAS are overwhelmingly negative. The Oregon Death with Dignity statute recognizes the presumption against PAS in the large number of restrictive definitions and conditions imposed on patients and physicians. There are over seventy restrictions or conditions mentioned in the statute.

The actual content of a "just PAS" ethic must only be constructed on the foundation of *a common agreement or moral presumption against PAS*. What makes the development of an ethic of "just PAS" possible is that reasonable people of good will are open to the possibility that the moral presumption against PAS can and perhaps even should be overruled in certain cases. As we have done on other issues, we can articulate relevant conditions that establish justice-related criteria that would have to be satisfied to claim a "just PAS" ethic. The Netherlands euthanasia law and the Oregon Death with Dignity law model

---

7. Section 293 (2) of the Dutch Criminal Code, as cited in Bert Gordijn and Rien Janssens, "Euthanasia and Palliative Care in the Netherlands: An Analysis of the Latest Developments," *Health Care Analysis* 12, no. 3 (September 2004): 196.

what an actual justice-related, rule-governed ethic would look like. Such an ethic might take form as follows:

Reasonable persons of good will universally agree that ordinarily physicians ought to promote and preserve the lives of patients and not act in accordance with a direct intention of causing a patient's death. This presumption against PAS (and, as in the case of the Netherlands, euthanasia) may, however, be lifted in a specific case if the following conditions are met:

1. The patient makes the request fully informed of his or her situation and prospects.
2. The patient's condition is terminal and death is imminent, with the prospect of six remaining months of life being a generally accepted medical time frame for defining "terminal."
3. The patient's request is not prompted by depression, as determined by a psychological evaluation.
4. The resources of palliative care will not provide a dignified death or prove fully efficacious in the final period of the end stage.
5. The patient's autonomy is to be respected throughout, and patients can withdraw the request for PAS at any point in the process.
6. The physician who participates must be willing to participate and have no mental reservations about involvement. There must be no coercion placed on the physician or patient by relevant or interested parties: family, the state, other medical authorities, or insurance companies.
7. The actual means of dispatch must be swiftly acting and painless.
8. Laws must exempt the physician who follows these guidelines from any prosecution for wrongful death, and the family of the patient must be protected from those who would seek to benefit from PAS, like an insurance company that seeks to renege on a death benefit due to the patient's suicide.
9. PAS must be approached as a last resort that is designed to preserve the value of physician beneficence and autonomous patient decision making in the face of imminent and intractably painful death.
10. Actual use of PAS must be publically reported in a timely and regular way so that any statistical trends showing abuse or discrimination against particular groups because of race, age, sex, or class status can be subjected to investigation and the practice of PAS halted if evidence of abuse becomes apparent.[8]

These criteria, if satisfied, would morally justify lifting the presumption against PAS. Satisfying the criteria does not mean that the individual would have to then commit suicide. Satisfying the criteria means that patients would now have the choice to end their own lives, and it is clear from the Oregon experience that some people in a situation of terminal illness want to have the option even if they do not exercise it. The Oregon Department of Health reported the following for 2012:

- Under the Oregon law 115 prescriptions were written in 2012, and 77 people chose to hasten their deaths.
- This accounts for 0.2 percent of all deaths in Oregon.
- The major concerns people expressed to their doctors when requesting the medication were centered around wanting control over their final days.
- Of the end-of-life concerns expressed, the *least* common was "financial implications of treatment."

People who request the medication under Oregon's law are receiving high-quality end-of-life care, as these statistics demonstrate:

- Compared to the 45 percent of deaths in the United States now under hospice care, 97 percent of the people who died using Oregon's law in 2012 were enrolled in hospice.
- Over 97 percent of the people who used the law died at home.[9]

One of the great social benefits of the Oregon debate over its Death with Dignity law is that it informed the citizenry about hospice care and alternatives to aggressive end-of-life interventions that many people do not want pursued on their behalf. The social utility of the debate over PAS in Oregon is not to be denied. That fact does not address all of the ethical issues surrounding PAS, but it is an important consideration because the information that was made available to the public in the heated debates over the legalization of PAS made some of

8. These criteria are slightly modified from those advanced in Steffen, *Ethics and Experience*, 127.

9. Melissa Barber, "Oregon's 2012 Death with Dignity Report," Death with Dignity National Center, January 25, 2013, http://www.deathwithdignity.org/2013/01/25/oregons-2012-death-dignity-report; see also Oregon Public Health Division, "Oregon's Death with Dignity Act—2012," 2013, http://public.health.oregon.gov/ ProviderPartnerResources/EvaluationResearch/DeathwithDignityAct/ Documents/year15.pdf.

the options people were wanting to have at the end of life—including palliative, noncurative care—available.

The criteria listed above will not respond to the Kantian who holds that suicide is irrational and that the person (physician) who assists is involved in an unjust killing, but it might persuade some Kantians, concerned to emphasize autonomous decision making, of the need for beneficent care to persons who have good reasons to think that they have no future. That is, some Kantians could hold that reason itself leads to the PAS process and that a suicide could be rational. The "just PAS" ethic laid out above is meant to be of assistance to those who are not caught in an absolutist perspective on this issue but who are willing to consider a reasoned and morally moderate position. That moderate position is not insisting that an individual take the medications once prescribed, only that by following the guidelines they are in a moral position of choice that others can and should respect.

The criteria above are rather limited compared to what is found in the actual Death with Dignity Act itself, which imposes safeguards against abuse with seventy-two different qualifications, restrictions, authorizations, and conditions. The Oregon law presents us with a legalized version of a "just PAS" ethic, and we could show that by simply listing the seventy-two conditions. That would present us, however, with a rather unwieldy ethics tool. It is unmistakable in my view that the Oregon law does incorporate a "just PAS" ethic by stating numerous qualifications, stipulations, and requirements that must be satisfied in order to have claim to a justified exception to the moral (and legal) presumption that physicians ought ordinarily not participate in their patient's suicides. Failure to satisfy the criteria laid out in the statute would render any instance of PAS illegal and, on my analysis, immoral as well. The Oregon statute stipulates that only competent adult residents of Oregon suffering a terminal illness that will lead to death within six months are candidates for PAS. It then sets up specific and highly qualified criteria that must be satisfied prior to physician involvement in a patient request to commit suicide. The "just PAS" ethic addresses all of the issues deemed legally relevant in the actual Death with Dignity Act, and out of 32,475 deaths in Oregon in 2012, only seventy-seven were attributable to physician assisted suicide under the Death with Dignity Act, indicating that actual use is rare—that 0.2% of all Oregon deaths mentioned above.[10]

Approaching the ethics of PAS by articulating a common agreement against PAS yet allowing exceptions when they meet various justice criteria will

10. The state death statistics are taken from https://public.health.oregon.gov/BirthDeathCertificates/ VitalStatistics/death/Documents/dage12.pdf.

be unsatisfactory for those who are opposed to PAS absolutely, the same way a pacifist might object to the prospect of a just war. What is at stake here is a fundamental commitment to seeing the moral world in a certain way. Does one see a world in which it is possible to live and act with moral purity and with absolute moral certainty, or does one see the world as tragic, difficult, and complex, requiring that human persons use practical reason to confront moral issues with reflection, analysis, and some inevitable uncertainty, knowing that we cannot know everything. The "just PAS" ethic seeks to preserve our basic moral agreements, which, in this case, include a presumption against PAS, yet it also acknowledges that in the tragic circumstances of life certain cases of PAS might be permissible. This approach urges people to engage their own moral views with public policy options. The Oregon law was approved by a referendum (Ballot Measure 16, approved in 1994) where just such public engagement took place prior to the actual law being signed in 1997. The approach to moral thinking represented by a "just PAS" ethic, rather than resolving particular cases, invites deliberation. This form of moral reflection is a form of citizen engagement; rather than cutting off debate by the assertion of moral absolutes, it expresses an approach to moral deliberation that respects the strengths of democracy.

RELIGIOUS REACTIONS TO PAS

Physician-assisted suicide does not enjoy widespread religious support. According to Christina L. H. Traina:

> Across the major traditions there is a history of opposition to PAS/ euthanasia, for related but slightly different reasons. In each case the practices must be seen in the context of the tradition's beliefs about death and the ways in which we ought to prepare for a good death. And in most cases, the incredible existential weight accorded the "natural" process of dying is traceable to a belief that our final days or hours have profound significance for reincarnation, afterlife, or resurrection.[11]

In response to an article by Damien Keown on Buddhist perspectives on assisted suicide and euthanasia, R. E. Florida states: "Keown is clear that the Buddhist tradition is remarkably diverse and that his paper presents only one Buddhist

---

11. Christina L. H. Traina, "Religious Perspectives on Assisted Suicide," *Journal of Criminal Law and Criminology* 88, no. 3 (Spring 1998): 1148.

perspective, one based on his interpretation of relevant passages from the Pali canon. However, there is a real danger that those readers who are perhaps not broadly read in Buddhism could be misled to think that the position presented in Keown's paper is *the* Buddhist view rather than *a* Buddhist view."[12] I cite this comment because it makes an important point relevant to discussions of PAS in Buddhism as well as in Hinduism, Christianity, and Judaism—namely, that there is no one view that can be put forward as the final teaching of a whole religious tradition. Anything said about assisted suicide from the perspective of a particular religious tradition must therefore be qualified and accepted as a generality that does not speak for all in the tradition and definitely not for the tradition itself. I can offer some broad generalities that doubtless would find support from many in these traditions, but there is much detail to go into, and within the traditions there are strikingly different points of view among individual believers and practitioners. So with that heavy qualification let us consider how this idea of assisted suicide is addressed in various religious traditions.

Suffering has a divine purpose in Islam, and the Qur'an ties killing and suicide to Allah's condemnation: "You shall not kill (yourselves or) one another. Allah is merciful, but he that does that through wickedness and injustice shall be burnt in Hell-fire."[13] Suicide leads to damnation. The belief that life is sacred because Allah gives life is connected to the idea that Allah alone has the prerogative to choose the length of life for individuals, and it is therefore impermissible for human beings to interfere with Allah's will in this matter. Muslim jurists and theologians condemn suicide as irrational and impermissible although "some interpretations in classical sources intimate a degree of extenuation, especially when coping with circumstances," and terminal disease at the end of life could be such a circumstance.[14] Islamic biomedical ethics will allow that death can result as a double effect from pain management where there is no direct intent to kill. Withdrawal of treatment that will inevitably lead to death is also permissible with the consent of all relevant parties, but "in the final analysis . . . there are no grounds for the justifiable ending a terminally ill person's life, whether through voluntary active-euthanasia or physician assisted suicide in Islam."[15]

12. R. E. Florida, "A Response to Damien Keown's 'Suicide, Assisted Suicide and Euthanasia: A Buddhist Perspective,'" *Journal of Law and Religion*, 13, no. 2 (1998-99): 413.

13. Qur'an 4:29, *The Koran*, trans. N. J. Dawood (New York: Penguin Books, 1981), 368. The insertion is from other translations—this verse is often cited as an "anti-suicide" verse from the Qur'an.

14. Abdulaziz Sachedina, *Islamic Biomedical Ethics*, 168–69.

15. Ibid, 170–71.

The teachings of the Buddha obviously do not address PAS specifically, but Buddhist teaching and values in general support a prohibition on suicide that is reflected in the "middle way," which on this issue would involve a presumption that life should be neither intentionally destroyed nor preserved at all costs.[16] The dying process can provide an opportunity for reflection on the body, its impermanence, and one's own attachment to it. And because of the cycling of life, so important to Buddhism (and Hinduism) in the doctrine of reincarnation and in the idea of karma, the question can fairly be asked whether killing a patient at the end of life or allowing a suffering patient to commit suicide actually ends the suffering. PAS or euthanasia could extend the suffering into rebirth, and if the sickness a patient is experiencing is itself the result of bad karma, the PAS is unlikely to end the suffering—Buddhist teaching would be inclined to say that it is better to deal with the suffering in the life one has.[17] Hindu teachings have concerned themselves with the consequences that would follow the physician who assisted in killing a patient or assisted with a suicide since such actions would create negative karma harmful to both patient and physician. The concern is expressed in both Hinduism and Buddhism that PAS offends against the principle of ahimsa, which entails the meanings of "respect for life as well as of 'doing no harm.'"[18]

In Buddhism and Hinduism, PAS creates a conflict between compassion for the suffering patient and the karmic consequences of killing, which could extend suffering into another lifetime. Buddhist ethics focus attention on intentions and motives, and in general, even when done from compassionate motives, the tradition stands opposed to PAS. That opposition rests in the fact that PAS negates the value of life, connects the will with death, and "negate(s) in the most fundamental way the values and final goal of Buddhism by destroying what the tradition calls the 'precious human life.' . . . [T]o choose death over life is to affirm all that Buddhism regards as negative [and to] reject the goal of flourishing and fulfillment described by the Third Noble Truth (nirvana) and the due process by which this is attained."[19]

As in Islam, there are teachings in Judaism that advance the view that suffering is an occasion for self-examination, and "the pious person observes

16. Damien Keown, "Suicide, Assisted Suicide and Euthanasia: A Buddhist Perspective," *Journal of Law and Religion* 13, no. 2 (1998–99): 405.

17. Peter Harvey, *An Introduction to Buddhist Ethics*, 297.

18. See the note about Hinduism at "Religion and Spirituality," Death with Dignity National Center, http://www.deathwithdignity.org/historyfacts/religion#sthash.FuNQE2Tk.dpuf, and the ahimsa discussion in Keown, "Suicide, Assisted Suicide and Euthanasia," 399.

19. Keown, "Suicide, Assisted Suicide and Euthanasia," 387.

the commandments with love for God and accepts suffering with joy."[20] But if we had to take note of differences of viewpoint within Buddhism, how much more striking will such a qualification be in examining Judaism, a religion of the Rabbis who teach and learn through a disputation process vital to the faith itself. So despite perspectives, some very old, that shine a positive light on suffering as an opportunity to deepen faith and understanding of God, there is a strong counterpoint to such a position, and "today there are some authorities who justify suicide because of extreme suffering or to avoid the commission of a cardinal sin. In such cases there would perhaps also be justification for assisted suicide and euthanasia."[21] In Judaism—and not for one's own benefit but for the sake of God—death is to be preferred to being forced to commit a cardinal sin, which includes idolatry along with murder and sexual immorality. The mitzvot that oblige persons to prevent *chillul hashem* (desecrating God's name) and to observe the commandment of *qiddush hashem* (sanctifying God's name) allow suicide as an exception in the circumstance of martyrdom, but otherwise suicide is forbidden, as is assisting someone in committing suicide.[22]

In general, Judaism holds that God is the owner of the human body, that God has imposed requirements to preserve life and health, and that to injure oneself—or kill oneself—harms what belongs rightly to God. Judaism, in general and by tradition, therefore opposes assisted suicide, some instances of which can be equivalent to murder. Applying traditional understanding and core Jewish values, a general Jewish perspective would oppose assisted suicide on the grounds that allowing a suffering person to live is redemptive or that assisting in suicide transgresses God's decision about when an individual sufferer should die. Jewish opposition to PAS is vested in the idea that life is God's and that human beings lack authority to tread on God's prerogatives having to do with life and its possible curtailment. Judaism's core values are life-affirming, and to that end Jewish teaching has held that all of Jewish law may be set aside to save lives (the law of *pikkuah nefesh*).[23] Judaism would emphasize the need for palliative care in terminal cases but not assisted suicide. The Union of Orthodox Jewish Congregations and the Rabbinical Council of America both opposed the Oregon Death with Dignity law and even filed amicus briefs opposing PAS when the law went before the Supreme Court, which then upheld the Oregon law in its 2006 decision.[24] Despite such concerted effort in voicing opposition

---

20. Ze'ev W. Falk, "Jewish Perspectives on Assisted Suicide and Euthanasia," *Journal of Law and Religion* 13, no. 2 (1998–1999): 379.

21. Ibid., 383.

22. Eliott N. Dorff, "Assisted Suicide," *Journal of Law and Religion*, 13, no. 2 (1998–1999): 268.

23. Ibid., 276.

to assisted suicide, PAS has received support, particularly from Reform rabbis, and in general the issue remains a topic of disputation among laity and rabbis alike.[25]

Among the perspectives that can be found in Christianity on the issue of PAS is the Roman Catholic teaching found in the 1995 encyclical *Evangelium Vitae* (The Gospel of Life), which states,

> To concur with the intention of another person to commit suicide and to help in carrying it out through so-called "assisted suicide" means to cooperate in, and at times to be the actual perpetrator of, an injustice which can never be excused, even if it is requested. In a remarkably relevant passage Saint Augustine writes that "it is never licit to kill another: even if he should wish it, indeed if he request it because, hanging between life and death, he begs for help in freeing the soul struggling against the bonds of the body and longing to be released; nor is it licit even when a sick person is no longer able to live."[26]

A 1992 statement adopted by the Church Council of the Evangelical Lutheran Church in America offered the following view: "We oppose the legalization of physician-assisted death, which would allow the private killing of one person by another. Public control and regulation of such actions would be extremely difficult, if not impossible. The potential for abuse, especially of people who are most vulnerable, would be substantially increased." Yet that same statement also said this:

> The deliberate action of a physician to take the life of a patient, even when this is the patient's wish, is a different matter. As a church we affirm that deliberately destroying life created in the image of God is contrary to our Christian conscience. While this affirmation is clear, we also recognize that responsible health care professionals struggle to choose the lesser evil in ambiguous borderline situations—for

---

24. *Encyclopedia of Religion in American Politics*, ed. Jeffrey D. Schultz, John G. West, and Iain S. MacLean (Phoenix, AZ: Oryx, 1999), s. v. "Euthanasia," 94.

25. See, for example, Rabbi Phil Cohen's support for PAS in a debate over PAS in *Reform Judaism Online* (Summer 2013), http://reformjudaismmag.org/Articles/index.cfm?id=3250.

26. John Paul II, *Evangelium Vitae* (The Gospel of Life), encyclical, March 25, 1995, para. 66, http://www.vatican.va/holy_father/john_paul_ii/encyclicals/documents/hf_jp-ii_enc_25031995_evangelium-vitae_en.html.

example, when pain becomes so unmanageable that life is indistinguishable from torture.[27]

Statements in favor of choice for PAS have been made in the United Church of Christ and by some American Methodists. "The Episcopalian (Anglican) Unitarian, Methodist, Presbyterian and Quaker movements are amongst the most liberal, allowing at least individual decision making in cases of active euthanasia."[28]

There are diverse viewpoints about PAS among Christians, but in cases where physical pain and cognitive impairment are at issue, the more conservative and fundamentalist Christians are—and this applies to Catholics as well as to Protestants—the more likely are they to desire life-extending treatment in end-of-life situations.[29] The Massachusetts Council of Churches, which is comprised of seventeen Protestant and Orthodox denominations, issued a statement on PAS that included the following statement and conclusions:

> Physician assisted suicide is not the answer. A right and good answer is found in the creation of measures that will effectively diminish suffering, so that the terminally ill patient can live and die with a maximum of consciousness and a minimum of pain. . . . Medical heroics all too often represent a kind of bio-idolatry, a vitalism that seeks to preserve mere biological existence, in spite of the patient's wishes or the cost to society. Unqualified respect for the patient as a bearer of the divine image is paramount. This means that in the final analysis the decision must have as its final aim, the surrender of the person into the loving and merciful hands of God with unwavering conviction that God, and God alone, should determine the limits of life and death.

The statement goes on to support life as a gift from God, to oppose "extraordinary means of keeping a dying patient alive though "technological

27. ELCA, "End of Life Decisions," http://download.elca.org/ELCA Resource Repository/ End_Life_DecisionsSM.pdf.

28. "What Are Christian Perspectives on Euthanasia and Physician-Assisted Suicide?," Pro-Con.org, http://euthanasia.procon.org/view.answers.php?questionID=000154.

29. Shane Sharp, Deborah Carr, and Cameron Macdonald, "Religion and End-of-Life Treatment Preferences: Assessing the Effects of Religious Denomination and Beliefs," Social Forces 91, no. 1 (September 2012): 275–98.

wizardry," and to call for affordable health care, optimum palliative care options, and additional funding for hospice efforts.[30]

In general, Christians will support reasonable alternatives to PAS, especially palliative care, and although some churches, including the Unitarian Universalist denomination, support the autonomy of persons seeking PAS, the idea that PAS "is not the answer" does reflect the views of many Christians.

COMMENTARY

COOLEY:

What roles do the subjective and objective play in determining futility? Is there a standard that applies to all people that is not somehow bound to how the individual or her proxy feels about the situation? Is there something wrong with allowing the individual to say it is futile even when most physicians would say it is not futile?

STEFFEN:

Philosophically, the distinction I would draw in defining these terms is this: objective truths are those acknowledged to be objective in public ways, but subjective truths, by being designated as such, are not publically available or acknowledged. That does not mean, however, that they are not objective or that it is impossible to translate a subjective experience into language that relates in meaningful ways "what is the case" so that it is understandable to others. What is at issue is people's ability to use the language and make meaning public, the way taking a course in auto mechanics would allow me to start talking the "hidden" language of the shop with my mechanic when earlier I had not understood what mechanics were talking about. The language was always "objective" and pointed to "what is the case" with fuel injection versus carburetors, but I lacked the facility to do anything with such language because I didn't understand it and had not developed my capacity to use that language meaningfully. So let's go to your question with this understanding of "subjective" as a form of objectivity in mind.

30. Massachusetts Council of Churches, "Physician Assisted Suicide: A Christian Perspective from the Massachusetts Council of Churches," adopted unanimously by the board of directors of the Massachusetts Council of Churches on November 30, 2000, http://www.masscouncilofchurches.org/docs/doc_suicide.htm.

Let us first consider end of life as an objective reality. According to the *Medicare Claims Processing Manual*, terminal illness and eligibility for hospice care is determined by a physician who certifies that a patient has a terminal illness defined as "a life expectancy of 6 months or less if the disease runs its normal course."[31] That may not always be the case, and surely some physicians who have given their best medical prognosis have missed the six-month mark. Medical science is art as well as science. Nevertheless, this looks like an "objective" determination of what constitutes a terminal illness—it is a public statement based on a consensus of medical judgment about how a terminal disease typically proceeds, and such a definition is practically helpful in deciding, for instance, who is eligible for the palliative care of hospice. The definition of "terminal" looks to be "objective" and based on medical science, and in large part it is.

A definition of futility would operate the same way. If we have an operationalized definition accepted within the profession and recognized publicly—and, for this issue, that would include legally—that definition would guide physicians in their examination, diagnosis, and prognosis of a patient. Physicians, who are given room to disagree with one another, can examine a case and determine that in their best judgment, with all the experience they bring to bear and with the knowledge of a patient and the patient's condition, a situation is futile. Physicians can come to an agreement that the case before them is futile. Although we might want to say that the definition of futile to which the physicians appeal is objective, the application of that definition to a certain set of medical data is subjective; that is, it relies on physicians as human subjects using experience and expert knowledge to evaluate and determine whether futility should be applied to the case before them. I believe that, in general, we have good reason to trust that professional physicians are able to examine a patient and the entire situation involving the patient and come to an agreement that a particular medical condition is, in fact, futile. Not every case will meet with physician consensus, and some cases may be disputed because of ambiguities in the medical record or interpretive differences regarding the medical data. But determining futility is not a process lacking objectivity when agreements involving expert knowledge and deep experience are reached. Determining futility involves physicians who work in a community of medical care professionals who themselves bring to the assessment of individual cases expert knowledge and a depth of patient care

---

31. "Processing Hospice Claims," ch. 11 of *Medicare Claims Processing Manual*, rev. January 31, 2014 (Baltimore, MD: Centers for Medicare and Medicaid Services), http://www.cms.gov/Regulations-and-Guidance/Guidance/ Manuals/downloads/clm104c11.pdf.

experience, so that what might appear as the subjective nature of determining futility finally yields to, and even entails, objective assessment.

This gets at some of your question but not all of it. You also ask about patients who might claim that their situation is futile when the physicians do not agree. My response here is that listening to human subjects is central to good patient care, and determining futility should not overlook patient input as if medical science must always have the definitive word. Most often, futility situations will arise with a comatose patient physicians think will no longer benefit from any treatment, so determining futility is something that will involve families who then have to decide whether to take the practical step of withdrawing or withholding further care. Your question, however, asks us to consider a conscious and, I also have to assume, rational individual who asserts futility over a doctor's medical objection.

The task here is to consider the situation facing a patient who is arguing for futility. It is certainly possible that a patient can lose the will to live. Let us imagine that the patient considers the combination of physical and mental deterioration, illness, and factors in the individual's biography as leading to the conclusion "life is not worth living." Let's listen to the patient. Perhaps the patient's spouse has died, the patient's children are struggling financially, and the patient does not want to be a burden on them, especially financially. Furthermore, most of the patient's friends have predeceased the patient; age and Parkinson-like symptoms have destroyed the ability to play the piano, the patient's former occupation and avocation; and severe hearing loss has made listening to music—the love of the patient's life—impossible. The patient cannot envision a future worth living and feels, as ethicist James Rachel's once wrote, that the "biography is ended." Now all those details about the patient's condition look as if they are subjective and private factors having nothing to do with "objectivity," yet I would say that those "subjective factors" are very much "what is the case" with the patient. Those details, which seem so personal and individual, constitute the objective reality the patient is facing. Should we not take seriously the claim of this patient if the patient said, "My life is over. I am ill and in pain—both in my body and in my soul. I don't have anything to live for since everything that was important and meaningful to me is gone. I don't want to be a burden on those whom I love. I'm grateful for the life I had, but I cannot live that life anymore, and I am ready to move on. I am without a future."

In this example we have an objective statement about futility by a human subject who is suffering, sees no future, and is ready to die. The six-month window may or may not be in play, but the explanation for why this patient says "life is not worth living anymore" ought not be dismissed as an unreliable or irrelevant statement. The statement is subjective in the sense that it is a report on the inner life and evaluations of a human subject about his or her own life—we have subjectivity in that sense of inner experience. Because of this report of inner experience, we now have access to data that had been hidden; the subjective experience is now public and understandable by others—I understand it, don't you? I think this "subjectivity" is very relevant to determining "what is the case" and should affect ethical decision making and even the approach to treatment and medical care.

Making decisions about patient care and treatment at the end of life ought to take into account patients' understanding of their own medical, psychological, spiritual, and even financial situation, for that subject-related contribution is included in the objective reality of the patient situation as it presents to us "what is the case" and thus should affect decisions about patient care.

COOLEY:

Second, is voluntary euthanasia a form of suicide?

STEFFEN:

You ask if voluntary euthanasia is a form of suicide. I think it is a *form* of suicide the way killing another person in self-defense is a form of homicide. I do not *equate* voluntary euthanasia with suicide, as if they were synonymous, but we face some issues with language and the moral connotations of these highly charged linguistic terms. Suicide is usually thought of as an intentional self-killing committed for some specific reason, often related, as Kant pointed out, to problems in one's life. As we have said before, Kant believed that because killing oneself to solve problems eliminated the person who would benefit from the solution—the suicide victim—suicide was inevitably a contradictory and thus irrational act. As we have mentioned several times already, Kant could not conceive of rational suicide, hence the freight of moral negativity on the term *suicide*. But with medical technology extending life beyond the point where a human person is able to pursue or enjoy the goods of life, it seems to me possible for there to be such a thing as rational suicide; and voluntary euthanasia, as an intentional act of decision making leading directly to one's own death, could be deemed a rational suicide in various circumstances.

Perhaps we should opt for other terminology altogether, like *voluntary life sacrifice*. The soldier who sees the grenade tossed in the foxhole falls on it to save fellow soldiers and dies—a spontaneous act performed with certain knowledge that it will lead directly to the soldier's own death. The soldier voluntarily sacrifices his life for another. This is an ideal held up, by the way, in the teachings of Jesus: "No greater love has a person than to lay down his life for a friend" (John 15:13), so rather than being condemned, the act is deemed praiseworthy. Practically speaking, we do not condemn this act of "sacrifice" even though it is also a self-killing. The victim is hailed as a hero. It will be said as the soldier receives posthumous medals that this was the ultimate sacrifice. We ascribe to the soldier altruism and even interpret the act as one of supererogation.

I see suicide, voluntary euthanasia, and even the grenade sacrifice example as related acts. All three present us with an agent exercising autonomy and consenting to a lethal act that the patient knows will result in death. And more than the will is involved in these decisions. A patient's request for voluntary euthanasia, for example, arises from the agent's self-understanding, perceptions, and choices; and it would involve a complex act of cognition that involves self-assessment, concern for others, and a realistic appraisal of medical and psychological conditions. I think the person who requests voluntary euthanasia engages cognition even more than volition—perceptions, understanding, and evaluations, which then engage the will for action. Many details would be involved in particular cases, and there are always questions to ask about coercion, freedom, and the suicide agent's competence and rationality. How those are sorted out will affect the language we decide to use to describe the act, but your question does allow us to consider once again the kind of moral connotations that attach to a term like *suicide*, which may be less negative in the future as end-of-life issues press on more and more families and on individual end-of-life sufferers who want options other than morphine-induced unconsciousness.

COOLEY:

Third, is there a right to life, and, if so, do physicians violate it in PAS?

STEFFEN:

The question about a right to life and its potential violation by a physician participating in a patient's voluntary suicide (PAS) leads me to talk also about persons. It makes sense to me to talk about a right to life because we have reached moral agreement that "persons" are rights-bearing agents. We have done this in ethics but also in law. If we are going to have persons defined as rights-bearing agents, then persons are able to enjoy the goods of life, including the good of life itself to which all persons are entitled, because they hold the status of person. Persons do have a claim on that good (a right to life) inasmuch as reason is able to discern goodness and life itself as a good of life, which all persons have a right to pursue and enjoy. So I would acknowledge a right to life as it is related to the moral category of "person."

Does a physician violate the right to life by participating in PAS? PAS does not involve the physician in the decision a patient makes to commit suicide but involves the physician as a drug prescriber and as an information source. Physicians who have prescription pads and drug manufacturers who provide medications that can be used by patients to kill themselves are part of the PAS process, but the decision about what to do is the patient's, and that decision is only possible at the end of a highly regulated and restricted process—individuals with a terminal illness must *qualify* for the PAS option.

I myself do not see the physician as violating a right to life. My moral description would be that the physician is acting in the best interests of a patient who is exercising autonomy by seeking to meet the numerous conditions that are required in order for the physician to actually write a prescription. Similarly, I would not hold drug manufacturers morally liable. The fact is that the patient is free to choose whether to use the drug to end his or her own life; again, we know from Oregon statistics that there are more prescriptions written than are ever actually used. It seems there is comfort in people facing difficult terminal situations with the knowledge that they could exercise the option if they needed to do so.

So if a physician prescribed a lethal drug that was not used for its intended purpose, would the physician be violating the patient's right to life? I think not, and neither would the physician if the patient decided to use the drug, although in both cases there would be an intention known to the physician of the patient's willingness to end his or her own life with a drug overdose. The decision is the patient's, not the physician's; the physician's decision is whether to become involved in the process, and physicians are free to participate or not. The move to PAS, however, seems to me to be patient driven, and the final decision to proceed with the S part of PAS once the drugs are acquired is the patient's, not the physician's.

STEFFEN:

Does PAS worry you in the sense that declaring a *right* to PAS, which is now a *legal right* in some states, may create an *expectation* that then becomes a *duty*? Are you concerned about the slippery slope in this case leading to a duty to die?

A second question: if palliative care really can assist persons in dying by means of caregiving rather than killing, don't you think that we should presumptively endorse palliation and put PAS on the back burner? In other words, has the new emphasis on palliation—which, ironically, has been made dramatically more available because of the PAS debate and Jack Kevorkian—rendered PAS irrelevant with respect to attending to patient well-being, pain management, and general care at the end of life? Does not palliative care almost eliminate the need for further attention to physician-assisted suicide?

COOLEY:

The slippery-slope argument for PAS moving from a moral right to a moral duty is of great concern to anyone who worries about how human beings will react when we permit actions that hasten death. Basically, the idea is that once people become accustomed to something that had been morally repulsive, they will seek to increase what is permissible because that no longer seems so bad.

Physician-assisted suicide is no different. In 1994, Margaret Battin wrote about circumstantial and ideological manipulation that can make physician-assisted suicide a rational action, even though it would not be an ethical action because it was manipulated.[32] A rational action, of course, is one that makes sense given the situation in which the person finds herself. It is rational, for example, to eat garbage when garbage is the only thing one can eat to remain alive, but it is not rational to do it if there are healthy food sources readily available. It is rational for a potential serial killer to be very careful not to be caught after his first murder because that would prevent him from fulfilling his goal to be a serial killer. But, as one can clearly see, the serial killer's action is not ethical; it merely makes sense given the particular circumstances and the goals the killer has.

Battin was worried about the manipulation of the situation in which a person finds herself or the alteration of social beliefs and conventions that would make it rational for people to choose suicide if it became a legal option. If people began to believe that physician-assisted suicide was a duty as the

---

32. Margaret Battin, *The Least Worst Death* (New York: Oxford University Press, 1994), 196–98.

result of PAS being legal and it becoming the norm of expected behavior, then the society's core beliefs have been manipulated to create a rational but unethical choice for the terminally ill person. This is a form of ideological manipulation. Circumstantial manipulation might happen if the ill individual's living arrangements became so extreme that PAS is the only rational choice she has to escape.[33] Perhaps they would make it obvious to the terminally ill person that she is not acting according to what is expected and is being a burden on them, which would then result in rather cruel treatment of her. For both types of manipulation, the "choice remains crucially and essentially voluntary, and the decision between alternatives free."[34] The manipulation thereby renders the decision to die a rational one, and we could therefore not intervene on the grounds of the person's choice being irrational and harmful in the manner we can for many suicides. As a predicted consequence, the number of PAS cases would increase as social norms changed and people began to consciously or unconsciously make the circumstances in which terminal patients exist bad enough that it becomes rational to choose PAS.

Rosemarie Tong worried about the undue burden placed on women by a right to die, and the even greater burden on them if there is a duty to die, especially if it is a PAS duty. Since women tend to live longer than men and therefore will have to face poverty from reduced financial circumstances and illnesses that happen most often to the very elderly, women will have to make decisions about terminating their lives in greater numbers than men will. Therefore, women will more frequently have to choose PAS, especially if a "duty to die" social norm develops. Second, women in most societies are the caregivers to families and friends, which make women more vulnerable to a duty to die. As Tong correctly points out, "it seems inappropriate to hinge the duty to die on whether one is fortunate enough to be enmeshed in a thick web of meaningful human relationships."[35] But those relationships will be part of the circumstantial and ideological manipulation. Women will try to do what is best for those they care for, even if that means that they have to choose to die earlier than they otherwise would. As we know, end-of-life care is among the most costly forms of care, and many women in care relationships would not want to subject those for whom they care to this burden. Third, given the power of physicians over their patients, the fact that many doctors are men and many of the PAS potential patients will be women, and the power men often have

33. Ibid. 200.

34. Ibid.

35. Rosemarie Tong, "Duty to Die," in *Is There a Duty to Die?*, ed. James M. Humber and Robert F. Almeder, 135–36 (Totowa, NJ: Humana, 2000), 135–36.

over women through social custom, there is an inherent danger that women will be coerced into selecting PAS by male physicians. This duress need not be conscious discrimination, but it will effectively alter decisions so that some women would choose PAS when they otherwise would not. These three factors would therefore make PAS result in sexism of the most vicious kind as women are pushed into physician-assisted suicide in far greater numbers than men. The very poor might be subject to the same sort of manipulation, but on slightly different grounds.

Although the concerns about sliding down the slippery slope into dangerous moral grounds will always be with us on the issue, the experiences of those jurisdictions that have permitted PAS show that the slide need not happen if the system is set up correctly. Two different studies of the Netherlands and Oregon found that there was no significant increase in the rates of physician-assisted suicide.[36] In fact, people were grateful for the opportunity to have this option, and many of the terminally ill patients involved in the studies spent a great deal of time discussing the options and making their own decisions. There were a fair number who decided not to make use of PAS. I think that if we keep doing a very good job of educating people about PAS and having very carefully drawn decision procedures in place with adequate monitoring, then we can avoid turning a right to use PAS into a duty to commit physician-assisted suicide.

As for the palliative care question you raise, I think that palliative care can eliminate some of the pressure for PAS but should not replace physician-assisted suicide as an option. Palliative care works for a great number of people facing the end of their lives. It is something that they autonomously choose so that they can end their lives on their own terms. Since palliative care works so well for those dying, and it allows them to finish writing their life's narratives in ways they desire, it might need to become a standard of practice.

However, there are two significant problems with replacing all PAS with palliative care. First, the cost could be considerably higher than that of PAS. As I stated earlier, end-of-life care is often the most expensive that there is. Campbell et al. found that hospice stays for younger decedents with cancer entail savings for Medicare, but expenditures increased for those without cancer and those

---

36. See Margaret P. Battin, Agnes van der Hiede, Linda Ganzini, Gerrit van der Wal, and Bregje D. Onwuteaka-Philipsen, "Legal Physician-Assisted Dying in Oregon and the Netherlands: Evidence Concerning the Impact on Patients in 'Vulnerable' Groups," *Journal of Medical Ethics* 33 (2007): 591–97; and Frances Norwood, Gerrit Kimsma, and Margaret P. Battin, "Vulnerability and the 'Slippery Slope' at the End-of-Life: A Qualitative Study of Euthanasia, General Practice and Home Death in the Netherlands," *Family Practice* 26, no. 6 (2009): 472–80.

greater than eighty-four years of age.[37] Those with dementia and relatively nonspecific diagnoses cost the most.[38] Austin and Fleisher argue that there is no consensus among experts that hospice saves money over futile medical intervention.[39] So it might be that palliative care is something we should try to achieve, but it might be too financially costly in an era in which people are living far longer lives and dying from dementia and other medically expensive diseases. As we know, there are limited health care resources available to health networks. We need to do what we can to produce the most efficient results while respecting the moral worth of those people in the system.

The larger problem is the cost of removing PAS as a legitimate alternative to palliative care. There are individuals, such as those found in the studies on the Netherlands and Oregon cited above, who want PAS and others who would like to have the power to choose PAS if they want to do so. They want control over the end of their lives. Even if they do not use it, there are those who desire PAS as an option, much as many people want insurance. The importance of their wishes should not minimized merely because we like palliative care better based on our reasoning. And I make this argument on the grounds of autonomy. Although I would not want to do something and might even think it is a bad choice for another to make, if I respect the person, then I must let him write his own narrative for his own life. For example, I can never understand why some people smoke cigarettes. It has been shown to reduce lifespan, causes health problems, and is costly in other ways. However, if this is the decision they have made for their lives, then others should not interfere with it as long as that decision does not illicitly affect others' autonomy.

Having control over the end of one's life is even more important. The end of one's life is literally the final thing that we do and the final action that we can take. It should be under our individual control. I would like to see as many options open to people as it is practical to have, which would include PAS.

COOLEY:

Do you think that a physician or other health care provider has a moral duty to try to talk patients out of PAS if the health care provider's religion forbids it? Should the religious qualms even be mentioned to the patient?

---

37. Diane E. Campbell, Joanne Lynn, Tom A. Louis, and Lisa R. Shugarman, "Medicare Program Expenditures Associated with Hospice Use," *Annals of Internal Medicine* 140, no. 4 (2004): 269–78.

38. Ibid.

39. Bonnie J. Austin and Lisa K. Fleisher, *Financing End-of-Life Care: Challenges for An Aging Population* (Washington, DC: AcademyHealth, 2003), 3, http://www.hcfo.org/pdf/eolcare.pdf.

STEFFEN:

The question about a health care provider having a moral duty to try to talk patients out of PAS if the health care provider's religion forbids it raises the issue of professionals doing what conscience forbids. Physicians and medical caregivers, including pharmacists, are already exempted by law from participating in medical procedures that violate their own values, conscience, and religious beliefs. So no doctor who believes abortion is wrong has to perform an abortion, no pharmacist who has personal moral qualms has to dispense a birth control pill, and the Oregon "Death with Dignity" law specifically exempts any physician who objects to participating in the PAS process. These are protections for conscience and I think they would apply in the situation you raise.

But to go one step further, health care providers are not authorized to preach their own personal morality at patients. This violates the canons of professional behavior, and a professional medical caregiver, one who abides by the guidelines of contemporary medical ethics, needs to respect patient autonomy. Patients must be provided with information to make their own decisions, and if a physician or nurse or pharmacist has qualms of conscience about what can even be told to a patient with respect to information and options for action, those medical professionals should simply absent themselves from any further consultation. I think that is a fine way to proceed. A physician who objects to PAS should not deal with end-of-life issues where PAS is an option but should turn the patient over to others who do not carry such a burden of conscience. Professional caregivers, like everyone else, have moral viewpoints shaped by philosophical and religious commitments, and they themselves should not be coerced into acting contrary to them, except as professional obligation may require. This was discussed in a prior chapter, but it is worth mentioning again. If a woman were in need of a therapeutic abortion to save her life, a physician who objects to abortion has a professional obligation to undertake the procedure if no other physician is available. "Conscience" is therefore not absolute; and I believe professional obligations can and should trump conscience in certain dire circumstances.

In reflecting on this question I am reminded that we should also consider a related issue: the physician who acts from conscience in defiance of social norms. This can be dangerous of course—Nazi medical professionals willingly participating in cruel death-dealing experimentation would come under such a heading. But let's presume such defiance is done out of respect for patient autonomy and as beneficence, which allows us to take Nazi medical experimentation off the table. Now the question with respect to PAS is not the physician who objects to PAS on the basis of personal conscience but one who, on the basis of conscience and as beneficent action that is also respectful of autonomy, does what, say, Dr. Jack Kevorkian did. Kevorkian objected to the legal restrictions that prevented him from helping patients who came to him wanting to die. He directly involved himself in patient dying without protection from "conscience clauses"; and he was prosecuted and sent to prison for doing what he thought was in the patients' best interests. That is something to think about when we consider how philosophical and religious values can affect what a caregiver can and cannot do—and how far they can, and should, go.

7

The End of Life II: Futility/Euthanasia

INTRODUCTION

Medical science has extended life in ways that could not have been imagined a mere hundred years ago. Medical technologies, advanced life-sustaining treatments, new drug therapies, and all kinds of emergency interventions have contributed to holding death at bay as people face the end of their lives. Sometimes the difficulties surrounding end-of-life situations come to widespread public notice, as happened with Terri Schiavo in the most famous medical ethics case of recent years. Due to the success of EMTs who defibrillated her seven times before transporting her to the hospital, Terri Schiavo was kept alive and then went on to live in a persistent vegetative state for fifteen years.

Postponing death and extending life continue to be subjects of medical research, but as we have reflected on Terri Schiavo and cases like hers, serious ethical questions arise. Yes, we can keep people alive, but at what cost? Consider the expense involved in drug therapies that gain extended life but at a price so high that health care costs increase for everyone, or, in another light, consider how diverting end-of-life dollars could be used in public health campaigns to inoculate, vaccinate, and prevent disease in a younger population so that end-of-life costs are diminished. For patients who have exhausted normal treatment for prostate cancer, a regimen for the drug Provenge costs $93,000 and provides about four additional months of life compared to a placebo; the drug Avastin, which is used to treat advanced breast cancer, delayed the median time at which tumors started to grow worse from one to five months at a cost of $88,000 a year—in addition to inciting some difficult side effects like gastrointestinal perforations and hemorrhaging.[1]

---

1. Editorial, "Extremely Expensive Cancer Drugs: Treatments with Limited Medical Benefits for Some Patients Could Be a Drain on Medicare," *New York Times*, July 7, 2011, http://www.nytimes.com/2011/07/07/opinion/07thu2.html?_r=0

Extending life and improving the quality of life are not the same thing, and while keeping death at bay is a professional medical objective and a worthy one to be sure, patients with terminal illness, along with their physicians, their family and friends, their spiritual advisers, and even their attorneys, face some difficult moral perplexity about what to do—and what not to do—in individual cases. For families, these decisions will focus not on cost-benefit abstractions but on the well-being of their loved ones. Dying is a complicated and difficult process, not only biologically but sociologically, psychologically, spiritually, and financially, and ethical perspectives raise questions about how, whether, and under what circumstances life should be extended.

This chapter opens by directing attention to end-of-life issues with a focus on the ethics of treatment, withdrawal of care and life support in futility situations, family involvement in decision making, and the value of hospice care, along with a brief mention of how different religions approach these issues.

STEFFEN

MEDICAL FUTILITY AND END OF LIFE AT THE BEGINNING OF LIFE

If we were to articulate a "common moral agreement" pertaining to individuals who have actively entered the dying process, we could agree that such patients ought to receive medical care and that decision making should involve patients or their surrogates, families, caregivers, and in some cases even legal authorities. The care might be directed toward treatment aimed at restoring the patient to health, or "curing" them; it might focus on caregivers observing advance directives in which a patient spells out what is to be done if he or she is comatose or incapacitated and thus unable to articulate directions; and it might involve an effort to care for the patient by means of palliation. The options for treatment and providing care are many and will depend on the medical details, the patient's involvement and wishes, family input, medical diagnosis and prognosis, ethical issues, and even legal directives.

Note that the idea of a "presumption of treatment" can present caregivers with a legal directive in the absence of an advance directive from a patient. In the Commonwealth of Pennsylvania, for instance, a law that went into effect in January 2007, Act 169, governs end-of-life decision making and advance directives. The assumption is made that any patient coming into a hospital would want hydration and continued nutrition. Only an advance directive or a clearly stated directive from the patient can legally overrule this assumption. Accordingly, the Pennsylvania law does not include hydration and artificial nutrition under its definition of "life sustaining treatment" because these are presumptively given every patient and can be withheld only by explicit direction of the patient. Making patient decisions about nutrition and hydration clearly involves ethics—ethics is about decisions and why we make the ones we do—but end-of-life situations can be difficult for all of those involved in decision making. The need for clarity about values and ethical priorities has led to court and legislature involvement, so decision making is referred to legal requirements that have been put in place to protect patients and guide the actions of medical caregivers. Medical ethicists and bioethicists are often involved with legal issues, as are hospitals, families, and the dying themselves. Medical futility at the end of life is a particularly thorny issue, and law makers have not provided medical professionals and citizens dealing with end-of-life issues with much in the way of legal guidance. In the United States, only Texas has in place a law designed to resolve conflicts around the issue of medical futility.

Discussing futility requires that we first take note that in general medical situations, patients are assumed to be competent to make decisions about their care. This springs from one of the four regnant principles of medical ethics, respect for patient autonomy, which acknowledges the patient as a self-governing person whose decisions are to be respected even in the face of disagreement from family or medical caregivers. (The other principles of medical ethics, incidentally, are nonmaleficence or "do no harm," beneficence or promotion of patient well-being, and justice.) At the end of life, evidence of patient incapacity will affect decision making, which will be redirected from the patient to an advance directive or "living will" the patient has prepared. Following the patient's stated wishes then becomes the way to respect the autonomy of the patient and do what the patient wants done. If no advance directive is available, decision making authority may go to a patient representative or surrogate, usually a family member, who has a durable power of attorney and was authorized by the patient—when the patient was competent—to be the decision maker about the course of care and treatment.

At the end of life, persons facing end-stage disease and incapacity (mental incoherence, unconsciousness, or the permanent unconsciousness of a persistent vegetative state) may be deemed incapacitated and thus incompetent. An advance directive specifying the patient's wish for certain kinds of medical interventions—or the withholding of them—directs the course of treatment. A surrogate decision maker can direct treatment and the withholding of treatment and also specify what life-saving measures, if any, are to be taken. Sometimes courts can be involved in appointing such a surrogate if no family member is available or a surrogate has not been appointed. The question of who decides difficult medical issues at the end of life has often wound up in the courts because decision making involves protecting the interests of the patient when the patient is unable to do so. At issue in end-of-life legal cases are patient's wishes, issues about patient vulnerabilities, conflicts between the values of the patient (or patient's family) and an assessment of the best medical care for the patient, and of course legal liabilities for medical professionals. Unless the law protects those who go through a documented process of consultation and consent for medical actions, the act of "pulling the plug" to withdraw care on a patient for whom future treatment is futile could lead to medical personnel facing serious legal consequences, including prosecution on charges of murder. This has actually happened.[2]

In the 1994 case of Baby K, the District Court for the Eastern District of Virginia faced an end-of-life problem involving the presumption of care, if we can call it that, which was our starting point for this discussion. To say again, the presumption of care is an ethical agreement shared by all reasonable people of good will that ordinarily an individual facing an end-of-life situation should be given care. However this finds its way into the specifics of law in various jurisdictions, the presumption of care is a matter of law as well as of ethics, and it provides the moral support for laws like Pennsylvania's Act 169.

Baby K was born with anencephaly, a severe handicap condition involving absence of the cerebral and cerebellar portions of the brain, so that she was permanently unconscious with no hope of cure or even a treatment that could improve her situation.[3] Baby K did not have any higher brain activity or neocortical capacity for such activity—the baby could not feel pain. Baby K, however, did have brain stem activity and reflex actions so that she could suck, swallow, and cough. Because the technical definitions of brain death in the United States include both higher brain function and brain stem cessation, Baby K did not meet the definition of brain death, so she was therefore placed on a ventilator to help her breathe. Baby K's medical prognosis was futile, but the

2. See Lewis M. Cohen, *No Good Deed: A Story of Medicine, Murder Accusations, and the Debate over How We Die* (New York: Harper, 2010). This extraordinary book tells about the murder charges leveled against two nurses who were treating a patient for pain and who were accused by a nursing assistant of murdering the patient.

3. Baby K has been written about extensively. See Peter A. Clark, "Medical Futility: Legal and Ethical Analysis," *Virtual Mentor* 9, no.5 (May 2007): 375–83; and for a brief description see "Baby K," Ascension Health,

http://www.ascensionhealth.org/index.php?option=com_content&view=article&id=237&Itemid=173.

laws governing such a situation mandated that the baby receive intervention treatment, including ventilation.

The medical staff approached the baby's mother about imposing a Do Not Resuscitate (DNR) order so that if Baby K stopped breathing or her heart stopped, intervention measures to keep Baby K alive would not have to be taken. The medical staff was hoping that this move would allow the baby to die sooner rather than later, and die naturally, but the mother refused to grant a DNR. Baby K was gradually taken off the ventilator and taken to a nursing home, but inevitable medical problems required her readmission to the hospital for surgery, which the mother wanted to have performed. When the mother insisted on surgical care, which in the situation was deemed aggressive care, the hospital went to court to ask that medical personnel be relieved of treating this baby any further and do so without legal penalty. The district court refused to grant the hospital's request. The baby, of course, eventually died but was kept alive much longer than was normal for a baby with this condition. The baby had no awareness and felt no pain, and the hospital believed that that keeping the baby alive was "medially and ethically inappropriate."[4] The courts rejected the hospital's position.

The hospital was not seeking to kill the baby but rather to withdraw and withhold treatment in the face of a hopelessly futile medical situation. In the Baby K case we can see the medical ethics principles of autonomy, nonmaleficence, beneficence, and justice coming into play, albeit in different ways on each side of the dispute. Both the hospital and the mother were acting to do no harm to the baby (nonmaleficence) while also seeking to promote the good of the patient through kind and beneficent action. The mother assumed paternalistically the role of decision maker—after all, she was the parent and was exercising autonomy on behalf of the child. The hospital and direct medical team caregivers respected that autonomy but disagreed with the mother about the appropriate course of medical intervention given the catastrophic medical situation. In holding that the medical treatment options were "futile," the hospital was also making a case that further aggressive treatment, such as surgery, was a misappropriation of resources, a justice issue. The mother obviously did not share this view.

The medical staff interpreted the application of the central principles of contemporary medical ethics differently from the mother in this case because each was dealing with a different interpretation of empirical matters relevant to medical care and each was coming at the issue from a different emotional context. Because of the disagreements between the parties, a neutral voice to

4. Clark, "Medical Futility," notes 3 and 6.

arbitrate the conflict was sought in the courts. To have overruled the mother and withdrawn treatment without seeking a legal remedy in the courts would have put the hospital and individual staff members in danger of litigation and legal prosecution. The hospital interpreted medical intervention as futile, so that continued medical intervention was of no benefit to the patient and cruel to the caregivers. The patient was incapable of any relation or future relation with the external world, so the hospital staff was not in relationship with what is ordinary thought to be—in philosophical terms—a person. In the eyes of the medical staff, surgery defied beneficent care, and the hospital could argue that continued care in a hopeless situation was an unjust allocation of precious medical resources. And although the hospital staff could acknowledge the mother's paternalistic exercise of autonomy on behalf of her baby and disagree with her expressed desire for continued care and medical intervention, they nonetheless respected the mother even as they sought legal authority to overrule her decisions. In this case, autonomy, represented by the mother, came into conflict with beneficence, nonmaleficence, and justice.

The courts decided to look only at how the law as written was to be observed, and that is what determined its judgment against the hospital. But if we were concerned only about the ethics of the case, we could ask whether a neutral or objective observer evaluating the hopeless medical situation would object to the interventions Baby K's mother insisted her baby receive.

Two things can be said in response to this question. First and most importantly, many of the troubling medical ethics situations that arise at the end of life are not so much ethical quandaries as they are conflicts centered in the relational dynamics of the family. One could easily surmise that the mother in the Baby K case was concerned with more than losing her baby, tragic as that would be. For example, would it be unreasonable to suspect that the mother might have been unable to face being the one who approved of actions leading directly to her baby's death, and would she even consider such a course of action if she had not done all she could to save the baby's life? Medical staff who confront difficult end-of-life decisions deal with these family conflicts all the time, and these disputes are often the critical factor in what presents an "ethics dilemma." Ethics students who study the famous Terri Schiavo case come to understand that the core of the conflict over law and ethics, requiring scores of court cases and involving the Florida governor, legislators in Florida and in the United States Senate, and even the president of the United States, was a family conflict involving loving parents unable to accept the terrible burden of condoning any action that would lead to the death of their daughter.

Second, the ethical framework I support and have offered as a helpful and even "best solution" to ethics problems can be constructed and applied to the Baby K case. Modern medical science has successfully intervened in numerous neonatal medical problems to preserve life and contribute to a neonate's eventual flourishing as a member of the moral community. So we can start by acknowledging a presumption of care—that is, identifying a common moral agreement that ordinarily we ought not consider withholding or withdrawing treatment to medically distressed newborns. There might be good reasons to consider an exception to this common agreement, however, and a diagnosis of futility would clearly suffice to prompt such consideration. But in order to justify an exception, attention would have to be given to justice-related criteria that would ensure that the patient's interests would be protected and that any action taken, even that of withholding treatment, was in the patient's best interest. I would propose the following as guidelines for thinking through the possibility of a justified exemption to the presumption of care:

1. The life of the neonate patient is deemed clearly a burden to the infant itself.
2. The intention to withdraw or withhold treatment must be to serve the best personal, social, and spiritual interests of the patient.
3. Descriptions of the patient's medical condition must establish both severity and futility of treatment. The determination must be made that the prospects of enjoying the goods of life, including the very basic good of life itself, are negligible. Reasonable hope that the neonate will flourish as a functioning, interactive human being in relationship to others is not present, and there is little hope that medical intervention will raise the medical condition to even the most minimal level required for flourishing. Medical intervention will, to the contrary, contribute to the burdens that patient must bear rather than relieve those burdens.
4. The decision to withdraw or withhold treatment should be, in the first instance, patient centered and not determined by the burdens the patient imposes on others—the medical staff, the family, or society at large.
5. The decision must be made by those who represent the various interests of the patient, including family, physicians, medical care personnel, and spiritual advisers.

6. By withdrawing (or withholding) treatment, one is trying to preserve respect for the good of life rather than diminish it, and nontreatment will reasonably accomplish this end.[5]

By satisfying these criteria, it seems reasonable to me that Baby K could have been withdrawn from aggressive life support, given palliative care, and prevented from receiving a futile surgical treatment. The medical situation was such that the presumption for care could in this case be lifted, and the reason would amount to this: doing so would have been in the best interests of the neonate and was ethically justified. The mother in this case was not willing to see anything short of continued life as in her baby's best interest, and one might surmise that more effort was needed to help her understand the terrible, tragic, and catastrophic medical situation that led the medical staff to advocate for less, rather than more, treatment. The ethic described above is a reasoned and reasonable ethic, but it cannot simply persuade a person gripped by the powerful emotions of fear and grief and thoroughly unsettled by the guilt of having approved action that would lead to the death of an infant—the person's own child.

FUTILITY AT THE END OF LIFE: A GENERAL ETHICAL FRAMEWORK

In natural law ethics, the good of life is itself a preeminent good because all other goods depend upon it. The Baby K situation points out that there are medical situations of such catastrophic consequence that the good of life can be placed into conflict with other goods, and preserving life at all costs and without consideration of the other goods that make life meaningful is neither wise nor morally "other regarding." A patient whose medical situation is such that treatment cannot provide benefit and the patient cannot improve "on the whole," so to speak, should be deemed futile. According to Lawrence J. Schneiderman, treatments that only preserve unconsciousness or cannot end dependence on intensive medical care are likewise to be deemed futile.[6]

Life is never an absolute good, despite its status as preeminent, and sometimes allowing to die is the morally preferable course of action. In medicine, some outcomes can be judged worse than death. In the case we just examined, Baby K has no future. In fact, given the tragic brain deficit, there is

---

5. I developed these criteria in a book chapter dealing with severely handicapped newborns in Steffen, *Ethics and Experience*, 134–35.

6. Lawrence J. Schneiderman, "Medical Futility: Its Meaning and Ethical Implications," *Annals of Internal Medicine* 112, no. 12 (1990): 949.

in a very real sense no Baby K present or even possibly present to experience the world—there is no sense of self or any capacity for engagement with the world or others, no possibility of Baby K being "in relation" with others. Dire medical situations in which a biological life cannot in any way develop or improve to become a relational partner in the moral community, or that are marked by disease, defect, or injury so catastrophic that they will permanently prevent a person from engaging in human relationality and enjoying—even experiencing—any kind of future, certainly seem to qualify as "worse than death" scenarios.

That we accept an obligation to care for persons who are severely handicapped is a strong moral presumption, and it should be strong—it should be difficult to overrule or lift that presumption grounded in the common moral understanding of reasonable people of good will. But the presumption is challenged when some medical conditions at the end of life are so severe that treatment is reasonably regarded by medical evaluators as being incapable of improving a "futile" regimen of therapeutic or curative care. Baby K has raised this issue with respect to beginning-of-life futility (in infancy), but futility at the end of life can involve caregiving and decision making about treatment options in other kinds of difficult situations. The broad moral question is whether a diagnosis of futility should prompt us to revisit our common moral agreement about care for medically distressed individuals in these other situations. Should we consider lifting the presumption of interventionist care, turn to palliative care, and help persons at the end of life die with dignity, without pain or any illusion that the care given is aimed at restoring them to health? The diagnosis of futile would seem to eliminate the possibility of reasonably pursuing any therapy option aimed at curing or restoring to health. The moral difficulty is that a determination of "futility" would authorize physicians to withdraw care without the consent of patients or their families. Futility rests on the medical ethics principle of beneficence, which can conflict with autonomy.

The issue of futility brings ethics into important conversation with laws aimed at preventing euthanasia and addressing patient vulnerability and potential abuse. Medical evaluators can examine a patient, conclude that death is near, and advocate withholding aggressive interventionist care. The problem is that laws embodying our common moral agreement that patients should receive care even if their situation is dire can, as laws, prove inflexible and unresponsive to particular situations. Since upholding a common moral agreement is important and ought to be difficult to overrule, states that have refused to enter into detailed discussions about what constitutes futility as a matter of law cannot be seen as unreasonable. How are legislators to determine as a matter of law when a medical situation is "hopeless"? And since it is certainly possible, given the reality of second opinions, that physicians can disagree with one another, what stance is the law to take in resolving conflicts over definitions of what is—and what is not—futile?

The Terri Schiavo case was a situation involving futility. Terri was kept alive after a still-mysterious collapse in her Florida home, and nutrition and hydration were provided for a period of fifteen years. Terri's condition was diagnosed as a persistent vegetative state, so no neurological possibility existed that she could return to health. The case became a way of integrating issues related to personhood and abortion back into the political realm and into the nightly news cycle for months as courts weighed in on the situation. (Was Terri Schiavo akin to an innocent fetus that Terri's husband and the government were willing to see killed in the act of withdrawing hydration and nutrition?) The process of trying to determine futility can be met with disagreement, but in general it identifies a medical determination that continued treatment is worthless and should be withdrawn or withheld. Defining futility as a matter of best medical practice and legal directive is and should be difficult. The question is whether movement to an ethic and a public policy governing physician actions and liabilities is possible. Courts and legislatures have found formalizing a definition of futility formidable, and when they turn for advice to the medical community, they receive the American Medical Association's determination that futility "cannot be meaningfully defined" and may be subjective, given the fact of physician disagreement over prognosis.[7]

Yet futility is an important concept even if it is hard to define—its boundaries are fuzzy, and the term can be used in a way that confuses futility with interventions that are harmful and ineffective.[8] Only one state law—Texas's 1999 Advance Directives Act—actually deals with futility as a matter of law. This law addresses the conflict between the patient or patient representatives who want to continue interventionist treatment and the physicians and other health care professionals who believe that on medical grounds the most appropriate next step is to withdraw treatment. As we think about ethics at the end of life, as did the legislature in Texas, we should, first of all, have in mind a reasonable definition of futility, such as this one put forward by Drane and Coulehan: "an action, intervention, or procedure that might be physiologically effective in a given case, but cannot benefit the patient, no matter how often it is repeated. A futile treatment is not necessarily ineffective,

7. American Medical Association, "Opinion 2.035 Futile Care," in *Code of Medical Ethics, 2008–2009 Edition.* (Chicago: AMA, 2008), 15–17.

8. Clark, "Medical Futility," 4.

but it is worthless, whether because their medical action itself is futile (no matter what the patient's condition) or the condition of the patient makes it futile."[9]

The ethical perspective I have been advancing in this book holds that we can articulate common agreements about moral meaning and appropriate guides for action. Based on that perspective, we can now ask whether there is a way to sort out what a "just futility" ethic might look like.

If medical staff determine that a patient can no longer benefit from medical interventions and that interventions aimed at restoring to health are not appropriate, the judgment of futility directs that such interventionist treatment can be withdrawn or withheld so that palliative care can commence. In order to bring this about, the following conditions should be met:

1. The condition of the patient must lead to a reasonable conclusion that the patient can no longer benefit from therapeutic intervention. This medical evaluation should be confirmed by at least one other physician.

2. Continued medical intervention is disproportionate to the end of restoring health or even of supporting a "good death," which would include some notion that life should not be prolonged when it is no longer enjoyable or capable of being enjoyed.

3. Every reasonable effort must be made to clarify the medical reasons for the judgment of futility and why withdrawal of treatment is being considered as a next medical option.

4. The autonomy of the patient or the patient's family or surrogates can be respected, but futility allows beneficence to trump autonomy, and this must be explained clearly.

5. Physicians and consultation members must explain that the determination of futility does not require the consent of the patient or family but that options exist if the patient or family do not want to stop medical intervention.

6. Physicians and caregivers should discuss the medical situation with the patient's family or surrogates (with the patient, if possible), and they must make the case that continued therapeutic intervention is providing no reasonable benefit to the patient.

9. James F. Drane and John L. Coulehan, "The Concept of Futility: Patients Do Not Have a Right to Demand Useless Treatment. Counterpoint," *Health Progress* 74, no. 10 (December, 1993): 29. Quoted in Clark, "Medical Futility," 4.

A futility policy is, from a moral point of view, a "just nontreatment" policy. The heart of the futility issue is actually an evaluation of the patient's medical condition. As we noted, there can be problems in communicating the medical issues to the family, and medical personnel can have difficulty understanding the emotional context of a family having to make decisions about treatment and nontreatment. The Baby K case, as well as that of Terri Schiavo, indicates how hard it can be for families to come to grips with medical futility, and religious views can come into play as people are trying to understand what can and cannot be done. Religion in general reinforces the value and preciousness of life and condemns the evil of intervening to cause or hasten death.

No one, religious or not, wants to be a "killer." No reasonable person wants to take responsibility for intentionally causing the death of another human being. A declaration of futility should not be about killing but about "letting die." It should be a recognition that the limits of medical care aimed at restoring to health have been reached, even exceeded, and that now "care" involves removing the technological interventions that stand between an individual and the natural processes that would lead to death.

Determining futility is the result of a medical evaluation, and medical professionals have an obligation to clearly explain why additional intervention is worthless and futile from a medical standpoint. Continued curative intervention will not meet a psychological or qualitative goal or lead to an improvement in quality of life but might actually lead to a decrease in the quality of life. This must be explained to the family, and at least two physicians must concur on the diagnosis. A judgment of futility does not ignore patient autonomy—autonomy is still in play for patients and their surrogates—but it reframes the withdrawal or withholding of interventionist therapies as beneficent action toward the patient that serves the best personal, social, and spiritual interests of the patient. Such withdrawal must be explained as a move that will not burden the patient with pain or cause the patient additional harm. Care itself is not stopping but rather changing form with different objectives due to medical futility. Palliative care is now a medical specialty, and more education needs to be done with medical personnel to integrate palliative care into the well-ordered conduct of medical practice, doctor training, and continuing medical education.[10]

10. See Diane Meier, Stephen Isaacs, and Robert G. Hughes, *Palliative Care: Transforming the Care of Serious Illness* (San Francisco: Jossey-Bass, 2010).

RELIGIOUS PERSPECTIVES ON END-OF-LIFE CARE

A well-known medical situation, one that contributed to the creation of the contemporary bioethics field, concerned Karen Ann Quinlan, who, in 1975 at the age of twenty-one, collapsed into a coma after arriving home from a party. Diagnosed with extreme hypoxia (lack of oxygen to the brain), her condition was deemed irreversible and her family was informed that she was in a persistent vegetative state. Karen was kept alive on a ventilator for several months without improvement, but her parents, having been informed that there was no medical possibility of a restoration to health or consciousness, did not want Karen's suffering to continue. As a result, they requested that Karen be removed from the ventilator, which was deemed an "extraordinary means" for keeping Karen alive. Karen's parents wanted her to die naturally. The hospital balked, and the case wound up in court. Medical experts who testified before the court believed that taking Karen off the respirator would cause her death, so the court was facing what it believed was a life-and-death decision. In *In re Quinlan*, the first major judicial decision to hold that in appropriate circumstances life-sustaining medical treatments could be discontinued even if the patient is unable or incompetent to make the decision, the New Jersey Supreme Court ruled that the ventilator could be removed.[11] The respirator was then removed, but Karen did not die as many expected. She continued breathing on her own, and she continued to receive ordinary life-sustaining nourishment and hydration until she died of pulmonary failure in a New Jersey nursing home in 1985. (Nourishment and hydration became issues in the Terri Schiavo case, and the courts ruled that they could be discontinued in the face of that futile medical situation.)

The Karen Ann Quinlan case raised headline issues about civil rights, euthanasia, and legal guardianship, but ethics and religion were very much a part of the broad cultural discussion. The Quinlan family was Roman Catholic and sought counsel from the church. Those preparing amicus briefs raised issues of moral theology for the court to include in its deliberations, and the court decision actually discussed theological ethics in determining a course of action in this difficult end-of-life case. Highlighting some of the issues as they came to the court from Catholic moral theology reveals how one religious ethic looks at issues of futility and what is at stake morally and theologically.

---

11. *In Re Quinlan* (70 N. J. 10, 355 A. 2d 647 [1976]; 355 A.2d 647). Case is available at https://www.uta.edu/ philosophy/faculty/burgess-jackson/In re Quinlan, 70 N.J. 10, 355 A.2d 647% 20(1976).pdf. The decision of the Supreme Court of New Jersey was entitled, "In the Matter of Karen Quinlan, an Alleged Incompetent."

The New Jersey Supreme Court took note of an address Pope Pius XII delivered to anesthesiologists on November 24, 1957, when he dealt with a question about keeping a patient alive by means of treatment deemed "extraordinary" (artificial respiration via ventilator) "even against the will of the family."[12] The pope made the following comments, distinguishing between "ordinary" and "extraordinary" means and between euthanasia (a direct and intentional killing) and letting an individual die naturally:

1. In ordinary cases the doctor has the right to act in this manner [that is, using the extraordinary means of artificial respiration], but is not bound to do so unless this is the only way of fulfilling another certain moral duty.
2. The doctor, however, has no right independent of the patient. He can act only if the patient explicitly or implicitly, directly or indirectly gives him the permission.
3. The treatment as described in the question constitutes extraordinary means of preserving life and so there is no obligation to use them nor to give the doctor permission to use them.
4. The rights and the duties of the family depend on the presumed will of the unconscious patient if he or she is of legal age, and the family, too, is bound to use only ordinary means.
5. This case is not to be considered euthanasia in any way; that would never be licit. The interruption of attempts at resuscitation, even when it causes the arrest of circulation, is not more than an indirect cause of the cessation of life, and we must apply in this case the principle of double effect.[13]

Note in this analysis the presumption that acting to directly kill the patient (that is, euthanasia) is not permissible and, as the pope declares, is "never licit," yet it can be accomplished by appealing to the principle of double effect. The principle of double effect states that if a good action has a bad secondary consequence, it is morally permissible to proceed with the good action as long as the bad secondary consequence (the double effect) was not intended, even if foreseen.[14] This is the doctrine that allows physicians to provide morphine to patients for the good end of pain control even if it

---

12. Ibid.

13. Ibid.

14. Double effect is drawn from the Catholic moral tradition, originally from Thomas Aquinas, *Summa Theologica* II-II, Q 64, A7, who asked "Whether It Is Permissible to Kill a Man in Self-Defense?"

causes the patient to lose consciousness and even die as a foreseen consequence of respiratory suppression. Pope Pius XII gives us an ethic for deciding to withhold or withdraw treatment and allow a person to die in accordance with ordinary and natural means. His argument follows the natural-law-based form of ethical reflection I have advocated in these pages: articulating a common moral agreement (opposing euthanasia) but then giving criteria for allowing action that does lead knowingly to a foreseen death. The pope's opposition to euthanasia is put in absolute terms, yet with the doctrine of double effect in play, the prohibition on a physician helping a patient die "naturally" does not appear to be absolutely restricted.

This ethical reflection by Pius XII allows us to see that Roman Catholicism endorses a view that action can and even should be taken at the end of life to avoid needless suffering when such suffering is created by employing "extraordinary" technological means that interfere with the natural dying process. The tradition holds that dying and death are natural parts of human life and should be respected as normal or "ordinary" events that ought to follow their course. And, of course, the dying need to be cared for—the Catholic Church is the originator of the medieval European hospital, designed as a care facility for the sick and dying, so the idea of palliation is consistent with religious values and commitments of care. This is a Roman Catholic view, but Christians in general would subscribe to the idea of tending the dying, offering them care and relief from suffering, and even finding action that helps avoid unnecessary suffering. Extending life at any cost for the purpose of eking out another moment of life regardless of the quality of that life is not an end-of-life Christian value.

Let us consider briefly the perspectives that Buddhism and Islam bring to bear on the end-of-life issues we have been discussing.

Buddhism

In Buddhism, learning to die is learning to see life as a cycle of beginnings and endings, of births and deaths and rebirths, so the Buddhist learns not to fear death. Dying itself is thought to be a process of letting go. In extreme end-of-life situations, Buddhist teaching goes so far as to suggest that a patient can act to hasten his own death by avoiding interference. The *Vinaya* commentary includes these lines: "But of whom there is great illness, long-lasting, (and) on the attending monks are wearied, are disgusted, and worry, 'what now if we were to set (him) free from sickness?': if he, (thinking): 'this body being nursed does not endure, and the monks are wearied', stops eating, does not take medicine, it is acceptable (*vaṭṭati*)."[15]

Ordinarily, treatment should seek to improve a person's condition. In Japan feeding tubes are often kept in infants with severe abnormalities, and removing them would not be morally permissible, regardless of whether the tubes improve the patients' situation. Buddhist ethics would not always support such a treatment protocol, however, for as Peter Harvey, a scholar of Buddhist ethics, has written: "Where a child's condition is such that he or she would be constantly battling with infections or other medical complications, and this would be painful and expensive and tie up scarce medical resources, then perhaps he or she should be allowed to die—for example by not having infections treated—if this is what the patient wants."Harvey goes on to note that a patient who has directed nonresuscitation should have that request honored.[16]

Buddhist teaching distinguishes between a person being dead and a person being in a state of cessation, which is when breathing stops and "all functions of the mind shut down." Buddhist interpretations hold that a person may be alive yet show no detectable breathing or mental activity. The distinction between death and the "cessation of identification and feeling" is made because advanced Buddhist practitioners can actually attain this latter state through meditation. The persistent vegetative state (PVS) shares some features of this cessation state, but as we saw in the Karen Ann Quinlan case, a patient in PVS can continue to breathe without the aid of a ventilator. "Buddhism would clearly not regard one in such a state as dead, then, and to remove intravenous or tube feeding from such a person would be to kill him or her."[17]

Whether feeding a person who is in PVS constitutes medical treatment is of course a debated issue. While Buddhism regards life as precious, and people should not take life or aid others in taking their own lives, Peter Harvey wisely notes that "euthanasia scenarios present a test for the implications of Buddhist compassion."[18] But he also concludes that "at a certain point in terminal illness, though, it may be appropriate to abstain from futile treatments that reduce the quality of life on its last short lap." It may also be appropriate to deal with mounting pain in such a way that death is a known but unintended and unsought side effect of increasing drug dosages. "Any help for the dying that does not include the intention of bringing death is acceptable."[19] Thus,

15. *Vin. A.* 467, quoted in Harvey, *An Introduction to Buddhist Ethics*, 290.

16. Ibid., 304.

17. Ibid., 306–7.

18. Ibid., 309.

19. Ibid., 310.

Peter Harvey invokes on behalf of Buddhist end-of-life ethics an endorsement of palliative care along with what amounts to a doctrine of double effect to deal with situations of medical futility requiring increasing dosages of pain medications.

Islam

In Islam, death is an inescapable aspect of the human condition, and although the faithful are instructed to prepare for death, The Prophet is said to have forbidden any desire for death: "None of you should long for death because of a calamity that had befallen him, and if he cannot but long for death, then he should say: 'O my God, let me live as long as life is good for me, and take my life if death is good for me.'"[20]

Muslim jurists concerned themselves with determining the meaning of death—both the symptoms of death and the state of death—regarding death as the cessation of the functions of an integrated body.[21] However, two states of life, stable (*mustaqarr*) and unstable (*ghayr mustasqarr*), provide juridical categories for determining movement toward death, with "unstable" indicating decreased cardiac function and blood flow seriously threatening continued viability. Determining death requires the irreversible cessation of both cardiac and respiratory functions, and the presence of a heartbeat in a situation of "unstable" life is held to be continuing life. Abdulaziz Sachedina, author of a fine analysis of Islamic bioethics, has pointed out that jurists have rejected "brain death" criteria for determining death, although he notes that the discussion about brain death among Muslims, "adopted from Western languages, is fraught with persistent ignorance of the facts of brain death" and "it seems unlikely that that any well-considered criteria for or definitions of brain death will emerge among Muslim jurists."[22] Brain death definitions are important for discussions of organ transplantation, but they are also critical for the end-of-life issue of futility. When can expensive life-prolonging technological equipment be turned off?

Sachedina's analysis is that practical considerations like proportionality and refusal to harm govern the decision to stop treatment in the face of futility. While Christianity and Buddhism recognize autonomy as a major principle to observe in end-of-life decision making, in Islam that decision is

---

20. Sachedina, *Islamic Biomedical Ethics*, 148. The hadith saying is from *Sahih Bukhari*, Volume 8, Book 75, number 362), at http://www.islamicity. com/mosque/sunnah/bukhari/075.sbt.html::

21. Ibid., 149.

22. Ibid., 164.

made by the patient, the family, the physician, the community, and all who are in relation with the patient: "Whether a physician can prolong life by introducing aggressive invasive treatments without causing further harm is decided by all parties connected with the patient."[23] The decision to die is held in sharī'a to be God's decision, so there is to be no assistance in dying, either actively or passively. No right to die is recognized because life is God's gift not to be terminated by any active human intervention; the length of days is determined by Allah's decree, which cannot be overruled by human action: "However, with its emphasis on promoting or seeking what is in the best interest of all concerned (*istislah*), Muslim jurists have recognized the possibility of arriving at a collective decision through consultation (*shura*) by those involved in providing health care, including the attending physician and the family."[24]

Islam provides no immunity for the physician who assists a patient in dying, although two situations seem to allow a terminally ill patient whose condition is medically futile to receive assistance. Providing pain relief that could shorten life is permitted in Islamic law but only if such assistance is administered with the intention to address pain and not to kill. In such a circumstance, if there is no intention to cause death, a physician is protected against any liability, including criminal liability.[25] So Islam too invokes a principle of double effect. Islamic law also holds that no culpability attaches to a withdrawal of treatment in a situation of futility if the intention is to benefit the patient and cause no further harm. A permissible withdrawal of treatment would involve patient, family, physicians, and others in a decision-making process focused on the reality that continued treatment can work against the patient's benefit. The problem arises, of course, in distinguishing between having an intention and not having an intention to see the patient die, and while some jurists have recognized the validity of a "living will" or advance directive, this appeal to autonomy is qualified by the relationship of the patient to the physician. The physician's expert medical opinion would provide grounds for turning off a ventilator, and "the death is regarded to have been caused by the person's underlying disease rather than the intentional act of turning off the respirator."[26]

In Islam, consultation involving the patient, family, physicians, and others is critical for providing the kind of care necessary for a patient's welfare and

23. Ibid., 166.
24. Ibid., 169.
25. Ibid., 170.
26. Ibid.

for avoiding any acts that could be construed as disobedience to God. The well-being of the patient must be uppermost in the hearts and minds of the caregivers. Allowing persons to die when they are facing untreatable and intractable suffering is permissible if the patient's welfare is the primary concern and if the consultation process has proceeded so that all relevant voices have been heard. Patient care at the end of life without any further attempt to cure—palliation—is of course provided and endorsed as proper medical practice; Islam does not support voluntary active euthanasia or physician-assisted suicide.[27]

COOLEY

Since many of the philosophical arguments for and against euthanasia have been covered above or will be addressed below, I will mention only a few.[28]

PHILOSOPHICAL ARGUMENTS AGAINST EUTHANASIA

1. One consequentialist argument focuses on the harm caused to the person who is killed as well as the injuries to others and even to the society in which euthanasia is practiced. There are several different ways that people other than the deceased can suffer. I will mention but a few of these. First, and possibly most importantly, those who have to help kill or make the decision for another person to commit euthanasia suffer guilt or other negative emotional reactions as a result of what they did, even if they think that the action was justified. Moreover, those acting or deciding in these ways do not want the person to die because everyone is reluctant to kill another person when that person could live. The reluctance increases as the positive emotional relationships between the two increase. Finally, there might be serious social and legal consequences as the police investigate the death, which might end with legal charges, conviction, and imprisonment, as well as the social condemnation given to those who assist in another's death.

27. Ibid., 171.

28. Many of these positions are argued in more depth in Robert M. Baird and Stuart E. Rosenbaum's edited anthology, *Euthanasia* (Buffalo, NY: Prometheus, 1989).

2. If we assume for the moment that euthanasia can be morally permissible, allowing it for morally allowable cases might create a slippery slope in which we start killing people because they cannot have the types of lives that those in power think are worth living. The danger of going too far is always present and, as we have seen from the history of humanity at its worst, seems inevitable.

3. Morally irrelevant conditions, such as race and ethnicity, play a role in making end-of-life decisions.[29]

PHILOSOPHICAL ARGUMENTS FOR EUTHANASIA

1. To minimize pain and suffering for the dying person, he should be allowed to die early in a way that is efficient and less painful than would be the case if he continued to a "natural" death.[30] In addition, there is a great deal of pain and suffering endured by the dying person's loved ones. As anyone who has had to undergo the experience knows, watching a loved one finish out his or her life takes a great emotional toll on people, especially if the death takes place in a way not keeping with the person's dignity.

2. Another consequentialist argument looks at a set of costs different from those of pain and suffering. End-of-life care takes an enormous amount of financial resources.[31] If those resources are engaged in prolonging a life no matter what the costs, they cannot be used for those patients whose health could be improved or whose deaths could be averted with the use of relatively minimal medical resources. For example, providing prenatal care and other health care to children can help them lead much better lives in the long term and is a more efficient use of resources than treating them when something dire has occurred to them later in life.

29. Amy S. Kelley, Susan L. Ettner, Sean Morrison, Qingling Du, Neil S. Wenger, and Catherine A. Sarkisian, "Determinants of Medical Expenditures in the Last 6 Months of Life," *Annals of Internal Medicine* 154, no. 4 (2011): 235–42.

30. What is natural and unnatural is difficult to agree on. Many times the distinction is between the artificial—or humanmade—and the natural. However, this definition entails that everything people do is unnatural because it is done by humans. Because we are part and parcel of nature—and thus part of the natural process—we need a better definition of the natural.

31. A. S. Kelley, K. McGarry, S. Fahle, S. M. Marshall, D. Qingling, and J. S. Skinner, "Out-of-Pocket Spending in the Last Five Years of Life," *Journal of General Internal Medicine* 28, no. 2 (2012): 304–9.

Early prevention, therefore, can produce much better results than reparative or therapeutic care.[32]

CONDITIONS FOR EUTHANASIA

Although euthanasia could be relevant to a much wider set of circumstances, I am going to limit my discussion of it to those cases in which all of the following conditions are true. First, the person on whom euthanasia might be used is near death or in some state in which being alive is much worse than being dead. Of course, what it means to be near death is open to interpretation, but let us assume for the sake of discussion that the credible prognosis is death within six months.

As for the latter criterion, what it means for death to be better than life in a certain state is also open to interpretation. However, let us stipulate that it means the person cannot flourish if he continues to exist, perhaps because he is unable to do the things that most people take for granted as part of flourishing, such as being able to care of oneself or interacting in meaningful ways with others. It would be important here to use subjective and objective measurements of flourishing. We should take into account what the agent or his representative thinks about the agent's potential to flourish, which is subjective. By using objective benchmarks about what the human species needs in general to function—food, water, security, and so on—we can reign in overly optimistic or pessimistic subjective judgments about the potential to flourish.

Second, the death has to be inevitable, as far as inevitability exists in the actual world. If there is something that could be done to save the person, such as a simple medical procedure that would eliminate the prognosis of near death, then that should be taken instead of euthanizing the individual. However, we cannot make this criterion too hard to achieve, which is why the futility criterion discussed above is so useful. There might be a cure or therapy that is helpful, but those involved might have no reasonable way to know about it. For example, there is probably a cure for liver cancer, but no one knows what it is. Therefore, to make this requirement practical, we must say that the something is a procedure that a reasonable person in that position should know about, and then leave it at that.

Third, the prognosis must be credible, which requires that it be made by those who have the relevant medical expertise. Also, the prognosis must

---

32. A. Leaf, "Preventive Medicine for Our Ailing Health Care System," *Journal of the American Medical Association* 269, no. 5 (1993): 616–18.

be based on the best available evidence that can be practically obtained in the situation, and the evidence must be sufficient and reliable to support the prognosis beyond a reasonable doubt.[33]

Fourth, the person making the decision to use euthanasia must be competent to make such a choice as a reasonable person. This person might be the dying individual or someone who is acting as a proxy for that individual. To be competent as a reasonable person, the individual would, among other characteristics, be sufficiently informed to make a reasonable decision and, at the same time, be free enough from coercion to make the choice freely. This is not to say that such things as internal forces, such as emotions, and external forces, such as relationships to others, do not have a role to play, but they cannot overwhelm the person's ability to come to a justified judgment using reasonable decision-making processes.

Finally, the means of death must be an effective method that does not horrify the vast majority of reasonable people. It should kill the person in a way that does not produce unnecessary pain and suffering and in a manner that is not disgusting, as using a guillotine would be. The death should be dignified and calm so that the person who is dying and those in relationship with her may reduce their suffering from the death as much as is practical. If all five conditions are met, then the euthanasia's moral permissibility can be entertained, although it should not be thought to be settled.

Euthanasia comes in a variety of forms, all of which should be delineated because each has its own moral factors that make it unique. In fact, the morality of some of the forms might be different in the same situation because of the difference in circumstances considered to be relevant by each type. First, there is a distinction between voluntary euthanasia and involuntary euthanasia. There is another distinction between active euthanasia and passive euthanasia. Finally, mercy killing can be distinguished from assisted suicide. Hence, because of the various euthanasia forms, we cannot say that euthanasia is morally right or wrong without knowing which type we are discussing in the circumstances.

Voluntary and Involuntary

First, let us examine the differences between voluntary and involuntary euthanasia. In voluntary euthanasia, the dying individual makes the decision

---

33. It would take too much time here to detail all that is required to fulfill these conditions. However, once again, we can rely on the reasonable-person standard for these determinations. Although not every reasonable person would agree, at least some of those who are experts and reasonable would reasonably believe that the evidence is sufficient and reliable.

about whether she will be euthanized, although she might not die by her own hand.[34] In general, this euthanasia type is less controversial than the involuntary variety because the agent's autonomy is involved in making the decision to end her life. If we remember the five criteria necessary for euthanasia to be considered morally permissible, including death's inevitability in the near term and a competent person making the decision, then respecting each person's medical choices and the other decisions that affect her life provide greater evidence that this form of death is permissible if not an actual right. After all, we make many choices about our lives as we are entitled to do. No one else can make such decisions without our consent because, if they did, our value as autonomous agents or people would not be respected. Therefore, even though we might not make the same choice in the case as the dying person, she still has the right to do so because it is her life, and she should be the one to write her own narrative of how it is lived up to and including her death.

Involuntary euthanasia is more expansive than voluntary euthanasia: it includes cases ranging from the patient actively opposing being euthanized to the patient not having an opinion on the matter at all. The latter type of person might be in a permanent vegetative state or otherwise incompetent to make medical decisions. Involuntary euthanasia is much more controversial in these cases because the individual is not ultimately deciding her own fate, which has to be one of the most important decisions a person can make. If a person, especially a competent person, is euthanized against her wishes, this killing is much worse: it becomes a murder.

Even if the person is incompetent, her desire not to die should still be taken into account by the proxy in the moral decision-making process. The incompetent individual is a moral subject, and we have the duty to act in his best interests because that he has intrinsic moral worth as a moral subject. In other words, the moral subject's value should be protected *because* it is worthy, which means, all things considered, that we should take measures to guard that worth by acting in the intrinsically valuable entity's best interests. If the moral subject does not want to die, then we should at least see if we can satisfy that desire even though the moral subject is incapable of making competent choices for himself. In this case, keeping the subject alive respects his value by preserving it. Euthanizing him would not.

The mere fact that someone acts as a proxy for the incompetent person does not mean that the proxy's decision is uncontroversial in a way that a choice made by the individual freely and knowingly deciding for herself would be. If

34. Daniel Brock, "Voluntary Active Euthanasia," *Hastings Center Report* 22, no. 2 (1993): 10–22.

the person chooses for herself, then we can say that autonomy has been used and should be respected. However, although the standard is that a proxy must act in the person's best interests, we ought to acknowledge that acting in the person's best interest is not the only way to fulfill one's duties in these situations. Perhaps it would be better to act as the incapacitated person would have acted had he not been incapacitated rather than worrying about what would be best for him. That is, the proxy should try to do whatever the person would have done even if that would not have been in the person's best interests. By acting as the dying subject would have done, the subject's narrative would end as she would have ended it rather than being made artificial by having goals and values alien to the subject. An example might be helpful in making clearer the difference in which standard we ought to use to make decisions in these cases.

Suppose we have an incompetent seventy-nine-year-old man with congestive heart failure and aneurysms who has six months, at most, to live. The man has to be hydrated intravenously and is on a respirator. We are given the choice of either letting him die by removing the hydration or respirator, or keeping him on both until his heart fails or one of the aneurysms bursts. If we remove the hydration or respirator, he will go to sleep, never to reawaken. If his heart fails or one of the aneurysms bursts, the death will be much more painful. Now suppose we know that the person was a fighter in life who wanted to live for as long as possible no matter how much the personal cost to him. If we select the best interest criterion, then we do what is best for him, which would allow him to die painlessly and more quickly. If we select the criterion to act as he would act, then we must keep him alive because he would have chosen that if he had been competent to make the decision. The latter would be much more painful for him and not add to his flourishing, but it fits with his life narrative. In these cases, it is hard to decide which standard to use. Both have their advantages, while at the same time neither is perfect. Doing what is best might not be what the person would do, and doing what the person would do might not be in the person's best interests. I will address this issue later on when discussing how to make end-of-life decisions such as these.

Active versus Passive Euthanasia

There is also thought to be a difference between active and passive euthanasia, which seems to be based in the same thinking that makes a distinction between positive and negative rights. Active euthanasia is characterized by someone actively killing another person in some way, such as giving her a morphine overdose. As with positive rights, people must perform an act of commission or go out of their way to do something above and beyond just letting something happen. On the other hand, passive euthanasia is generally thought of as allowing people to die, which is an act of omission.[35] Acts of omission merely do not interfere, much as the negative right to privacy is thought to be characterized by the government and others not interfering in one's life. Palliative care, in which pain is alleviated as far as practical, is based on the same idea of allowing people to die of "natural" causes rather than artificial or human-made actions. No further attempts to treat the illness claiming the life of the individual are made, but the person is not required to undergo any more pain than is necessary during the dying process.

However, there is no moral distinction between allowing someone to die and actively killing him. Both are actions. Both are undertaken with the end goal of shortening a person's life; that is why each is a form of euthanasia. Some people mistakenly believe that allowing something to happen is different from actively bringing it about, or that the former is ethical whereas the latter is morally wrong. The only real difference is that the number of calories burned by the person actively killing is higher than the number burned by the person standing by to allow the person to die. So people's argument for the moral superiority of allowing someone to die on the grounds that it is passive euthanasia appears to be merely a fig leaf to assuage their guilt.[36]

In fact, in many cases active euthanasia can be considered to be the right thing to do and better than passive euthanasia because of what is entailed by each action type. Suppose we return to the example of the seventy-nine-year-old man with aneurysms but change it a bit so that we no longer know how he would have wanted his life to end. If the person is passively euthanized, then his death will be a miserable, painful ending to his life. Actively euthanizing him, on the other hand, will eliminate this potential suffering. Given that the outcomes will be the same, we have to ask ourselves which is the more humane thing to do. Should we allow someone to suffer needlessly so that we can give ourselves the illusion that we did not cause his death, or end that life more quickly with as little pain as possible?

The Pragmatic Principle can provide some help to us here. Obviously, Reasonable Person Consequentialism would say that at least one reasonable

---

35. Others make passive euthanasia more active: "Passive euthanasia is moderated suicide when subjects choose to facilitate death and to pass naturally but comfortably, without technology prolonging onset of death." L. Z. G. Touyz and S. J. J. Touyz, "An Appraisal of Life's Terminal Phases and Euthanasia and the Right to Die," *Current Oncology* 18, no. 2 (2011): 65–66.

36. Making a distinction between killing and allowing to die remains controversial. Bonnie Steinbock and Alastair Norcross, eds., *Killing and Letting Die* (Bronx, NY: Fordham University Press, 1994).

person would reasonably believe that the best outcome would result from active euthanasia. Other reasonable people can disagree, but remember that the standard is not that all reasonable people come to a consensus on the issue. The Quasi-Categorical Imperative states that when doing the action, those entities with intrinsic value must be respected to the proper degree and in the appropriate way required by that value. Given the inevitable death and pain from the passive euthanasia alternative, it is hard to see how selecting this action would respect the seventy-nine-year-old man. Let us say that he has no loose ends in his life that he must address, no one needs him to stay alive so that the survivor can go through an emotional process that will assist the survivor's flourishing, and there are no other vital interests that will be served by the dying man's extended existence. In this case, the main moral factors are the intrinsic worth of the person and his pain, suffering, and death in each alternative. Since passive euthanasia will make the dying man's end so much worse than it needed to be, selecting that alternative cannot respect his value. If we believe that each person as a person should receive the best end that is practical—which includes dying peacefully and with dignity—then active euthanasia is the only alternative that would satisfy both of PP's conditions.

Assisted Suicide versus Mercy Killing

Our final distinction is between assisted suicide and mercy killing. Mercy killing is a more expansive term that includes all assisted suicides, while the category of assisted suicide is more limited, requiring that the action be undertaken voluntarily by the dying person. First, we should get a good understanding of what mercy killing is. Mercy killing is performed primarily as an act of kindness, forgiveness, or compassion for someone over whom the person acting has power. Another person believes the dying person must be killed in order for the dying person to avoid a more calamitous ending than necessary. That is, if the dying person is allowed to live, then much worse things will happen to her than would be the case if she died earlier through active or passive euthanasia. Of course, mercy killing can be involuntary or voluntary, but the person who commits the action must be doing it as a mercy for another person without the help of that person.

One interesting fact to note about mercy killing is the use of mercy. Mercy is something that is neither deserved nor earned; it is a gift of grace. Suppose that you have done something unethical and deserve punishment from the person you have wronged. If the person forgives you for what you have done, then the person is acting mercifully. You deserved punishment, but the person expunged your debt. There was no obligation on the person's part to act in this manner, which makes the action supererogatory, or above and beyond the call of duty. Mercy is something that can never be required in a particular circumstance; therefore, mercy killing can never be required. It can be morally permissible and morally right, but it cannot be a moral obligation if we hold to the true meaning of mercy.

Assisted suicide occurs when the dying person needs help killing herself and is thought to require active euthanasia. Unlike mercy killing, the dying person is an active participant in her own death in some way beyond deciding that she wants to die. To make it a suicide, she has to do something to carry her decision out, such as asking someone to help her, buying the pills, or otherwise acting in a significant way to take her own life.

More controversial is to say that if the killing is voluntary, then passive and active euthanasia are both forms of suicide because each has the requisite mental states required to make it suicide. And what are these mental states? First, the clearest case is when the person intends his death and then takes actions to ensure that the death is accomplished. The most obvious cases are when someone intentionally overdoses, shoots himself, and so on. Less prevalent but still suicides are instances in which the agent forces another to kill him, such as "death by cop" in which the person acts violently in such a way that a police officer shoots him in the belief that the person will kill the officer if the officer does not first take the person's life.

There are other types of suicide in which the requisite intention is not fully formed as an explicit, conscious intention. For example, consider a noble person who sacrifices her life in order to save other people. To make this a heroic act, the noble person must be aware that her actions are highly likely to cause her death, such as would be the case by jumping on a live grenade. When the person throws herself on the ordnance, she does not intend her death, but the knowledge of the almost-certain outcome must be accepted by her in some way although she need not fully consent. I would say she needs at least to acquiesce, which is to passively accept the action's consequences. By accepting that her death will be the result of her heroic action, she now makes the outcome hers in a way that an unforeseen consequence can never be.[37] Therefore, when people act heroically to save others even if it costs the former their lives, then they are committing suicide.

When someone seeks passive euthanasia, she acquiesces to the hastening of her death by her own hand. Refusing treatment or those goods required to keep her body alive results in her death just as much as taking an overdose or

---

37. See the chapter on suicide for a more detailed discussion of this topic.

shooting herself would. Each suicide requires both a conscious, active decision and an action to fulfill the decision. In refusing something needed for life, one is performing an act of commission just as much as actively overdosing or acting in a similar manner. Therefore, both voluntary passive euthanasia and active euthanasia are forms of suicide whose only difference is whether they are active or passive in bringing about the resulting death. Hence, they must be treated identically. Either both are permissible on these grounds, or both are impermissible.

The complexity of the euthanasia debate can be seen by how finely we must parse what type of euthanasia we are discussing in a particular context. Sometimes, we will discuss voluntary, active euthanasia performed as mercy killing. Sometimes, we will examine assisted suicide of the active variety. There are a number of combinations we can consider. We should, hence, take great care to determine which one is under discussion before venturing an opinion or claim on its morality. More importantly, on the grounds of complexity, it might be impossible to make any moral judgments on euthanasia's morality in general.

The Morality of Types of Euthanasia

That being said, it is practical to make some claims about the morality of the various types of euthanasia as suicide. These claims are not true in all cases, but they seem accurate enough in the majority of situations to make them useful. Let us begin with the assertion that voluntary, active euthanasia is generally less problematic and more likely to be morally permissible than any of the other varieties. This moral status is based on respecting autonomous people's self-determination and minimizing their and others' suffering, which intuitively appeals to many of us and is required by the Pragmatic Principle. However, this type becomes more problematic if the person requires help bringing about his death. Recall that helping others to die often causes the survivors a great deal of mental strife that does not occur if the issue is dealt with by the person who is taking his own life. Therefore, in general, suicide is preferable to mercy killing and assisted suicide.

Voluntary, passive euthanasia without palliative care is generally a worse alternative than voluntary, active euthanasia. Since in many instances voluntary, passive euthanasia can involve a great deal more suffering because of the prolonged nature of the death, it can create a less valuable world than would have been the case with a quicker, less painful ending. However, it can be better in some circumstances, especially when the survivors need additional time to begin the process of managing their grief and other emotions caused by the impending death. In these situations, the dying person, in addition to trying to produce the best result, cares for his survivors' flourishing in a way that respects their dignity as intrinsically valuable entities. Time is often needed by those for whom we care to make amends, come to terms, and otherwise bring their business of living to a close in a way that causes the fewest ripples to their long-term well-being.

The morality of the involuntary types of euthanasia depends on what is happening to the dying person. If the person is in great pain that passive euthanasia will not alleviate quickly enough and staying alive is not part of the person's life narrative, then active euthanasia is to be preferred. If passive euthanasia allows for the best end as determined by a reasonable person coming to a reasonable belief about potential outcomes, then this alternative is generally the right one.

Since the deaths are involuntary, these types of euthanasia also need to take into consideration the needs and intrinsic value of the proxy making the life-and-death decision. She must consider what the impact of the decision and the resulting consequences, such as the death process and its aftermath, will mean to her and to the other survivors. In the absence of sufficient information to know precisely enough what the dying moral subject would have wanted or what is in the moral subject's best interests, the proxy might need to use whichever method of hastening the death would foster the proxy's own flourishing. This might require passive euthanasia so that the proxy feels better than she otherwise would about the process. It also might entail active euthanasia if the proxy requires that for her own flourishing. Though the moral subject should often be of primary consideration, we should never forget that these actions involve other people and interrelated and interdependent relationships. Those, too, need to be respected and preserved, if worthy of such activity.

Although euthanasia's morality as a whole is a topic far too large to address fully here, there are a few general rules that are helpful for making moral decisions in this area. First, use the Pragmatic Principle. The principle requires that every intrinsically valuable being affected by the action be respected in the proper way—which is never a bad thing—while simultaneously trying to do the best we can—another good thing. Each of these components is necessary for dealing with a situation in which the outcome is death for a person or moral subject. In fact, it would be impossible to come to any reasonable solutions without involving these elements in some significant manner. Pursuant to the Pragmatic Principle's two criteria, we should always consider the flourishing of family and survivors, as well as that of the dying person. This is required to respect each good in and of itself and to make the world a better place.

Second, the death should be as dignified as possible. No one wants to perish in a way that makes a mockery of his life, nor does such a death deliver the proper respect.[38]

The first two rules lead us to a third rule: look at the life narratives the people involved in the situation have developed. When progressing through the decision procedure, it is important to ensure the decision is consistent with the lives those involved are leading. If the dying person has created a life story for herself that would never allow her to expire painfully while desperately scrambling for a few more moments of life, then that story should inform the decision. If possible, the life stories of others involved should affect the decision as well, although the dying person's story should be of primary consideration. It is, after all, her death, and she should take priority. However, by making the decision consistent with other life narratives, the survivors will be better able to handle the loss. Instead of being more disruptive to the person's life, the decision is consistent with who she is, thereby making it easier to incorporate into her story. That respects her and makes flourishing easier for everyone affected by the decision.

COMMENTARY

COOLEY:

Here are my questions. First, "futility" seems to be an emotionally charged word. Who should be the ultimate judge as to whether a treatment is futile? Some folks might want more time, such as in the case of African Americans and Hispanics. In the past, racism was used to hurry nonwhites to their deaths, which has caused quite a bit of resistance from some people of color to any speeding up of the dying process. Also, how much should a person's religion figure into determinations of futility? Finally, we would think that religious folks are the most likely to declare futility early and let the person go to his or her reward. But do you think that is the case?

38. T. S. McClemen, H. M. Chochinov, T. Hack, T. Hassard, L. J. Kristjanson, and M. Harlos, "Dignity Therapy: Family Member Perspectives," *Journal of Palliative Medicine* 10, no. 5 (2007): 1076–82.

STEFFEN:

Your question concerning the ultimate judge of "futility" leads me to respond that there is no "ultimate judge." Futility is a conclusion that continued treatment will not yield medically significant improvement in a patient's condition. Suppressed in that conclusion is the idea, I think, that continued interventionist care could actually be harmful to the patient by causing extended or even aggravated pain, distress, and discomfort without any reasonable hope of benefit. Continued care also imposes a burden on families while representing an unjustified expenditure of medical resources. A declaration of futility redirects medical care from cure and restoration to palliative care in which the medical directive is to keep a patient free of pain and comfortable. The expert knowledge and experience of physicians would establish a futile medical condition.

A determination of futility would result from physicians agreeing that medical intervention aimed at restoring a patient to health is not going to happen. The Texas law, the only futility law we have at the moment, makes it clear that physicians consulting about a patient's condition can disagree with one another. Additionally, family members can disagree with the expert opinion of physicians about futility. Families are free to remove their loved one from a facility where their loved one's treatment has been declared futile. The law actually gives them a time period within which to seek such alternative care. A declaration of futility would allow physicians to stop treatment and impose palliative care even over family objections, but if families are free to find alternative medical care where aggressive treatment would continue, then a final decision to withdraw care seems not to be in the hands of those who would ordinarily determine futility—namely, the physicians. In the event of disputes, the courts could get involved; in the Terri Schiavo case, the decision to withdraw treatment was actually made by the courts. Maybe an actual judge is the "ultimate judge" in cases where futility is disputed.

The facts of a patient's medical situation should, ordinarily, be clear enough that physicians from different specializations can agree on futility status, but there is widespread discomfort with the idea of physicians holding the authority to make a decision to stop treatment and turn to palliative care even over family objections. That we do not have futility laws to govern this kind of end-of-life situation is telling. We seem not to want to formalize or codify this power despite the fact—and it is a fact—that physicians actually do make recommendations to families to suspend interventionist care and move to palliation, often hospice care. How would anyone even get into hospice if physicians did not determine and discuss with families that on the medical front all that could be done has been done and now it is time to think about another approach to patient care?

Your question, however, asks whether the process of declaring someone's treatment futile could be abused, and you raise the specter of the influence of racist attitudes, which could certainly be included along with discrimination against the poor and the disabled. Could the power to declare a patient's treatment futile be abused? Yes, of course. Medical ethics is mindful of the history of physicians visiting terrible abuses on patients. Notorious examples of abuse include the following: The eugenics movement that in the United States began in the early twentieth century had, by the outbreak of World War II, led to more than thirty-six thousand "mental defectives" being sterilized—Nazi medical experimentation, associated with Dr. Joseph Mengele, involved many other physicians who would be tried as war criminals for their abuses of power. And in the Depression-era "bad blood" experiment in Tuskegee, Alabama, human subjects—all black men—were deceived and not treated for syphilis even after drugs had been developed that would have cured them.[39] It is of course relevant to any such discussion to point out that the power of a physician over a patient can become abusive.

Even though we both address physician-assisted suicide, or PAS, in a separate chapter, let me appeal to PAS to respond further to your question about abuse of power. The Oregon law, which models PAS, does actually observe and respect our common moral agreement that ordinarily physicians should not get involved in helping patients end their own lives. But because PAS is directed to patients facing the kind of death they do not choose to die—a death without dignity that has been created in large part by medical technology—the Oregon legislators imposed numerous and strict conditions that are meant to safeguard the patient from any kind of abuse. A physician is not authorized under the regulations to suggest PAS or to lead a patient to PAS; the request for consideration must come from the patient in writing, and then the process—the seventy-two steps—must be observed. This is required so that patients have a choice about what they can do facing death in their terminal situation. The point is not to see to it that a suicide is committed. We can imagine scenarios where states might authorize physicians to "dispatch" persons who have been identified as "undesirable"—they could be blacks or Asians or whites, or Jews or gay people, or the poor or those who are disabled. History provides ample evidence of political and even religious powers holding to ideological

---

39. Daniel Kevles, *In the Name of Eugenics: Genetics and the Uses of Human Heredity* (Cambridge, MA: Harvard University Press, 1995), 116, cited in Gregory E. Pence, *The Elements of Bioethics* (New York: McGraw Hill, 2007), 185.

perspectives that "dehumanize" persons from various groups and thus make disrespectful, harmful, and even murderous treatment possible. In a debate I witnessed over PAS at a national gathering of the United Church of Christ, a resolution calling for support of physician-assisted suicide did not get out of committee, and the main reason was the opposition of those who feared that PAS would lead to a slippery slope of discrimination and possible elimination of disabled persons. Those who objected to PAS did not believe that disabled persons could be guaranteed protection from being labeled "undesirable" and thus targeted for unjust treatment and even wrongful death.

I believe that the dangers of possible abuse in terminal medical situations are well-known and that the only way—the Oregon way—to proceed confident that such abuses will not occur is by heavy regulation by the state and medical profession, including commitment to a process that requires vigilant attention and continued "checking in" with any patient pursuing the PAS option. Physicians can lie to patients. Patients can be misled and misunderstand their medical situation. Patients who are medically and psychologically vulnerable can be manipulated; they can feel pressure from families and be subject to subtle coercion. Patients can receive medical attention, unknowingly, from racist, anti-Semitic, or homophobic physicians or even from a rogue physician who personally wants all disabled persons to be eliminated. All of these things are possible. But if the process is working and well regulated, I think these abuses can be practically, if not theoretically, eliminated. Awareness of abuse is behind the heavy regulations in Oregon and also behind the moral presumption that physicians ought ordinarily not be working to assist patients in ending their lives. That common agreement is the strong standard of moral direction—the ethical rule—that in its diligent and scrupulous observance makes an exception in certain cases a reasonable and morally justifiable possibility.

In response to your question about how much a person's religion should figure into determinations of futility, I am forced to say that it depends. Religion is, in many ways, about death—so said the great Swiss Protestant theologian, Karl Barth, in the early twentieth century. Therefore, it seems that religion not only brings comfort to the living when they confront the deaths of loved ones but also helps individuals to confront their own mortality. A determination of futility requires the processing of medical information and then the acceptance of the life project that will lead to death. How that project is undertaken will be different for different people, and I don't think we can say this is how Jews do it, Hindus do it another way, and so on.

Dying is as personal a thing as can happen to an individual. Religion provides pathways to make the project of dying more easily understandable and acceptable, and some religious people can actually so undertake this project of living toward death that they come to welcome death. Dying can become a growth experience, even in the midst of a terminal illness. I do not think it follows that Christianity as a religion—or Buddhism or Judaism or any other religion—endorses this attitude toward the death project as a benefit of belief or practice. People who happen to be Christian or Buddhist, Jewish or Muslim, however, may achieve this understanding. Remember that the prospect of death can be shocking, disorienting, and debilitating, and people are psychologically and spiritually equipped to handle this moment in their lives in different ways. The prospect of death, when it becomes real or immediate, can give rise to denial and defiance as well as acceptance, and it is the person, not the religion, that is at issue. People will interpret the assistance religion offers in certain ways and react as they will, as they are able. One need not be religious to make of death and dying a life project of acceptance and personal growth, and this project is not something automatically received upon acceptance of a religious point of view. I don't think religion can require or instill in its adherents the idea that the ideal way to die is to undertake a personal growth project aimed at accepting and perhaps even welcoming death. When I say "it all depends," I mean it all depends on the person—not on the religion.

In your last question you suggest that religious people are the most likely to declare futility early because the idea of an afterlife is attractive, so people will find themselves wanting to move on. You ask me if I think this is the case.

I think some religious people, Christians and Muslims particularly, are so invested in resurrection ideas or simply in the idea of a life after death that they see the hope of a promised life after death as attractive. I would never try to disabuse a person of such a belief—what kind of argument based on evidence to counter it could possibly prove convincing? The one thing we know for certain is that we do not know anything for certain about life after death (and I say this elsewhere in these pages but it is worth saying again). Do such ideas come as a consequence of consciousness and the inability to conceive of nonbeing because being, conscious being, is all we know, or have we had intimations and intuitions that something of our lives, our selves, will be continuing? Our moral relations to the dead continue after biological death (as when we honor wills), so maybe we come to trust insights, teachings, and religious leaders who claim to have had experiences of more spiritual intimations with life after death.

You've raised the life after death question in other parts of this conversation, and it is clear to me that this is important to your understating of religion. That I understand, but I also think there is a diversity of opinion on this topic among religious people. What religious people believe or do not believe can affect how they live, but how we live—how we should live—is essentially a moral question. To the extent that a belief in an afterlife contributes positively to human flourishing and helps persons to live in a world that is often hostile and definitely finite, then that belief has moral weight and practical value. In terms of the life project to accept death, which entails not fearing death, it is possible that some religious people, as a consequence of believing in life after death, undertake that life project toward death and have an inclination to accept or even welcome death, even "earlier" with PAS. But I just cannot commit to the view that this is an offshoot of religion itself as if this understanding is religion's to give as an inevitable benefit of belief or consequence of practice. Coming to such an understanding is the result of a task, a project, which falls to individuals to create and develop and accept.

Dying well is an achievement. It is a project that can go well or not so well. Religion can help with developing that project—or not. In any case, it is the project that is important because dying can be, as I have claimed, a growth as well as learning experience. It can also be an experience of tremendous physical and psychological suffering for oneself and for one's loved ones. Religion can provide comfort to the dying and to the grieving; it can even help with the life project of dying well, and it can provide ideas and hopes and beliefs that emphasize the connection of the individual to larger transcendent realities. But, in general, I don't think the diagnosis of a terminal illness would lead many religious people to opt for PAS just because they want to get to heaven earlier. First of all, who says they are going to heaven? Second, the moments after a diagnosis of a terminal illness are life moments, and those moments are to be lived. I think religion rather broadly would support that claim as would any universalizable ethic.

STEFFEN:

Your distinctions between passive and active, voluntary and involuntary, and mercy killing and assisted suicide are clear and helpful. You claim, however, that involuntary, active euthanasia can be a preferable option in some situations begs a question about whether "a preferable option" could become a duty. If active euthanasia is the preferable thing to do, all things considered, both because of pain management issues for the patient and because of the patient's lack of a future, then why would not the most morally sound thing be to pursue active euthanasia as a duty? Would those physicians evaluating the medical situation have an obligation not only to recommend it as preferable but to enact it? I would think that making active euthanasia a duty is a problem because obligating physicians with a duty to kill is asking too much—our moral agreements against killing go too deep to require that. I think certain situations of active euthanasia could be morally justified, but that is ethics work and that option would be one choice among others. Hence, killing would not become an obligatory act—a duty—as the only rational and moral thing to do. It sounded to me like you think it could be a duty if it is the preferable course of action to take, the act that most fully realizes goodness.

Do you think we need to rethink our language around end of life?

I think physicians who specialize in palliative care would object to their work being included under the heading "passive euthanasia." Is this pointing to another language issue, or are there conceptual differences between palliation and passive euthanasia, so that letting a person die (passive euthanasia that does not actively intervene to cause death) is conceptually distinct from offering palliative care?

And do you think a person who is judged to be in a futile medical condition is, by such a diagnosis, a candidate for euthanasia, whether active or passive?

COOLEY:

While waiting outside a hospital room, I had time to look through the hospital's brochure on palliative care.[40] What struck me was the extreme vagueness of its language and information. Death, dying, and end-of-life care are mentioned once each in the entire thing. What was emphasized was that the focus is on care, comfort, and transition and that the palliative care unit will become like a home for patients and their families. It was also partially filled with the testimonials of palliative care patients, one of whom is the only one to mention that death is the ultimate end in these programs. The professionals who wrote the brochure do not use the word *death*, although they do mention dying in one of their self-asked questions. The question is whether the need for palliative care also means the person is dying. The response is not an affirmative, nor does it give any sign that the vast majority of folks in palliative care are near their deaths. The brochure merely talks about improving the quality of the patients' lives.[41]

40. I will not name this very large hospital chain in the Midwest because its material is very similar to that of other hospital chains throughout the country.

41. Since this is a book on death and dying, I am setting aside palliative care that deals with chronic illnesses.

The reason I have spent so much time here discussing this brochure, which accurately reflects other organizations' perceptions and the literature on palliative care, is that it indicates something that concerns me a bit: Why not be frank? Why not clearly and forthrightly address the fact that people are dying, that palliative care is intended to ease their dying process, but that there is really nothing medically that will be done to keep the person alive? Why not acknowledge that the people interested in this care are either dying themselves or helping make decisions for their dying loved ones and that these decisions and what they will go through will be emotionally difficult for everyone, then make their argument for why palliative care might be the best or right decision for them? Why not say that treatment is futile, death is the outcome, and now you have to deal with it? Instead, the issue is addressed through several thick layers of obfuscating language that hides the bare facts. In fact, a person reading the brochure might be forgiven for believing that his life will be extended or that there is a future for him after he leaves this unit. This misconception is generally addressed by staff members who discuss the brochure and the processes with those who are making the final decisions, but why create a situation in which confusion needs to be abated?

I believe terminal palliative care is discussed in such a limited way to cushion as much as possible the emotional blow death and dying causes. This approach might be the correct one if we consider that many people in the Western world are uncomfortable, to say the least, with confronting their own mortality or that of their loved ones. Hastening one's death in any way is often thought of as a sign of weakness or moral failure on the part of the person who does it. When a fatal disease is not fought to the very bitter end, the person is often believed to be a quitter on life and, perhaps more importantly, as someone who betrays the survivors by not doing enough to keep their relationships in existence and flourishing. In addition, those who assist are often thought of as murderers, at worst, and callous, unethical people at best.

To cope with our inability to deal with death and dying as they are, we have built up a new set of terms to allow us to understand sufficiently what is going on so that we may function but avoid the starker language that makes clear the facts of the matter. For example, "passed away" is often used in place of "died" as if dying is something that is so indecent we need a euphemism in its place. We use "palliative care" in terminal cases rather than "end-of-life care," "care to ease dying," or "palliative end-of-life care." "Terminal palliative care" might even be too strong for some in the field. If one helps to cause a death or shorten a life, even if such an end is not intended, there is a shying away from calling it passive euthanasia in favor of the less emotionally charged "ending futile treatment" or "not using cost ineffective treatment." Perhaps this gives the individual doing it a sense that she has clean hands, that she has not acted unethically.

I question the need for and moral prudence of such indirect language and thinking about death. Firstly, it might confuse people who have to make end-of-life decisions that fit with their narratives and the flourishing of themselves and others. If they truly believe that there is a prolongation of life or decent chance of it, then they might not choose to draw their lives to an end in the way they want and morally need, all things considered. For instance, they might not make amends or mend relationships as they would have if they had fully grasped that they would be dying in a very short time.

Secondly, I am worried about a slippery slope of adding more and more layers of obfuscating language to death and dying. When more and more people actually begin to know what terminal palliative care is, will we have to protect their emotions and sensibilities further by coming up with additional nomenclature that removes us from what is actually going on? That is, when people figure out that palliative care has the very same effect as passive euthanasia without the exact same intentions, will palliative care get as bad a reputation as passive euthanasia has?

Thirdly, we should address the issues involved with death and dying clearly and forthrightly. We all will die, and that is a fact that each and every one of us should accept. Doing so gives us greater autonomy when making large and small decisions that will affect our life narratives. It is likely to maximize utility because we will make better decisions rather than those based on obfuscation and wishful thinking. Although it might sound emotionally cold, having a brute-fact understanding of death and dying puts our life and those of others in a much clearer perspective, clarifying what life is, what happens in it, and how it should end. It helps us plan flourishing lives by helping us to figure out what goals are important and then to pursue those in a reasonable manner. Such knowledge would help us to value what we should value—such as life and its relationships in their very nature—instead of incorrectly imagining we have unlimited time and opportunities. Perhaps dealing with death as it is will assist all of us, and society as well, to be more honest brokers with ourselves and others, which might in turn eliminate some of the unnecessary culturally and individually inflicted emotional tribulations associated with death and dying.

I think that those professionals involved in palliative care would object strenuously to my claim about the similarities between passive euthanasia and terminal palliative care. They do not want the stigma associated with passive euthanasia to attach to palliative care, and they truly believe that one is essentially different from the other. First, palliative care is defined as a method of care whose primary intent is to comfort patients, and nothing else. Second, they rely on a very narrow definition of passive euthanasia that many have adopted with three essential characteristics:

1. There is a withdrawing or withholding of life-prolonging treatment.
2. The main purpose (or one of the main purposes) of this withdrawing or withholding is to bring about (or "hasten") the patient's death.
3. The reason for "hastening" death is that dying (or dying sooner rather than later) is in the patient's own best interests.[42]

Futile treatment is not passive euthanasia on these grounds because the treatment is not in the patient's best interests and the main purpose is not to aim at the patient's death. Moreover, treatment withheld because it is not cost effective fails to instantiate the second essential condition because there is no intention that the patient dies.[43] Therefore, those engaged in palliative care in these cases can claim that their hands are clean of any moral impropriety from hastening another person's death.

Although I have the highest respect for those who try to bring comfort to the dying or those with lives determined not to be worth living, I cannot agree that there is a necessary moral difference between passive euthanasia and palliative care in terminal cases.[44] In palliative terminal sedation situations in which a patient is sedated into a nonresponsive state and generally dies from a lack of food or water rather than his disease, there is no question that the action is euthanasia.[45] However, all terminal palliative care shares other similarities with passive euthanasia. Both determine that disease treatment is futile in some way, perhaps using one or more of Brody and Halevy's four definitions of futility, or that the treatment is not cost effective. Both intentionally choose not to treat the disease or engage in other life-extending actions. Both end in the hastened death of the patient, which is a direct result of not giving the patient treatment.

42. E. Garrard and S. Wilkinson, "Passive Euthanasia," *Journal of Medical Ethics* 31 (2005): 64–68, at 65.

43. Ibid.

44. I am not alone in this view. I interviewed a person who has worked over thirty years in nursing and hospice care about palliative care as a form of passive euthanasia. She stated, "People just refuse to see it. They want it all warm and fuzzy."

45. Torbjorn Tännsjö, "Terminal Sedation: A Substitute for Euthanasia?," in *Terminal Sedation: Euthanasia in Disguise, ed.* Torbjorn Tännsjö (Dordrecht, Netherlands: Dordrecht, 2004), 15–30.

The only real difference in most cases between terminal palliative care for these cases and passive euthanasia seems to be the intentions of the various practitioners and a version of the doctrine of double effect. For palliative care, for the sake of argument, let us say that the intentions are solely on comfort of care, which explains why the definition of palliative care here must focus solely on care and not on the outcome. There is an awareness that death will occur, but that is merely foreseen. On the other hand, those who are involved in passive euthanasia might have a larger set of intentions. There will be those who merely foresee that their deaths will be hastened because of their refusing treatment or taking other actions that will shorten their lives. Their primary intention is to eliminate the pain or undesirable state in which they find themselves, which entails their death. There will also be those who intend to die as a result of refusing treatment and so on. These individuals go beyond mere foresight to a much more committed plan of action required by intending something to happen. Their deaths would be an intended result of their act. I assume that the latter cases are rather rare, given that most people, even in the end of life, do not want to die.

But in all passive euthanasia and palliative care cases dealing with shortened lifespan, we should see that the hastened death is intentional although it might not be intended, which makes terminal palliative care a form of passive euthanasia. When a person foresees that an event will occur as a result of her action, which is intended to bring about another event but does not intend the former event, then the foreseen event is intentionally brought about. That is, all parts of an intended act are intentional, although they might not be individually intended. If, for example, I shoot a gun intending to scare away crows from my garden and foresee that firing the gun will cause the neighbor to be injured, then the neighbor's injury is intentional but not intended by me. And if it is intentional, then I am responsible for it in a way that I would not be if I had not accepted the action and its consequences by performing the action. The mere fact that I chose to perform that action with those consequences makes me responsible for all the foreseen and intended events caused solely by me and flowing from my action.

In order for those involved in terminal palliative care to act rationally, they have to accept the fact that what they are doing is hastening the death of their patients by not using medical intervention to preserve life for as long as possible. Although it might be neither a primary goal nor intended, it is an intentional result for which the person is responsible. It is permissibly done because it is performed with the proper respect for persons and maximization of utility in the framework of the flourishing of individuals and society, but it is intentionally done. There is an awareness that treatment might give the patient more time to live, but the treatment will be futile to some stated goal, such as retaining some other positive characteristic, or too costly. For example, the person will never be able to defeat her disease or it will give very limited benefit at enormous cost to others. Therefore, terminal palliative care in these cases must be both a method of care and a form of passive euthanasia that allows a person to die by not giving her treatment that would keep her alive longer than if she had not been given that treatment.

Making this link between terminal palliative care and passive euthanasia is a good thing. To accept that one's action hastens another's death is to accept the reality of the situation rather than trying to mask it as something more mentally palatable. It is taking responsibility for one's actions and their consequences, which is required of all moral agents. Acceptance also will prevent a backlash against terminal palliative care when others discover that its results and processes are identical to passive euthanasia—although not all forms of passive euthanasia. The only real difference between other forms of passive euthanasia and terminal palliative care is that palliative care's primary focus is on comfort of care during the hastened dying process without really emphasizing the death aspect. And that is the main piece of evidence that makes terminal palliative care preferable in many cases over other forms of passive euthanasia that might be faster or involve greater discomfort.

The only time that terminal palliative care is not a form of passive euthanasia—because passive euthanasia is necessarily about shortening ill people's lives by not giving them something they need to continue living—seems to be in cases in which any and all medical intervention is futile to prolong life even for a moment. Palliative care in these cases, and I think that there might be very few of them, would merely be a form of treating patients rather than allowing a person to die sooner than she otherwise would. We could pick palliative care or something else to manage comfort levels, but the maximum time for living would be at least as great in the palliative care case.

My main concern with the possible cases just described is how we can *know or reasonably believe* that we have encountered such an instance in which palliative care is not a form of passive euthanasia. We would have to know or reasonably believe that any and all medical intervention could not extend the life of the patient sufficiently longer than would palliative care. We have to have sufficient evidence for our belief—and because this is a literal life-and-death matter, the standard for such evidence would have to be much higher than if we were making a much less important decision. In fact, the standard might make it impossible to know the lengths of time involved in the various alternatives open to us, which would make it difficult for us to claim with any reasonable certainty that the palliative care approach is not shortening the patient's life. Therefore, it might be best overall not to muddy the waters further and merely accept that we should treat terminal palliative care as a form of passive euthanasia, even when in rare cases it is not.

COOLEY:

Although the issue raises many questions I would like to ask, I have two that I am especially interested in. First, if people are dying, then why don't they take that as a sign that their divine entity wants them to die? Why would they try to stay alive, especially when trying to do so will be futile? A person might think that not accepting terminal palliative care or passive euthanasia would be a rejection of their faith rather than an affirmation of it. How do you resolve this issue if it can be resolved?

Second, palliative care seeks to eliminate or reduce pain as much as possible, but what if the divine entity wanted that pain to be there in the first place? Perhaps it is part of an overall plan that we do not understand. If we remove that pain, then we how do we reasonably believe that we are not interfering in something far more important?

STEFFEN:

My responses here will be short compared to what they could be if we really go into a disputation about the question about God and human suffering. On your first question, I would say that many, if not most, theists (and that is the kind of religion we are talking about) would not interpret their own dying as a sign that God wants them dead. I would propose two reasons for this claim. First, most theists hold that God is a good and life-affirming God, and this view of God is supported in sacred Scriptures by such texts as this one from Deut. 30:19: "I have set before you life and death, blessing and curse; therefore choose life, that you and your descendants might live" (RSV). Dying theists would not presume that a good God who affirms life would actually want them dead; God is the author and creator of life and would be presumed or believed to be on the side of life. Theologically considered, life is a gift that God gives and human beings receive as such.

That said, let us consider the terminal medical situation where much suffering is involved. When suffering is added to human experience, the good of life can come into conflict with other goods of life, such as the good of bodily integrity and mental equipoise. The problem you raise then becomes a conflict in values. I think a theologian open to the idea of palliation and passive euthanasia would say that a good God who expresses care for the creation can see good not only in life itself but also in the cessation of suffering. This would mean that a person of faith who opted to withdraw life support and die is not acting contrary to "the nature of things" as divinely created and ordered. In such a situation, the individual is, rather, allowing nature to take its course without undue interference. Medical interventions that keep life going beyond the capacity of persons to live their lives in a meaningful way presume morally that the good of life trumps all other goods. But that is not necessarily the case. The good of letting nature take its course and allowing suffering to end can be, it seems to me, conformed to a theism that asserts God as good, kind, and compassionate. Could not such a God discern value conflicts and even endorse actions (and inactions) that put an end to the gift of life? After all, when we give a gift, we let go of it and allow others to use the gift as well as they can. If life is a gift from God, would God not want us to use this gift as well as we can, even to give it up and let it go when problems have arisen and we can no longer use it as a gift? This is not to say that we can peer into the divine mind and say that God wants someone dead. I would argue that God could and would agree that it would be good for suffering and pain to stop, but that is because I am anthropomorphizing God at the moment, and I think a good God could see that pain and suffering can come into conflict with the good of life itself.

This leads to my second point. Our ideas about God are, ultimately, ours. There are theistic believers who hold that the gift of life is sacrosanct and cannot be violated even to end suffering. There are others who would say that a loving God has provided human beings with reason, and reasonable persons with good and compassionate hearts who are concerned for the well-being of others should not be prevented by absolutist strictures from allowing persons to die. Perhaps there are even occasions when the just and compassionate action would be to assist in expediting death due to the circumstances of the situation.

Not everyone has faced such situations. Those who have not faced them do not know what they would do in such a troubling situation where one option is to allow palliative care or passive (or active) euthanasia. People will hypothesize and imagine what they would do, but they do so along a continuum of possible responses. Decisions for passive euthanasia occur all the time in hospitals, and what interferes with them is usually a family conflict—not a moral conflict—in which guilt comes to play an important role. Family members can easily resist becoming involved in a decision that leads directly to a loved one's death, for it is a serious matter to take on the responsibility for stopping medical treatment and allowing death to come. But you ask about God's will. How God will affect theists as they think through these issues will depend on how they allow a conflict of values to play out in the divine nature, and on that issue, even theists cannot claim to know with certainty. Human beings do not have access to God's own mind as God has access to it—our theistic religious traditions all share that view. To assume knowledge of God's will with such certainty would be the height of arrogance in the context of faith. God, theists believe, is only known through revelation, and the problem with knowledge and certainty is that what is revealed must be interpreted—human beings, last I checked, are notoriously fallible when it comes to interpreting the divine will. So fallible human beings cannot know the divine will or at least cannot know it for certain.

In answer to your questions, then, I am willing to say it is *possible* that God would want someone dead and also that God would inflict pain and suffering on an individual for some purpose (or perhaps allow it to happen, as in the case of Job in the Hebrew Bible). But all of this then begs a philosophical and theological question about the nature of God: would a good God want an individual dead? If so, why does God not simply hit the "smite" button and dispense with the person? Does God require human agents to work the divine will? Isn't that to put a qualification on God's power, and, if such a qualification occurs, is God not then limited? If God is limited in such a matter, how else is God limited? Now God is not fitting the picture of God insisted on by traditional theists. While that is not a particular issue for me because I believe that God—if there is a God—is limited, that picture of a limited God would cause enormous problems for traditional theists.

The same with your question about suffering: if God has some purpose in inflicting or even allowing suffering, then what is that purpose and why should God hide it? The human supposition that suffering is a "test" of faith, the idea that an experience of suffering will increase human wisdom, or the notion that the believer's task is to accept and endure suffering as God's will—these "explanations" provide a place to make some sense of things in the midst of the experience of suffering, but they hardly satisfy the requirements of the moral point of view. Asking a person to suffer the discomfort of a tooth extraction for the good of health is one thing, but to suffer the loss of a child or a spouse or a loved one on the understanding that such loss is "God's will"—without further explanation—is not only morally unsatisfactory but cruel. Then the hard question in response to your second question is this: is interfering with a divinely sanctioned suffering actually an effort to resist God's cruelty?

In the end, I think the most reasonable position for a theist to take is that God is good, that God does value life and values it highly—for that is the faith affirmation of those who believe themselves to be created in God's image and who believe they in some way share in the divine nature. Furthermore, if the divine nature is that of loving-kindness and compassion, the way out of the dilemmas your questions create is to say that God not only takes no pleasure in suffering but experiences suffering with those who suffer, shows compassion and offers comfort to those in pain, and relies on human beings to translate a vision of such a divine reality into the values human beings can and should enact in everyday life. All of this depends on how one conceives the divine nature, and people just have to decide that because, as I said, our ideas about God are, ultimately, ours.

8

The Value of Death

Lloyd Steffen

Death is a value-laden term. The term reaches our ears shrouded in negativity; and to hear the word 'death' uttered can, as W. H. Auden put it, "stop all the clocks." Death, even the mention of it, can be trusted to arouse feelings of apprehension as we suppress the anxiety that attaches to it and try to avoid thoughts of death, especially as those thoughts turn personal and the death that comes into view is our own. When we do confront death, we often do so with wariness, a sense of unreality and even fear. Death is a mystery to us—despite all we might claim to know about it and despite the certainty we attach to claims about what we believe and profess to know.

Religion provides people with practical frameworks (i.e., rituals) and organized belief systems that offer explanations and make sense of death in the context of ultimate realities. Religion helps people to confront the threat of nonexistence and the anxiety of helplessness in the face of our natural movement toward what looks to be, from the point of view of nature, personal extinction. From a moral point of view, religion is one of the cultural assets that makes it possible for people to create meaning and to transform anxiety and fear of death into a powerful life-affirming impulse. When life projects integrate honest confrontation with human mortality, and rely on philosophy and religious thought to do so, the sharp sting of death anxiety can be blunted. Many people experience death through religion, for religion has power to affect a transformation in values and even alter the meaning of death itself. Religious people will often appeal to the values of hope and love, claiming that in those values lies a power even stronger than death.

Such a reflection tells us more about the value of religion in relation to death than it does about the value of death itself. So how death comes to have value in human existence seems to be a question worth asking.

Keeping in mind that death is an experience for the living, let me suggest just a couple of ways, both positive and negative, that death has value in human life

On the negative side, when the constant anxiety over death is realized in an actual human experience of death, the sense of sadness, loss, and grief can, if the death is of a loved one, provoke the most profound and disorienting of human experiences. Testimonials to the shocking and horrible experience of grief are legion, but let me just offer one, a letter Ralph Waldo Emerson wrote the day after his son, Waldo, died in January 1842:

> My boy, my boy is gone. He was taken ill of Scarlatina on Monday evening, and died last night. I can say nothing to you. My darling & the world's wonderful child, for never in my own or another family have I seen anything comparable, has fled out of my arms like a dream. He adorned the world for me like a morning star, and every particular of my daily life. I slept in his neighborhood & woke to remember him. . . . My angel has vanished. . . . You can never know how much daily & nightly blessedness was lodged in the child. I saw him always & felt him everywhere. On Sunday I carried him to see the new church and organ & on Sunday we shall lay his sweet body in the ground. You will also grieve for him.[1]

In another letter that same morning, Emerson shared this with Margaret Fuller: "My little boy must die also. All his wonderful beauty could not save him. He gave up his innocent breath last night and my world this morning is poor enough. . . . Shall I ever dare to love anything again?"[2] Emerson visited his son's grave regularly, but it is not is not known if he opened the casket to view his son's face as he had done in the wake of the death of his first wife—his wife of sixteen months.[3] The loss of a loved one occasions sadness and grief; the loss of a friend is a deep sorrow.

Death interrupts life with the experience of profound loss, and that death should so deeply affect us allows us to see that death is what helps us become aware of what we most value in life. Without death, we would not know what those most valuable things are. And if there really were no death, a

1. Ralph Waldo Emerson, *The Letters of Ralph Waldo Emerson in Six Volumes, Volume 3*, ed. Ralph L. Rusk (New York: Columbia University Press, 1939), 7, 8.

2. Ralph Waldo Emerson, *The Selected Letters of Ralph Waldo Emerson*, ed. Joel Myerson (New York: Columbia University Press, 1997), 263.

3. See Richardson, *Emerson: The Mind on Fire*, 3.

notion sometimes entertained in film, such as Frederick March's 1934 feature *When Death Takes a Holiday*, or a novel, such as José Saramago's *Death with Interruptions*, we would quickly see how dependent we are on death for the continuation of meaningful and orderly life. In Saramago's fanciful fiction, death ceases on January 1 in an unknown country. The absence of death threatens the country with economic peril, not only for the mortuary business, where business stops, but in health care, where the burdens of caring for the aging-but-not-dying present unimaginable obstacles. As the novel concludes, death—not the cosmic death of the universe but the pesky little death who visits individual human beings—falls in love with a cellist who seems unable to die. The novel ends: "Death went back to bed, put her arms around the man and, without understanding what was happening to her, she who never slept felt sleep gently closing her eyelids. The following day, no one died."[4]

Does this recapitulate in fictional form a profession of faith in the idea that love is stronger than death?

The impetus for creating such fields of human inquiry and endeavor as medicine, economics, government and politics, agriculture, and psychology—so many of the things human beings do and think about—are aimed in tacit, even unconscious ways at preserving life and providing the means for sustaining life so that the terrible experience of death can be avoided and postponed. It is a good thing to put death off, and that is so natural and widely accepted a view that it establishes the sometimes unexamined ground beneath all of our ethical reflection on living and dying. So death's crushing negatives—grief and the pain of profound loss—are always in relation to those things that human beings do, those constructive and creative things that aim to keep death at bay. Yet even saying this, we need to say more. Against this negative value we attach to death is the positive value that death is a natural aspect of life itself, something nature itself cannot flourish without.

The dialectic of death with its positive and the negative evaluations is only seen in a vastly broad perspective. The positive and negative are hard to separate. In our individual lives, the negative value of death is ever present, is usually overwhelming, and is, when experienced, more often than not traumatizing. Talking about any positive value we might attach to death seems absurd, especially since we experience death most closely in relation to those we love—the pain of loss is all the more real and likely to fracture our worlds because of the closeness of death to love. But in that imagined and perhaps fictional "larger perspective," just as the forest needs to undergo the clearing

---

4. Jose Saramago, *Death with Interruptions*, trans. Margaret Jull Costa (Orlando: Harcourt, 2008), 238.

of accumulated waste through the destructive action of fire—a natural process that only becomes a great evil when human beings are affected—in order to grow and renew itself, so too does life renew and flourish in the wake of death. It is too much to ask of human beings affected by death to see death through such a larger perspective, for to see it we would have to let go of our attachments and allow love itself to take a holiday. Yet in religion, as in nature, death is a necessary condition for the creation of new life. Christianity embraces resurrection; and the Hindu divine triad of Brahma (creator), Vishnu (sustainer), and Shiva (destroyer) are all three necessary for life. Each of the three affects the others—creation yields to destruction, destruction gives way to creation, and life and the Dharma are preserved until Shiva intervenes—interrupts—again, clearing the ground for new life.

The examination of the ethics of death undertaken in these pages has tried to confront the problems and dilemmas that human beings face in those aspects of life where we encounter death, foresee death, and evaluate actions that can lead to death. Both authors have tried to respect the grounding so important to ethical reflection—that death is experienced as negativity, even an evil. But both of us have also, at times, challenged that assumption, especially when human beings have done things to make some forms of life worse than death. The dialectic of death is ever present, or could be, if we could but question our assumptions and open up new conversations. Our hope is that this book will contribute to doing precisely that.

Both religious thought and philosophy engage in the act of encounter and confrontation with meaning and value as they pertain to the topic of death. And both prescribe actions for how human beings could best construct their life projects in the face of a death reality that cannot finally be avoided. If these last pages have invoked the insight of a novel and a divinity myth to consider the question of death's value, it is because religion is itself a poetry, and it requires for deep understanding a kind of poetic sensibility not only to the meaning of what people do (ethics) but to the values that human beings ground in what they believe to be transcendent realities. Those transcendent realities can be described as cultural phenomena, but they are not accessed at the experiential and subjective level by science or through the scientific temperament. Much as that temperament might be tempted to exceed its competence and deny them any hold in reality beyond wishful thinking, they are, or so practitioners of religion assure us, accessible through more poetic sensibilities, where we confront death as something other than biological cessation, as a loss attached to those things in life most important to us, those things we love that, as Emerson put it, "fled out of my arms like a dream."

Index of Names

Index of Subjects